ENCYCLOPEDIA OF THE
ANCIENT WORLD

Editor
Shona Grimbly

FITZROY DEARBORN PUBLISHERS
LONDON • CHICAGO

For information write to
Fitzroy Dearborn Publishers
310 Regent Street
London W1R 5AJ
UK

or

Fitzroy Dearborn Publishers
919 North Michigan Avenue
Chicago, Illinois 60611
USA

British Library Cataloguing in Publication Data.
A catalogue record for this book is available from
the British Library

A Cataloging-in-Publication record for this book
is available from the Library of Congress

ISBN 1-57958-281-8

This edition first published by
Fitzroy Dearborn Publishers 2000

Printed in Singapore by C.S. Graphics, PTE

For Brown Partworks Ltd

Editor:	Shona Grimbly
Design:	Wilson Design Associates
Picture research:	Veneta Bullen
Text editors:	Mark Fletcher
	Chris King
	Sally MacEachern
Managing editor:	Lindsey Lowe

Maps

Red dots on the maps show the location of ancient sites and
cities. Present-day cities are indicated by blue dots.

Picture credits:
Brian & Cherry Alexander: 104tr. AKG London: 20, 78, 85br, 91, 97, 108, 144tc,
146, 151, 164tr, 169, 183, 204br, 215, 218, 226bl, 230, 232, 237tr, 239tr; Erich
Lessing 4, 6, 9, 13tl, 25, 29, 30, 33, 36, 38, 39, 45, 53, 63, 68tr, 69, 74bl, 75, 76, 79,
81, 82, 90, 100bl, 144bl, 173, 176tl, 177, 217br, 224br, 231tr, 234, 235, 236, 238,
241tr, 243tr, 245; Hilbich 110; John Hios 62, 86, 87. Ancient Art & Architecture:
13br, 210, 229, 231bl. Art Archive: 12, 14, 23b, 31, 35, 83, 85tr, 107br, 109, 114,
117, 119, 121tl, 128, 129, 130bl, 131tc, 136, 141, 185, 188, 197, 209, 212tr, 216,
217tl, 219tc, 223, 224tl, 226tr, 247br. Corbis: 168; Bojan Breceli 21; Richard A
Cooke 163, 165; Dave G Horner 171tr; Archivio Iconographico 54; Angelo
Hornak/National Museum, Dehli 243br; Institute of Archaeology Inc 213tr; Jiangi
Provincial Museum, Nanchang, China 133; Wolfgang Kaehler 66, 72; Kimbell Art
Museum, Fort Worth, Texas 145; Museo Archaeologica Nazionale, Italy 214; Gianni
Dagli Orti 10, 42, 73, 74tr, 158bl, 224; Neil Rabinowitz 203; Seattle Art Museum
246br; Brian Vilkander 142; Adam Woolfitt 55, Roger Wood 26, 65; Michael S
Yashashita 43. CM Dixon: 16, 61. Mary Evans Picture Library: 80, 118. Eye
Ubiquitous: 137tr; B Battersly 59; David Cummings 123, 124tc; James Davis Travel
Photography 140, 150, 162, 195; L Foroyce 170. Getty Images: 201; Glen Allison
134; Christopher Arvesen 132; George Grigorian 51; John Higginson 5; Richard
Passmore 22; Hugh Sutton 18; Penny Tweedie 198. Robert Harding Picture Library:
40, 124br, 125, 147, 199; Gavin Heller 17; P Icoch 127; Robert Frerch/Odessey,
Chicago 41; Ian Tomlinson 1. Sonia Halliday Photographs: 67, 96, 225tr; FHC
Birch 57, 68bl, 70, 77, 106; David Morgan 64. The Hutchinson Library: 24, 27, 28,
88, 92, 178, 222; Michael MacIntyre 115, 153, 206; Sarah Murray 189. Image Bank:
89. Panos Pictures: 139; Morris Carpenter 207. Portfolio Pictures 131bl. Poseidon
Pictures: Michael Nicholson 157. NJ Saunders: 159. Mick Sharp Photography: 101b,
102, 103; Jean Williamson 56. South American Pictures: 190, 192, 193; Kathy Jarvis
160, 161; David Horwell 202tl; Charlotte Lipson 164br; Chris Sharp 182, 175, 227;
Tony Morrison 196, 213br. St Edmunsbury Borough Council/West Stow Anglo
Saxon Village 116.Travel Ink: Ronald Budkin 107tl. Werner Forman Archive: 19,
44tr, 48, 50, 52, 101tr, 113, 120, 121bl, 122, 137br, 154, 155, 171bl, 184, 200, 202br,
212, 220bl, 237br, 242, 246tl; Anthropological Museum, Veracruz University 158tr;
Art Gallery of New South Wales, Sydney, Australia 134; Art History Museum,
Shanghai 225bl; Bibliteca Universitaria, Bologna 209; British Museum 44bl, 100tr,
211; Charles University, Prague 32; courtesy of the Entwhistle Gallery, London 46,
205; Field Museum of Natural History, Chicago 167, 179; Eugene Fuller Memorial
Collection 156; Greenland National Museum 104b; Hermitage Museum, St
Petersburg 60, 239, 241bl; The Louvre, Paris 221; Museum of the American Indian,
Heye Foundation, New York 180, 181cr; National Museum of Anthropology,
Mexico City 187tr; National Museum of Ireland 98; National Museum of New
Zealand, Wellington 204tl; Museum für Völkerkunde, Basel 247tr; Museum für
Völkerkunde, Berlin 186, 187br, 194; Private Collection 176bl; Ohio State Museum
166; Roberts Peabody Foundation for Archaeology 181cr; San Francisco Museum of
Asiatic Art 148.

Cover images: Werner Forman Archive; AKG London/Erich Lessing; James Davies
Travel; Corbis/Roger Wood; The Hutchinson Library.

Artworks: Salamander Picture Library, Mark Topham, and Colin Woodman

Contents

Introduction 4

Middle East and Africa 5

Europe 51

India and the Far East 122

The Americas 157

Oceania 197

Across the Cultures 206

Timeline 248

Further Reading 252

Index 253

Introduction

In the space of just a few thousand years human beings have made the transition from Stone Age hunters to the sophisticated technocrats of today. This book tells the stories of the peoples of the ancient past and shows how they laid the foundations of the modern world.

In the remote past human beings lived in wandering tribes that hunted animals and gathered seeds, fruits, and grasses from the wild for food. They lived in rock shelters or primitive dwellings and moved from place to place to find more food. Archaeologists call people who lived like this "hunter-gatherers."

Over a long period of time some of these hunter-gatherers found that there were things they could do to increase their food supply. The Aborigines of Australia, for example, discovered they could use fire to burn off existing vegetation. This encouraged fresh young grass to grow, which attracted grass-eating animals and so made hunting easier. Other Aborigines discovered that they could improve the supply of yams by breaking off the top of the tuber and putting it back in the ground, where it would grow again. And so, gradually, hunter-gatherers became farmers who deliberately planted crops and stayed in the same place to wait for the harvest.

With farming came settled villages, which gradually grew larger. The harvests of crops were stored so that food was available for everyone throughout the year. Because not everybody had to work on the land to grow enough food to feed the population of the village, some people had time to develop crafts, or mine metals, or trade with other peoples. In this way the society—particularly the chief—became richer.

ABOVE: The ruins of ancient Rome, capital of the Roman Empire, which was perhaps the most powerful empire of the ancient world. At the height of its power Rome dominated most of Europe and much of north Africa. Its cities, roads, army, and administration were more advanced than any others in ancient times.

➛ THE FIRST CITIES ➛

The first cities emerged in the Middle East in the region that is now Iraq. Many historians believe the city was an essential feature of a civilization. A city provided protection for its citizens and an assured supply of food. It also had a powerful ruler, a body of officials to keep order and collect taxes, craftspeople to produce goods and forms of art, and very often a slave labor force. As cities grew more powerful, states came into being in which one ruler controlled a large region made up of many cities.

A state needed a very complicated organization to control it. There would be an army to keep order, a large bureaucracy, and many merchants carrying out the trade on which the wealth of the region usually depended. Other features often thought of in connection with civilization are writing—which was necessary for keeping records of taxes paid—and highly developed religious beliefs and art forms.

But there were other peoples who did not take this path toward an urban society. They nevertheless developed an advanced culture, with sophisticated beliefs and art forms, and many had a quality of spiritual life that is envied by some people living in today's cities. The stories of some of these peoples are included to show that "civilization" does not necessarily mean urbanization.

Each of the first five chapters of the book looks at the cultures and civilizations that developed in one particular region of the world. The last chapter looks at some general aspects of life in the ancient world, such as agriculture or legal codes, and examines them in different cultures. At the end of the book there is a timeline, which shows how civilizations in different parts of the world relate to each other in time, plus a list of further reading, and a comprehensive index.

Chapter 1:

Middle East and Africa

The first known settlements of the ancient world grew up in the Middle East in the Neolithic (later Stone Age) period. The Neolithic village of Çatal Höyük in Anatolia was the world's first substantial settlement. It was to be followed by other settlements that grew into cities in Mesopotamia, the fertile land that lay between the Euphrates and Tigris rivers in the region that is now Iraq. The people who lived in these cities were clever and inventive, and it is to them that we owe some of the most important discoveries of humankind—such as the ox-drawn plow, the wheel, and writing.

BELOW: The landscape of Anatolia (present-day Turkey) where Neolithic Çatal Höyük was located. This dry and barren land was once covered with lush growth.

Jericho

Jericho in present-day Israel is thought to be the world's first true town and its history dates back to about 10,000 B.C. It features in the story in the Bible in which its walls fall before the trumpets blown by the oncoming army of Joshua, an event dated to about 1200 B.C.

The town of Jericho is a mound (or "tell" in Arabic) at the western edge of the Jordan River Valley, not far from the Dead Sea. It lies near Ain Musa, an everlasting spring that is sometimes known as the "Spring of Moses."

When the British archaeologist Kathleen Kenyon excavated the site in the 1950s, she worked her way through many layers stacked one on top of the other, each layer the remains of an ancient town or village. At the bottom she found a small village that was first populated almost 12,000 years ago.

The first inhabitants of Jericho were not true farmers. They hunted wild animals and collected cereals from the surrounding countryside. However, unlike earlier hunter-gatherers, they lived in permanent homes—round, single-roomed houses that were semisubmerged in the ground. It was these houses that formed the basis of the first Jericho.

➤ THE WALLS OF JERICHO ➤

The second oldest settlement dates back to about 10,000 years ago. The people who lived in this village had learned how to farm, growing wheat and barley in the highly fertile surrounding land.

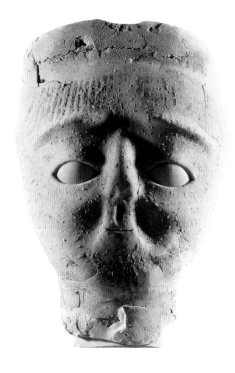

LEFT: A human skull found at Jericho, covered in plaster. The people of Jericho had distinctive burial customs. When someone died, the body (without its head) was buried under the floor of the house. The skull was covered with plaster and shaped to recreate the face of the dead person, with black paint for hair and shells for eyes. The plastered skulls were placed in a special room that became a kind of shrine to the dead.

The village held around 500 people, a very large number for those times. The inhabitants of Jericho had also begun to work together to build large structures in stone.

The most impressive of these structures was a huge wall that ran all the way around the village. The wall stood 16 ft (5m) tall and 10 ft (3m) thick, and was made up of no fewer than 10,000 tons (9,070 metric tons) of building material. In front of the wall ran a ditch 26 ft (8m) wide. Many parts of the wall survive to this day.

As if these feats were not enough, the villagers also built a solid stone tower just inside the wall. The tower rose 35 ft (11m) into the air and was over 30 ft (9m) wide at the bottom. To get up to the flat top, the villagers made a staircase. So well did they build the tower that it remains solid even after 10,000 years.

Some archaeologists believe that these early farmers built the wall and tower to protect the village against an enemy attack. Others think that the wall may have been intended to protect the villagers against floods, while the tower had some kind of ritual significance. Whatever their true purpose, these buildings are still spectacular examples of early stonework.

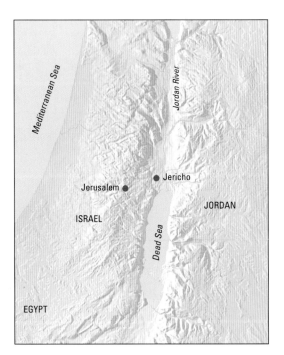

LEFT: Jericho is located in Israel near the Jordan River, a few miles north of the Dead Sea.

Çatal Höyük

Çatal Höyük is another very ancient town. It was built by Neolithic people in southern Anatolia (now Turkey) about 8,000 years ago and lived in for over 800 years, between about 6250 and 5400 B.C. Excavations begun in the 1960s showed that much of the town had been preserved.

The first builders of Çatal Höyük were nomadic hunters who had started to farm. To do this they needed to live in a settled community. The first houses they built were made of timber and sun-dried mud bricks. These houses did not last for very long, and as they crumbled, people built new houses on top of them. Over the centuries, the layers gradually built up to form a giant mound of earth.

The site of Çatal Höyük covers an area of 32 acres (13ha) and consists of two mounds ("höyük" means an earth mound containing ancient remains). In the early 1960s a team of British archaeologists, led by James Mellaart, started to excavate the great mound of Çatal East, and at its heart they uncovered a Neolithic town. It consisted of a honeycomb of primitive one-roomed dwellings, all built back-to-back with no streets in between. The houses were made of timber, mud brick, and plaster, and had flat roofs. Each dwelling had one large room, usually about 20 by 13 ft (6 by 4m) with one or two small storerooms. The main room had raised platforms for sitting and sleeping on, and an oven for cooking. Small windows were set high up in the walls and let in a small amount of natural light.

➤ WORKING THE LAND ➤

Most people in Çatal Höyük worked as farmers, watering the fields around the town by channels that they dug by hand. They grew barley, wheat, peas, and lentils, and also kept domesticated animals such as pigs, sheep, and goats. Apples, almonds, pistachios, and other nuts and fruits were gathered in the surrounding area.

At its largest, Çatal Höyük had between 5,000 and 6,000 inhabitants. The town was sufficiently large to support some citizens who did not farm but worked as craftsmen or traders. These new classes of people became richer and started owning luxury goods such as jewelry. Çatal Höyük prospered with its wealth based on trade.

BELOW: The houses of Çatal Höyük were built so close together that the town had no streets. Because there were no streets or ordinary doorways, people had to walk over the roof terraces and enter their homes through openings in the roofs. Wooden ladders made access easier and also made the settlement simple to defend. When the town was threatened by invasion, the ladders could be pulled up quickly to present the enemy with an invincible barrier of high, blank walls.

Çatal Höyük's main resource was obsidian, a black, glassy volcanic mineral found in the volcanic mountains nearby. The rock can be chipped like flint to form a tool with a sharp, jagged edge. Obsidian was prized for making axes, knives, and polished mirrors. It was traded as far away as Jericho, a distance of over 500 miles (805km), and would have been carried on pack animals such as mules and donkeys. In return the merchants received shells and flint—items that were highly prized by the citizens of Çatal Höyük.

Many pieces of pottery and modeled or carved small figures were found at the site. The pottery was molded by hand, since the potter's wheel had yet to be invented. The people also made textiles, which they may have decorated with patterns, using clay stamps. Metalworkers worked local copper and other metals to make jewelry, such as beads, and simple tools.

➤ RELIGION AND BURIAL RITES ➤

Each section of Çatal East had its own shrine room where religious rites were held. The walls of the shrines were decorated with bulls' heads molded in plaster, and geometric patterns were also painted on the walls. The bulls' heads may have been the focus of religious ceremonies.

Clay figures of boars and other animals marked with stab wounds were also found, and this suggests that the people of Çatal Höyük practiced sympathetic magic to bring success in hunting (which was still one of their main sources of meat). Some of the shrine walls at Çatal Höyük were decorated with wall paintings showing hunting scenes, with beasts and leaping warriors.

As well as carrying out magic rites, the people of Çatal Höyük may also have worshiped an earth goddess who brought fertility. Many pregnant female figurines were found, made of various materials like terracotta, marble, and volcanic stone. The most famous pregnant figure was a stone statuette of a large earth goddess seated on a throne of leopards.

The dead of Çatal Höyük were buried inside the houses, after undergoing an elaborate ritual. First the bodies were exposed in the open to be pecked by vultures. When the bones were picked clean they were wrapped in animal skin, cloth, or matting, and tied up with rope or leather. They were then left in a mortuary. In the spring, when the houses were redecorated, the skeletons were placed under a platform inside the house. They were often buried with jewelry, such as shell necklaces, and covered with colored powder.

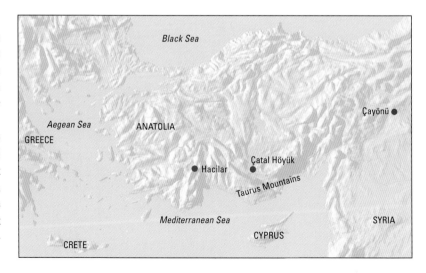

Mesopotamia

The name Mesopotamia comes from a Greek phrase meaning "between the rivers."
The culture of ancient Mesopotamia, which is also known as Uruk, began in a fertile valley
between two great rivers, the Euphrates and the Tigris, in the region that is now Iraq.

Here a number of cities grew up around 6,000 years ago. The citizens of these settlements were clever, skillful people who made several vital discoveries. They are believed to have invented the wheel, the ox-drawn, metal-bladed plow, and most important of all, the art of writing.

The lands around the Tigris and Euphrates rivers were low-lying plains where the soil was deep and fertile. Each year in spring the rivers flooded their banks, depositing a layer of rich silt over the land. Yet this region, now part of Iraq, was too dry to be ideal farming country. In summer little or no rain fell, and the earth baked hard. Without water no crops would grow. Mesopotamia could only be farmed successfully when the local people learned how to control and regulate the flow of life-giving water.

Some time around 5000 B.C. the people of the land of Sumer in south Mesopotamia learned how to do just that. They built a system of dikes, canals, and reservoirs to store water and carry it to their fields. This enabled them to grow dates, vegetables, barley, and wheat. These crops could be stored and eaten long after harvest, so freeing the people from the danger of starvation. So the early Sumerians thrived; their numbers increased, and their communities grew larger.

Thanks to irrigation Mesopotamia became a land of plenty. The people fished in the rivers, caught wildfowl in the marshes, and kept livestock such as pigs, sheep, and goats. As they watered and plowed more land, their crop yields increased, leading to a surplus. This meant that some members from each community could be freed from farm work and could follow other occupations, becoming priests, administrators, craftsmen, and traders. This specialization is one of the first signs of civilization.

➤ BEGINNINGS OF TRADE ➤

Specialization also meant that craftsmen could produce desirable goods that could be traded. Mesopotamian potters molded the local clay into pots from which to eat and drink. They also produced loom weights for weavers, bead ornaments, and tools. Sumerian merchants began to travel

LEFT: This large vase—it is three ft (90cm) high—was found in a temple in Uruk and dates from about 3000 B.C. Made from alabaster, it shows (on the center strip) a procession of priests bearing offerings for Inanna, the goddess of love and war. Other strips show pictures of sheep and goats, date palms, and cereal crops.

Cylinder Seals

Cylinder seals developed in ancient Uruk about the same time as writing. They were small cylinders of stone or ivory carved with pictures that left a print when the seals were rolled over wet clay. They were used to stamp official documents, as well as sealed jars, chests, and doorways to mark ownership of property. A wide variety of scenes was carved on these tiny seals, showing great skill in the craftsmen who made them. The pictures included scenes from everyday life, as well as events from the lives of gods and heroes from myth and legend. Like writing and other inventions, these seals were soon widely used beyond the borders of Mesopotamia.

A carved cylinder seal from Mesopotamia (on the right) together with the picture that it makes when rolled over damp clay. The carving on the seal had to be done in reverse, and on a curved surface, and required extraordinary skill and patience on the part of the craftsman. Many of these tiny seals have been found, and they are an important source of information about life in ancient Mesopotamia.

BELOW: This map shows the main cities of ancient Mesopotamia, and also the shoreline at that time before it was altered by changing sea levels.

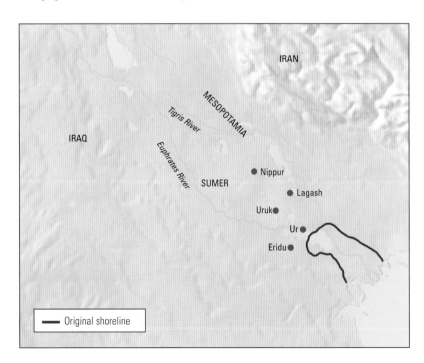

Original shoreline

widely, setting up trade links with distant regions such as Anatolia, Syria, and India. These traders were able to exchange Mesopotamian crops and handmade goods for important materials that the Mesopotamians lacked—such as timber, building stone, and metals.

As the network of canals grew, villages began to cooperate to run and maintain their waterways. Society grew more complex. At the same time, war became more common as villages were raided by neighboring settlements or by tribes from outside the region. More and more people were driven to live in large settlements for protection, and they began to fortify them with high walls. And so, around 4500 B.C. some of the world's first cities developed. A new, urban age dawned, named after one the largest settlements.

➤ THE CITY OF URUK ➤

This was Uruk, which held about 1,000 citizens around 4500 B.C. By 3000 B.C. it had grown to a great city covering 250 acres (100ha) and was home to many thousands of people. The settlement was protected by six miles (9km) of stout brick walls. The great temples on the mound dominated the whole city. They were dedicated to Anu, the sky god, and Inanna, the goddess of love and war. The main feature of the temples were mighty columns decorated with patterns made from thousands of nails—painted black, red, and white—that had been hammered into the plasterwork. Archaeologists digging at Uruk discovered priceless treasures, including a female head carved in white marble, which may have represented Inanna, and a tall alabaster vase showing religious scenes.

In times of war the men of Uruk and the other cities banded together to form armies. They elected chiefs called *lugals* to lead them into battle. These war chiefs probably developed into the first Sumerian kings, who soon ruled over the cities. In turn, each city came to dominate the surrounding region, forming a little kingdom.

In the cities most homes were made of mud bricks dried in the sun. Kings and important citizens such as priests and noblemen may have lived in grand dwellings. But the most impressive buildings were the temples, which were built on earth mounds that raised them well above the settlement and the surrounding lowlands. Some of them were massive: Uruk's temple terrace took up one-third of the city.

Some archaeologists believe that the temples were originally warehouses for storing the harvest. Since they also contained the community's sacred objects, they became the focus for religious ceremonies as well as trading. Soon the priests became responsible for the smooth running of the city. Farmers brought their crops to the temple each year and gave part to the priests as an offering to the gods. Priests also controlled trade and even the network of waterways.

➤ GREAT INVENTIONS ➤

Around 4000 B.C. Uruk civilization entered a new phase, marked by many brilliant inventions. By 4000 B.C. Sumerian smiths had learned how to extract copper from copper ore by heating it to high temperatures. By 3500 B.C. they were making bronze, a harder metal, by heating copper and tin together. Craftsmen made tools, ornaments, and weapons by pouring molten copper, bronze, and gold into molds. Around the same time, farmers improved the plow, which up to then had been pulled by men, by hitching it to teams of oxen. Metal blades made plows even more efficient, allowing farmers to cultivate more land.

Around 3500 B.C. Uruk craftsmen invented the potter's wheel, a wooden turntable that could be rotated to make the fashioning of clay pots easier. About 300 years later the wheel was in use on wooden carts pulled by oxen—which was the world's first wheeled transportation. The wheels were made of solid wooden sections, so the first carts must have been cumbersome and heavy. Even so, a cart pulled by a mule or donkey carried three times as much grain as a farmer could load on the animal's back.

Ziggurats

Many ziggurats were built in Mesopotamia. These massive pyramidlike structures were used as platforms on which temples stood. Like the one at Ur, which was built by the Babylonian king Ur-Nammu, they were made of sun-dried bricks and then encased in baked bricks to protect them from the extreme weather. The most famous ziggurat was the one dedicated to the god Marduk at Babylon. It had eight levels and many staircases leading to the summit. The temple at the top was believed to contain a couch on which Marduk slept. At night the temple was deserted except for a priestess who stayed in the building to keep the god company.

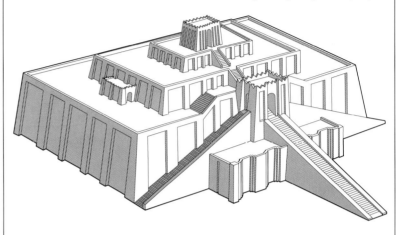

A drawing of a reconstruction of a ziggurat. Most ziggurats have disappeared because they were built of mud brick, which soon crumbles away.

Some time around 3300 B.C. the Mesopotamians invented writing. The first written records were accounts of trading and tallies of farm produce that were delivered to the temples. To make these records, scribes made marks on soft clay tablets with a pointed tool called a stylus, and then left the tablets to dry in the sun.

This simple record-keeping gradually developed into a more sophisticated form of writing, which meant that people could send messages and instructions over great distances and pass on information from one generation to the next.

It took about 500 years for writing forms to develop from simple signs into a more complicated system. The earliest forms were simple picture signs (pictograms), which showed images of real objects. So, for example, a bull was represented by a drawing of its head. Gradually, the bull sign came to mean strength as well as the animal itself. Finally, a system of wedge-shaped symbols developed, called cuneiform writing. These new symbols were phonetic—they conveyed the sounds of speech, either of whole words or of syllables. This was a very important step toward the system of writing we use today.

Sumerians

From about 3000 to 2000 B.C. Mesopotamia was dominated by the city-states in the south of the region, a land known as Sumer. The people of this region, who were called the Sumerians, created one of the greatest of the early civilizations.

The Sumerians were pioneers in both writing and mathematics. They also constructed magnificent buildings, including the huge stepped pyramids called ziggurats. And they produced outstanding craftsmanship, carving small statues, for example, and inlaying wood with a variety of precious stones.

No one knows how it was that the Sumerians rose to such prominence in what was such a barren region of land. Although the two great rivers —the Euphrates and Tigris—provided rich silt for farming when they flooded their banks, the area was not blessed with natural resources. Timber was scarce, and there was no stone for building or metals for making tools or weapons.

However, Sumer did have a good food supply, especially of wildfowl and fish. Also, over the course of time the Sumerians learned to make better use of their rivers. They dug canals and reservoirs and made dams, and so were able to bring water to their fields and grow many crops. To carry out projects like these, they needed good organization and leadership—qualities that may have helped create the first towns.

From about 3500 B.C. onward the cities of Sumer grew in size and importance. They included Ur, Eridu, Lagash, Uruk, and Nippur. The citizens of these cities thought of themselves as Sumerian, but there was no central government that united them all. Instead, each city was the head of its own small state, in a way similar to the city-states of ancient Greece. Sometimes one particular city would grow strong and dominate others. Then power would swing to another city.

We do not know what form of government the cities had at first. It was believed at one time that the remains of large temple complexes indicated that the priests actually ruled their respective cities. Although this is no longer thought to be the case, many historians do still believe that the great temples played a major role in the lives of the citizens.

At some point, perhaps about 2800 B.C., kings emerged as rulers of the cities. The Sumerian word for king is *lugal*, which literally means "great man." It may be that a *lugal* was originally

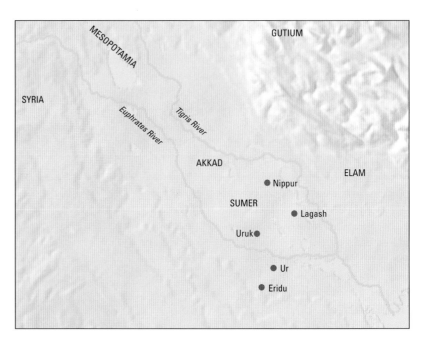

appointed during a crisis such as a war, and that in time the role became permanent.

Sumer's cities continued to exist independently until 2370 B.C., when disaster struck: the land was invaded and conquered.

‑ THE AGE OF SARGON ‑

The leader of this invasion was Sargon, king of Akkad, a state that lay about 150 miles (240km) north of Sumer. Sargon was originally descended from Semitic peoples who had migrated to Mesopotamia centuries before. According to legend, Sargon's mother had abandoned her baby

ABOVE: Sumer did not have a capital city. Instead, it contained a number of great cities whose wealth and power fluctuated over the centuries.

LEFT: A limestone tablet from about 2500 B.C. showing Ur-Nanshe, king of Lagash, with members of his family.

son in a basket in the Euphrates River. He was later rescued by a shepherd, who brought him up.

Sargon grew up to become a powerful leader. He conquered not only all of Mesopotamia but also parts of Syria. He built himself a capital at Agade, and he made Akkadian the accepted language of the region.

Sargon's family's reign over Sumer lasted until about 2200 B.C., when it was invaded by a mountain people known as the Gutians. After a further century of chaos the Sumerians regained power under the leadership of a king of Ur named Ur-Nammu. For the next 100 years the region prospered. Temples were built; standard weights and measures were introduced; and a new calendar was put into use. In about 2000 B.C., however, the Elamites invaded from the east, destroyed Ur, and brought the age of Sumer to a close.

➤ SUMERIAN SKILLS ➤

The Sumerians were highly skilled builders and architects. Their cities were sturdily built, with strong walls for defense. Inside, large temples and palaces were set among streets crowded with houses. Buildings were made primarily from sun-dried mud bricks, although stronger, fired bricks were also used. For the poor, houses were small one-story dwellings, while the rich had larger structures on two levels, with more spacious rooms and quarters for slaves. The second story also had a balcony built around it.

To help them build and transport materials and goods, the Sumerians made use of the wheel—and were the first people in the world to do so. They had both two-wheel and four-wheel carts, of which small clay and bronze models have been discovered. Apart from carts that were used

for agricultural and building purposes, they also had chariots that they used for warfare.

Sumerian society was divided into different classes, with the king, priests, and nobles at the top and slaves at the bottom. In between came the traders, craftsmen, and farmers. Kings conducted wars, dealt out justice, and made sure that the canals, dams, and reservoirs—vital for keeping the land well watered—were kept in good repair. At first it seems that the Sumerians elected their kings. Eventually, kingship was passed on from one generation to another on a hereditary basis.

For wealthy Sumerians life did not just consist of work. Those who were rich could afford to throw lavish banquets and hire musicians to play lyres, harps, or tambourines to amuse their guests. There were also lively religious festivals throughout the year, especially the one at New Year, which lasted for several days. On the other hand, the discovery of a board game and counters at Ur shows that the Sumerians enjoyed quiet indoor pursuits as well.

LEFT: A clay tablet dating from 2500 B.C. inscribed with cuneiform writing. The tablet acted as a bill of sale for a field and house, and makes it clear that the house was paid for in silver.

The Temples

Sumerian cities were dominated by their temples, which were built on the huge stepped pyramids known as ziggurats. The temple was in fact a great complex, almost like a small city in itself, with cooks, brewers, gardeners, blacksmiths, scribes, and administrative staff to keep it running smoothly. It is recorded that a temple at Lagash had to supply bread and beer to 1,200 people a day. The temple was also, of course, the religious center of the city, dedicated to its patron god. Priests carried out the necessary rites and rituals, and celebrated holy festivals. They also recited prayers, sang hymns, and sacrificed animals. The priests were considered the servants of the gods, who were thought to reside in the temple itself.

The remains of a temple found at Uruk, one of the main Sumerian cities.

Sumerian Farming

Most Sumerians worked on the land as farmers. Because the land was dry with little rainfall, they transported water from the rivers to the fields through man-made canals. In fact, the world's first known canal was built by the Sumerians. It was constructed under the orders of the governor of Lagash in around 2500 B.C. and can still be seen today as part of the Al-Gharrif waterway. The Sumerians also built smaller irrigation channels and dams.

Barley was the most important crop, but the Sumerians also grew onions, dates, cucumbers, pomegranates, and melons. To break up the earth on their fields, the Sumerians used a simple wooden plow. To this they attached a funnel that was used to sow seeds. Sheep were kept for their wool and oxen for their ability to pull plows and carts as well as for their hides. The Sumerians also kept pigs and goats—and onagers to pull war chariots.

BELOW: One of the long decorated panels on the box known as the "Standard of Ur," which was found in a royal tomb at Ur. This side shows a Sumerian army—in the center strip is the

Sumerian artists and craftsmen formed themselves into guilds to support each other. The work they produced was of an extraordinarily high standard. Goldsmiths were able to beat gold into thin strips and cut them into shapes of leaves or stars. Sculptors made small statues using a method called the lost-wax process. For this, a figure was modeled in wax, placed in a container,

writing. The earliest existing writing in the world was found on inscribed clay tablets at the city of Uruk. They date from about 3300 B.C. and consist of bookkeeping lists and accounts.

At first writing was in the form of small pictures—for example, a simplified image of an ox's head would mean "ox." In time these pictures became more abstract. They were produced by imprinting a wedge-shaped, or "cuneiform," stylus into tablets of soft clay which was then left to harden. Small inscribed cylinders were also used. These were rolled over soft clay to produce pictures and writing, and were often used to seal an official document.

The system of word signs gradually developed to express more complex ideas. A picture of a star, for example, originally simply meant "star." Later it could also mean "god," and later still "high." Sumerian was the first language to be written down in the cuneiform script. After the conquest of Sargon, however, cuneiform was used to write the Akkadian language.

As the pool of Sumerian skills increased, it became important to educate young people in these skills. In early times temple priests were

infantry, wearing helmets, while the lower strip shows four-wheeled war chariots drawn by onagers. In the top strip the large figure of the king is shown being presented with prisoners of war.

and covered with clay. It was then fired so that the wax melted and ran out of small, ready-made holes. This left a hollow mold made of the fired clay. Molten metal was then poured into the mold and took the form of the original wax model.

➤ THE FIRST WRITING ➤

As the Sumerian cities grew in size, their organization became more complex. A need arose for careful records, which in turn created a need for

responsible for educating the young. Over the years, however, schools were removed from their direct influence. Evidence uncovered from a school at Ur, dating from about 1800 B.C., shows that pupils learned to read, write, and do arithmetic. Among the clay tablets unearthed were ones with multiplication tables inscribed on them. Education was strictly practical, however, and the aim was to produce the scribes, traders, or businessmen of the future.

Ur

In 1923 a British-American expedition was launched to excavate the Sumerian city of Ur in southern Iraq. Situated close to the Euphrates River, Ur had flourished between 3000 and 2000 B.C. It was one of a number of city-states within the land of Sumer in ancient Mesopotamia.

Despite its buildings having disappeared beneath the desert, Ur's name had been preserved because it was mentioned in the Bible as the birthplace of Abraham. It was not until the early 20th century, however, that archaeologists could be sure that Ur was located in Iraq. This was due to the discovery of some clay tablets inscribed with writing that had been found at a site known locally as Tell al-Muqayyar. When the tablets were deciphered, it was found that they referred to a king named Ur-Nammu, who was known to have become king of Ur in about 2112 B.C. So when they began excavating at al-Muqayyar the archaeologists knew the site's ancient name. However, they had no idea of the treasures they would discover.

The leader of the expedition was a Briton named Sir Leonard Woolley, who was one of the most outstanding archaeologists of his time. Excavations at Ur occupied him for 12 years and were the high point of his career. Working tirelessly with up to 400 local laborers, Woolley and his team soon unearthed floor plans of houses and temples, and rescued many everyday objects from the sand and dirt. They discovered that Ur's streets were narrow. Some had been laid out in a plan, others simply twisted around groups of small buildings. Houses were made of mud brick and built around a central courtyard. Floors were covered with reed mats. Furniture consisted mostly of low tables, stools, and chairs.

➤ THE ROYAL CEMETERY ➤

The most spectacular finds, however, were made in the royal cemetery. It contained more than 1,800 graves, most of them for the common people. But 17 of these graves were larger than the others and more sturdily built out of stone or brick. They also contained a wealth of precious objects made from gold and silver, often inlaid with gems. Only two of the 17 graves had escaped being plundered by tomb robbers in the past. But inscriptions of the names of kings were found, and this discovery convinced Woolley that they were the graves of Ur's royal rulers.

The archaeologists used great care in the excavation. One of their techniques involved pouring paraffin wax over delicate objects to keep them from falling apart when lifted up. Soon marvellous objects, more than 4,500 years old, were being brought to light. They included statues, necklaces, beads, and women's headdresses

BELOW: This panel from the "Standard of Ur" box shows a celebratory banquet given by the Sumerian king in about 2500 B.C. In the top strip the king is shown facing his guests, who raise their cups while a musician plays a lyre. The other strips may show some of the food that is to be eaten at the banquet—goats, fish, cows, and sacks of grain or other provisions.

decorated with wafer-thin gold shaped into leaves of willow and beech. There was also a helmet of hammered gold once worn by a king named Meskalamdu. It had small holes drilled around the rim for fastenings that attached a cloth lining, traces of which were found inside.

Perhaps most fascinating of all the finds was a small wooden box that became known as the Standard of Ur. This was inlaid with shell and lapis lazuli, and may have been the sounding box of a lyre. What makes the box fascinating for scholars are the inlaid pictures on each of its long sides and the light they shed on Sumerian life. One of the two main panels shows a royal feast, while the other shows a war scene. The two end panels are also elaborately decorated. One of them shows a ram being sacrificed to the gods.

➤ TRADING NETWORKS ➤

Apart from the insight they give into Ur's burial rituals and the skill of its craftsmen, the finds show the city's trading patterns and partners. Lapis lazuli, for example, is known to have come from Afghanistan, which may have also provided tin. This metal was specially prized because when mixed with copper, it produces bronze. Shell came from the Persian Gulf. The red stone carnelian was brought from what is now Iran. And timber was fetched from the Amanus Mountains in northwest Syria via the Euphrates River.

If Woolley was able to gather a lot of information from Ur's artifacts and burials, he gained even more from the collection of over 200 written records preserved on clay tablets. There were lists of animals and materials, such as fish, sheep, goats, and trees, as well as the names of individuals and their professions. They indicated that Ur had people working in many specialized occupations—including carpenters, metalsmiths, gardeners, cooks, and bricklayers. The tablets also described aspects of law. If a man wanted to divorce his wife, for example, he only had to pay a sum of money. Also, he was allowed to sell his children into slavery if he wanted to.

Ur's golden age lasted for about 100 years under the reigns of Ur-Nammu and his successors. This king was responsible for rebuilding the city's great temple—a stepped pyramid, or ziggurat. Although only its base remains, excavations showed that it was a solid structure made of brick. It rose up to 70 ft (21m) in three tiers, all connected by exterior staircases. On its summit was a small shrine where holy rituals took place. This ziggurat, like others in the region, was built to resemble a sacred mountain—a place where humans could stand closer to the gods. At Ur the patron god was Nanna, god of the moon.

The end of Ur finally came in about 2000 B.C. A people called the Elamites invaded from the west and destroyed the city. Over the centuries it decayed and was totally covered by sand. Yet some 4,000 years later it was destined to yield up its treasures to the light of day.

RIGHT: This statue representing a ram in a gold thicket was found in the Great Death Pit. The face and legs are of gold, while the horns, eyes, and fleece are lapis lazuli—all inlaid over wood.

Egypt

The people who lived on the plains of Egypt close to the Nile River around 3000 B.C. were fortunately placed. Although the Nile Valley was surrounded by desert, the river brought life to ancient Egypt, allowing a vibrant civilization to grow up and flourish around its banks.

Every year the Nile, fed by winter rains higher up the river, broke its banks and flooded the Egyptian fields with water and fertile silt. When the water retreated, the farmers were able to sow their seeds in rich, moist earth. Warmed by the spring sun, the crops grew quickly and provided an abundant harvest. Farmers made up about 95 percent of the Egyptian population, and the success of their crops was vital to the economy.

The major crops grown were wheat, barley, and flax, which was woven into a fine linen cloth for which the Egyptians became famous. The abundant harvests meant that a large population could live in a relatively small area, and in turn, this meant that there was a large labor force available for building great stone monuments, such as the royal tombs.

The Nile River was also important as a natural transport system. Great cargo boats could travel north using the flow of the river or, by hoisting a sail, travel south using the north wind. This made it easy to transport the large quantities of materials the Egyptians needed to build their enormous stone pyramids and temples.

Egypt was also very rich in other natural resources that would shape its civilization, such as gold and limestone. Gold was so abundant that a king of a neighboring state wrote enviously to the pharaoh, "In your country gold is like dirt."

➤ EARLY HISTORY ➤

Little is known about Egyptian history before 3100 B.C. It is thought that the land of Egypt was a collection of small kingdoms populated by similar peoples who spoke the same language but had no political unity. Some time between 3100 and 3000 B.C. Egypt became a unified country ruled by a single king. This unity may have been brought about by the conquests of a king called Narmer, from the southern city of Hierakonpolis.

BELOW: The Nile River brought life to the plains of Egypt in the middle of a desert region.

He was the first king to claim the right to wear the crowns of both Upper (southern) and Lower (northern) Egypt. After Narmer's conquests a new capital city, Memphis, was established where the broad Nile Delta meets the narrow Nile Valley—on the other side of the river from the modern Egyptian capital of Cairo.

In later times the legendary founder of Egypt was said to be Menes, "the one who establishes." He was the first king, or pharaoh, of the First Dynasty. Some historians think that Narmer and Menes may be the same person, but this is not certain. Altogether there were 31 dynasties of kings who ruled Egypt until the conquest of Alexander the Great in 332 B.C. These dynasties are grouped into periods of stability (called the Old Kingdom, Middle Kingdom, and New Kingdom) and periods of confusion (intermediate periods) when the right to the throne was disputed between various claimants.

The king was believed to be the chosen of the gods and was the highest source of authority. He was commander-in-chief of the army, chief priest of all the gods, and the sole lawmaker. When the king died, his body was placed in a special tomb, which was usually a pyramid.

⏤ THE PYRAMIDS ⏤

The Old Kingdom (2650–2150 B.C.) was a period of peace, prosperity, and culture. The only one of the Seven Wonders of the ancient world still standing, the Great Pyramid of Khufu at Giza, dates from this time. It is the largest of the Egyptian pyramids but not the oldest. This honor goes to the pyramid built by Zoser of the Third Dynasty, whose seven-step pyramid is the oldest large stone building in the world. It was built at the site of Saqqara, which is one of a number of cemeteries clustered along the desert edge just to

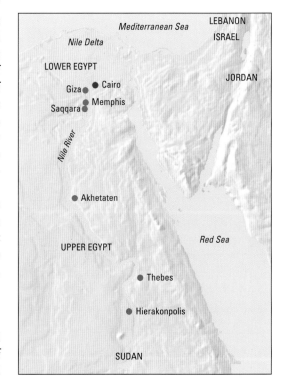

the west of the Old Kingdom capital at Memphis. Later kings of the Third Dynasty also built step pyramids, but it was not until the beginning of the Fourth Dynasty that straight-sided, or true, pyramids appeared. The first were built by Snefru, whose experiments in building royal tombs resulted in no fewer than three pyramids. Snefru's son Khufu (known to the Greeks as Cheops) built the largest pyramid of all, at Giza, the first of three famous pyramids at that site. Khufu's pyramid was about 480 ft (146m) high and was constructed from more than two million huge limestone blocks.

Pyramid building must have required massive organization and effort—all the energies of Egypt were directed toward the construction of these great stone tombs for their god-kings. Labor was brought from all over Egypt to work on these enormous pyramid projects, probably during the season when the Nile River was flooding the agricultural land, and the farmers were therefore unable to work on it.

The kings of Egypt were not the only people to have special tombs built for them. High-ranking members of the royal court were buried around the pyramid in large, low, rectangular tombs called *mastabas* (from the Arabic word for "bench," which they resemble in shape). The *mastaba* tombs, unlike the pyramids, were decorated with carved and painted scenes showing the owner of the tomb receiving food offerings to feed his *ka* (the soul that remained in the tomb).

These tombs were visited by relatives of the dead, who could enter the tomb to leave food

The Social Structure

In ancient Egypt the king was believed to be a god made human, and he had supreme power. His commands were carried out by advisers, scribes, and other officials. The king's deputy was the vizier, who was responsible for supervising the day-to-day running of the country.

Egyptian society was highly structured. The royal family was at the center of a court that was attended by the nobility. Below the nobility were the scribes, priests, and court servants. Below them were the merchants, craftsmen, and soldiers. Apart from slaves, the lowest members of society were agricultural laborers and miners. Women had a far higher status than in any other civilization in the region. With rare exceptions, they could not be officials or scribes, but most other occupations were open to them. They could also own property and were even allowed to divorce their husbands.

Stairway to the Sun

The Egyptians believed that when a person died they would continue to live in an afterlife. So when a king died, his body was placed in a special burial chamber inside a pyramid, with everything he needed for life in the next world—furniture, clothes, and other personal belongings. The burial chambers were quite small compared to the massive exteriors of the pyramids.

The first pyramids were built in such a way that the outside rose up in steps, whereas the later pyramids of the Fourth to Sixth Dynasties were straight-sided. The Pyramid texts (which were painted on the walls of the burial chambers inside pyramids from the Fifth and Sixth Dynasties) seem to give reasons for these designs. In the Old Kingdom the most important god was Re, the sun-god. The king was thought to spend eternity crossing the sky every day in the boat of Re. The texts tell of a "stairway" that enabled the king to ascend into the sky and also of rays from the sun being strengthened to form a ramp that the king could walk up. Some historians think that both the step pyramids of the Third Dynasty and the later "true" pyramids are huge models of these staircases and ramps for the king's use after death.

The great wealth buried with the kings meant that all the royal tombs were broken into and robbed. This may be why the kings stopped building pyramids and instead were buried in secret rock-chambers in the Valley of the Kings.

---

offerings in front of a statue of their relation or in front of a false stone "door," which only the *ka* could pass through. The corpse was placed in the burial chamber below the *mastaba* in a stone coffin. The body had to be preserved in order to be a "home" for the *ka*, so the soft internal organs such as the brain, lungs, and intestines were removed. The body was then covered with salt and dried. Finally, it was wrapped with bandages and spices in the process of mummification.

Mastaba tombs grew in size during the Old Kingdom, and the increased wall space was used to depict a wide range of activities from everyday life. As the tombs of the nobles became larger, the pyramids became smaller, which may mean that the kings were becoming less powerful.

The Old Kingdom collapsed shortly after the reign of Pepy II and in the First Intermediate Period that followed the local rulers of different parts of Egypt all struggled to gain control of the whole region. The eventual victors were the rulers of the southern city of Thebes, and Nebhepetre Mentuhotep became king of all Egypt in 2040 B.C.

The early rulers of the Middle Kingdom reunited Egypt, reopened trading links with other countries, and increased the power of the throne. They started building pyramids again near Memphis, but the status of Memphis was starting to be challenged by Thebes. The later rulers of the Middle Kingdom were less powerful, and gradually the kingdom fell into chaos again.

During the Second Intermediate Period (1640–1550 B.C.) the north of Egypt was occupied by Semitic kings (called "Hyksus" by the Greeks), and Thebes became a focus of resistance to alien rule. When Ahmose drove out the Hyksus and took the throne in 1550 B.C., it heralded the beginning of the New Kingdom.

➤ THE NEW KINGDOM ➤

During the New Kingdom Thebes was the heart of a great Egyptian empire that conquered and controlled most of what is now Sudan and Israel, and parts of Jordan, Lebanon, and Syria. Under great kings such as Thutmosis III and Amenhotep III of the 18th Dynasty and Ramses II of the 19th Dynasty, Egypt became the international superpower of the late Bronze Age, with military victories abroad and extensive building projects at home. Egypt was also part of a greater economic system, which included almost all regions of the eastern Mediterranean, the Middle East, northeast Africa, and southeast Europe.

With prosperity people began to desire exotic goods. Merchants and sailors were willing to cross great distances in small boats to satisfy this demand. A constant stream of boats must have sailed from Egypt to Lebanon, Cyprus, and Greece, and back to Egypt, trading the specialties

BELOW: A royal sarcophagus from around 800 B.C. Such coffins were always elaborately decorated, as befitted a king's status.

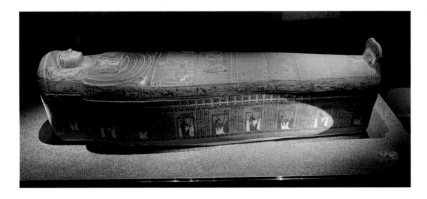

Sacred Writing

The Egyptians had a number of different ways of writing. The most common was called hieratic. This style was made up of a series of simple individual signs, which were easy to write with a reed pen on papyrus (made from reeds) or on fragments of pottery called *ostraca*.

The best-known form of writing was hieroglyphics, which means "sacred writing" in Greek. This was the writing used for monuments such as temples and tombs. The Egyptians called this script "the god's words." It had hundreds of signs that were basically drawings of things in the real world:

people, animals, parts of the body, and furniture. Each sign could have a phonetic use (representing a sound), or it could be an ideogram (representing an actual object). The signs were used together to form words and sentences. Hieroglyphics provide us with a vivid picture of daily life in ancient Egypt.

Hieroglyphics found inscribed on a tomb in the Valley of the Kings. Hieroglyphics were chiefly used for inscriptions on sacred sites and objects.

of each region—timber from Lebanon, copper from Cyprus, wine and olive oil from Greece, gold from Egypt, and ebony, ivory, and ostrich eggs from Africa.

— THE RISE OF THEBES —

During the period of the Middle Kingdom Thebes had become an important royal center. The temple of Karnak was built on the east bank of the Nile at Thebes and dedicated to the god Amun. Formerly Amun had been merely a local god, but he was now promoted to being king of the gods and the patron of the Egyptian Empire. Amun was believed to live within a statue kept in the heart of the temple—the sanctuary—where it

was washed, clothed, and offered food and drink every day. King after king competed in showing their devotion to Amun by adding to his temple. These additions usually took the form of courtyards, which were surrounded by rows of pillars and had massive tower-shaped gateways.

The temple became one of the largest religious complexes ever built and eventually covered five acres (2ha). Much of the early 18th Dynasty work at Karnak was carried out by Hatshepsut, one of the few women to rule Egypt.

On the west bank of the river a new form of tomb was built for the kings of the New Kingdom. Underground chambers were cut into the rock of a hidden valley, which was now called the Valley of the Kings. These new tombs may have been built to hide the royal bodies from grave robbers, for the kings knew that the pyramid tombs had been entered, and many items stolen. However, even here, in the Valley of the Kings, only the tomb of the boy-king Tutankhamun survived unplundered until the 20th century.

As at Memphis, in the Old Kingdom, high-ranking officials of the New Kingdom wished to be buried close to the king. They were not actually buried in the Valley of the Kings—it was kept almost exclusively for royalty—but in the cliffs of the Theban hills, not far from the royal valley. Although the form of the tombs—a rock-cut "T" shape—was different from those at Memphis, the walls were still decorated with detailed pictures of everyday life.

When Amenhotep IV became king in 1360 B.C., he turned his back on many of the old traditions, including worship of the god Amun. Instead, he favored a new god, Aten. Unlike the old gods, Aten was not depicted as an image of a person or an animal but as the sun. In order to promote his new religion, the king changed his name from Amenhotep to Akhenaten ("Living Spirit of Aten") and moved the capital of Egypt to a new location halfway between Thebes and Memphis. He called this new city Akhetaten ("Horizon of Aten"). Unfortunately for Akhenaten, this enthusiasm for Aten was not widely shared. After the king's death Akhetaten was abandoned, Thebes once again became the center of power, and Amun the chief god.

After the New Kingdom collapsed in 1064 B.C., the kings were unable to keep order, and the country once again slipped into a time of internal chaos called the Third Intermediate Period. For the next 700 years Egypt was ruled by separate local dynasties and foreign rulers until the invasion of Alexander the Great, the Macedonian leader. From 332 to 30 B.C. Egypt was part of the Hellenistic (Greek) world, ruled by the descendants of Ptolemy, Alexander's general, after which it became part of the Roman Empire.

➤ EVERYDAY LIFE ➤

Archaeologists have been able to discover far more about the great royal tombs of ancient Egypt than about the houses, villages, and towns of ordinary Egyptians. This is for practical reasons. The Egyptians, fearing the Nile's annual flood, built their cemeteries high up in the desert where the flood water would not reach them. The tombs, made of stone blocks, were cut into the solid rock or dug into the desert and were intended to survive forever. Less care was taken over ordinary houses. People needed to be near the Nile, which provided water for them and their animals and a natural sanitary system, and they also needed to be near their fields.

The Nile also provided the mud bricks that were used to make almost every building—from animal sheds to palaces. Mud from the edge of the river, or from a convenient canal, was formed into brick-shaped lumps using simple wooden molds and then left to dry. Although mud provided a cheap and convenient material for housing, it was easily destroyed if the annual flood was higher than usual. This was not considered to be a huge problem since destroyed villages could easily be rebuilt. However, it means that the only villages and towns to survive in a good enough condition for exploration by archaeologists are those in unusual places away from the Nile. The best-known of these are the towns set up to house people involved in building and maintaining Old Kingdom and Middle

BELOW: A view of the massive columns inside the temple of Karnak at Thebes. The main parts of the temple complex were built by the kings and queens of the 18th Dynasty (1550–1298 B.C.), but the buildings were continually modified by later generations.

Kingdom pyramids and, most famous of all, the village of Deir el-Medina, which for 500 years housed the workers who dug and decorated the royal tombs in the Valley of the Kings.

The terraced houses of Deir el-Medina were clustered closely together and surrounded by a high wall. The houses were small and mostly had four small rooms, one behind the other. The kitchen at the back may not have had a roof. There was usually a cellar, where jars of food and drink and any valuables could be stored, and a staircase up to the roof. Few poor people had much furniture aside from wooden headrests. However, the warm, dry climate probably meant that people carried out many domestic activities, such as food preparation and laundry, outdoors.

Egyptian Art

Egyptian paintings are instantly recognizable, but the human figures seem stiff and twisted to the modern eye. This is because the Egyptian artist was not trying to create a realistic painting. The purpose of Egyptian art was religious—it was done to decorate the walls of tombs and temples.

The Egyptians believed that a painting or a statue was magical and could be a substitute for the thing that it represented. After death the *ka*, or soul, of a dead person lived on in the tomb. The *ka* needed to have a home—ideally, it would be the body of the dead person; but if that should rot away, pictures could provide substitute homes. However, the pictures needed to be as complete as possible and—this was vital—have appropriate captions naming the owner of the statue or picture.

In order to show as much of the body as possible (each arm, leg, hand, foot, and finger), the painter would depict an oddly distorted form (head in profile, eye from the front, shoulders face on, waist from the side). The artists used flat colors and did not attempt to add shading or highlights. This style of Egyptian statues and paintings remained nearly unchanged for thousands of years.

An illustration from the Nedjemet Book of the Dead, *which dates from about 1090 B.C. Scrolls such as this were placed in tombs to help the dead make their journey to the afterlife.*

Tutankhamun's Tomb

Most of Egypt's pharaohs are remembered either because they were great conquering soldiers or because they built massive temples and tombs. Tutankhamun was neither a great soldier nor a great builder, yet he is probably the best-known of all the pharaohs.

This is because of the dramatic discovery of his tomb in 1922. Unlike all the other royal tombs, it had never been plundered and so was full of the most magnificent treasures.

Tutankhamun was born about 1341 B.C. He reigned for only nine years, and died before he was 20. Although it is not known for certain who his parents were, the most likely candidates are Amenhotep IV (later known as Akhenaten) and his queen, Nefertiti.

Given the name Tutankhaten, the child was brought up at the new royal capital of Akhetaten. His probable father Akhenaten had rejected the traditional gods of Egypt in favor of a new god, Aten, and moved his court from the old capital of Thebes. Unlike the old gods, Aten was not depicted as a person or an animal but as the sun. Tutankhaten's close connection with the royal family is emphasized by his marriage to Akhenaten's daughter Ankhesenpaaten, who was much older than him and was probably his sister. This marriage would have made Tutankhaten's claim to the throne more secure.

When Akhenaten died, it seems that Tutankhaten's brother Smenkhkare became pharaoh for a very brief time before Tutankhaten, aged about nine, succeeded him. His name was changed to Tutankhamun, and the city of Akhetaten was abandoned. The removal of the royal court to Memphis and Amun's reinstatement as the chief god of Egypt suggests that the young king's advisers were opposed to his father's ideas and wanted to restore the old ways.

Tutankhamun died when he was about 18 years of age. Whether this was the result of a plot against him is unknown, but his body bore no unusual signs of violence. His death was certainly unexpected, since no tomb had yet been prepared for him in the Valley of the Kings. Instead, a small nonroyal tomb—perhaps intended for a favored courtier—was hastily pressed into service and quickly decorated during the 70 days required for embalming the body.

The modest nature of the tomb meant that, unlike some of the larger, more magnificent tombs in the Valley of the Kings, the tomb of Tutankhamun was ignored and then forgotten, especially after the rubble waste from the nearby

LEFT: The funeral mask of Tutankhamun, made of solid gold and decorated with blue glass and lapis lazuli. The mask was only one part of the great treasure found in the Burial Chamber. The mummified body was contained in a series of coffins, one inside the other like the layers of a Russian doll. Inside a sarcophagus made of quartzite was a coffin of cypress wood covered with a thin layer of gold. Inside this was a second coffin of gilded wood elaborately decorated with precious materials, including faience, obsidian, and lapis lazuli. Finally, there was a coffin of solid gold that weighed 243 lb. (110kg). When the lid of this was lifted, it revealed the king's mummified body and the golden funeral mask. The king's hands were also covered with gold, and the mummy wrappings concealed huge quantities of jewelry.

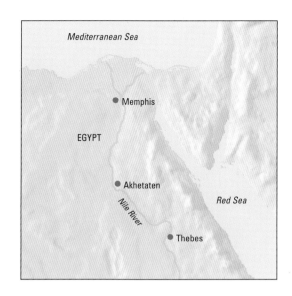

tomb of Ramses VI was dumped on top of it. The boy-pharaoh lay undisturbed for over 3,500 years until his tomb was discovered by the English archaeologist Howard Carter in 1922.

‐ THE DISCOVERY OF THE TOMB ‐

Sponsored by the aristocrat Lord Carnarvon, Carter had been working in the Valley of the Kings since 1915. On November 4, 1922, workmen discovered a set of stone steps leading to a blocked doorway. The seals on the doorway were intact and named the owner—Tutankhamun. Beyond this sealed door a corridor led to a second door. Carter cut a small hole in it to see what lay ahead. What he saw was, in his own words, "everywhere the glint of gold." He was looking into the first of four rooms that, although small, were crammed full of treasure.

The first room, or Antechamber, measured 25.7 x 11.6 ft (7.8 x 3.5m). The most noticeable items in this room were three gilded ritual couches in the form of sacred animals stacked against the rear wall and, to the left of the doorway, a tangle of six dismantled chariots. Two further doorways led out of the Antechamber. The first led to a small room called the Annex, which seems to have been where the dead king's food, wine, and oils were stored. The other doorway was completely blocked and was guarded by a pair of life-size wooden statues of the king. This doorway led to the greatest prize of all—the Burial Chamber.

Like the other chambers, the Burial Chamber was very small for the tomb of a pharaoh—only 20.9 x 13 ft (6.37 x 4.02m). It was the only room in the tomb to have painted decoration on its walls. More importantly, it was here that Tutankhamun himself lay.

Beyond the Burial Chamber was yet another small chamber. It was called the Treasury, mainly because of the superb quality of the objects found within it, which included model boats, gold shrines, and jewel cases. Also in the Treasury were two miniature coffins, each containing a mummified fetus. Were these the stillborn children of the pharaoh, and was this why Tutankhamun did not leave even an infant heir to succeed him? The mystery may never be solved.

Lord Carnarvon was never to know what lay inside the sarcophagus of Tutankhamun; he died in April 1923, and by then the lengthy task of emptying the tomb and conserving the objects that came from it had scarcely begun. The work was finally completed in 1932 by Carter, who died seven years later. Carnarvon and Carter's memorial is the wonderful collection of objects from the tomb of Tutankhamun and the story of what must be one of the most exciting and spectacular archaeological discoveries ever made.

LEFT: Tutankhamun's tomb lay in the Valley of the Kings, on the west bank of the Nile River at Thebes. As a boy Tutankhamun was brought up in Akhetaten, which was the royal capital at that time. However, during his reign the site of the royal capital was moved to the ancient city of Memphis.

BELOW: This detail from the back of Tutankhamun's golden throne shows the pharoah and his wife Ankhesenpaaten. The couple wear elaborate jeweled crowns.

Nubians

The ancient Nubians lived in a region of northeast Africa, in the southern part of modern Egypt and the northern part of the Sudan. Nubia was bounded to the west by the Nile River and the Sahara Desert, and to the east by the Red Sea—an area which today is the Nubian Desert.

The kingdom of the dark-skinned Nubians was invaded around 1920 B.C. when King Senusret of Egypt sent his armies up the Nile River. The Egyptians called this region Kush, and to them it was an important source of valuable metals and minerals—especially gold. For hundreds of years there was a string of raids between the two kingdoms, and the Kushites managed to capture some Egyptian treasures, which they took back to their capital, Kerma, near the third cataract of the Nile in present-day Sudan.

At that time Kush was a powerful state, ruled by kings who lived in luxury. Evidence of this was discovered early in the 20th century when the American archaeologist George Reisner uncovered a castle structure and a royal cemetery with many burial mounds containing the skeletons of

ABOVE: Models of Nubian archers found in an Egyptian tomb. The Nubians were expert archers, and the Egyptians referred to Nubia as the "land of the bow."

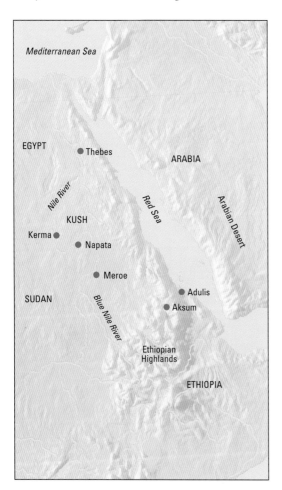

sacrificed animals and humans. The kings were found buried in larger tombs. The body of the king was laid on a bed in a small chamber, and near him were found the skeletons of hundreds of men, women, and children, who were all buried with the king as a sacrifice. Historians believe that they may have been buried alive.

The Kushites adopted some of the religion, art, and customs of the Egyptians. Then, about 740 B.C., the Kushite king Piankhi managed to conquer Egypt itself. The Kushites founded Egypt's 25th dynasty, but their rule did not last long. By 654 B.C. they had been driven back south by the Assyrians. The Kushites were now forced to set up their capital much farther south, at Napata, near the Nile's fourth cataract. At that time the Kushites adopted Egyptian as their official language and began to build pyramids for their royal tombs, as the Egyptians had done many hundreds of years earlier.

➤ THE KINGDOM OF MEROE ➤

But perhaps Napata was too close to Egypt, for in 590 B.C. the Kushites once again moved their capital, this time to Meroe, between the fifth and sixth cataracts. Their smaller kingdom flourished again, free from Egyptian influence. Here the Kushites found iron ore, which they smelted to make iron tools and weapons (this may have been

LEFT: Over the centuries the Nubian capital was moved southward down the Nile River, first from Kerma to Napata, and finally to Meroe.

where the practice of iron-smelting began in ancient Africa). Meroe and Napata were joined by an ancient caravan route.

At Meroe the Kushites built a royal palace of brick and stone, as well as a riverside quay and many steep-sided pyramids. These were built on top of tombs and were smaller and steeper than their Egyptian equivalents. Unfortunately, some 19th-century explorers lopped the tops off many of the pyramids as they searched in vain for hidden treasure. The Meroites also built temples to the Egyptian sacred bull Apis and to the goddess Isis, who represented the female force of nature. A further temple was dedicated to a god that was much more African and seems to have belonged only to the Meroites: the lion god Apedemak.

The Meroites gradually became less influenced by Egypt. They created new styles in art and architecture, used their own language, and developed their own alphabet and system of writing from Egyptian hieroglyphics. Their Meroitic symbols cover stone slabs, but scholars have not yet been able to decipher them fully. Meroe's merchants traded their excellent ironware with both the Mediterranean region and Asia. Farmers outside the city channeled water from the nearby Nile and used waterwheels driven by oxen to transfer the water to their fields. They grew cotton and other crops, as well as raising cattle.

In 45 B.C. Amanishakhete became queen of Kushite Meroe, and she and her successors increased contact with Egypt. But in 30 B.C. the great Egyptian kingdom fell to Rome, and seven years later the Roman prefect Petronius led an expedition into the Meroe region. The Romans captured several towns and destroyed Napata. They soon withdrew north to Egypt, but from that time Meroe's power and wealth gradually fell away. This decline may have been due to a fall in crop yields—the land may have been stripped of trees and overfarmed, so that desert spread across the region. By the third century nomads from the Arabian Desert had moved into the area. Then, about A.D. 350, forces from the powerful kingdom of Aksum destroyed Meroe itself.

➤ THE RISE OF AKSUM ➤

The city of Aksum was located 375 miles (600km) to the southeast of Meroe, in the northern highlands of present-day Ethiopia. The mountainous kingdom surrounding the city lay between the Blue Nile River and the Red Sea, stretching to parts of present-day Eritrea, Djibouti, and Sudan. By the first century A.D. the people of this region had become a strong trading power. They used

The Stelae of Aksum

Aksum is famous for its giant granite stelae—ancient pillars with carved inscriptions that resemble narrow skyscrapers. The monuments date from before the fourth century A.D., and their carvings show scenes that include Aksumite buildings of limestone, mud, and wood similar to those that can still be seen in villages in the highlands of northern Ethiopia.

The tallest stela still standing today is 65 ft (21m) high. Some of the stelae may have been even higher, but they now lie shattered on the ground. Historians are not sure what their purpose was, but some believe they marked royal Aksumite graves. In the 1970s archaeologists found a series of tombs running under the stelae, some of them 25 ft (8m) deep.

One of the largest stelae was removed by the Italians in the 1930s, during their occupation of Ethiopia as part of Italian East Africa. This ancient Aksumite monument now stands in Rome near the Arch of Constantine.

Many of the giant stone stelae put up by the kings of Aksum are still standing.

their port of Adulis on the Red Sea to trade with the Roman Empire, Arabia, and India. The conquest of Meroe gave the Aksumites more control over trading routes in the Nile Valley.

At about the same time as the conquest of Meroe, King Ezana of Aksum converted to Christianity. His kingdom became an ally of the Eastern Roman Empire that was administered from Constantinople. Over the next few centuries Aksum increased its power and conquered part of Arabia. The capital's monuments, churches, and 20,000 inhabitants were supported by taxes from conquered lands and their own successful traders. But after the Persians conquered Arabia in A.D. 575, it became difficult for the Aksumites to trade along the Red Sea. In the seventh century Muslim Arabs conquered the Persians, destroyed the Aksumite fleet, and cut Aksum off from the rest of the Christian world. The Aksumites could not compete with the Muslims' might, and by the year 1000 their civilization had lost all its power.

Akkadian Empire

The Akkadians set up the first known unified kingdom in Mesopotamia over 4,000 years ago. Before the rise of the Akkadians Mesopotamia was made up of many city-states, each of which had its own king, territory, and towns.

In the south of Mesopotamia were the Sumerians, and in the north were peoples who spoke a Semitic language. This language was quite distinct from the language spoken by the Sumerians, but otherwise the northerners were similar to their Sumerian neighbors.

In around 2334 B.C. a Semitic-speaking official at the court of the king of Kish, one of the city-states in Mesopotamia, overthrew the king and assumed the royal powers himself. He called himself Sargon (meaning "true king"), and from Kish he marched against the strongest ruler in the region—the Sumerian overlord and king of Uruk, Lugalzagesi. Sargon defeated Lugalzagesi and then attacked and defeated three more cities in southern Mesopotamia—Ur, Lagash, and Umma—and tore down their walls. He then marched his army to the shores of the Persian Gulf and, to show that his authority was unchallenged from Kish to the Gulf, washed his weapons in its salt waters.

⚊ A NEW CAPITAL CITY ⚊

Sargon built his new royal capital at Agade (or Akkad) on the Euphrates River near present-day Baghdad. His kingdom, Akkad, and its people the Akkadians were named after the city. People came from all over the empire to Agade to trade their goods, such as goats, cattle, and asses. The city had a vast port, and ships from as far away as Egypt and India docked there.

Sargon led more victorious campaigns—to Elam, in the mountains east of Mesopotamia, and westward toward the mountains of Lebanon. In the west the Akkadians gained access to important resources, such as silver and cedarwood. In the east the Akkadians made the Elamites move their capital from Elam to Susa and forced them to speak Akkadian.

Sargon the Great, as he now called himself, ruled over his empire until 2279 B.C. However, his authority grew much weaker in the later years of his reign, when he had to face revolts from some of his subjects in Sumer. But he succeeded in crushing them and handed over his mighty empire to his son Rimush.

Rimush ruled from 2278 to 2270 B.C. He had a troubled reign, but like his father he was successful in subduing rebellious cities. In the end, however, he was killed by his courtiers, who stabbed him (according to the story) with their cylinder seals. He was succeeded by his brother Manishtusu, who ruled from 2269 to 2255 B.C.

BELOW: A portrait head in copper of the first Akkadian king, Sargon the Great, who ruled his empire in Mesopotamia for more than 50 years.

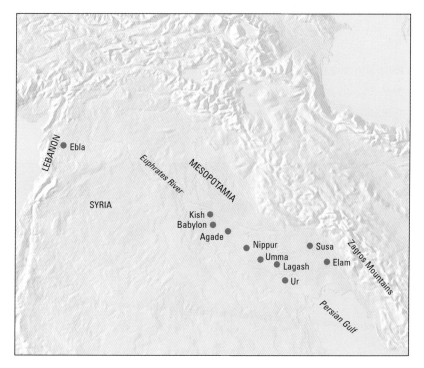

Lullubi, who lived in the foothills of the nearby Zagros Mountains.

The Akkadian Empire did not survive long after the death of Naram-Sin. His successor, Shar-kali-Sharri (ruled 2217–2193 B.C.), was killed by his own people, and after his death strife among his own successors, together with invasions by tribes from the Zagros Mountains, brought the Akkadian Empire to an end.

⬩ AKKADIAN MIGHT ⬩

The Akkadians ruled their empire with the help of a mighty army—King Sargon had 5,400 soldiers. The army was ruthless. The Akkadians tore down the walls of cities that rebelled, massacring all their citizens. Many stone monuments show victorious Akkadian soldiers carrying off booty and leading prisoners away to be killed.

Sargon's power rested on changing the traditional Sumerian system of government. The Sumerians had ruled their cities by appointing

ABOVE: A map showing the main cities of the Akkadian Empire and the nearby enemy city-states of Ebla and Elam.

RIGHT: A relief sculpture from the walls of the palace of King Sargon showing an Akkadian huntsman shooting birds with a bow and arrow.

Manishtusu found that although Elam had been defeated, the western part of the empire had recovered its independence. This threatened the routes Akkadian traders used in search of metals to make bronze. So the king led an expedition to the eastern end of the Persian Gulf, where he found an alternative supply of the metals needed.

Manishtusu's heir was Naram-Sin (ruled 2254–2218 B.C.), who spent most of his reign at war. In the west he brought northern Syria back under Akkadian rule. In the north he conquered the Assyrians and defeated the Hurrians. In the east he put down a revolt among the Akkadian subjects around the waters of the Persian Gulf. He also defeated his most powerful enemy, the

governors from among the leading families of the towns themselves. Sargon, instead, appointed other Akkadians who were sent to the cities with royal warrants as governor.

By turning the Sumerian city-states into a major military power, Sargon spread Sumerian culture across the Middle East. Cuneiform writing was widely adopted as a writing system and the Akkadian language became the semiofficial language of Mesopotamia and the Middle East.

The Clay Tablets of Ebla

When the site of ancient Ebla in northern Syria was first explored in 1964, archaeologists found the remains of a city dating from about 2500 B.C. It had been destroyed and burned to the ground either by Sargon or his grandson Naram-Sin.

The most exciting find was the archive room of the royal palace, which contained nearly 20,000 clay tablets inscribed with cuneiform writing. They were the state records, and from the information they contained it was possible to build a vivid picture of life in this Bronze Age society. The tablets made it clear that Ebla was the capital of a powerful state with its wealth based on trade and agriculture. The people grew vines, olive trees, and barley, and herded as many as two million sheep and half a million cattle. They traded in textiles and gold, silver, and bronze. Some of the tablets recorded laws, decrees, and treaties, showing that Ebla had an efficient administration.

Babylonia

The Babylonian Empire was one of the great empires of the ancient world. The Babylonians were highly sophisticated people who built great cities and invented astronomy, the lunar calendar, and the zodiac. They were also masters of algebra and advanced math.

The capital of Babylonia was the city of Babylon, which stood on the Mesopotamian plain surrounding the Euphrates River. The first Babylonian dynasty was founded in about 1890 B.C., when a king of the Amorite tribe established a kingdom around his capital, Bab-ilu, which was situated close to the Euphrates River. This was the beginning of the Old Babylonian Empire, which lasted until about 1600 B.C.

In 1792 B.C. an energetic young king called Hammurabi inherited the throne. Gradually, Hammurabi built a large empire that stretched from Assyria in the north to the Persian Gulf in the south. To keep order in his empire, Hammurabi developed an elaborate code of law. He set up efficient systems to organize defense, administer justice, collect taxes, and control trade and farming. This was a golden period of the Old Empire during which arts and sciences flourished in Babylonia.

After Hammurabi died in 1750 B.C., Babylonia came under attack. Eventually, in 1595 B.C., the capital was sacked by the Hittite people from Anatolia. However, it was not the Hittites but the Kassites, from the east, who finally inherited the kingdom. For the next 440 years Kassite kings ruled Babylonia until they were expelled in 1155 B.C. This began an unsettled age for Babylonia during which a series of powerful dynasties ruled, each for only a short time.

ABOVE: This relief sculpture carved in stone is from the palace of Nebuchadnezzar. It shows a governor of Babylon praying to the larger figures of the god Adad and the goddess Ishtar.

At the beginning of the first millennium B.C. the power of the Assyrians in the north was at its height. In the seventh century the Assyrians sacked Babylon and took control of the region. But the Assyrian Empire was now in decline, and in 626 B.C. a general from Chaldea (a southern region in Mesopotamia) called Nabopolassar recaptured the capital and restored Babylonia's independence. His victory marked the start of the greatest period of Babylonian history.

━ THE NEW EMPIRE ━

Nabopolassar, who ruled from 625 to 605 B.C., claimed he was "the son of a nobody," but under his leadership Babylonia became a mighty empire again. Helped by his allies, the Medes from Persia, Nabopolassar defeated the Assyrians and claimed their lands. In 605 B.C., his son Nebuchadnezzar defeated the Egyptian army at the Battle of Carchemish and was crowned king shortly afterward. His reign (605–562 B.C.) was the high point of the New Babylonian Empire.

Nabopolassar had begun a program of rebuilding in Babylon. Now the new king

Gods of Destiny

The Babylonians worshiped many of the same gods as the Sumerians. Their deities represented the powerful forces of nature or heavenly bodies such as the sun, moon, and stars. Ishtar, the goddess of love and war, represented the planet Venus, while Adad was the god of storm and winds. Each Babylonian city had its own patron god or goddess. The patron god of Babylon was Marduk, the Creator.

The Babylonians believed their gods were responsible for their destinies. Signs in the heavens, dreams, and unusual happenings foretold future events. For this reason the Babylonians rapidly became expert astronomers, studying and recording the movements of the stars each night. They could predict eclipses of the sun and moon, and they invented many of the names of the star constellations we use today.

Babylonian Law

The Babylonians had a comprehensive legal code, which was administered all over the empire. The law was literally set in stone—it was carved on stone tablets. The most famous set of laws was King Hammurabi's code, which was written down around 1760 B.C. The code was very long—it contained 282 articles, and its stated purpose was "to cause justice to prevail in the land, to destroy the wicked and the evil, that the strong may not oppress the weak."

The law was not the same for everyone, however. The same crime carried different penalties according to who had committed it and whom it was committed against. For example, if one aristocrat harmed another, the rule was "an eye for an eye, and a tooth for a tooth"—in other words, the criminal would suffer the same injury that he had caused his victim. However, if an aristocrat hurt a commoner or slave, his penalty was lighter, and he only had to pay a fine.

Punishments in Babylonian law included fines, beatings, mutilation, and execution. Imprisonment and forced labor did not exist. If a surgeon killed a patient during a major operation, he could have his hand cut off. Architects whose buildings collapsed and caused the death of the house-owner could be executed.

There were also laws governing family life. Men could divorce their wives and were allowed to have mistresses. They could also sell their wives and children into slavery. Wives, however, could only divorce their husbands if they could show they had been abused or treated cruelly—they risked death if they could not prove their case. Children were also covered by the law—a son who hit his father could have his hand cut off.

The legal code of King Hammurabi was carved on this stone column in cuneiform writing. At the top of the column a relief carving shows Shamash, the god of justice (seated) handing the laws to King Hammurabi (standing).

Nebuchadnezzar continued his father's work. He built stronger defensive walls, new palaces and temples, and the beautiful Hanging Gardens of Babylon for his wife.

Nebuchadnezzar also enlarged his father's empire, defeating Syria and the kingdom of Phoenicia on the shores of the Mediterranean Sea. He continued south to conquer Israel and Judah, capturing the city of Jerusalem in Judah in 597 B.C. After this conquest, the king of Judah and thousands of Jewish citizens were taken to Babylon in chains. When Jerusalem rebelled 10 years later, the city was sacked, and once again many of its citizens were deported to Babylon.

After Nebuchadnezzar, Babylon's glorious history declined. The last king was Nabonidus, who ruled from 556 to 539 B.C. He was a mysterious figure—an elderly scholar who seemed to be more interested in religion than in solving Babylonia's problems. Around 550 B.C., without warning, Nabonidus went to live in Taima, an oasis in the Arabian desert.

He stayed there for 10 years, leaving his eldest son, Belshazzar, in charge of Babylon. In 539 B.C.

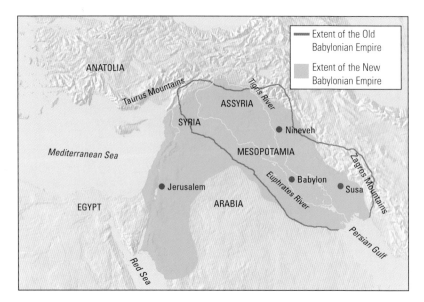

the Persians invaded Babylon, and in the battles that followed both Nabonidus and Belshazzar were killed. Babylonia was taken over and became a province of the Persian Empire.

ABOVE: This map of Mesopotamia shows the extent of the Old and New Babylonian Empires.

BABYLONIAN SOCIETY

Babylonian society was made up of three distinct groups—aristocrats, free citizens (commoners), and slaves. The aristocrats were generally government officials, military leaders, priests, wealthy landowners, and rich merchants. The free citizens were the craftsmen, traders, farmers, and scribes. Slaves were at the bottom of the hierarchy, but certain slaves had limited rights—they could own land and even in some instances buy their own freedom. Women, too, could own land, but otherwise they had few rights. They were never educated, for instance—only boys were allowed to go to school.

Most people in Babylonia worked as farmers. The flat plain between the Tigris and Euphrates was very fertile, since each spring the rivers flooded, spreading rich silt over the low-lying land. When the flood waters receded, a network of man-made channels carried water from the rivers to irrigate the fields. Farmers grew crops such as barley and sesame, vegetables, and fruits. They also kept bees for honey, and grew flowers such as lotuses and lilies to make perfume. Herds of goats, sheep, and cattle grazed the rich pastures. Much of the land was owned by the king, or by priests and noblemen, so many farmers leased the plots of ground they worked.

Many city-dwellers were either merchants or craftsmen. The merchants traveled great distances to trade, exchanging textiles, grain, and manufactured goods for wood, stone, and

BELOW: A necklace from Babylon made of gold and lapis lazuli, with a sculpted female head as a pendant.

precious metals. There were not many building materials in Babylon, so wood and stone were very valuable.

Craftsmen were highly skilled, and the members of each craft belonged to a guild. Boys had to be apprenticed to a master craftsman to learn the trade before they could be admitted to the guild.

SCIENCE AND MATH

The Babylonians were accomplished scientists and mathematicians. They invented the lunar calendar, which divided the year into 12 months based on the phases of the moon. Months were divided into weeks of seven days, and each day was divided into 24 hours. Like the Sumerians, they divided the hour into 60 minutes.

In mathematics they excelled at geometry and algebra, and understood square roots and fractions. They were skilled doctors and left detailed medical records of the symptoms of many illnesses and their cures. They had a good knowledge of anatomy and understood the circulation of the blood in the human body.

The Babylonians spoke Akkadian, a Semitic language. They wrote in cuneiform script, the system of writing developed by the Sumerians. Several thousands of documents written on clay tablets have been discovered. Many are business records, listing legal contracts, receipts, and loans. Others record military victories, mathematical proofs, prayers, or works of fiction.

Babylon

From about 2000 to 500 B.C. Babylon was the capital of the Babylonian Empire and a major center of religion and trade. It was also the site of the legendary Tower of Babel and the Hanging Gardens of Babylon, which were considered among the Seven Wonders of the World.

The city of Babylon was famous throughout the ancient world. When the Greek writer Herodotus visited the city around 450 B.C.—after it had been conquered by the Persians—he claimed that it "surpasses in splendor any city of the known world." The glories of the capital included immense, decorated temples and palaces and the brick-built ziggurat that was supposed to be the Tower of Babel mentioned in the Bible.

The site of Babylon lies in Iraq, 55 miles (88km) south of the city of Baghdad. Between 1899 and 1913, Babylon was excavated by the German archaeologist Robert Koldewey and his team. Brick by brick, they gradually built up a picture of the ancient city. Their research revealed Babylon as it had been in its final years, during the reign of King Nebuchadnezzar II. Below the ruins of Nebuchadnezzar's Babylon lay the remains of cities from even earlier eras.

During the 1700s B.C., Babylon had been the center of a large empire under King Hammurabi. Koldewey's team found that Hammurabi's Babylon contained fine temples and palaces, and a maze of narrow streets lined with houses. All the buildings were made of mud bricks set on top of burned brick foundations. Hammurabi's capital was protected by strong walls.

After the reign of Hammurabi, Babylon passed into the hands of people called the Kassites, who ruled Babylon from about 1600 to 1150 B.C. Then, in the seventh century B.C., the Assyrians captured and sacked the city.

➤ NEBUCHADNEZZAR'S CITY ➤

It was not until the Babylonian general Nabopolassar defeated the Assyrians in 626 B.C. that Babylon was restored to its former glory. He and his son Nebuchadnezzar rebuilt the capital and transformed it into the finest city in the ancient Middle East. Nebuchadnezzar's capital covered an area of 2,100 acres (850ha), which made it larger than many modern towns. In its heyday, up to 250,000 people lived there.

The rectangular city was enclosed by a double line of mighty walls. The outer walls were 85 ft (26m) thick. The inner walls were equally sub-stantial—according to Herodotus, two chariots pulled by four horses each could ride side by side along the top of them.

Eight bronze gates led into the city. The most magnificent of them was the Ishtar Gate. Its walls and gateway were decorated with bright blue glazed tiles and with reliefs of animals that symbolized the Babylonian gods. Ishtar, the goddess of love and war, was represented by a lion; Adad,

ABOVE: This reconstruction of the Ishtar Gate stands in a Berlin museum. The gate was covered in blue-and-yellow tiles showing images of bulls and dragons, which were both symbols of gods.

RIGHT: A map of Babylon
in the time of King
Nebuchadnezzar showing
the outer walls, main
streets, and the sites of
the palace, temples,
and ziggurat.

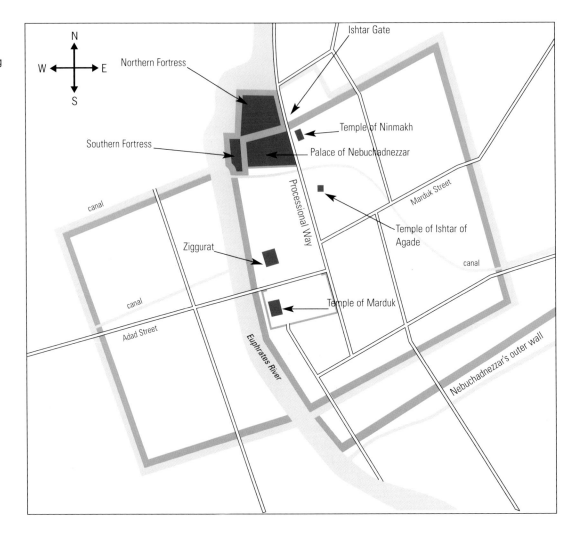

the god of storms, was symbolized by a bull. A horned dragon represented Marduk, who was an important god and patron of the city.

In Nebuchadnezzar's time the Euphrates River flowed through the city, dividing it in two. The two halves were linked by a stone bridge over the river. The western part contained houses for many of the citizens while the eastern part contained palaces and temples.

Nebuchadnezzar's palace stood close to the Ishtar Gate. Known as the "Marvel of Mankind," it was built around five courtyards and its walls were decorated with glazed tiles. On the ground in one of the courtyards the archaeologists found a huge sculpture of a lion trampling the body of a man. This statue symbolized Babylon's triumph over its neighbors.

South of the palace lay the temple of Marduk, which was linked to the Ishtar Gate by a wide avenue called the Processional Way. This temple was the focus for the city's most important festival, which took place at New Year and lasted for 11 days. At its climax the king would lead a procession carrying a statue of Marduk through the Ishtar Gate to a shrine outside the city. North of the temple of Marduk stood a towering brick ziggurat, or pyramid-temple, supposed to be the origin of the Tower of Babel mentioned in the Bible. It rose to a height of 300 ft (91m) and was topped by a smaller shrine to Marduk.

→ THE LOST GARDENS →

The archaeologists could find no trace of the famed Hanging Gardens of Babylon. According to ancient writers, the gardens were built by Nebuchadnezzar to please his wife, a princess from Media who missed the forests and meadows of her native land. The gardens probably grew on rooftop terraces that have long since crumbled.

After Nebuchadnezzar, Babylon's power faded. The city first fell into the hands of the Persian Empire in 539 B.C., and then in 331 B.C. it was conquered again, this time by the Macedonian general Alexander the Great. It became his capital; but when Alexander died, the region passed to his general Seleucus. Seleucus built a new capital, Seleucia, on the Tigris River, and Babylon was abandoned.

Assyrians

The Assyrians were a warlike people from the northern region of Mesopotamia. Over a period of about 1,500 years they fought and defeated many of their neighbors, building an empire that stretched west as far as the Mediterranean Sea and east to the Persian Gulf.

The original home of the Assyrians was in the north of Mesopotamia (present-day Iraq) around the Tigris River. This was a land of rolling hills and fertile valleys where the people grew crops of barley and sesame, and kept herds of animals such as cattle, goats, and sheep.

The history of Assyria is usually divided into three periods: the Old, Middle, and New Empires. In the Old Empire (2000–1450 B.C.) the Assyrians set up city-states, notably Ashur on the banks of the Tigris River. Each city was a collection of houses, temples, and palaces built inside a city wall. Assyrian merchants grew rich by trading copper with the people of Anatolia in the northwest—and many Assyrian colonies grew up along the trading routes.

From 1813 to 1781 B.C. Assyria was ruled by a warrior-chief, Shamshi-Adad, who increased the extent of Assyrian lands through conquest. However, during his son's reign Assyria was attacked and conquered by Hammurabi, King of Babylon, which ended the Old Empire. Assyria was then ruled by Babylon and later, around 1450 B.C., by the Mitannians from northern Syria.

In 1363 B.C. King Ashur-uballit I restored Assyria's independence, marking the beginning of the Middle Empire, which lasted until 1000 B.C. During this time Assyrian kings fought against their neighbors and won new lands. At the same time, Assyrian culture was enriched by neighboring civilizations, and its influence increased.

⤙ THE NEW EMPIRE ⤚

During the period of the New Empire (1000–612 B.C.) Assyrian power reached its greatest height. The empire was ruled by a series of ruthless warrior-kings who showed no mercy in their search for new lands to conquer. One of the fiercest, Tiglath-pileser III, conquered and destroyed the main cities of Israel and the Mediterranean kingdom of Phoenicia during the eighth century B.C. Prisoners were either killed or exiled to other parts of the empire, so that there would be no resistance to Assyrian rule.

Conquered lands became provinces of the empire, ruled by governors appointed by the king. Each year the provinces were forced to send gold, silver, food, animals, or fine cloths and

BELOW: A stone relief carving from a wall of the palace of Nineveh, showing Ashurbanipal II and his queen being served a victory feast.

luxuries to the Assyrian capital. Tiglath-pileser's successors used the same tactics. In the eighth century B.C. Assyrian kings conquered Israel and the state of Urartu in Anatolia. In the seventh century B.C. even Egypt was conquered, and the cities of Babylon, Thebes, and Susa were sacked. By now, however, the Assyrian Empire had become so vast that it was difficult to rule.

The Assyrians had also made many enemies and now these enemies attacked their oppressors. In 614 and 612 B.C. Babylonians and Medes from Persia invaded Assyria and sacked the cities of Ashur and Nineveh. By 608 B.C. the Assyrian Empire had been destroyed.

➤ A DEADLY ARMY ➤

At its height during the New Empire the Assyrian army was one of the deadliest and most efficient fighting forces the world had ever known. In earlier years, most Assyrian soldiers had been part-time—peasants and farmers forced to fight in times of war. But during the eighth century B.C. the army was reorganized into a regular force of full-time soldiers.

The main part of the army comprised foot soldiers, who were provided by landowners and the conquered provinces. But there were divisions of cavalry and chariot troops too, who came from the rich elite. Soldiers were issued leather or chainmail armor and shields, plus spears, slings, battleaxes, maces, swords, and daggers for hand-to-hand fighting. Each unit of 50 men was led by a captain. Special units of archers were protected by their own soldiers who carried large shields and spears.

Usually the king led the army into battle himself. By the eighth century it had become customary for the king to lead a new campaign every year, either to collect taxes from distant parts of the empire or to conquer new lands. Every campaign was carried out with minimum use of force to save Assyrian lives. When he had decided to conquer a new region, the king would select a target city and lay siege to it to cut off its supplies. When the enemy was weakened, the assault would begin.

During the assault the archers of the army and other soldiers with slings kept the defenders at bay with a hail of arrows and missiles. While this was going on, wooden siege engines were rolled up to batter the gates and walls. Soldiers also scaled the walls with ladders to get into the city.

Once the city was taken, the Assyrians showed no mercy to its citizens. They took some prisoners, to be taken away to be slaves. But most of the citizens were massacred, and their mangled bodies set on stakes around the edges of the city to scare the whole region into surrender. Back in the

RIGHT: This stone relief from King Ashurnasirpal's palace at Nimrud shows a scene from a royal hunt, with the king in his chariot taking aim with his bow and arrow at a lion that is attacking him. Hunting was a favorite sport of the Assyrian kings—the king and members of his court would ride out on horseback or in chariots, carrying long spears or bows and arrows to kill their prey. They hunted elephants, wild bulls, or lions, all of which roamed the Syrian plain at that time. The hunts were dangerous, since a cornered lion could well turn and savage the attacking horse and rider.

Assyrian capital, the king would lead a triumphal procession through the streets to the temple to give news of the victory to the warrior-god Ashur.

➤ MAGNIFICENT CITIES ➤

The Assyrians built many fine cities. Throughout the centuries, the capital of the empire was located in different places by various kings. During the Old and Middle Empires Ashur was the capital and held the kings' tombs. Around 880 B.C. King Ashurnasirpal II built a new capital further north at Nimrud.

Craftsmen from all over the empire were brought in to work on the buildings of the new city. When the royal palace was finally completed, King Ashurnasirpal celebrated by giving a huge banquet to which he invited 69,500 guests. The feasting lasted for 10 days, and during this time the guests consumed 10,000 vessels of wine and ate 14,000 sheep.

In the seventh century B.C. King Sennacherib moved the capital again, this time to Nineveh, which was also set on the banks of the Tigris River. There he built a "palace without rival," with beautiful gardens.

Each of the Assyrian capitals was protected by high city walls and held temples to the chief gods and a ziggurat—a temple mound shaped like a pyramid with steps. The halls and shady courtyards of the palaces spread over several acres. The throne room was the most impressive building in the palace. The king's throne was guarded by giant statues of winged lions or bulls with human heads. The palace walls were decorated with carvings showing battles, scenes of conquered peoples bringing tributes, or lion hunts.

Assyria's position at the crossroads of east-west and north-south trade routes meant that it was well placed for trading with its neighbors. The Assyrians exported textiles and imported wood, wine, precious metals and stones, horses, and camels. Goods were exchanged using a system of barter based on different metals—such as silver, tin, and copper.

The Assyrians wrote using cuneiform script, the system of wedge-shaped symbols developed by the Sumerians. During the seventh century B.C. King Ashurbanipal built up a large library of clay tablets that came from all over Assyria, Babylonia, and neighboring countries. Some of the tablets were historical accounts of Assyrian conquests; others were legal documents, medical records, or records of myths and prayers.

The Assyrians worshiped some of the same gods and goddesses as the Babylonians. They

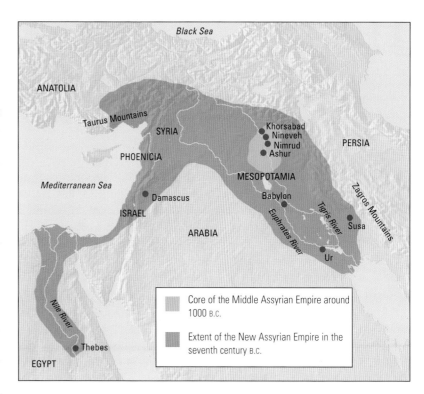

revered Ishtar, the Babylonian goddess of love and war, the storm god Adad, and Ninurta, the god of war and hunting. However, their main god, the warrior-god Ashur, was their own. The king was the religious head as well as the head of state—he held the position of chief priest as well as being ruler and commander of the army.

Most Assyrians were farmers or herders. They kept flocks of goats, sheep, and cattle, and grew crops such as barley, sesame, vegetables, and grapes in irrigated fields. In the cities people might work as craftsmen or traders. They, too, grew fruit and vegetables in little gardens outside the city walls. Everyone, from wealthy landowners to peasants and slaves, had to follow the strict code of Assyrian law. The law punished wrongdoers harshly. Penalties for crimes ranged from beatings to mutilation, and even death.

ABOVE: A map showing how the Assyrian warrior-kings of the New Empire dramatically increased the extent of their territory.

Assyrian Crafts

The Assyrians were skilled craftsmen. They learned many of their techniques from the Babylonians, but they developed their own style. Assyrian sculptors were very good at carving relief sculptures in stone on walls. When they were first done, the reliefs were painted in bright colors, but today only the lines of the bare stone remain.

The Assyrians also worked with gold, bronze, and other metals, and made smaller carvings in ivory, stone, and wood. They used small cylinders with pictures carved on their surface to make impressions on clay tablets to seal important documents. These delicate impressions show many scenes from myths and legends.

Hittites

An aggressive people, the Hittites were based in ancient Anatolia (present-day Turkey). With the help of their superior fighting forces they built an empire that stretched from Anatolia east as far as Mesopotamia (present-day Iraq) and south into Syria and Cyprus.

At its height the Hittite Empire rivaled the empires of ancient Egypt and Babylon, and the Hittites were a powerful force in the Middle East for about 500 years—between around 1700 and 1190 B.C. Despite this, almost all knowledge of their civilization was lost for thousands of years, until recent archaeological discoveries restored the Hittites to their place in history.

The Hittite capital, Hattusas, lay in the west, near the modern city of Ankara in central Turkey. Yet the Hittite people did not originally come from this region. They were an Indo-European race from the barren steppes of Central Asia. Some time before 2000 B.C. they pushed southwest and finally settled in an area of Anatolia called Hatti. The name "Hittite" comes from the area they conquered.

The forerunner of the great Hittite kings was a prince called Anittas, who carved out a small kingdom in central Anatolia around 1850 B.C. Anittas conquered the city of Kanesh and then the mountain settlement of Hattusas, which dominated the northern region. He completely destroyed Hattusas and declared it cursed ground. However, the site was a natural fortress in a key position, making it far too useful to be abandoned for long. After a few generations a Hittite king named Labarnas reoccupied the site and then rebuilt the city, making it his capital. Labarnas even changed his own name to Hattusilis, which means "man of Hattusas," in honor of the place.

─ FOUNDING AN EMPIRE ─

Hattusilis was the real founder of the Hittite Empire. During the 1700s B.C. he conquered the windswept plateaus of Anatolia south of his new capital, then led his armies across the rocky barrier of the Taurus Mountains and down to the southern Turkish coast. Next, his forces marched east to subdue the cities of northern Syria, which were ruled by the kings of Aleppo, one of the powerful Syrian cities.

His grandson, Mursilis I, capped his grandfather's achievements by conquering Aleppo itself. In 1595 B.C. Mursilis continued east along the Euphrates River, entered Mesopotamia, and sacked the great city of Babylon.

However, this proud victory was to cost the Hittites dearly. As they were returning home along the same route, the exhausted Hittite troops were attacked and routed by the Hurrians, a fierce warrior-race from the region around the upper Euphrates River. In addition, Mursilis's control over his kingdom had been fatally weakened by his long absence, and on his return he was murdered by his own brother-in-law. Later Hittite kings failed to hold onto the lands that Mursilis had conquered, and they, too, fell into the hands of the Hurrians.

Then in 1375 B.C. a young, energetic king called Suppiluliumas opened a new, glorious chapter in Hittite history. Suppiluliumas had

LEFT: A Hittite couple carved in stone on a funeral stela. In Hittite society the choice of a marriage partner was made by the couple's parents and was based mainly on financial considerations, but a woman was allowed to reject her parents' choice.

many talents. He was a brave warrior and also a clever diplomat. Although the young king had inherited a weakened empire threatened by powerful enemies on all sides, in a relatively short space of time he and his successors built an empire that was powerful enough to rival any in the ancient Middle East.

Suppiluliumas began his conquests by retaking the old Hittite territories in southern Anatolia. His armies then moved south to subdue the Syrian city-states, reaching as far as Damascus. Finally, they turned east to settle their score with the Hurrians.

Suppiluliumas defeated the Hurrians in a battle fought at Carchemish and installed a minor prince, who had sworn loyalty to him, on the Hurrian throne. He then strengthened this alliance by marrying his daughter to the prince.

← CONSOLIDATING THE EMPIRE →

Through a combination of military force and shrewd politics Suppiluliumas managed to establish a large empire made up of many smaller kingdoms. Each of these kingdoms was ruled by a vassal who swore an oath of political loyalty and obedience to the Hittite king. The loyalty of these vassals was often reinforced by arranged marriages to members of the Hittite royal family. While Suppiluliumas offered his vassals the "protection" of the mighty Hittite Empire, the vassal princes in return had to send a yearly tribute to the capital and a quota of men to swell the ranks of the Hittite army.

Suppiluliumas's son, Mursilis II, continued in his father's footsteps. He conquered the kingdom of Arzawa in western Anatolia, extending Hittite influence as far as the Aegean Sea. The next king,

RIGHT: Hittite gods were usually represented—like this one—wearing a cone-shaped hat and a short kilt. This gold pendant probably served to protect its wealthy owner.

Muwatallis, attacked the might of Egypt, which was ruled by Ramses II at that time, and inflicted great damage on the Egyptian army at the Battle of Kadesh in 1275 B.C. Afterward the Hittites made peace with both Egypt and Babylon, and the Hittite Empire entered a period of great prosperity and power. But not for long—to the east the powerful Assyrian Empire was growing ever stronger, while warrior-races known as the "Sea Peoples" threatened Anatolia from the west. Around 1190 B.C. the Sea Peoples overran Hittite lands, and the capital city of Hattusas was sacked. The empire of the Hittites was destroyed forever.

← HITTITE SOCIETY →

In the Hittite Empire most people worked as farmers. High on the Anatolian plateau, with its harsh climate, the main crops were wheat and barley; but onions, peas, figs, olives, grapes, and apples were also grown. Cattle, pigs, sheep, and

The Hittite Army

The Hittite army had a reputation as a formidable fighting force. During major campaigns the army numbered as many as 30,000 men, and the king himself led his forces into battle. Noblemen and officers led smaller units of 10,000 and 1,000 soldiers.

The chariot divisions were among the most effective fighting units in the ancient Middle East. In other armies, such as that of the Egyptians, chariots carried two men: a driver and a warrior armed with a bow and javelins for medium-range fighting. Hittite chariots held three men: a driver, a shield-bearer, and a soldier armed with a stabbing spear for close-range fighting. Weighed down by three soldiers, the Hittite chariot was less maneuverable, but the extra manpower made it deadlier in the thick of battle. The army also had divisions of foot soldiers armed with bows, axes, spears, or sickle-shaped slashing swords. Helmets and shields helped protect the men from the blows of the enemy.

LEFT: The remains of a Hittite temple. The temples were built of huge blocks of stone like the ones seen here, carved with relief figures, and they often contained monumental stone statues, which were also carved in relief.

goats were kept for wool, meat, and dairy produce. The main foods were breads and cakes, porridge, and meat or vegetable stews.

In addition to farmers there were workers with specialist trades, such as carpenters and builders, and craftsmen such as metalworkers and potters—who produced slim-necked jugs and wide, shallow cups, or vases modeled into the shapes of birds and beasts.

⇀ CRAFT SKILLS ⇀

The Hittites were well known for their metalwork. From the people of Anatolia they learned bronzeworking skills and also the art of smelting—the technique of extracting iron from iron ore by heating it to high temperatures. The Hittites may have guarded this precious secret closely; certainly, it formed the basis of their trade. Iron ore was dug out of local mines and formed into rough ingots on site. The ingots were then transported to the towns to be refined and shaped into tough, long-lasting tools and weapons. However, iron remained scarce, and most of the Hittite weapons and armor were made of bronze. (It was only after the downfall of the Hittite Empire that the true Iron Age began.)

The Hittites were also skilled stonemasons and sculptors. Indeed, their giant stone carvings of gods, humans, and animals are the most impressive record of their civilization. Most Hittite sculptures were relief sculptures—carved into a flat stone surface—and designed to be seen from the front only. However, smaller bronze figures, and even some large stone statues, were carved "in the round."

Wool was spun and clothes were made in the home. For everyday wear men wore a long-sleeved, knee-length tunic that was fastened at the shoulders with bronze pins. For outdoor wear women threw long cloaks about their shoulders to cover the lighter garments they wore indoors. Both men and women wore jewelry.

At festivals Hittite men wore calf-length tunics called "Hurrian shirts," which were ornamented with embroidery or bronze decorations.

BELOW: At the height of its power the Hittite Empire extended over a large area that included much of modern Turkey, Syria, and Iraq.

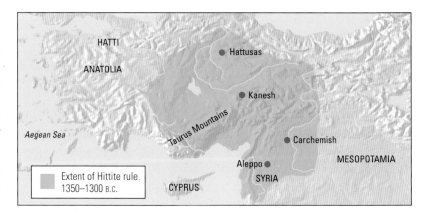

Hattusas

The capital city of the Hittite Empire was the great city of Hattusas. Its ruins today cover roughly 400 acres (162ha) of rugged crags and hillside, but it was originally one and a half miles (2.4km) across. It was built at a place where many streams rush down the mountainside and the Hittites carved cisterns out of the solid rock to store the water. The town's builders did not lay out the streets on a regular grid but made use of any land that could be built on. To create more flat ground on the uneven hillsides, they constructed earth terraces.

The houses of Hattusas were built of mud bricks and stone, with flat roofs of brushwood and mud laid over timber beams. The homes must have been very dark inside, for there were few windows. The largest houses, built for noble families, were minicastles, perched on rocky outcrops and fortified by strong walls. As well as dwellings, the city also contained many workshops, taverns, eating houses, and granaries.

Throughout the Hittite Empire most people worked as farmers, but in Hattusas many people earned their living by following a specialized profession. There were merchants, soldiers, watchmen, inn-keepers, doctors, tailors, and cobblers, together with craftsmen such as potters, stonemasons, and gold- and coppersmiths.

At the height of the empire the streets of Hattusas would have been crowded with townspeople, priests, warriors, and slaves hurrying about their business. Farmers, bakers, and fishermen would rub shoulders with other citizens as they sold their wares. Merchants leading their pack ponies through

Part of the ruins of the city of Hattusas in central Turkey. The remains of the Great Temple can be seen on the right.

the nearby hills would know they had almost reached their destination when they saw the curls of woodsmoke rising from a hundred hearths and heard hammers ringing on iron, the shouts of soldiers, and the barking of the city's dogs.

Enemies of the Hittites, approaching Hattusas on less peaceful missions, would have been daunted by the town's defenses. Circling the city were four miles (6km) of high earth ramparts, topped by stout stone walls. Some of the boulders built into the walls were so massive that later visitors believed the city had been built by giants. A long, secret tunnel built under the walls enabled the defenders to mount counterattacks on invaders.

The gates that led into the city were guarded by towers and battlements. Of these the southern gates near the crest of the ridge are the best preserved. Each was decorated

by sculptures carved into the giant stones. The Sphinx Gate was decorated with twin sphinxes (borrowed from Egyptian mythology), while the Lion Gate had two snarling lions that give the impression they are about to charge straight out of the rock. The King's Gate held the finest sculpture—the figure of a young warrior dressed in a pointed helmet and short tunic, and holding a battleaxe. Today, this statue is in the Ankara museum, and only a copy remains at the site of the ancient city.

Inside the southern gates was a group of temples and castles, as well as more humble dwellings. Farther down, a fortress called the Citadel stood on a rocky outcrop. It included the king's palace, with its pillared walkways. Even lower down the hillside was the Great Temple, which was undoubtedly the setting for important Hittite festivals.

On state occasions it seems that the kings may have worn the high, cone-shaped hats normally reserved for Hittite gods.

➤ LANGUAGE AND WRITING ➤

The Hittites spoke an Indo-European language—one of a group of languages related to Sanskrit, the ancient Indian tongue. Classical languages such as Latin and Greek developed from this group. Then, in turn, they gave rise to English, French, and other European languages. Some ancient Hittite words are very close to their modern English equivalents: for example, the Hittite word for water is "watar," and the word for daughter is "dohter."

From other civilizations of that time, such as those of the Hurrians and Babylonians, the Hittites learned the art of writing in both hieroglyphs (picture symbols) and in the cuneiform script of wedge-shaped signs. It was the thousands of hieroglyphic and cuneiform tablets found at Hittite sites in the 20th century that enabled historians to piece together some of the lost history of the Hittite Empire.

Persian Empire

The Persians were originally nomads from Central Asia. From the sixth to the fourth century B.C. they pursued an aggressive policy that resulted in an empire stretching from Egypt and Anatolia east as far as India—the largest state the world had ever known.

LEFT: A glazed brick relief from King Darius's palace at Susa showing the Persian royal guard. Armed with spears, bows, and arrows, the royal guards were known as the Immortals because any who fell in battle were swiftly replaced.

The Persians were fair rulers who treated the peoples they conquered better than any previous overlords, such as the Assyrians, had done. When the Persians were finally defeated by Alexander the Great, their tolerant attitude was adopted by their Greek conquerors, and many of their values became part of Greek society and so passed on to the modern world.

The Persians were originally a nomadic people who came from the steppes of Central Asia. Around 1000 B.C. they moved west to settle in Elam, the land of the Elamites. Their new home, which is today part of Afghanistan and Iran, was mainly high, dry, dusty plateau. The newcomers pastured their flocks in the highlands and grew crops in the valleys. Like other nomadic peoples, they were expert riders and horse-breeders. By 800 B.C. the Persians and another related group of

people called the Medes had established dominance over the original inhabitants of Elam.

During the 700s B.C. the Medes created the kingdom of Media, northeast of Mesopotamia. To the west of Media lay the mighty empires of Assyria and Babylon, where civilization had thrived for thousands of years. In 612 B.C. the Medes made an alliance with the king of Babylon and invaded Assyria. They overran the country and sacked the capital, Nineveh.

⇀ CYRUS THE GREAT ↽

However, in 550 B.C. the Medes were themselves defeated by Cyrus, the chief of the Persians. By uniting the Medes and the Persians, Cyrus laid the foundations of the Persian Empire. He called it the Achaemenid Empire after one of his ancestors, Achaemenes, who had founded his royal

The Behistun Inscription

The story of Darius's struggle to win the Persian throne is recorded on a giant rock near Behistun in Iran. The rock carving shows a picture of Darius, protected by the chief Persian god, Ahura Mazda, receiving homage from nine rebel kings.

The inscription on the rock was written in cuneiform script in three ancient languages: Persian, Babylonian, and Elamite, all of them unreadable in the early 1800s. The English scholar Henry Rawlinson succeeded in deciphering the Persian and Babylonian scripts in the 1850s and in doing so, he cracked the secret of the ancient cuneiform script of wedge-shaped characters, making the Behistun rock as famous in archaeological terms as the Rosetta Stone, which was the key to understanding Egyptian hieroglyphs. Thanks to his work archaeologists were able to read the clay tablets and other inscriptions from Assyria, Mesopotamia, and Sumer, greatly increasing knowledge of the history, religion, economy, science, and literature of the ancient Middle East.

line. Cyrus was an ambitious statesman and a clever general. During his reign Persia grew from a small kingdom into a mighty empire.

First, he set out to conquer the kingdom of Lydia in west Anatolia. Lydia was rich in gold, and its king, Croesus, was fabulously wealthy. Before Croesus went to war, he consulted the oracle at Delphi in Greece, to discover whether he was likely to win. The oracle told Croesus that an empire would fall if he crossed the Halys River to wage war. Pleased by this news, Croesus crossed the river to fight the Persians, but the empire that fell was his own. Cyrus took over Lydia and the Greek cities of Ionia in Anatolia.

About half a century later, around 500 B.C., the cities of Ionia rebelled, helped by mainland Greece. The rebellion was soon crushed, but the incident was to cause lasting hostility between the Greeks and the Persians.

In 539 B.C. Cyrus captured the city of Babylon and took over the whole Babylonian Empire, including Palestine and Syria. He treated his conquered peoples fairly and was soon popular. He also set free the Jews who had been held captive in Babylon, allowing them to return to their homeland in Palestine and rebuild their temple.

In 530 B.C. Cyrus was killed in battle and was succeeded by his son, Cambyses. The new king conquered Egypt but ruled more harshly than his father had. In 522 B.C. Cambyses died on his way back to Persia. His death was followed by a time of turmoil, as Achaemenid princes fought one another for the Persian throne and many parts of the empire took the chance to rebel against Persian rule. In the end a nobleman called Darius defeated his rivals, put down the rebellions, and was crowned king in 522 B.C.

➤ KING DARIUS ➤

Darius's first task was to reestablish control over all parts of his realm. He divided the empire into provinces called *satrapies*, each one ruled by an official called a *satrap*. He established a just code of law, a new tax system, a uniform system of coinage, standard weights and measures, a postal service, and a common calendar. He also built royal capitals at Susa and Persepolis.

Having sorted out his affairs at home, Darius launched a campaign to win more land. On the eastern borders of Persia he continued to conquer territory until his empire reached the Indus River. Then he turned west and defeated the kingdoms

BELOW: A carved limestone slab from Persepolis showing Darius I on his throne.

of Thrace and Macedonia on the borders of Greece. After an unsuccessful war against the Scythians, who lived in the region around the Caspian Sea, he set his sights firmly on Greece itself. At first, his army and navy were victorious, but in 490 B.C. the Persian forces were crushed at the Battle of Marathon.

Darius died in 486 B.C. while preparing for another war against the Greeks. He was succeeded by his son Xerxes, who led an army of 70,000 men against Greece. The Persians were victorious and even managed to capture Athens. However, in 479 B.C. they were beaten at the Battle of Plataea and driven from Greece. This defeat marked the end of Persian expansion in Europe and the Middle East.

In contrast to his predecessors, Xerxes was a heavy-handed ruler, and his reign was marred by revolts of the city-states in Anatolia. In 465 B.C. he was assassinated. His death began a century of civil war and rebellion in Persia as members of the Achaemenid dynasty plotted and murdered each other to win power. The Persians were never to regain full control over their vast empire.

In 336 B.C. a new king, Darius III, succeeded to the Persian throne. Persia was now threatened by a new force—the armies of Alexander the Great, king of Macedonia, who was eager to carve out his own empire. Alexander won three battles against the Persians, then marched on Persepolis, the Persian capital. He feasted at the royal palace there—before burning it to the ground.

Alexander's triumph spelled the end of the Achaemenid Empire, but not the last of the Persian kings. After nearly five centuries of foreign rule a new Persian dynasty called the Sasanians took power in A.D. 225. This line of kings ruled Persia for 400 years until A.D. 636, when they were conquered by the Arabs.

━ ENLIGHTENED RULE ━

Despite their power, the Persian kings did not rule through terror but with the help of a council of nobles. Conquered peoples were treated justly and allowed to keep their own laws and customs, provided they acknowledged Persian rule. Each *satrapy*, or province, was ruled by a governor responsible for collecting taxes and maintaining law and order. Each region had to send a yearly tribute to the king in the form of gold or silver, ivory, animals, or slaves. It also had to supply soldiers to serve in the Persian army.

In return for the regional taxes the Persian government carried out a program of public projects throughout the empire. It improved

drainage and irrigation, digging an underground network of channels to carry water through the desert. During the reign of Darius I the Persians built a canal that linked the Red Sea with the Mediterranean Sea.

Workers also constructed excellent roads that linked all parts of the empire. The best-known was the Royal Road, which ran from Sardis in Lydia to the capital, Susa, a distance of 1,550 miles (2,500km). All major routes had staging posts where travelers could eat, rest, and change horses. Soldiers and the king's messengers could travel at speed along the roads, and relays of messengers on horseback provided an efficient postal

ABOVE: One of the magnificent stone relief carvings that decorated the walls and staircases of the city of Persepolis. The building of the city was started in 516 B.C. by Darius I, and eventually completed in 465 B.C.

LEFT: The Persians excelled in fine goldwork and jewelry—this gold armlet is decorated with griffins and originally would have been inlaid with semiprecious stones and colored glass.

RIGHT: A Roman mosaic based on a fourth-century B.C. Greek painting. It shows the Persian army under the command of Darius III fighting against Alexander the Great at the Battle of Issus in 333 B.C.

service. The fifth-century Greek historian Herodotus wrote of the Persian messengers, "Neither snow, nor rain, nor heat, nor gloom of night stays these couriers from the swift completion of their appointed rounds."

The ancient Persians worshiped many gods of nature, such as the sun. Around 1000 B.C. a prophet named Zoroaster called on the Persians to abandon their deities and worship the supreme god Ahura Mazda. He also stressed the importance of good deeds. By the sixth century B.C. Zoroastrianism had become the state religion.

The Persians were great builders and built many magnificent cities. The finest were Pasargadae, Susa, and Persepolis, all of them capital cities. Each city had a royal palace built with skills and materials drawn from all parts of the empire. The palace at Susa, for example, was designed by Babylonian and Median architects and then built with the help of Lydian and Egyptian craftsmen. It used timber from India and Lebanon, gold from Lydia and Bactria, ivory from Africa, and silver, turquoise, and precious stones from many distant lands.

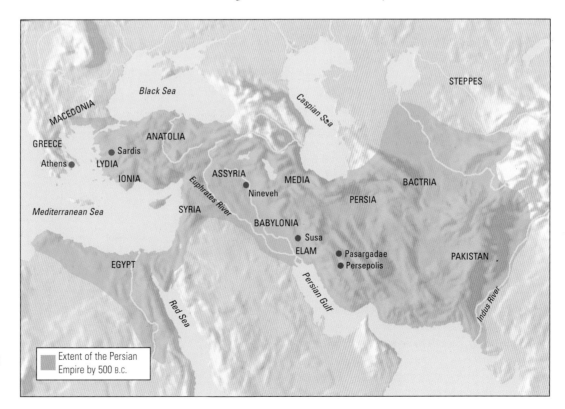

RIGHT: A map showing the extent of the Persian Empire in 500 B.C. and the position of its three capital cities—Susa, Persepolis, and Pasargadae.

Africa

The beginnings of civilization in the African continent south of the Sahara Desert can be traced from about 1000 B.C. At that time southern Africa was still in the Stone Age, and hunters and farmers had only stone tools to help them in their work.

The region of sub-Saharan Africa at this period consisted of two types of land. Savanna—consisting of grassland with few trees—covered most of the northern part of the region and some parts of the south. Small farming communities lived in the northern fertile area, which was suitable for growing crops and raising livestock. Most of the southern part was covered by tropical forests, and here, along the coastal areas, people lived as hunter-gatherers.

About 2,500 years ago peoples from northern Africa started moving into southern Africa, bringing a new way of life with them. These tribes lived in settled villages, grew crops like sorghum and millet (grains), beans and cowpeas, and herded cattle, sheep, and goats. They also knew how to use iron, and each group made pottery with its own distinctive style.

This was the beginning of the African Iron Age. Iron was the first metal used by Africans living south of the Sahara Desert, and it was spread through Africa by farmers. It was used to make tools for clearing land and for carving wood, as well as for weapons. Africans also began working in copper and gold. From around 200 B.C. towns, kingdoms, and states started to emerge.

➤ THE EARLY CULTURES ➤

The Nok culture, which lasted from about the sixth century B.C. until the first few centuries A.D., was the earliest known ironworking community in West Africa. The Nok grew sorghum and kept herds of cattle. Some of the Nok replaced their houses of wood and grass with mud dwellings. Nok craftsmen made striking terracotta sculptures, some of which were life-size sculptures of people with elaborate hairstyles, wearing necklaces, bangles, and anklets.

Around 250 B.C. in Mali in West Africa a small settlement was built on the Niger River. This gradually grew in size until around 800 A.D. it was a rich trading center called Jenné-Jeno. The town was enclosed by a mud-brick wall 13 ft (4m) high and over one mile (2 km) long. The wall was probably not built for defense but to protect the town from floods, to control access to the market,

Trade Across the Sahara

Some time in the first millennium B.C. traders probably started to cross the Sahara Desert using horse-drawn chariots. Crossing in this way would have been very slow and difficult. When the camel started to be used as a pack animal, things changed dramatically. This was because the camel could go for several days without water and could cover up to 20 miles (32km) a day.

By the ninth century A.D. trade across the Sahara was well established and trading stations were set up in the desert. The people of West Africa traded gold, slaves, ivory, and animal products and in exchange bought salt, cloth, pottery, glass, fruit, and horses. Gold was a very important export—until Europeans discovered gold in the Americas, African gold was almost the only gold sold in Europe.

or even to identify the town as an important and prestigious place to live. Inside the wall the town was a maze of narrow alleys and tightly packed houses. When a house fell down, the people simply built another one on top of its ruins.

About 27,000 people may have lived in Jenné-Jeno and the surrounding area. There were craft specialists, including mud-brick masons, potters who made elegant bowls with black or white

LEFT: The Nok people sculpted life-size heads like this one out of baked earth. The head shows how Nok men and women tied their hair up in elaborate styles.

RIGHT: Villages in ancient Mali consisted of houses built of thick mud-brick walls, and probably looked very similar to this present-day village.

designs, and smiths who made iron, copper, and gold objects. The wealth of the town was based on its farming activities—herding sheep, cattle, and goats, fishing, and growing sorghum, millet, and African rice.

The town was abandoned during the 13th century. Today all that remains of it is a huge mound up to 26 ft (8m) high, littered with pieces of mud-brick walls, pottery and clay toys, and iron and copper ornaments.

By the ninth century West African wealth was concentrated in the hands of a few people. The town of Igbo-Ukwu in the forests of southern Nigeria became a rich center for trade where remarkable copper and bronze items were produced. A burial chamber found there consisted of an underground room lined with wooden planks and matting. The corpse had been placed on a stool in one corner. In his hands were a fanholder and a flywhisk, and he was wearing a beaded headdress, a copper crown and chestplate, and wristbands of blue beads set in copper wire. Buried with this obviously high-ranking person were over 100,000 beads and a mass of objects made from iron, copper, bronze, ivory, and bone.

➤ THE KINGDOM OF GHANA ➤

As trade developed and a wealthy class of people grew more powerful, states were established in West Africa. The kingdom of Ghana grew up between the Niger and Senegal rivers in present-day Mauritania and Mali well before the eighth century A.D. This ancient kingdom was far away from the modern African country of Ghana.

Ghana's wealth came from trade in gold and salt, as well as taxes on goods passing through the area. The Soninke people of Ghana acted as middlemen between the gold miners to the south and Muslim traders in the north who supplied salt to the miners. Salt was in such demand by the miners that they were willing to give gold equal in

The Lost-Wax Method of Bronze Casting

When an important burial chamber was excavated at Igbo-Ukwu in southern Nigeria, many magnificent bronze objects dating from the ninth century A.D. were found. They had been made using the "lost-wax" process, a technique used by the West African metalworkers to produce very complex shapes in bronze. The first stage in the process was for the sculpture to be shaped in wax. This wax object was covered with a layer of clay. The clay was then fired, so that it became a rigid clay mold. The heat also melted the wax, which was poured out, and the clay mold was placed in sand. Hot molten metal was then poured into it. When the metal had cooled and solidified, the clay was smashed, revealing a bronze sculpture.

weight to the salt they received. This contact with Muslim neighbors led Ghana to become an Islamic state.

The capital of ancient Ghana was at Kumbi Saleh, now on the southern border of present-day Mauritania. It was a prosperous town full of mosques and houses that were lived in mainly by traders from the north. These buildings were made from stone cemented with mud and were decorated on the inside with yellow plaster. The king lived in a separate area. Early writers told stories of an impressive royal court.

The king sat in a pavilion surrounded by horses dressed in gold cloth, pages holding gold-mounted swords, and princes with gold braided into their hair. The king would listen to his subjects' complaints while they knelt before him and poured dust over their heads. Foreigners clapped their hands to show respect.

The ordinary people lived in thatched mud houses, grew crops such as millet, and fished. They were often required by their king to fight neighbors or undertake raids to capture slaves. Ghana was conquered by the Sanhaja Berbers from the north in the 11th century.

THE EMPIRE OF MALI

The successor to Ghana was the ancient empire of Mali, which occupied more or less the same area as present-day Mali. By the end of the 13th century Mali had a permanent army of professional soldiers and was the richest and most powerful state in the region. During the reign of Mansa Musa (1307–1332) many impressive buildings were built in Mali.

This came about because Mansa Musa went on a pilgrimage to the Muslim holy city of Mecca in Saudi Arabia. There he met a Spanish poet and architect, Es-Saheli, who Mansa Musa persuaded to go back to Africa with him to build great mosques and palaces in his capital city. Es-Saheli used the baked red bricks now common in West Africa for many of his buildings.

After Mansa Musa's death the empire of Mali grew weaker. In the 15th century it was conquered by Sanni Ali, a warlike king of the Songhai peoples from Gao on the Niger River. His new kingdom was called the kingdom of Songhai.

When Sanni Ali died an army general, Askia Mohammed, took over the throne and developed a very effective system of running the empire and collecting taxes. He appointed inspectors to ensure that the weights and measures used in markets throughout the kingdom were the same. Trade and learning flourished. The university at

ABOVE: This bronze head is thought to be of Oni, ruler of the kingdom of Ife. It was made by the Yoruba people using the lost-wax method of casting.

Timbuktu became so famous that it was visited by scholars from all over the Islamic world and beyond. However, the kingdom was shortlived. In 1589 it was overthrown by a leader from Morocco, El Mansur, who crossed the Sahara Desert with his gun-toting followers and defeated the Songhai army, which was armed only with spears and swords.

THE YORUBA PEOPLE

Farther south in West Africa cities grew up in the forest in places where people would be safe from attack by animals or other people. The city of Ife in southern Nigeria was one of these. It flour-

The Lydenburg Heads

In the 1960s some fragments of pottery were found by a schoolboy near Lydenburg in northeastern South Africa. Years later, when the boy had become a college student, he told one of his tutors what he had found. The bits of pottery turned out to be the remains of seven hollow, decorated ceramic heads that had been made in the eighth century A.D. They were probably used in initiation rites—the two larger heads could have fitted over a person's head, while the smaller ones may have been placed on poles. At the end of the ceremony they seem to have been deliberately smashed and the pieces thrown into deep pits.

One of the Lydenburg pottery heads. Similar heads were found in other parts of South Africa, suggesting the rites may have been widespread.

BELOW: A map of West Africa showing the extent of the early African cultures—Nok, Ghana, Mali, and Songhai.

ished between the 11th and 15th centuries. The Yoruba people of Ife lived in sun-dried mud-brick buildings that had courtyards paved with huge quantities of broken pieces of pottery. They produced sculptures in terracotta, bronze, and stone, and traded these and forest products. The realistic figures in terracotta and bronze that they sculpted seem to have been of religious importance and were placed on altars in houses.

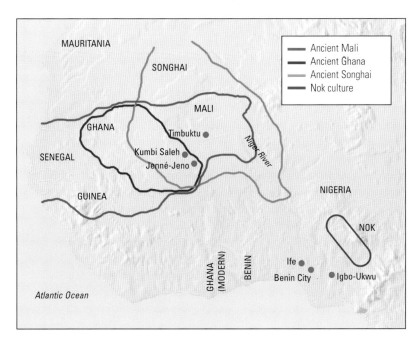

In the forest southeast of Ife another city-state was built at Benin around the 11th century. It was ruled by an *Oba*—king—who had a large army and many officials to help him govern. From the late 16th century the *Oba* became very rich by trading in brass, ivory, and coral. European visitors to the town in the 17th century were greatly impressed by its size and its main street, which was four miles (6km) long, as well as by the palace, which had towers topped by huge birds and decorated with large brass pythons.

➤ EAST AFRICA ➤

In the ninth century or even earlier, traders belonging to an Islamic African society called the Swahili ("people of the coast") set up trading stations along the East African coast. These people were expert sailors, and used the monsoon winds to sail to India and back. They took goods like ivory, gold, and iron from the African interior up the coast in small boats to northern East African ports. Then they sailed to Arabia and India, where they traded these goods for glass beads, ceramics, and cloth. As a result of this trade, the Islamic rulers became very wealthy.

Swahili society was divided into several distinct groups. The ordinary Swahili people were farmers, growing millet, rice, and sorghum, and fruits such as oranges, pomegranates, and figs. Then there were the rulers, who were descended from Arab and Persian traders; craftspeople who were native Africans but spoke the Swahili language; and slaves. The Swahili were also excellent builders, constructing stone palaces and mosques.

About the year 1000 newcomers set up a new trading capital for the kingdom of Schroda, which was located near the place where present-day South Africa, Zimbabwe, and Botswana meet. This settlement followed a pattern called the Central Cattle Pattern: in the center were "male" areas like a court and cemeteries for important people, while surrounding these were buildings such as houses and granaries that were mainly associated with women. However, when the capital moved about four miles (6km) to the south to Mapungubwe ("Hill of the Jackals") in about 1220, the leader did not follow the Central Cattle Pattern. He settled on a hilltop with his family, leaving the ordinary people to live in the valley below. This pattern of building became known as the Zimbabwe Tradition.

Mapungubwe was abandoned in about 1270 and Great Zimbabwe then emerged as the most powerful trading kingdom. It was abandoned in its turn about 1450.

Great Zimbabwe

Great Zimbabwe is a dramatic ruined town surrounded by a massive stone wall in the southern African country of Zimbabwe. In the Shona language spoken by Zimbabweans, "zimbabwe" means the home, court, or grave of a chief. More than 150 zimbabwes are known, but Great Zimbabwe is the largest and most impressive of them all. At its height in the 14th century it was the capital of a Shona empire that stretched from what is now northern South Africa to beyond the Zambezi River, and from western Mozambique to eastern Botswana.

The site of Great Zimbabwe was first occupied between A.D. 500 and 900 by early Iron Age farmers. They probably settled there because there was plenty of water, grass for their cattle to graze, and fertile soil in which to grow crops. The Shona people arrived at Great Zimbabwe around A.D. 900.

Between 1270 and 1450 the town grew to become the region's largest and most important trading center. From the number of house mounds and garbage dumps found there, archaeologists think that it reached its height in the 14th century, when the town covered about 1,700 acres (700ha) and was occupied by some 18,000 people.

In the early days Great Zimbabwe's wealth was based on cattle, and the ruling classes may have won their power originally by gaining control of the cattle herds and the grazing land. The ruling classes kept their power by controlling trade with merchants on the East African coast. The kings of Great Zimbabwe became very rich by exchanging gold and ivory for foreign imports like cloth, glass beads, and Chinese ceramics. The gold was panned from streams or mined from hazardous tunnels and was an important source of Great Zimbabwe's wealth.

At Great Zimbabwe, unlike many other southern African societies at the time, rulers and their families, as well as important officials, lived separately from ordinary people. The houses of the king, members of his family, and important officials, as well as places of religious importance, were found in a series of stone-walled enclosures now known as the Hill Ruin, which stood on top of a large granite hill called Zimbabwe Hill. The

The Great Enclosure in the central area of the valley is one of Great Zimbabwe's most impressive structures. It may have been used as a school for young people where they could be prepared for life as adults.

location of the king's house on top of a mountain was considered to be symbolic of his high status.

Noblemen lived in houses on the lower slopes of the hill, which is partly surrounded by a wall. Another wall in the valley below the hill encloses a vast central area, where the numerous royal wives lived under the control of the king's first wife. It is thought that some powerful Shona kings may have created political allegiances by marrying as many as a thousand wives.

Also in the central area in the valley is a huge structure known as the Elliptical Building or Great Enclosure. It is the most famous part of the site. The outer wall is over 825 ft (250m) long and consists of at least 900,000 stone blocks. It seems to have been built in stages. Inside lies a giant tower and a series of stone passages. Historians believe that this impressive building may have been used as a school for young men and women to learn the privileges and responsibilities of adulthood before they married.

The ordinary people lived in densely packed, round, thatched houses in the valley. Each family homestead consisted of a large house for cooking, eating, and shelter, with

smaller buildings for sleeping in, all linked together by stone walls. The houses were decorated inside—many of the stone walls as well as steps, seats, fireplaces, and posts were plastered with painted and sculptured mud. Excavations of these houses have uncovered everyday items such as pottery and farming tools, as well as ornaments like glass beads and metal bangles.

While the dress of ordinary people was quite simple—probably just a small skin apron—officials are thought to have worn garments made from imported silks. Historical accounts suggest that the king himself dressed in a length of fine cotton cloth with one end thrown over his shoulder. From the discovery of hundreds of pottery disks used as spinning weights it is clear that much cotton thread was spun at Great Zimbabwe.

The importance of Great Zimbabwe began to decline after about 1450. It is thought that people moved away from the town because the large number of people living there had exhausted local resources like firewood, bark (used for nets, bags, and blankets), and fertile soil. The competition for resources would probably also have caused considerable social problems.

Chapter 2:

Europe

By 4000 B.C. the Neolithic peoples of Europe were farming and living in settled villages, and had started building tombs of great stone blocks and circles of massive standing stones. The first European culture with palaces and a complex administration was that of the Minoans, which developed around 3500 B.C. Other cultures followed, culminating in the great civilization of the Greeks and the impressive empire of Rome. After the fall of Rome, Europe fell into anarchy from which some stable kingdoms emerged, notably those of the Anglo-Saxons and the Vikings in Britain.

BELOW: One of the most famous buildings in the world, the Parthenon sits on top of a hill overlooking the city of Athens. Built of white marble in the Doric style, it represents the full flowering of the glory that was Greece.

Neolithic Europe

The early peoples of Europe started to farm later than the peoples of the Middle East. Agriculture first arrived in Europe around 6500 B.C. and by about 4000 B.C. there were settled farming communities throughout continental Europe, southern Scandinavia, and Britain.

Archaeologists call this period of early farming the Neolithic or New Stone Age in order to distinguish it from the earlier Old Stone Age of hunter-gatherers who constantly moved from place to place.

The earliest European farmers raised the same crops and livestock as those that had already been domesticated in the Middle East. Farming spread first from Greece westward through the Mediterranean basin and also northward into central and north Europe. Most of the early farmers around the Mediterranean Sea lived in coastal caves, suggesting that the local hunter-gatherer communities may have been in contact with each other by boat or along the shore.

These communities probably obtained sheep and grain through trade—they would then farm them while also fishing, hunting, and gathering plants. Eventually, these groups moved inland and established settlements in areas where there was more room to grow plants and raise livestock.

As farming communities spread north from Greece around 6000 B.C., they sometimes encountered groups of hunter-gatherers who had found areas that were rich in game and fish. One such group was located where the Danube River cuts through the Carpathian Mountains in a gorge called the Iron Gates. Here the inhabitants of sites like Lepenski Vir and Vlasac lived in large settlements of many small huts, each with a central, stone-lined hearth. The people of these settlements carved strange statues with fishlike heads out of stone. These hunter-fishers took advantage of the numerous wild animals on the surrounding mountain slopes and also relied on an abundant supply of fish in the rapids and eddies of the river. Eventually, they adopted agriculture from nearby farming communities.

BELOW: A view of the inside of a typical one-room Neolithic stone house at Skara Brae on the Scottish islands of Orkney. The central hearth and the furniture, such as the massive dresser against the wall, were all made of stone.

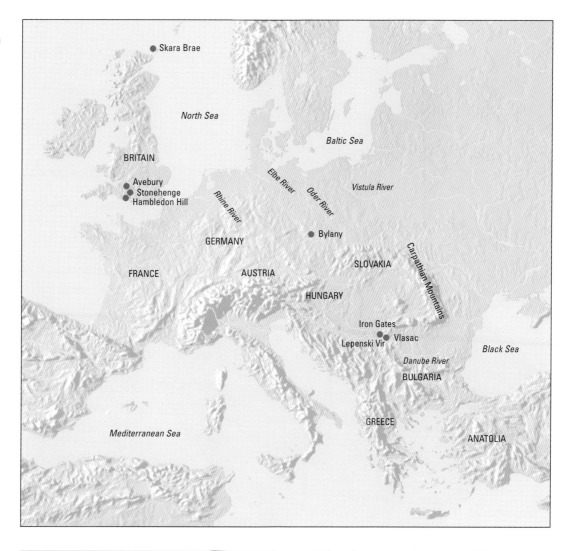

RIGHT: A map of Europe showing some of the main Neolithic settlements and ceremonial sites.

RIGHT: A stone statue of a man-fish from the Iron Gates settlements of eastern Europe. Fishing played a vital part in the lives of the Iron Gates people, and it is possible that the statue had a religious significance.

When farmers reached central Europe about 5500 B.C., they encountered only a few large groups of hunter-gatherers, so they were able to spread rapidly from Hungary westward to France and north up the valleys of the Rhine, Elbe, Oder, and Vistula rivers until they reached almost as far as the Baltic and North seas.

⚊ LINEAR POTTERY ⚊

These farmers had begun to make a very distinctive type of pottery called Linear, the thin walls of which were decorated with incised lines. The shapes of the vessels and their decoration were very similar all the way from Slovakia to France.

The Linear pottery farmers settled along small streams throughout central Europe. Their settlements, such as Bylany in what is now the Czech Republic and Schwanfeld in Germany, consisted of small clusters of long timber houses, each of which was occupied by a family, its livestock, its food supplies, and its equipment. The fields, where these farmers grew wheat and barley, were located in small clearings in the forest

ABOVE: In eastern Europe pottery was often painted and shaped to represent humans or animals. This decorated vessel with eyes and nose is from Bulgaria and dates back to around 6000 B.C.

people to keep animals for their milk. Some of the Linear pottery settlements were fortified with ditches and embankments.

Farther north, along the coasts of the Baltic Sea and the North Sea, small groups of hunter-gatherers lived close to the shoreline, where they could find plenty to eat.

➤ COASTAL PEOPLES ➤

These coastal peoples gathered shellfish in great quantities from the sea. The large mounds created from the shells that were thrown out after all these oysters, cockles, and clams had been opened were called "kitchen middens" by early archaeologists. These people also caught fish by using traps, which were baskets specially made so that the fish could swim in with the current through a small opening but could not swim out.

Inland the hunter-gatherers paddled dugout canoes on the lakes and rivers and speared fish with harpoons. Using a new invention, the bow and arrow, they also hunted waterbirds like geese and ducks. In the forests they found edible plants and mushrooms, along with deer and wild boar. Children could increase the family's food supply by gathering berries and nuts.

These coastal hunter-gatherers saw no reason to adopt agriculture, so for almost 1,000 years farming did not advance beyond the area settled by the Linear pottery farmers. The two groups traded, however, and wheat and barley began to be grown by some coastal communities around 4000 B.C. At first the coastal peoples may have practiced agriculture part-time, but eventually it became their primary source of food.

Along the Atlantic coast of France and in Britain the last hunters became farmers just after 4000 B.C. Little is known about the settlements of these new farmers, except in the few places where

where the trees had either been cut down or had been killed by removing the bark. Cattle were the most common animals kept by these Linear pottery farmers, although they also kept sheep, goats, and pigs. It appears that they were among the first

The Iceman

In September 1991 hikers in the Alps came across the body of a man lying in a pool of water that had melted from a glacier. The corpse was taken to the University of Innsbruck in Austria, where it was identified as that of a man who had died about 5,300 years ago—it had been preserved in the ice. Since he was found in the area called the Otztaler Alps, the man

became known as "Otzi," or simply the "Iceman." The Iceman seemed to have been crossing the mountains when he died (perhaps from exhaustion). He was carrying many belongings, which, together with articles of his clothing, had also been preserved in the ice.

The Iceman had a copper axe, a wooden bow, a leather quiver with 14 arrows, and a flint dagger. He

may also have worn a leather backpack. On his feet were leather leggings and shoes, which had been packed with straw to insulate against the cold. Lying nearby was a fur cap. Berries and some mushrooms were found in a birch-bark container. These objects have given archaeologists a "time capsule" that tells us much about everyday Neolithic life in the Alps.

Neolithic Ceremonial Sites

Besides building impressive tombs, the early farmers of western and central Europe constructed large ceremonial sites where they gathered for rituals. Initially, these were often situated on hilltops that had been surrounded by ditches and banks. One such site is Hambledon Hill in southwestern England, where several ditches enclose a hilltop. Within the ditches many partial or complete human skeletons have been found,

suggesting that bodies of the dead played a role in the ritual activities. Other enclosures found in Denmark, France, Germany, and the Czech Republic indicate that such sites were widespread between 3500 and 3000 B.C.

Over time the building of large ceremonial structures became more important. One such henge was at Avebury in southern England, where a deep ditch was dug to enclose an area about 990 ft (300m) across. The bank

formed from the excavated earth is still 25 ft (8m) high today, and the adjacent ditch was just as deep. Inside, upright stones were placed to form circles, and two avenues of stones led away from the ceremonial area. Dating from just after 3000 B.C., Avebury is believed to have been built a few centuries earlier than its more famous neighbor, Stonehenge, which is located about 20 miles (32km) to the south.

The important ceremonial site of Avebury in England as it is today, showing part of a stone circle and the bank behind it.

they have been preserved. One such settlement was at Skara Brae in the Orkney Islands off the coast of Scotland, which was established about 3100 B.C. There are very few trees on Orkney, so the single-room houses were all built of stone, as were the hearths, beds, and cupboards. Covered passages connected the houses. The inhabitants of Skara Brae and similar settlements nearby were primarily herders, and many bones of sheep and cattle were found in the excavations.

Not long after farming was established in western Europe, large megalithic tombs began to appear. These were built of large, flat boulders set upright to form the walls of a burial chamber, which could be either a simple box shape, or a long passage with side chambers. Earth was mounded up on the outside to form a ramp, and

then more large, flat stones were dragged on top to form a roof, which was then covered by earth. These tombs were used for many generations. When people died, the tomb was opened, and their bodies were placed among the bones of their ancestors. In some large tombs several hundred skeletons have been found.

Over time the early farmers found good sources of flint for making tools, and trade in flint connected many communities. Eventually, about 3000 B.C., farmers learned to harness their animals to pull plows and wagons. Finally, they discovered that certain rocks, when heated, would release molten copper. Copper was first used mainly for ornaments because it is a soft metal and does not hold its shape well, but eventually people began using it to make tools like axes.

Stonehenge

The mighty circle of massive standing stones that is Stonehenge is set in the lowlands of southern England about 75 miles (120km) from London. It is one of the most captivating but least understood archaeological sites in the world.

Stonehenge is just one of many stone circles that were built in Neolithic Britain over a period of more than 1,000 years. However, this particular circle of megaliths (large stones) has fascinated scholars for hundreds of years and has been the subject of many myths and superstitions. Anyone visiting the monument today is always impressed by the massive stones rising high in the air, and it must have had an even more overpowering effect on the Neolithic peoples who built it 4,000 years ago.

Stonehenge was built during the later part of the Neolithic period and the early part of the Bronze Age, between about 2950 and 1600 B.C., and it is almost certainly the best-known example of the megalithic monuments that were being built throughout western Europe at this time. It consists today of about 90 large stones, although it seems that about 50 more may have disappeared over the centuries.

The image that most people have of Stonehenge—a circle of upright stones supporting horizontal stones or lintels—is really only one part of a large and complex monument. In the center is a small horseshoe-shaped arrangement of upright bluestones that encloses the altar stone—the focal point of Stonehenge. Around the bluestones is another horseshoe shape of five massive trilithons, each consisting of two immense stone pillars with an equally immense lintel laid across them.

The trilithons are surrounded by a circle of small upright bluestones, which in turn is surrounded by yet another circle. This outer circle was once composed of about 30 large upright stones and an equal number of lintels. Like the

BELOW: Stonehenge still inspires awe and wonder 4,000 years after it was built. Even though many of the stones have disappeared, the monument remains a testament to the extraordinary engineering skills of the Neolithic people of Britain.

RIGHT: A close-up view of the trilithons that make up the horseshoe shape at Stonehenge, together with some of the smaller sarsen stones of the outer circle.

trilithons, they were made from a stone called sarsen. Many of them are still standing. Around the perimeter of this central area was an earthen bank and ditch.

➤ THE AUBREY HOLES ➤

Just inside the bank archaeologists found 56 holes that had been dug into the chalk beneath the soil, then filled in immediately afterward—no one really knows why. These holes are known as Aubrey holes. At four points this ring of holes is interrupted by an upright bluestone called a Station Stone. The main entrance to the area enclosed by the earthwork is marked by a large stone called the Heel Stone.

Many people do not realize that Stonehenge was built in several stages. First, the surrounding ditch and the Aubrey holes were cut into the chalk around 2750 B.C. For the next few centuries Stonehenge remained in this simple form. Then the four upright Station Stones among the Aubrey holes and the Heel Stone were erected

Why Was Stonehenge Built?

No one is sure what purpose Stonehenge served, although it is clear that it was a place of great importance for the Neolithic and early Bronze Age inhabitants of the surrounding countryside. It does not seem that people lived at the site, and only a few burials have been found among the stones and in the ditch. Yet something made the farmers and herders of this area devote their time and energy over a period of several centuries to building this massive construction.

In the 1950s and 1960s some historians suggested that Stonehenge might have been an observatory or a primitive means of predicting astronomical events. Indeed, the sun at the summer solstice, on June 21 or 22, rises almost directly over the Heel Stone.

Other than this, however, there is little evidence that Stonehenge was aligned on stars and planets, and most archaeologists today do not accept the idea that the monument was an astronomical observatory.

Instead, it seems more likely that Stonehenge was a gathering place or ceremonial area that gave the surrounding farmers and herders a powerful sense of community—it served as a visible and lasting reminder of their ancestors who had established their claim to this territory. The largest stones may have been erected by a powerful chief who wanted to make this the most elaborate monument in the region, visible from a long distance away across the surrounding plain.

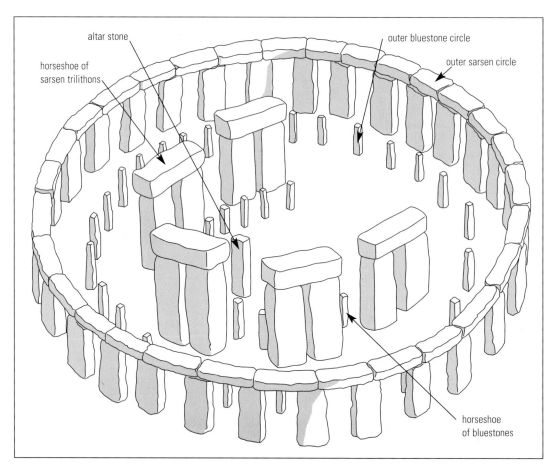

altar stone

horseshoe of
sarsen trilithons

outer bluestone circle

outer sarsen circle

horseshoe
of bluestones

around 2100 B.C. We now know that the bluestones came from about 125 miles (200km) away in the mountains of Wales and that they were probably transported by water on rafts for much of that distance. It was not until about a century later that the massive trilithons and surrounding circle of sarsens were set up.

⟶ ERECTING THE STONES ⟵

Putting these larger stones in place was a remarkable engineering feat. First, the stones had to be brought over land from about 20 miles (30km) away. No one is sure how this was done, but it seems they may have been hauled on rollers during the winter months when the ground was hard. Another theory is that the stones may have been transported on sleds, over specially built wooden trackways. Once on the site, they had to be erected in place. This was probably done by raising them to a vertical position, using a system of ramps, scaffolds, and levers, and then sliding them into ready-dug pits. The whole operation probably involved using the strength of hundreds of people and oxen.

The lintels were hauled into place by raising one end, putting timbers under the stone, then raising the other end and putting more timbers in place, then repeating this process over and over until the lintel reached the tops of the uprights and could be pushed into place. On the tops of the uprights the ancient builders chipped away the stone to make bumps that fitted into holes in the undersides of the lintels to hold them in place.

Historians have estimated that it would have taken 1,000 people to haul the larger stones to the site and that this third phase of building at Stonehenge would have required two million hours of labor in total.

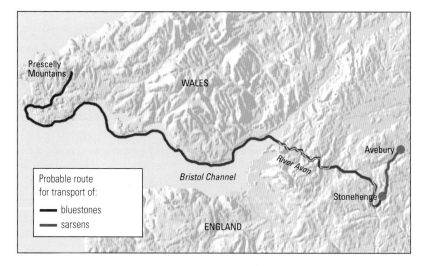

Prescelly Mountains

WALES

Bristol Channel

River Avon

Avebury

Stonehenge

ENGLAND

Probable route
for transport of:
— bluestones
— sarsens

The area surrounding Stonehenge had many monuments that reminded the people of their ancestors and chiefs. They buried their leaders under round mounds, or "barrows," often accompanied by artifacts made of gold and bronze. Bush Barrow, about one mile (1.6km) south of Stonehenge, contained the skeleton of a tall individual with two copper daggers, a bronze axe, and several gold ornaments.

About 1.5 miles (2.5km) from the main entrance of Stonehenge is an earthwork known as "The Avenue," which consists of two parallel ditches about 100 ft (30m) apart, from which the dirt had been thrown toward the middle to make a raised pathway.

About 19 miles (30km) to the north lies Avebury, where an enormous ditched enclosure some 985 ft (300m) across was built just after 3000 B.C. Within the Avebury enclosure, as at Stonehenge, is a circle of sarsen stones, although there are differences in how they are arranged. Avebury is also much larger than Stonehenge.

Near Avebury is the mysterious man-made earthen mound called Silbury Hill, which was built about the same time as Stonehenge. Many other such monuments probably existed in this area but have been destroyed over the last 4,000 years. Elsewhere in western Europe many megalithic monuments were being put up at this time. Small stone circles are common throughout England, Wales, and Scotland, perhaps continuing an earlier tradition of making circles out of upright pieces of wood stuck in the ground that have not survived.

Across the English Channel in Brittany, France, at the site of Carnac, many rows of thousands of upright stones were set up about the same time as Stonehenge was being built. At one location seven parallel rows of stones, of which 1,029 still stand, run for about 3,700 ft (1,130m) across the countryside. Nearby, at Locmariaquer, an enormous granite pillar once towered 66 ft (22m) high before it fell down, or was toppled, and broke into four pieces.

◄ THE DRUIDS ►

A popular misconception about Stonehenge is that it was built by the Celtic priests, commonly known as Druids, who were described by Roman writers who visited Britain. This romantic fantasy about the origins of Stonehenge began nearly 300 years ago and still persists today. Every summer solstice present-day Druids and other people who believe that the stones possess religious or mystical powers gather at Stonehenge to perform special midsummer rituals. Although their beliefs are not supported by any archaeological evidence, the fact that they are drawn to Stonehenge reflects the magical attraction felt by everyone who sees this spectacular monument.

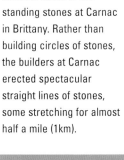

BELOW: Some of the standing stones at Carnac in Brittany. Rather than building circles of stones, the builders at Carnac erected spectacular straight lines of stones, some stretching for almost half a mile (1km).

Steppe Nomads

The steppes are a vast area of grassland stretching about 5,000 miles (8,000km) from southern Ukraine east to Manchuria. The herders who lived there around 3500 B.C. were the first people to ride horses, becoming raiders who were feared by everyone in the surrounding regions.

The climate of the steppes varies from freezing cold in the winter to baking hot in the summer, and there is very little rainfall. Because of this inhospitable climate farmers did not move into the region until about 4500 B.C., and even when they did so, they relied more on animals than on crops. The grasslands provided good grazing for cattle, sheep, and horses. By about 3500 B.C. these herders were using their horses for riding rather than food, making them the first people in the ancient world to do so.

The domestication of the horse had a great impact on the steppe-dwellers' society since it meant they could become fully nomadic, moving from place to place with their flocks. This development was also to have a great impact on other civilizations since armed groups of horsemen were able to attack settlements with ease, and the raids of the steppe nomads were soon feared in many parts of China, India, and Europe.

The earliest known steppe culture was that of the Sredny Stog (about 4400–3500 B.C.). These people lived in permanent settlements of timber-framed houses near the Dnieper River and were the first to domesticate the horse, although at this stage most horses were used for food. However, some people also began to ride them. By the third millennium B.C. steppe peoples were using ox-drawn wagons and were working copper. By about 1850 B.C. horses were being used to pull light two-wheeled carts, or chariots. This invention would later spread to the Middle East, where it would have a dramatic impact on warfare. By the first millennium B.C. the steppe people were almost completely nomadic.

Much of our knowledge of these steppe nomads comes from their burials, since their nomadic lifestyle meant that they lived in tents. Their belongings were light and portable; wagons transported household goods and tents. Sheep were an important source of their wealth and could be traded for all kinds of valuable objects. Horses were also vitally important to them and were often buried alongside their owners. At Pazyryk in the Altai Mountains of Siberia, for example, the burial of a steppe chieftain from the fifth century B.C. included a dismantled wagon and nine horses.

LEFT: This detail from a golden Scythian jar shows a rider undoing the shackles on his horse. The Scythians were expert goldsmiths, and many beautiful examples of their work have been found in the graves of their chieftains.

RIGHT: The steppes cover a vast area of land, stretching from Ukraine in the west to Manchuria in the east.

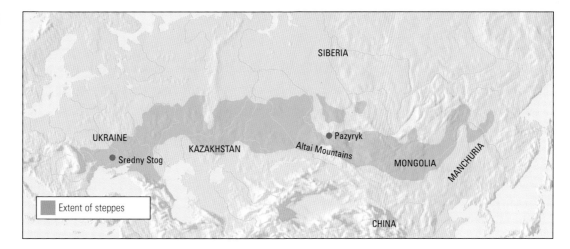

RIGHT: A felt wall hanging from around 400 B.C. Found in a tomb at Pazyryk, it gives us a rare glimpse of how the steppe nomads dressed.

⤙ THE SCYTHIANS ⤚

Greek writings from about 600 B.C. describe a people they called the Scythians. The Scythians consisted of mounted bands of warriors formed around strong chieftains. The group's loyalties lay with their leader, and rival bands would fight over grass and water. At times these bands would form a loose alliance under the control of the high king of a dominant group.

The Scythians were armed with iron swords, massive iron spears, and bows and arrows that were said to be able to pierce bronze armor. They were ferocious fighters, and the Greeks reported that the Scythians scalped their enemies and kept the scalps as trophies. However, with their defeat by King Philip II of Macedonia in 339 B.C. the Scythians lost their power, and their empire finally collapsed in the first century A.D.

The Scythians were by no means the last band of steppe warriors to terrorize the peoples of Europe. In fact, for much of the following 2,000 years a succession of steppe peoples launched devastating attacks on Europe to the west, India to the south, and China to the east.

Among the most noteworthy attacks were those of the Huns, who appeared in Europe around A.D. 370. Sweeping westward from the steppes, the Huns left a trail of destruction and death behind them. Under their most famous leader, Attila, who reigned between A.D. 434 and 453, the Huns created a huge empire, incorporating into their army the people they conquered. This force was so formidable that even the Roman Empire was forced to pay it tribute.

In the east, too, China was subject to similar attacks from a variety of warlike nomadic tribes. These barbarians were to be a continuing threat over the following centuries.

Frozen Tombs

About 400 B.C., on a high plateau among the Altai Mountains of Siberia, a people related to the Scythians lived a similar nomadic life. We know about these people because their bodies and possessions have been found in their tombs. They buried their dead in timber-lined tombs during warm weather when the ground was soft. Moisture collected in the tombs after they were built and froze during the icy winter—then the earth mound above kept the contents permanently frozen. In 1995 the preserved body of a man whom archaeologists nicknamed the "Warrior" was found in a log coffin with a set of bow and arrows, an axe, and a knife. He had a tattoo of a deer on his right shoulder and was wearing leather boots and a fur coat. Beside him lay his most important possession—his horse.

Cyclades

The Cyclades are a group of more than 200 Greek islands that are found in the Aegean Sea. The islands got their name from the Greek word *kyklos*, meaning "circle," because the ancient Greeks thought that they formed a circle around the central island of Delos.

Delos and the other islands of the Cyclades were first inhabited thousands of years ago. The earliest settlement we know about was on the island of Kythnos and may be up to 9,000 years old. The first people to settle on the islands came from Anatolia (present-day Turkey)—they were seafaring people, and because of this all the early settlements were very near the coast, even on the larger islands. In later times the Greeks referred to these people as "pirates."

⌐ THE CYCLADIC CULTURE ⌐

The ancient civilization of the Cyclades, which is also called the Cycladic culture, began when the people who lived in the region of the Aegean Sea discovered how to make bronze from a mixture of copper and tin. This was around 3000 B.C. and it marked the beginning of the Bronze Age.

During the Bronze Age islanders from the Cyclades became experts at carving stone. They carved female figures in a white marble that they dug up on Paros and on the largest island in the Cyclades, Naxos. The sculptors rubbed the figures smooth with stones of emery, a hard, dark rock found mainly on Naxos. Some of these figures are small, but others are almost life-size. Details were often added in red and blue paint. The figures were placed in tombs, and archaeologists think that they may have been the images of goddesses that were put there to protect the dead. Marble figures of men playing musical instruments have also been found.

On the island of Milos the inhabitants discovered another substance that was to prove useful to the whole region. It was obsidian—the black, glassy volcanic rock that could be used to make knives and scraping tools. This was a highly sought-after product, and the Milos islanders traded obsidian throughout the region.

Around 2500 B.C. the seafaring, fishing communities of the Cyclades started to move their settlements away from the coastal areas toward the middle of their small islands. They also began to build citadels, probably to defend themselves against any attack. At Kastri, on the island of Syros, a walled citadel has been found that was surrounded by six towers.

Archaeologists have also found many artifacts that throw light on the lives of the Cycladic people. At a cemetery near Kastri 500 tombs were discovered that contained many interesting objects, including bowls, vases, and other vessels made from terracotta, marble, and even gold. Silver and bronze pins used to fasten clothes were also found—these were engraved with designs similar to ones that have been found in Egypt and on the Greek mainland.

Historians believe that between 2000 and 1500 B.C. some islands of the Cyclades began to have increasing contact with the Minoans of Crete. Some of them may even have been ruled by the Minoans.

⌐ LIFE ON THE ISLANDS ⌐

The islanders were now farming as well as fishing, growing olive trees, vines, and cereals. Grapes from the vines were used to make wine. Farmers kept mainly sheep and goats but also some cattle and pigs.

People lived in two- or three-story houses with many rooms, separated by narrow streets

BELOW: A fresco from the buried town of Akrotiri. The painting on the left shows two boys boxing, while the one on the right is of a pair of antelopes. Many of the frescoes found in the Cycladic islands display strong Minoan influences.

that had sewage systems to remove household waste. At Phylakope, on Milos, there were spacious houses, and some were beautifully decorated with wall paintings (frescoes). One famous painting shows a school of flying fish.

The most complete set of Cycladic frescoes was found on the southerly island of Santorini. It was buried under layers of volcanic ash, which had come from a huge explosive eruption on the island around 1500 B.C. The eruption was so violent that volcanic ash and dust were blown high into the atmosphere and carried by winds as far as Crete, 68 miles (110km) away. The explosion also

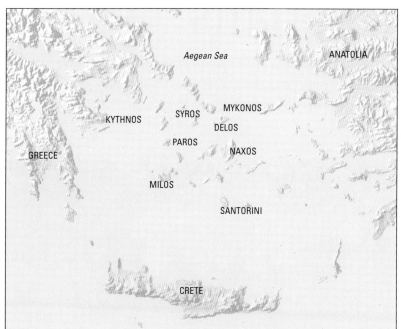

ABOVE: The Cyclades are a group of over 200 islands in the Aegean Sea, the largest of which is Naxos.

LEFT: A female idol carved in marble dating back to the 23rd century B.C. When these white marble figures were first sculpted, many of them were painted in bright colors.

blew Santorini apart—whereas before it had been one single piece of land, after the explosion it became one main island and four smaller ones in and around the mouth of the volcano.

On Santorini houses up to three stories high were discovered buried beneath 16 ft (5m) of volcanic ash at the ancient town of Akrotiri. Some of the buildings are very well preserved, and they offer many clues as to what life was like on the islands of the Cyclades before 1500 B.C. Many of the houses contained wooden furniture, large storage jars, pottery, and frescoes of festivals, battles, sports, and religious ceremonies.

➤ TIME TO ESCAPE ➤

Unlike the Roman city of Pompeii, which suffered a similar fate, excavations at Santorini did not reveal any jewelry or fleeing human figures. So it is thought that there may have been a series of minor earthquakes or small eruptions that would have warned the islanders and given them time to escape with their valuable possessions.

After 1500 B.C. the Cyclades began to be increasingly influenced by people of a different culture—the Mycenaeans from mainland Greece. The Phoenicians also used the islands as trading bases. They were interested in the islands' precious metals, as well as a special purple dye that was found in shellfish of the Aegean Sea.

By 1000 B.C. the Dorians from northwestern Greece had settled on Santorini and Milos, and the rest of the islands of the Cyclades were taken over by the Ionians from Anatolia. The Cycladic culture had come to an end.

Minoans

The first great civilization of Europe developed 4,500 years ago on the Mediterranean island of Crete. The Minoan kings built great palaces, splendidly decorated with wall paintings, and ruled their domains with the help of a large body of officials.

ABOVE: The ruins of the north side of the Palace of Minos at Knossos, which was the largest and most important of the Minoan palaces on Crete.

This civilization was given its name by the British archaeologist Arthur Evans (1851–1941), after King Minos of Crete. Evans was fascinated by the legend of the Minotaur—a monster with a man's body and a bull's head that was kept in a labyrinth by King Minos. Every nine years the Minotaur was fed seven young men and seven young women sent from Athens as a sacrifice. Eventually, Theseus, son of the king of Athens, offered to go to Crete as one of the seven young men. With the help of King Minos's daughter, Ariadne, he found his way into the center of the labyrinth and killed the Minotaur.

Evans believed that there was some truth behind the legend, and in 1899 he went to Crete in search of the mythical labyrinth. There he discovered and excavated the magnificent Palace of Minos at Knossos. With its 1,200 rooms and vast system of winding corridors, the palace certainly resembled a labyrinth, and it is quite possible that it provided the basis for part of the ancient legend. Evans's excavations produced a great deal of information about the Minoans and their way of life. Since these first excavations on Crete, other Minoan palaces and settlements have also been found and explored, giving us a much more detailed picture of the Minoan civilization.

The first people to settle in Crete probably sailed from Anatolia (present-day Turkey) in about 7000 B.C. They established settlements on the island, one of which was at Knossos—evidence of this has been found beneath the ruins of the Palace of Minos. The early Cretans were farmers, growing grain and rearing sheep and goats. They also grew vines and olives, which required less labor than other crops and were able to survive in relatively poor-quality soil. Wine and olive oil would prove to be important exports in later years when the Cretans began to trade with other Mediterranean countries.

Around 3000 B.C. the people of the Aegean Sea and Crete discovered how to make bronze from a mixture of copper and tin. During the early Bronze Age people began to use bronze to make tools and weapons. The Minoans became increasingly skilled at metalworking, and many beautiful gold artifacts have been found. Gold was cut and stamped into beads and ornaments, and jewelers also used decorative filigree and granulation techniques.

Early Bronze Age houses were made mainly of mud bricks. Many were very sophisticated, however, with separate kitchens, living rooms, and workrooms.

MINOAN CIVILIZATION

The Cretan civilization that we call Minoan began around 2500 B.C. The civilization is characterized by the great royal palaces built by the Minoan kings. The changes that led to the building of these palaces probably occurred among the people already living on the island. But some historians think that new groups may have arrived from the Greek mainland, Anatolia, or the shores of the eastern Mediterranean. Certainly, new types of olives and vines were introduced to Crete, and the island's population increased.

The early Minoans traded with other lands and imported fine stone vessels from Egypt. They also imported the volcanic glass obsidian from the island of Melos in the Cyclades and used it for cutting and scraping.

RIGHT: A faience (glazed pottery) statuette of the snake goddess, found at the Palace of Minos. She wears a typical Minoan dress and clasps a snake in each hand.

Minoan society was organized into different social groups. At the top was the ruler, who had his own palace. The greatest of the palaces, that of King Minos, was at Knossos. According to legend Minos's two brothers had their own royal palaces: the palace of Sarpedon was at Mallia, and that of Rhadamanthys was near Phaistos. The kings may have shared some of their power with their nobles—the provincial rulers who lived in country mansions.

Craftsmen formed another group, and merchants supplied them with imported goods to work with, such as ivory. There would have been a body of officials to organize and control the work of the craftsmen and merchants. Then there were the farmers, who produced many of the products that were stored at the great palaces. There was also a class of scribes—archaeologists have discovered three different types of script.

Religion played an important part in Minoan life, and there were many priests and priestesses at the royal palaces. Kings and queens may have shared some of the duties at religious rituals. The Minoans worshiped many gods, and even more goddesses. Arthur Evans believed that they worshiped one goddess above all others. This mother or earth goddess was a symbol of fertility. She

BELOW: Some of the key Minoan sites on the island of Crete.

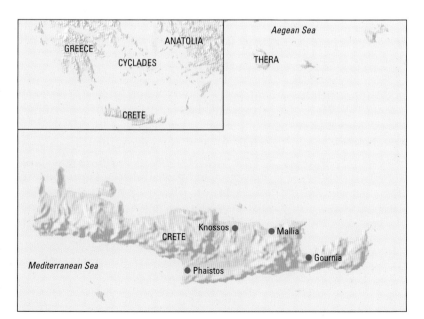

the bull was the focal point of some form of religious cult. This theory is backed up by several wall paintings that show young men and women leaping over charging bulls. Bull-leaping was probably part sport, part ritual and took place in the palace courtyards.

Minoan palaces and houses were decorated with bright frescoes (wall paintings) that were painted on plaster while it was still damp. Archaeologists have found scenes of birds and flowers, swimming dolphins, richly dressed court ladies, and processions of men carrying vases. In these pictures men are often painted red. This was not just an artistic convention; men often covered their bodies with a red powder called rouge for ceremonial purposes.

The frescoes have told us a great deal about daily life in ancient Crete. Women wore their hair braided with strings of beads and jewelry. Their dresses, which had an open bodice, left their arms and breasts bare, and had a long flounced skirt. They wore armlets, necklaces, bracelets, earrings, and rings. Men just wore a leather belt and a loincloth, though some wore kilts. Outdoors the men wore sandals or boots, but indoors they went barefoot. They had long hair but were clean shaven. Minoan clothes were mostly made of wool, and some frescoes show them woven with colorful designs, including pictures of animals and birds.

Women seem to have been the equals of men in Minoan society. They took part in many activities, including the dangerous sport of bull-leaping. Paintings and seals show that priestesses performed the main religious rites. Family names may have been passed down through the female line. In the great palaces the queen's and other noble ladies' quarters were richly decorated, and had well-plumbed bathrooms and toilets.

watched over animals and plants, and married a young god who died every year as winter drew near but came back to life in spring.

Another important Minoan deity was the snake goddess. Many statuettes of her have been found in the settlements and palaces. She was probably seen as a guardian of the house; and since a snake periodically changes its skin, she may have been a symbol of rebirth. Instead of building great temples to their gods, the Minoans carried out their religious ceremonies in special rooms in palaces, caves, houses, and especially at small stone shrines on Cretan hilltops.

Bulls played a major part in Minoan religion, possibly providing more fuel for the legend of the Minotaur. A large number of stone bulls' horns have been found on Crete, which suggests that

ABOVE: Part of the "Blue Ladies" fresco from the Palace of Minos, showing an elaborate hairstyle popular with Minoan women. Strings of beads were braided into the long hair, while a coronet kept forehead curls in place. Locks of hair were also curled over the ears.

◄ MINOAN POTTERY ►

The vases and other pottery found in these rooms were beautifully painted with spirals, animals, and fish. Potters sometimes also gave their work an overall wash of shiny dark paint and applied designs in lighter colors. This pottery is known as Kamares ware, named after a sacred cave on Mount Ida where vases of this kind were found (and where the god Zeus was born, according to some legends). In the great palaces potters made cups with thin walls and shiny, dark surfaces decorated with abstract designs in white, red, and orange—this is called "eggshell" ware.

Decorated Cretan pottery has been found in the eastern Mediterranean region and Egypt.

The Minoan Scripts

The early Minoans wrote in hieroglyphics, a script made up of signs in the shape of animals or objects. It was similar to the ancient Egyptian form of writing, though only a few Minoan signs are similar to those found in Egypt. Nevertheless, this Cretan picture writing might have been inspired by contact with Egypt or Syria.

From about 1700 B.C. the Minoans wrote on clay tablets in a new script, probably developed from the earlier hieroglyphics. Arthur Evans called this form of writing Linear A. This script used signs to represent the separate syllables of words. About 400 inscriptions using Linear A have been found, but as yet no one has been able to decipher it completely. Some experts believe that it developed from a language used by the seafaring Phoenicians. It is thought that the tablets may show stock-keeping records of grain, wine, and oil.

After about 1450 B.C. the Minoan tablets showed a different script, which Evans called Linear B. He could not decipher the script himself, but in 1936 a lecture given by Evans inspired a teenager to try to break the code. Michael Ventris, who became a scholar and architect, studied thousands of inscriptions and finally deciphered Linear B some 16 years later. It turned out to be an early form of Greek, with about 90 signs representing different syllables. Again, most of the inscriptions are lists and records of stocks. Tablets using Linear B have also been found at Mycenaean towns on the Greek mainland, which suggests that the Mycenaeans might have brought the language to Crete.

LEFT: The Minoans were skilled potters, producing very thin-walled pots with intricate decoration. Plant motifs, like the ones on this elegant pot, were popular, as was the sacred double-headed axe symbol also seen here.

Gournia—A Minoan Town

While Arthur Evans was excavating the Palace of Minos at Knossos in 1901, the American archaeologist Harriet Boyd Hawes was starting to dig up the remains of a Minoan town called Gournia, 38 miles (60km) to the east of Knossos. At Gournia she discovered winding streets and a jumble of small houses and courtyards. There was also a square with a shrine where religious ceremonies and public events probably took place. Workshops and craftsmen's tools were found, and from them it can be deduced that the town's community included carpenters, smiths, weavers, and potters. Farmers and fishermen also lived there.

The town of Gournia stood on a high ridge overlooking the sea. Its houses were built in either a square or rectangular shape, and had up to three floors and flat roofs. The living quarters were usually on the second floor, reached by stairs directly from the street, while the first floor had storerooms and possibly workshops. There was also one larger, grand house, which was probably occupied by the governor either of the town or this region of eastern Crete. Gournia was destroyed about 1450 B.C. Some of its citizens seem to have left in a great hurry—a carpenter's tool-kit was found where it had been dropped outside one of the houses.

The ruins of a house in the small Minoan town of Gournia—traces of the original limewash can still be seen on the wall on the left.

Some of the larger jars were exported with produce in them: olive oil, grain, wine, and honey.

Wool was also exported, showing how successful the Minoan farmers were. The mountainsides of ancient Crete were covered in cypress forests, which stopped rainwater from just running straight to the sea, as it does today. The coastal plains were well watered and fertile, which was good for farming. Efficient agriculture supported a large population, as well as producing a surplus for export. Trade, as well as craft and agricultural production, was probably under palace control.

BELOW: The Queen's Hall in the Palace of Minos was decorated with this colorful dolphin fresco. All the original frescoes found at the palace are now in a museum; the ones seen at the site are copies.

The Minoans were expert sailors. Their ships had a single mast carrying a square sail and were steered with a large paddle at the stern. Merchant ships had wide, rounded hulls with a long pointed prow, while warships were narrower, lighter, and faster. Some ships also had oars, probably for use near land. Minoan ships dominated the seas around Crete. This gave the Minoans the confidence to leave their towns and palaces unwalled, since they felt safe from attack. In later times the Greeks referred to Minos as the "King of the Sea." There may have been Minoan colonies on some of the Aegean islands, but we do not know whether they were ruled directly from the palace.

➤ THE PALACES ARE DESTROYED ➤

Around 1700 B.C. all the Minoan palaces were destroyed, probably by earthquakes. However, they were completely rebuilt and probably extended before much of Crete was damaged by fallout from the violent eruption of a volcano on the nearby island of Thera (present-day Santorini) in about 1500 B.C. The volcanic ash that fell on Crete ruined crops, and the eruption created huge sea waves that caused flooding and may have destroyed the Minoan fleet. Historians believe that this devastation weakened the Minoan civilization, perhaps tempting others to attack, particularly Mycenaean warriors from the Greek mainland. Whatever the reason, the Minoan civilization that had been centered on Crete for over 1,000 years was soon at an end.

Knossos

The Palace of Minos at Knossos on the island of Crete is one of the most remarkable archaeological sites in the world. It was discovered and excavated by the British archaeologist Arthur Evans, who devoted 30 years of his life to recovering a lost civilization.

LEFT: The several stories of the Palace of Minos were connected by a grand staircase, of which this landing was a part. It is called the Hall of the Royal Guard, and it was restored by Arthur Evans along with the rest of the staircase. One of the great achievements of Minoan architecture, the staircase was five stories high and lit by a light-well and double windows. The original columns were made of wood. The frescoes are of figure-eight-shaped shields.

Evans was familiar with the ancient Greek myths and legends, and the story that fascinated him most was that of Minos, the legendary son of Zeus, king of the gods. Minos was born on Crete and became king of the island. His wife, Pasiphae, fell in love with a magnificent bull and gave birth to the Minotaur, a monster with the body of a man and the head of a bull. King Minos kept the Minotaur in a labyrinth hidden in the depths of his palace.

Evans was 51 before he was able to go to Crete in 1899 and investigate the truth of the legend. In that year Crete obtained its independence from the Ottoman Turks, and Evans was able to buy a plot of land on a mound called Kefala (which the local people called Knossos). In March 1900 Evans began excavating in earnest.

His site was on the side of a wide valley, lying about 3 miles (5km) from the north coast of Crete. Digging started on the 23rd of the month,

and four days later Evans recorded in his notebook that he was convinced the city they were unearthing "goes at least well back to a pre-Mycenaean period." Evans and his colleagues had found blocks of rock that were engraved with strange, unrecognizable symbols. Within a matter of weeks it became clear that these blocks were part of a large prehistoric building. Furthermore, as frescoes and decorations were discovered, it was found that a recurring motif was that of a bull.

Evans was elated—he had no doubt that he had discovered the palace of King Minos. He called the building the Palace of Minos and named the civilization that had built it Minoan, after the Cretan king.

As the excavations continued, Evans could see that the palace was vast. It was five stories high in places, with 1,200 rooms, including storerooms, halls, and bathrooms. Corridors and staircases

connected the rooms, which were all grouped around a large central courtyard. The rather haphazard arrangement of the rooms must have reminded Evans of the legend of the labyrinth. It looked as if rooms and halls had been added onto the palace as they were needed, without anyone thinking much about a balanced design.

As the excavations continued, the bases of walls and doorways were uncovered, as well as many objects made by the Minoan craftsmen. Remains were found just a few inches below the modern surface, and this suggested that the building had suffered a great catastrophe. Evans wrote: "From the day of destruction to this the site has been left entirely desolate. For three thousand years or more not a tree seems to have been planted here; over a part of the area not even a plowshare had passed. At the time of the great

RIGHT: A plan of the palace at Knossos. It was built on several floors around a central open courtyard—its complex layout may have given rise to the myth about the labyrinth and the Minotaur. The palace included a throne room, where the king would receive visitors, separate halls for the king and queen, and a vast number of magazines (storerooms) which were used to store grain and olive oil.

northwest entrance

magazines

throne room

central court

west entrance and porch

grand staircase

corridor of procession

south entrance

Queen's Hall

King's Hall

overthrow, no doubt, the place had been methodically plundered for metal objects, and the fallen debris in the rooms and passages turned over and ransacked for precious booty. . . . But the party walls of clay and plaster still stood intact."

◄ RESTORATION ►

As he worked, Evans decided to fit pieces of the jigsaw puzzle together in a work of restoration that he called "reconstitution." Some archaeologists have since criticized this restoration work, but today's visitors certainly gain a better insight into the palace and the Minoan world because of it. Evans said some of the restoration was essential because the workers had to support what they had uncovered before digging deeper.

The palace had thick walls of stone and thinner brick walls; many were framed with wood, probably to help the building withstand earthquakes. The walls had collapsed, the thatch and clay roofs had fallen, and a lot of the wood had rotted. Evans replaced rotten timbers with con-

crete and painted it a buff color to make it resemble wood. He then rebuilt the walls, using the original stone blocks.

The western half of the palace had at least two stories, but only the first floor survives. In a courtyard near the western entrance were three large, round pits. They may originally have been for storing grain, or they might have been used for sacred offerings in religious ceremonies. The main entrance from the west led through a columned porch into a wide corridor covered with a procession of brightly colored frescoes of life-size young men carrying jars. Evans found many other beautiful frescoes at Knossos, and they tell us a great deal about how the Minoans lived. In an anteroom (outer room) beside the grand stairway there was a fresco of a figure called the "priest-king," though it may be a priestess.

On April 13, 1900, Arthur Evans got his first sight of an extraordinary room that led onto the central courtyard. Inside was a high-backed stone throne guarded by painted griffins. This throne room may have been where King Minos received important visitors, though some experts believe it was used by a priestess to worship the supreme Minoan goddess.

Evans found scattered vases here, and he thought that a ritual might have been taking place when disaster struck Knossos. A large stone basin was found a short distance away in a corridor. Evans moved it to the anteroom of the throne room because he believed the Minoans may have used the basin to purify themselves before entering the important throne room.

Much of the rest of the first floor of the west wing was taken up with narrow storerooms (the magazines), where grain, olive oil, wine, dried fish, and beans were kept in huge jars. The upper floor probably contained the main reception rooms and large columned halls used by the king for public audiences.

⇥ THE ROYAL QUARTERS ⇤

The eastern half of the palace was probably five stories high, some of which survive because they were cut into the side of the hill. The floors were connected by a grand staircase. Here were the royal living quarters. Evans called the king's room the Hall of the Double Axes, since these royal symbols were carved on some of the room's stone blocks. This double room had a light-well at one end and a large veranda looking out to the east. The whole palace was cleverly built to receive light, allow air to circulate, and offer protection from the fierce heat of summer. In winter, doors were closed, and hearths provided heat.

The nearby Queen's Hall contained beautiful frescoes of dolphins and a dancing girl. In one corner, enclosed by a half-wall, was a royal bathroom with an earthenware bathtub. The bath was probably filled by a female servant and emptied through a hole in the floor that led to the drains.

Next door was a room with a toilet. There was a hole in a stone slab in the connecting dressing room, and water would have been poured down this to flush the toilet. The toilet drain carried sewage to a stream below the palace. Evans wrote: "The elaborate drainage system of the Palace and the connected sanitary arrangements excite the wonder of all beholders. The terracotta pipes, with their scientifically-shaped sections, nicely interlocked, which date from the earliest days of the building, are quite up to modern standards."

As well as the king and queen, nobles, and priests, many other people lived at the Palace of Minos. There were many servants and slaves to look after the royal family and their courtiers.

Bull-leaping

One of the most famous frescoes found in the Palace of Minos shows a young man somersaulting over the back of a bull. A young woman waits to catch him, and another is about to leap over the bull's horns. Other scenes of bulls and bull-leapers have also been found on Minoan seals and bronze statuettes. Symbols of bulls' horns and vases and cups in the shape of bulls' heads were also found at Knossos.

Historians believe that bull-leaping may have taken place in the central courtyard of the palace, which measures about 164 x 82 ft (50 x 25m). The sport may have been part of a religious ritual as well as an entertainment, and the bull may have been sacrificed at the end. The practice of bull-leaping may have given rise to the legend of the Minotaur—the creature that was the Bull of Minos.

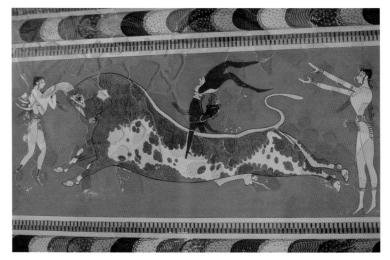

The famous bull-leaping fresco comes from the east side of the palace. Some historians have suggested that it may show the three stages of a successful leap. The athlete first grabs the horns of the bull, then somersaults onto its back, and finally lands on his or her feet.

Storekeepers, scribes, and accountants organized and recorded the vast stores. There were potters, jewelers, masons, carpenters, and painters—many of their workshops have been found. Smaller buildings lay outside the walls of the palace, which was not surrounded by fortifications or a defensive wall. Roads led away from the palace to the city of Knossos.

From the work done by Evans and others we know that the palace was built about 1900 B.C. It was destroyed, probably by an earthquake, about 200 years later. After being completely rebuilt and probably extended, the palace may have been damaged by the eruption of the volcano on the nearby island of Thera (present-day Santorini) in about 1500 B.C. Around 100 years later the palace was destroyed by fire and never rebuilt. The city of Knossos was taken over by Mycenaean warriors and became a leading Greek city-state until the Romans conquered Crete in 67 B.C.

Mycenaeans

The Mycenaeans were a sophisticated Bronze Age people who flourished in ancient Greece between 1600 and 1100 B.C. Their prosperity lasted for a period of 500 years, their wealth being based on sea trade with the countries lying around the Mediterranean Sea.

The Mycenaeans were not united by a single kingdom. They were a loose grouping of small states linked by a common language, religious beliefs, and way of life. Each state was ruled by a king from a fortified city.

In addition to the great city of Mycenae, the cities of Tiryns, Pylos, Thebes, Gla, and Athens were also important centers of Mycenaean life. The Mycenaeans were war-loving, but they were also skilled craftsmen and prosperous traders. Their kings were mighty and powerful, as we know from the glittering riches that have been recovered from their tombs.

The history of both the rise and fall of the Mycenaeans remains something of a mystery. The Mycenaeans came originally from central Europe—some experts believe they migrated to Greece around 2000 B.C. By about 1600 B.C. their influence had spread throughout the Greek mainland. The rise of the Mycenaeans coincided with the decline of the Minoan civilization, based in Crete, which had dominated ancient Greece since around 2200 B.C.

Around 1450 B.C. the Mycenaeans took over the island of Crete, which had been the center of the Minoan Empire. They also occupied many

ABOVE: The citadel of Mycenae as it is today. The deep shaft tombs discovered here date from about 1600 B.C. Their contents included gold, jewelry, and crystal scepters, indicating that they were probably royal tombs.

smaller Greek islands, including Rhodes in the east. On the Greek mainland their cities flourished, and Mycenaean trade and influence spread across the Mediterranean region.

Yet only 200 years later the Mycenaeans were facing some mysterious threat. Around 1250 B.C. huge stone walls were built to fortify their cities against attackers. By 1100 B.C. the Mycenaean civilization had come to a sudden, violent end. Whether the Mycenaeans were defeated by enemies invading from the north, overthrown by civil war, or even weakened by crop failure and famine, we do not know. For whatever reason, the cities were all destroyed by fire or abandoned.

RIGHT: These two pottery statues of female figures with their arms raised in prayer may represent the earth goddess, or they may have been left at a shrine to remind the deity to respond to a request for help or healing.

Schliemann at Mycenae

Heinrich Schliemann (1822–90) was the German archaeologist who excavated Mycenae in the 1870s. Armed with a copy of Homer's *Iliad*, he was searching for King Agamemnon's city when he started excavating a burial ground on a steep hillside in southern Greece. He found shaft tombs containing a treasure trove of gold,

silver, gems, and priceless objects. In the last tomb he found a mummified body wearing a golden mask. Schliemann lifted the mask and later claimed, "I have gazed upon the face of Agamemnon." However, experts have since proved that the golden mask dates to the 1550s B.C.—three centuries before Agamemnon's time.

The "Mask of Agamemnon" found at Mycenae by Heinrich Schliemann. It was made from a thin sheet of gold that was first beaten into shape and then sculpted by using hammers and punches.

Greece now entered a time of decline known as the Dark Ages, which lasted until the dawn of what is called the Archaic Period in 800 B.C.

➤ DISCOVERING THE PAST ➤

Much of what we know about the Mycenaeans comes from archaeological excavations. Digging began in the 1870s and still continues today. These digs have produced a second source of information—written records inscribed on clay tablets in an early Greek script called Linear B, which was developed from ancient Minoan.

The epic poem the *Iliad* contains information about the Mycenaeans, but experts disagree about whether the poem is accurate or not. Attributed to the ninth-century Greek poet Homer, the *Iliad* tells the story of a 10-year war between the Greeks, led by King Agamemnon of Mycenae, and the Trojans—the people of Troy, a city on the west coast of Anatolia (present-day Turkey). Some experts dismiss the *Iliad* as a heroic fantasy. Yet Heinrich Schliemann, the German archaeologist who discovered the city of Mycenae and uncovered the first evidence of Mycenaean culture, believed every word of the poem was true.

A fortified city lay at the heart of each Mycenaean kingdom. The cities were all built on hills that could be easily defended against enemy attacks. On the summit of the hill stood the acropolis, or upper city. During the troubled times of the late Mycenaean age huge walls 16 ft (5m) thick were built up around the cities. They were made of massive, irregular stones so heavy that Greeks of later times believed they could only have been set in place by giants. They called this style of stonework Cyclopean, after the Cyclops, a mythical race of giants. Imposing gateways set in the walls allowed traffic to enter and leave the city. The main gateway at Mycenae was topped with carved stone lions, thought to be a symbol of the king.

➤ THE ROYAL PALACE ➤

In Mycenae and other cities the royal palace dominated the acropolis. It acted both as a regional center and military headquarters. Built around stately courtyards, the palace held a throne room, halls, craft workshops, and storerooms as well as the royal living quarters.

The most important room in the palace was the *megaron*, a large hall where the king held court and conducted state business. A round hearth with a bright fire burned in the center. The walls of this impressive audience chamber were decorated with colorful frescoes that showed scenes from daily life.

In the palace workshops craftsmen produced fine pottery, jewelry, cloth, perfume, tools, and bronze weapons. Beyond the palace walls the streets of the acropolis were lined with ordinary houses. There were no large temples for public worship in the upper city. Instead, many homes contained a shrine. Like the Minoans, the Mycenaeans worshiped the earth goddess as their chief deity. Written records show they also revered Zeus, Poseidon, Athene, Hera, and Hermes deities who would feature in the reli gion of the Greeks of later times.

The hilltop fortress of Mycenae also contained royal burial grounds. There kings and nobles were laid to rest along with many of their valuable possessions that the Mycenaeans believed would be needed in the afterlife. Archaeologists digging in the ruins discovered gold and silver jewelry, crystal goblets and scepters, priceless vases, armor, and weapons set with precious stones. Five of the kings buried at Mycenae wore death masks over their faces that were made of thin, beaten gold. These burial hoards were among the richest finds the world has ever known.

Mycenaean kings were buried in two different styles of tomb. The earliest graves, dating from the 1600s B.C., were simple shaft tombs, sunk deep into the earth. Several generations would be buried in these tombs, along with their possessions. Then the tomb was roofed with stones, and the shaft filled in with earth. A stone slab might be placed on top to mark the spot.

From the 1500s B.C. more elaborate graves called tholos tombs were built by master craftsmen. They were large domed chambers shaped like giant beehives, built of stones and then covered with earth. Both styles of tomb were hard for grave robbers to break into, so many of the treasures they contained lay undisturbed until modern times.

The Mycenaeans were a warlike people. Their tombs contained armor, weapons, and paintings of battle scenes, which give many clues about war in Mycenaean times. Kings kept large permanent armies, who lived in the palace in times of peace. Rulers were expected to feed, arm, and clothe their men. Chieftains wore heavy

BELOW: The citadel at Mycenae was enclosed by a thick wall constructed of massive, closely fitting boulders. The Lion Gate shown here was the main entrance into the citadel.

bronze armor and leather helmets bristling with boars' tusks. The ordinary soldiers wore leather tunics and carried many weapons, including spears, swords, shields, and daggers. Chieftains rode into battle in chariots; the rest of the army went on foot.

In the countryside most Mycenaeans worked as farmers. On land that was owned mainly by the king, poor farmers and slaves raised crops or kept livestock like sheep and goats. Each year the farmers brought their harvest to be stored in the palace grain rooms—they also had to give a portion of their crops or herds to the king as rent for the land they worked. In the cities people earned their living in other ways. Some were priests, administrators, or soldiers. Others worked as merchants or craftsmen.

The Mycenaeans dominated sea trade in the Mediterranean region from the 1600s B.C. They set up trading posts in southern Italy and along the west coast of Anatolia, and traded with distant countries in the Middle East, North Africa, and Scandinavia. Merchants traded Mycenaean grain, pottery, cloth, and hand-crafted goods for metals like gold, copper, and tin.

➤ FINE CRAFTSMEN ➤

Mycenaean craftsmen were among the finest of ancient times. In art, as in writing and religion, the Mycenaeans were strongly influenced by the Minoans. Potters produced elegant drinking cups and wide-bodied vases in the Minoan style, painted with colored glazes showing sea creatures. War and hunting were also popular themes. Like the Minoans, the Mycenaeans made small statues of female figures dressed in long robes and with their arms raised in prayer. These statues are often found in graves, and some archaeologists believe they represent the earth goddess.

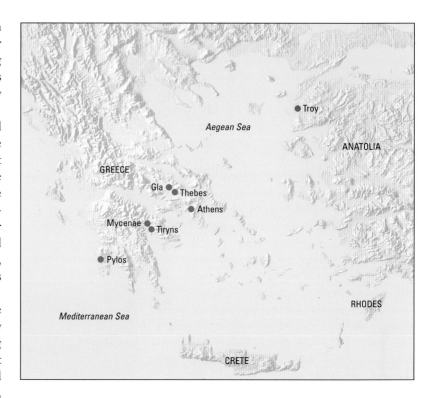

ABOVE: A map showing the main Mycenaean city kingdoms on mainland Greece and the site of Troy on the west coast of Anatolia.

LEFT: A Mycenaean pottery drinking vessel shaped like a hedgehog. Mycenaean potters were highly skilled and produced large quantities of pottery goods for trade with mainland Greece and other countries.

Troy

For centuries Troy was believed to be a city of legend, living only in the Greek epic poem the *Iliad*. Then in the second half of the 19th century the German archaeologist Heinrich Schliemann set out to prove that Troy had been a real city.

The *Iliad*, by the Greek poet Homer, is the story of the Trojan War, fought between the Greeks and the Trojans. After the Trojans lost the war, the city of Troy disappeared without trace, and by the 19th century most historians believed that it had only existed in ancient myth. However, Heinrich Schliemann (1822–90) was to prove the doubters wrong.

When he was just seven years old, Schliemann saw an artist's impression in a history book of how Troy might have looked, and it convinced him that the city really had existed and that its ruins must lie somewhere. Years later, Schliemann's studies of Homer's poem led him to the Aegean coast of western Anatolia and a hill called Hissarlik in present-day Turkey. A few other archaeologists had already suggested this as a possible site for Troy, and when he arrived there, Schliemann felt sure that they were right.

In 1870 Schliemann started digging at Hissarlik and soon found, 15 ft (4.5 m) beneath the surface soil, an ancient wall of huge stones. A year later he returned to continue the excavations, and made more finds. By 1872 Schliemann had more than 100 local workmen helping him. They found the remains of not just one ancient city but several cities built one on top of the other. It was clear that as each city had been destroyed, another had been built on the ruins. The diggers continued to find walls, urns, and fragments of pottery. But was this Troy? In June 1873 Schliemann thought he had the answer.

At the bottom of a wall he was excavating, Schliemann saw a gleaming piece of gold. When he got it out, he found that it was a gold diadem. Shortly afterward, he found another diadem, gold bracelets, a gold goblet, and a large silver container with thousands of small gold rings. Schliemann was elated, and convinced that he had found the treasure of Priam, the legendary last king of Troy.

After Heinrich Schliemann's death, excavations at Troy were continued by his colleague Wilhelm Dörpfeld and later by archaeologists from the University of Cincinnati. They found that the gold that Schliemann called "Priam's Treasure" was actually from a period about 1,000 years before King Priam and the Trojan War. It

ABOVE: The remains of the city walls of Troy VI, which flourished between 2000 and 1300 B.C. This version of the city was destroyed by an earthquake.

The Trojan War

According to Homer, the Trojan War began when Paris, the son of King Priam of Troy, stole Helen, the wife of Menelaus, king of Sparta. Menelaus's brother, Agamemnon, sailed to Troy with a huge army carried by a fleet of 1,000 ships to win Helen back. He laid siege to Troy for 10 years, but could not conquer the walled city. Then Odysseus, one of the Greek commanders, devised a plan. The Greeks built a huge wooden horse, placed it outside the walls of Troy, and then sailed away. The Trojans thought the horse was a sacred offering and took it into their city. But the wooden horse was actually full of Greek warriors who crept out under cover of night and opened the city gates for the rest of their army, which had sailed back from a nearby island. The Greeks took Helen back, killed King Priam and the Trojan men, took the women captive, and burned Troy to the ground.

RIGHT: Taken at the time of Schliemann's excavations, this photograph shows a collection of pottery storage jars found at Troy. They date back to the early Bronze Age and to the city known to archaeologists as Troy II.

came from the second of the nine cities that lay one on top of the other.

Archaeologists believe that Troy was founded in the early Bronze Age, which began about 3000 B.C. in Anatolia. Over the following centuries Troy became an extremely important trading center, mainly thanks to its location. It lay not only on a major land route between Asia and Europe but also on the sea route between the Aegean and the Black Sea. Because of this Troy became extremely wealthy, and historians believe that it served as the capital of the surrounding region, an area that we now know as the Troas.

Archaeologists divide the history of Troy into a series of distinct periods. The first Troy was a small fortified citadel to which local farmers and villagers moved in times of danger. The second Troy, built on top of the first city and called Troy II by archaeologists, was a larger and wealthier city, and traded extensively with the Mycenaeans of Greece. This city came to an end through fire, which led Schliemann to mistake it for Homer's Troy. The next three citadels were each larger than the previous one.

Troy VI had many new settlers and was far more heavily influenced by the Mycenaeans than its predecessors. It was destroyed by an earthquake about 1300 B.C. The next city, which is called Troy VIIa, was looted and burned around 1250 B.C. Archaeologists arrived at this date because Mycenaean pottery found at the site can be dated very accurately. Most historians believe that Troy VIIa was the city of King Priam that featured in the story of the Trojan War. Its successor, Troy VIIb, did not last long—it was abandoned about 1100 B.C. and left unoccupied for several centuries.

A new chapter in the history of Troy began at the start of the seventh century B.C., when Greeks from the nearby island of Lemnos reoccupied it. The city now became known as Ilium and prospered for many years. The Romans eventually sacked this city in 85 B.C. and built Troy IX, the final version of the city, which was abandoned around A.D. 400.

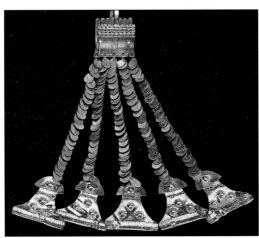

RIGHT: A gold earring that was part of a hoard of gold jewelry discovered at Troy and known as "Priam's Treasure." However, it actually dates back to around 2300 B.C., roughly 1,000 years before the time of the Trojan War.

Phoenicians

The Phoenicians were a nation of great seafarers and traders from the shores of the eastern Mediterranean Sea. No one knows where they came from originally, but it is thought that they probably arrived in the Mediterranean region about 3000 B.C.

The Phoenicians' homeland where they settled on the coast of the Mediterranean Sea was the narrow strip that is now divided between Syria, Lebanon, and Israel. The Phoenicians were renowned as merchants, navigators, skilled boatbuilders, and gifted craftsmen. They were also famous for their learning, inventing an alphabet that was adopted by the Greeks and was later to form the basis of all the alphabets used in the West today.

The name Phoenicia comes from the Greek *phoinix*, meaning red-purple. The Greeks called the Phoenicians *Phoinikes* (the red-purple men) because of their most important product, a purple dye that was used to stain cloth.

The Phoenicians, however, called themselves Canaanites. They were descended from the Bronze Age people of Canaan (an area that is now Syria and Palestine), and Canaan also means "land of purple" in the Semitic language.

➤ THE CANAANITES ➤

During the early Bronze Age (3000–2000 B.C.) the Canaanites built a number of great cities, including the ports of Byblos and Ugarit, which became important trading centers between 2000 and 1500 B.C. However, after 1550 B.C. the cities of Canaan were conquered and ruled by a series of foreign powers, including the Hittites, Egyptians, and Mycenaeans.

The history of Phoenicia really begins around 1100 B.C., when the Phoenicians seized an opportunity to gain their freedom. At this time the civilizations of southern Europe and western Asia were threatened by invading tribes called the Sea Peoples. These fierce warriors attacked the

ABOVE: The ruins of the city of Byblos. On the Mediterranean coast, Byblos was the main Phoenician port for the export of cedarwood. It was to remain a great trading center well into Roman times.

ABOVE: An artist's impression of a Phoenician trading ship. The Phoenicians built their merchant ships with a wide hull to hold plenty of cargo.

Egyptians, conquered the Hittites, and contributed to the downfall of the Mycenaeans in Greece. The Mycenaeans had dominated sea trade in the Mediterranean since the 1600s, and now the weakening of all these nations gave the Phoenicians the chance not only to reclaim their independence but also to win control of sea trade in the region.

◄ PHOENICIAN INFLUENCE ►

Over the next 250 years Phoenician power and influence spread throughout the Mediterranean region. Their cities set up trading stations, then colonies, in Cyprus and western Sicily, and at Gades (modern Cadiz) in Spain. Carthage, a port on the north coast of Africa, was another important Phoenician colony.

Carthage was founded in 814 B.C. by the city of Tyre, which, together with Sidon, grew into a wealthy city and an important center of learning.

Built on two offshore islands, Tyre was especially powerful because it was very difficult to attack. Nebuchadnezzar, king of Babylon, laid siege to it without success for 13 years during the 500s B.C.

During the 900s B.C. the king of Tyre made an alliance with the Hebrews under King David and his successor, Solomon. According to the Bible, King Hiram of Tyre provided cedarwood and craftsmen experienced in working "gold and silver, iron, stone, and wood, as well as purple, violet, and crimson yarn and fine linen," to help build Solomon's temple. Hiram sent shipbuilders to establish a Hebrew fleet on the Red Sea. From there Solomon's ships, manned by Phoenician sailors, went out on trading missions. Once every three years, the Bible tells us, "this fleet of merchantmen came home, bringing gold and silver, ivory, apes, and monkeys."

By about 850 B.C. the Phoenicians had colonized the Mediterranean islands of Corsica, Sardinia, Malta, and Gozo, and possibly also parts of the Greek mainland. They controlled the Strait of Gibraltar, where the Mediterranean Sea narrows to a distance of eight miles (13km) as its waters mingle with the Atlantic Ocean. Daring Phoenician sailors ventured beyond this strait to visit the Azores and possibly even Cornwall, on the southwest tip of England, which was a center for tin mining. Later, during the 600s B.C., Phoenician seamen led an Egyptian expedition that sailed all the way around the African coast, a voyage that lasted three years according to the Greek historian Herodotus.

The development of Phoenicia was influenced by its geography. To the west the waters of the Mediterranean Sea formed a natural boundary. To the east the mountains of Lebanon made another protective barrier between Phoenicia and its powerful neighbors inland. The great cities of Phoenicia—Tyre, Sidon, Byblos, Berytus (Beirut), and Arvad—began as small sea ports that grew rich on trading profits. But miles of rugged coastline separated these settlements and prevented Phoenicia from becoming a unified kingdom. Instead, it flourished as a chain of powerful city-states.

Although small, Phoenicia held rich resources. Cloth and timber formed the basis of Phoenician trade. The shallow waters offshore were a rich fishing ground and the source of the murex snails that produced the famous purple dye. Inland the coastal strip was well watered by streams and rivers. In this fertile soil farmers grew wheat, barley, grapes, and olives, and pastured their herds. But Phoenicia's greatest asset lay in

Royal Purple

The Phoenicians were famous for their purple cloth, which was in demand throughout the Mediterranean region because purple was the color worn by kings. The dye was obtained from murex snails, which were found in the sea. To make the dye, the shells of the snails were cracked, and the soft creatures inside removed. Their rotting bodies yielded a yellow liquid that darkened to purple when boiled and processed—Tyre and Sidon were notorious for the stench given off by the rotting snails. Each snail produced only a tiny drop of liquid, so up to 60,000 mollusks were needed to make 1 lb. (450g) of dye. Skilled dyers could produce a range of colors, from pale pink to deep purple. Tailors then made up the cloth into robes.

the mountains—the mighty forests that grew on the steep hillsides. The cedars of Lebanon were prized for their hard, long-lasting timber. The Phoenicians used the wood for their own ship-building and also sold large quantities for export.

⏤ TRADE GOODS ⏤

Phoenician merchants sold agricultural produce such as grain, oil, wine, and raisins. They also acted as middlemen, selling crops and goods produced by other peoples. Traders imported metals and other raw materials from around the Mediterranean for the skilled Phoenician craftsmen to make into desirable objects. Smiths cast and hammered gold, silver, and bronze into items that were much in demand, such as tools, weapons, and jewelry. Ivory brought from Africa was carved into delicate panels to decorate furniture, including chairs, beds, and chests. Glassworkers made glass objects from silica-rich sand and wood ash. To do this, they shaped the molten glass around a sand or clay mold and then allowed it to set before destroying the mold. Later Phoenicians may have invented glassblowing.

The Phoenicians worshiped a variety of deities, sharing some of their gods and goddesses with other ancient civilizations, including Egypt and Babylon. They worshiped the Egyptian sun god Re and goddess Hathor, and the Mesopotamian god of storms, Hadad.

The Phoenicians usually called their deities simply *Baal* (lord) or *Baalat* (lady). They offered animal sacrifices to the gods on altars that were called tophets.

RIGHT: This elegant glass container for perfume or ointment was made by Phoenician craftsmen in the fifth century B.C. using the sand-core method. To make glass objects by this method, they first poured layers of molten glass over a shaped sand mold. When the glass coating set, the sand was emptied out, leaving a glass vessel. To decorate it, colored glass was dripped onto the vessel, which was then rolled on a flat surface before the glass cooled.

BELOW: The Phoenician trading empire stretched as far as the Strait of Gibraltar, and possibly beyond it.

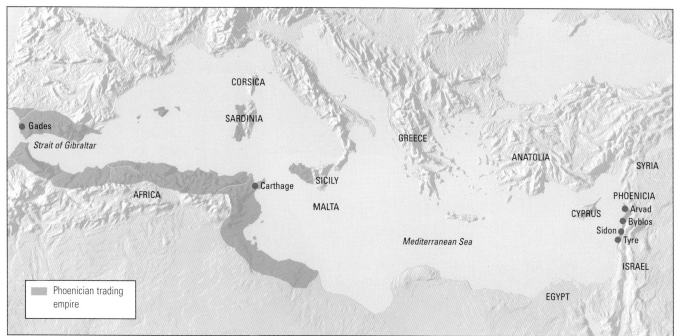

CORSICA

SARDINIA

Gades

Strait of Gibraltar

GREECE

ANATOLIA

SYRIA

AFRICA

Carthage

SICILY

MALTA

PHOENICIA

CYPRUS

Arvad

Byblos

Sidon

Tyre

Mediterranean Sea

ISRAEL

EGYPT

Phoenician trading empire

A New Alphabet

The Phoenicians spoke a Semitic language related to Hebrew and Babylonian. From the Babylonians they also learned cuneiform writing—the script of wedge-shaped symbols.

Around 1200 B.C. they developed their own alphabet of 22 letters, all of which were consonants. This was an immense improvement since the cuneiform scripts in use at this time could have as many as 600 different symbols. Later the Greeks adapted the Phoenician alphabet, adding vowels. From the Greeks the alphabet passed to the Romans, and through the Romans it became the basis of all Western alphabets. Some Phoenician words still survive in English and other European languages. The English words "bible" and "bibliography," for example, are both derived from the name Byblos, the Phoenician port that was famous for its trade in papyrus, the writing material of the ancient world.

In 842 B.C. Phoenicia was conquered by the Assyrian Empire and for the following 200 years Phoenician cities suffered under the harsh Assyrian rule. Eventually, during the 600s B.C., they passed first into the hands of the Babylonians, and then the Persians. The Persians allowed the civilizations they conquered many freedoms, so the cities prospered again, especially Sidon. The Phoenician fleet fought for the Persians in their wars against the Greeks, only to be destroyed by the Greek navy at the Battle of Salamis in 480 B.C.

In 330 B.C. Phoenicia was conquered again, this time by Alexander the Great of Macedonia. Under his successors Phoenicia thrived as a center of culture and commerce until 64 B.C. At this point it was absorbed into the Roman Empire and ceased to have a separate identity.

BELOW: A sacrificial altar in the city of Carthage. The Phoenicians used altars like this to sacrifice small animals to the gods. Some historians believe that parents may also have sacrificed their first-born child to the gods, although the extent of this practice may have been exaggerated.

Etruscans

The Etruscans lived in a central region of Italy from about 900 B.C. and developed a distinct culture with a unique language. They may have been native Italians, or they may have been descendants of the Tyrrhenians, who originally came from Lydia, west of present-day Turkey.

LEFT: Wealthy Etruscans were buried in elaborate tombs, which were often designed to look like houses and decorated with wall paintings. This rock tomb from the sixth century B.C. is at Tarquinia. It contains lively scenes of everyday life and a painted doorway to provide access to the world of the dead.

Before Rome became the dominant power in the Mediterranean region, there were three main sea powers—the Greeks, the Phoenicians, and the Etruscans. When the Etruscans allied themselves with the Phoenicians, they jointly defeated the Greeks at the Battle of Alalia in 540 B.C. and expelled the Greeks from the island of Corsica. This was to be the high point of Etruscan expansion.

By 510 B.C. the Etruscans had been forced out of Rome by the native Romans, and the entire Etruscan area was eventually absorbed into the Roman state in the first century B.C.

↠ ETRURIA ↞

The Etruscans lived in an area of Italy called Etruria, which was bordered to the south and east by the Tiber River and to the north by the Arno River. There were 12 main Etruscan towns. Some Etruscan towns, such as Tarquinia, Vulci, and Orvieto, can be found around present-day Italian cities. These settlements were usually built on easily-defended hilltops.

One of the best-known Etruscan towns is at Marzabotto near the present-day city of Bologna. This town, which was built in the sixth century B.C., was laid out with a street grid, and a specific area was set aside for the temples. The houses usually had a central courtyard that gave access to

the rooms. The walls were made of sun-dried mud brick, and the roofs of fired clay tiles. Traditionally, each town was ruled by a king, but by the fifth century B.C. a number of wealthy families had control of the towns. These nobles carried out specific administrative functions.

Etruscan temples were very distinctive, with two rows of columns at their front—this later became known as the "Tuscan" style of architecture. Many of the temples were made of mud

LEFT: This statue of a woman resting on a couch is from an Etruscan sarcophagus. Etruscan women seem to have enjoyed a high status.

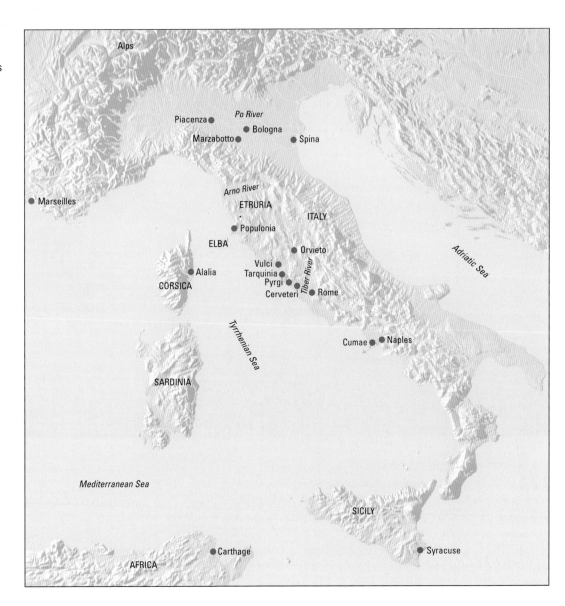

Alps

Po River
Piacenza ●
● Bologna
Marzabotto ●
● Spina

Arno River

Marseilles ●

ETRURIA

ITALY

● Populonia

ELBA

● Orvieto

Vulci ●
Alalia ●
Tarquinia ●
Pyrgi ●
CORSICA
Cerveteri ●   ● Rome

Tiber River

Adriatic Sea

Tyrrhenian Sea

Cumae ● ● Naples

SARDINIA

Mediterranean Sea

SICILY

● Carthage
AFRICA

● Syracuse

brick, and the roof was often decorated with mythological figures in fired clay.

We do not know a great deal about the Etruscans' religion, but it seems that one aspect of it involved studying the internal organs of animals as a way of divining the future. A find that seems to be connected with this is a bronze model of a lamb's liver discovered near Piacenza. The model was divided into sections. Each bore the names of several gods—in all, some 52 gods were named. The gods often resemble those known from Greece and Rome. The Etruscan goddess Menerva, for example, is similar to the Roman Minerva and the Greek Athena.

Sea trade played an important part in Etruscan civilization. The Etruscans had regular trading contact with the Greeks and the Phoenicians. They exported metals such as iron ore, which was mined on the island of Elba and smelted at the city of Populonia. They also exported more valuable items such as gold drinking cups. They imported rare goods from Africa such as richly decorated ostrich eggs and thousands of ceramic pots from Athens.

The Etruscan Language

For writing the Etruscans used an adapted form of the Greek alphabet, adding letters of their own. For centuries no one was able to understand their texts. Then a breakthrough came in 1964 when an Italian archaeologist discovered three gold plaques at the Etruscan port of Pyrgi. Two of the plaques had texts inscribed on them in Etruscan, while the third was in Punic (the language of the Phoenicians and the Carthaginians). Although the texts were not parallel (that is, they were not direct translations of each other), there was enough overlap to allow scholars to decipher the Etruscan part of the inscription. One of the longest surviving Etruscan texts—consisting of some 1,200 words—was written in a linen book and gives details of the Etruscan religious calendar.

RIGHT: This bronze statue
of a warrior is a fine
example of the Etruscans'
metalworking skills.

The Etruscans expanded northward and established the port of Spina at the mouth of the Po River. This gave them access to the Adriatic Sea and meant that they could trade easily with Greece, and in particular Athens. They may also have traded with central Europe, using the passes over the Alps.

The Etruscans seem to have exported wine and olive oil—Etruscan transport containers ("amphoras") have been found as far away as the south of France around Marseilles. A wrecked ship containing Etruscan amphoras has been found near Giglio Island (off the coast of northwest Italy); the ship was also found to contain metal ingots.

The presence of Greek traders in Etruria is indicated by the discovery of a stone anchor in one of the Etruscan sanctuaries at the harbor town of Pyrgi. The anchor was dedicated to the Greek god Apollo, probably by a man named Sostratos from the island of Aegina near Athens. The level of trade with Greece in the sixth and fifth centuries B.C. is also indicated by the thousands of Athenian pots in Etruscan tombs.

⤙ HOUSES FOR THE DEAD ⤚

Tombs are the best-explored Etruscan monuments. They were placed in large cemeteries outside the cities. Often the tombs resembled the insides of houses. At the city of Tarquinia the tombs consisted of a chamber cut into the volcanic rock and were decorated with elaborate wall paintings. The so-called Tomb of the Reliefs at Cerveteri is also cut from the rock and laid out as if it were a banqueting chamber. Cups and armor were hung on the walls. Around the room were rock-cut couches, fitted with cushions, on which the dead could be placed. The overall effect would have been one of a feast for the dead.

RIGHT: A wall painting of dancers from one of the Tarquinian rock tombs. Paintings like these are a valuable source of information about Etruscan activities, dress, and appearance.

Greece

The civilization of ancient Greece was possibly the greatest of the ancient world. In the first millennium B.C. Greek philosophy, politics, science, architecture, art, and drama were to provide the basis for much of Western culture through the succeeding centuries.

After the Mycenaean civilization came to an end, Greece entered a period called the Dark Ages (1100–800 B.C.). Little is known about this time because the art of writing was lost, and there was hardly any contact with other civilizations. However, around 800 B.C. Greek civilization began a new phase—the population started to increase, there was a rise in the standard of living, writing reappeared, and there was an upsurge in trade with other cultures.

The institution that formed the basis for this flourishing new culture was the city-state, or *polis*. A *polis* consisted of a city or town and the surrounding countryside. Some *polis*, like Athens, were large; others were quite small. All were supported by agriculture, which was the main occupation for most people. Even city-dwellers often owned farms.

The city-states shared a common language (Greek), although there were local variations, worshiped the same gods, and occasionally joined together to hold athletic games or fight invaders. However, the mountainous countryside made communication between cities difficult. This meant that people felt more loyalty to their own city than to other Greeks, so the cities often fought each other. Nevertheless, Greeks had a strong feeling of a common identity, and called all non-Greek people "barbarians" because they thought their language sounded like "bar-bar."

Athens is the best known of the city-states. This is partly because it was one of the most powerful and successful, but also because we have far more information about it. The Athenians were pioneers in politics, law, and administration, and by the middle of the fifth century Athens had become the intellectual center of the Greek world. Traditionally, Athens had been ruled by kings, but by the seventh century B.C. it was ruled by magistrates or *archons*. The *archons* and the ruling council were all aristocrats, who were wealthy landowners. In many city-states there was a huge gap between the wealth and power of the aristocracy and the poverty of the people. This situation led to rebellions and sometimes to the rise of an absolute ruler, who was called a tyrant. Some of

these tyrants were enlightened leaders who curbed the power of the aristocrats; others showed the kind of ruthless behavior that led to the modern meaning of the word. Phalaris, for example, was a sixth-century Sicilian tyrant who roasted his victims alive in a bronze ox.

➤ THE BEGINNING OF DEMOCRACY ➤

In 594 B.C., to prevent a threatened rebellion, the ruling council of Athens gave the *archon* Solon special powers to introduce reforms. Solon canceled all agricultural debts, restored freedom to Athenians who had been sold into slavery, and gave all citizens (only landowners could be citi-

ABOVE: The marble temple of Athene (now called the Parthenon) was built on a hill overlooking the city of Athens.

zens) the right to vote in the Assembly. Many consider Solon to be the founder of Athenian democracy. But after his death the Peisistratid family seized control of Athens in 561/560 B.C. Then in 510 B.C. they were driven out by a group of nobles led by Cleisthenes and helped by Athens' chief rival, Sparta.

Cleisthenes divided all the citizens of Attica (Athens and the surrounding area) into ten tribes (*phylai*). Each tribe was given three pieces of land—each piece of land contained many small villages called *demes*. The *demes* voted for the 50

people from each tribe who would form the Council. The tribes took it in turn to run the city, each holding office for one month. The ruling group (*prytany*) provided a number of individuals who were always available in case any crisis needed immediate attention. In addition, all adult male citizens served as members of the Popular Assembly, which met on the Pnyx, one of the hills of Athens. At least 6,000 members had to be present before any proposals of the Council could be voted into law. Under this democratic system much of the power of the *archons* passed to the

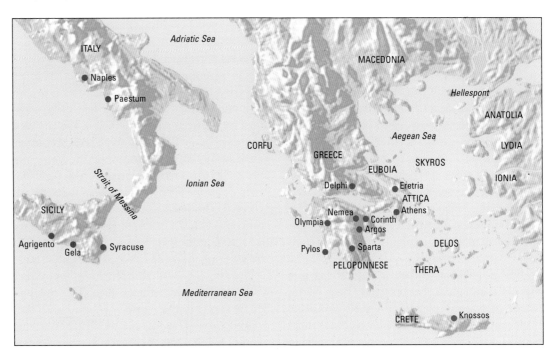

strategoi (military commanders). There were 10 of these, one from each tribe. They were elected annually (but could be re-elected) and carried out orders given by the Council and the Assembly.

Justice was also in the hands of the people. Magistrates were elected, juries were selected by lottery, and defenders and prosecutors had to speak for themselves—water clocks were used to limit the length of speeches.

The Athenians did not want any one individual to gain too much power, so they developed a system called ostracism. At a certain point in the year all the citizens were called together. If anyone wanted to expel someone, he wrote their name on a piece of pottery (*ostraka*) and cast it into a ballot box. If enough votes were cast against one person, the individual was expelled. Although the Athenian political system gave wide powers to the people and is the basis of the Western democratic system, it did not include women, slaves, or foreigners.

The population of Athens was divided into two main groups: free people and slaves. Slaves were completely in the power of their owner and could not own property or even marry without permission. Almost half the people who lived in Athens were slaves—most worked in the home, but others worked in stone quarries, docks, or workshops. On the whole, slaves were reasonably well treated, with the exception of the wretched slaves who worked up to 10 hours a day in terrible conditions in the silver mines of Laurion.

Free men were also divided into two groups: citizens and *metics*. A citizen was someone born to Athenian parents, and he was expected to participate in government whether he was an aristocrat or a farmer. A *metic* was someone whose parents were not both citizens. A *metic* had to be sponsored by a citizen and could live in the city on a long-term basis. They paid some taxes and served in the army but were not entitled to vote, own land or houses, or marry citizens. Although they could never become citizens, *metics* were socially accepted, entitled to protection under the law, and could follow a trade or profession. Women had the status of their husband or male relations and were not allowed to take part in public life.

Sparta, Athens's main rival in the Greek world, had very different values. The Spartans had always been a warlike people, and they evolved a way of life that was totally based around military ideals. At age seven all male children

ABOVE: The temple of Apollo at Corinth. The Greeks built their temples as homes for the gods. A room called a *cella* would contain a statue of the god, while a second room held a treasury for offerings. The altar for sacrifices was situated outside the temple, often at the main door.

were taken from home and trained in athletics and martial arts. At 20 all men became soldiers.

Sparta was ruled by two kings who led the army to war, but most of the power was held by five magistrates elected by an Assembly consisting of all citizens over 30. The Council consisted of 28 councilors over the age of 60 who were elected for life and the two kings. The Assembly voted for or against the Council's proposals.

Women were not able to vote but had much more freedom than Athenian women. They could also own property and represent themselves in court. Because all Spartan men were soldiers, all other work was carried out by *helots* (slaves) and *perioikoi* (foreigners). Unlike Athenian slaves, Spartan ones were harshly treated and resented their masters. Spartans were famous for their bravery, discipline, and loyalty, but they failed to produce any outstanding architecture, art, or literature. In time, however, many of the city-states turned to Sparta to curb the power of Athens.

⏤ COLONIES AND TRADE ⏤

During the sixth century B.C. many city-states sent out groups of settlers to establish new cities in unpopulated areas. The reasons for this colonizing movement are not clear, but it may be that the wealthiest families encouraged members to leave the cities and found colonies to relieve political tensions at home. The main areas colonized were in Italy and Sicily. In fact, so many cities were established there that the area became known as Great Greece. Colonies were also established as far afield as Massilia (Marseilles, France), Emorion (Ampurias, northern Spain), and in Anatolia (Turkey).

The Greeks were very active traders. We know this is so because so many Greek objects have been found far from home. A bronze *krater* (vase) found in a grave in Vix, central France, probably came from the colony of Massilia (on the south coast of France), which gave the Greeks access to central Europe along the Rhône River. During the sixth century B.C. the Greeks established a port in Egypt at Naukratis on the Nile Delta, and large quantities of Greek pottery have been found there. At the Greek port of Al Mina on the east Mediterranean coast warehouses have been found containing Greek pottery, which suggests this was one of the points of contact between the Greek world and the Middle East.

It was no doubt through ports like Al Mina that Greece started to receive exotic Middle Eastern objects, such as fine gold, silver, and bronze metalwork. Large quantities of sixth- and fifth-century B.C. Athenian figure-decorated

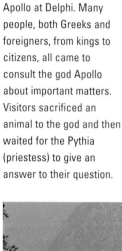

BELOW: The remains of the oracle (shrine) of Apollo at Delphi. Many people, both Greeks and foreigners, from kings to citizens, all came to consult the god Apollo about important matters. Visitors sacrificed an animal to the god and then waited for the Pythia (priestess) to give an answer to their question.

pottery have also been found in the Etruscan cemeteries of Tuscany, such as Cerveteri, Tarquinia, and Vulci.

The discovery of several ancient shipwrecks has shown how Greek trade operated. For instance, a fifth-century B.C. wreck off Porticello in the Strait of Messina, between Italy and Sicily, contained amphoras (pots for transporting wine or olive oil), lead ingots, and even a bronze head.

SANCTUARIES AND GODS

Although there was no concept of Greece as a nation, Greek identity was enhanced by shared sanctuaries (sacred places), which were used by all the cities. The best-known were at Delphi and Olympia. These sanctuaries held regular athletic games (every four years at Olympia) with a range of events such as running, boxing, and chariot-racing. A victorious contestant was awarded an olive wreath and given permission to commemorate his victory with a statue. Only Greek men could compete; slaves and women were not even allowed to watch. The Olympic games were held in conjunction with a festival in honor of the god Zeus. Heralds were sent to all the cities to announce the date and declare a universal truce, so that hostilities were suspended for a week.

In addition to sanctuaries, the Greeks built temples, which were thought to be the earthly home of the gods. In Athens the main temples were placed on the rocky outcrop in the heart of the city called the Acropolis. The patron deity of the city was Athene, and her main temple, the Parthenon, contained a huge statue of her in gold

RIGHT: This picture of a hoplite (foot soldier) is painted on a Greek vase. By the seventh century B.C. the hoplite was the most important part of the armies of the Greek city-states. He wore a bronze helmet, breastplate, and leg guards and carried a shield, stabbing spear, and short sword.

and ivory. The marble temple was decorated with sculptures, including a wonderful sculpted frieze that is now in the British Museum, London.

The Greeks worshiped many gods and goddesses. The 12 most important gods were believed to live on Mount Olympus in northeast Greece and were called the Olympians. In addition, each city-state had its own local gods. Zeus was the ruler of the gods and controlled the heavens. He was married to Hera, who was the protector of women. Poseidon was the brother of Zeus and ruler of the seas; Hades was king of the underworld, the kingdom of the dead.

The gods behaved like humans—they married, fell in love, and felt emotions like jealousy and rage. Many Greek myths record the stories of the gods. People prayed to the appropriate gods as they went about their daily lives and made sacrifices when asking for a particular favor.

THE PERSIAN WARS

In the seventh century B.C. there were two major powers to the east of Greece—Lydia and Persia. The Greeks had good relations with Lydia; and although they were less friendly with Persia, the two cultures traded goods. However, in 546 B.C. Darius, the Persian king, expanded his empire by conquering Lydia and the Greek colonies of Ionia. In 499 B.C. the Ionian cities rebelled against their Persian governors and called on their fellow Greeks for help. This was the beginning of a series of battles between Greeks and Persians that later became known as the Persian Wars.

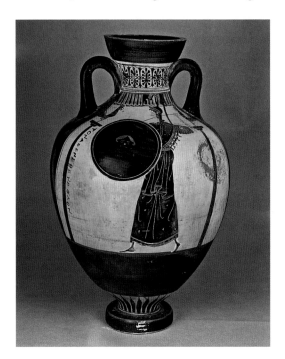

LEFT: A "black-figure" vase from the sixth century B.C. showing the goddess of war, Athene, with helmet, spear, and shield. The orange color came from the natural clay, while the black figure was painted on.

Greek Scientists and Philosophers

Early Greeks thought that the gods and goddesses were responsible for the way the world worked, but in the sixth century B.C. some men began to study the world on a more scientific basis. Their discoveries formed the foundations of our knowledge of science.

One such was Anaxagoras, who was expelled from Athens for proclaiming that the sun was not, in fact, a god but a white-hot stone. Anaximander went even further, proposing a theory of the universe that did not involve gods and suggesting that life began in warm mud, producing first reptiles, then land animals, and finally humans. In addition to asking questions about the physical world, men also debated about human behavior and the purpose of life.

Their ideas formed the basis of modern philosophy. Three of the most famous philosophers were Socrates, Plato, and Aristotle. Socrates (who lived around 469–399 B.C.) encouraged his students to question the established beliefs and practices. He never gave answers to his students; instead, he asked them further questions. The authorities considered his views dangerous, and he was forced to commit suicide. One of his pupils was Plato (about 427–347 B.C.), who wrote down many of Socrates's teachings as dialogues. Plato founded a school of philosophy, called the Academy, in a grove of trees outside Athens.

Plato's chief pupil was Aristotle (384–322 B.C.), who, in turn, was to start his own school, which was called the Lyceum. Aristotle wrote numerous books on almost every known subject. Between them Plato and Aristotle laid the framework for much of Western thought and knowledge.

A 19th-century painter's impression of the Lyceum, Aristotle's school of philosophy. Aristotle's method of teaching followed that of Socrates and Plato—he, too, ran into trouble with the authorities and had to flee Athens.

In the end, the cities managed to form an alliance, and the discipline and tactics of the Greek armies led to land victories at Marathon in 490 B.C. and Plataia in 479 B.C. In these battles the Greek hoplites (foot soldiers) became renowned for their disciplined battle line—the whole unit (phalanx) moved as one man, sweeping all before it. In 480 B.C. 380 Greek ships defeated 1,200 faster, larger Persian ships during a ferocious sea battle in the Bay of Salamis.

The Persian Wars were followed by an era of great achievement in Athens—called the Golden

The Theater

Western theater as we know it today began in ancient Greece at religious festivals. Festivals held for gods such as Dionysus included songs and dances that were performed by a group of men called a chorus. At first these festivals were probably performed in the market place or in temporary structures, but then a permanent theater was cut out of the hillside near the sanctuary of Dionysus.

The theater was semicircular in shape, with rows of seats going up the slope of the hill. In time, as drama developed, theaters were built throughout the Greek world and included buildings behind the orchestra (the area at the foot of the seats) and a raised stage. All the performers were men. At first a play consisted only of the chorus, then an actor was added to talk to the chorus, then more actors, until eventually the actors became more important than the chorus. The theaters were huge (most could hold around 18,000 people), so to help the audience identify individual characters, each wore different-colored clothes and a painted mask.

Greek plays soon developed into two types: comedies and tragedies. Aristophanes (about 450–385 B.C.) was the master of comedy. Many of his plays make fun of the politics of his time. The most famous are *The Wasps, The Birds,* and *The Frogs.* The three great tragedy writers were Aeschylus, Sophocles, and Euripides. Aeschylus (about 525–456 B.C.) wrote tragedies about gods and heroes. The most famous are three plays about King Agamemnon and his family, called the *Oresteia.* Sophocles (about 496–406 B.C.) was the first playwright to concentrate on human characters rather than gods. His most famous plays are *Antigone, Oedipus Tyrannus,* and *Electra.* Euripides (about 485–406 B.C.) wrote plays that include some powerful female roles. The most famous are *Medea, The Trojan Women,* and *Orestes.* Many ancient Greek plays have been lost (sometimes only fragments remain), but others are still performed today and have influenced writers through the ages.

The fourth-century theater at Epidaurus, which could seat 14,000 people in 55 rows of seats.

Age (479–431 B.C.)—when the city grew rich through trade and became a celebrated center for philosophy, architecture, sculpture, pottery, and drama. The Athenian leader during much of the fifth century was Pericles. He was a military general turned politician who encouraged many artists and intellectuals to come and live in the city. He also started a building program that produced some of the finest buildings in Athens, including those on the Acropolis.

Athens's prosperity and its position as the leader of the Delian League (an alliance of cities created to counter any new Persian threat) meant that the city began to dominate the entire Aegean Sea. This led to rivalries with the cities of Corinth and Sparta, and finally to the Peloponnesian War, which broke out in 431 B.C.

The war lasted for 27 years, ending in 404 B.C. when Sparta occupied Athens. The Spartans tore down the city walls, banned democracy in favor of an oligarchy, or rule by the few, known as the Thirty Tyrants, and put up an elaborate sculptural monument at Delphi to celebrate their victory. However, the costs for both sides had been high, and neither Athens nor Sparta ever completely recovered from the long struggle.

The Spartan victory failed to bring peace to Greece, and wars broke out again between the cities, which were then too preoccupied to notice the rise of a new power in Macedonia to the northeast. Philip II came to the Macedonian throne in 359 B.C. In the 23 years before he was assassinated in 336 B.C., he united his country and turned Macedonia into the greatest military power of the day. In the process of expanding his empire he defeated all the Greek cities and gained control over the whole of Greece.

The formation of the *polis* not only had a strong influence on the politics of the Greeks, it also shaped the way people lived and the environment they lived in. Where possible, streets were laid out in a grid pattern to form blocks, a convenient flat place became the main square (*agora*), and impressive public buildings were built in stone with tiled roofs. A popular type of building was the *stoa*. This was an aisled hall with a back and two short sides, a row of columns at the front, and a roof to provide shelter from sun and rain. *Stoas* were often built around the main square and contained shops behind the colonnade. Most cities also had a theater, a gymnasium, and a sanctuary dedicated to a local god.

⏤ DAILY LIFE IN GREECE ⏤

In contrast, private houses were usually made of mud bricks with a wooden roof laid with terracotta tiles. At the center of the house was an open courtyard from which doors opened into the first-floor rooms, while stairs led to the upper rooms. Very few houses have survived, so we do not know exactly what an average house looked like inside.

However, archaeologists have found a number of domestic structures in Athens. Some of these had workshops, where bronze-casting and sculpting took place. It is also possible to identify the men's quarters, which included a dining room where the men gathered for *symposia* (drinking parties). In these dining rooms couches would be placed around the walls of the room, leaving the central space free for the *krater* (vase) of water and wine. The furniture was usually made of wood and was simple in design. Wealthy people had more elaborate, decorated furniture, which might be carved or inlaid with silver, gold, or ivory. Their houses might also have a small bathroom containing a hip-bath—water came from wells and cisterns. Drains were rare, but many houses would have had a dung heap, which was collected at regular intervals.

Ancient Greece was essentially a man's world. Boys went to school to learn writing, reading, music, and athletics. Pupils were escorted to and from school by a slave, called a *paidagogos*. Schooling was not free, so poor boys probably did not get more than a very basic education. Girls stayed at home and were taught by their mothers how to prepare food and make clothing. At 18 Athenian boys were accepted into the *phylai* (tribe) and began two years of military training, while a girl was usually married at the age of about 15 to a much older man chosen by her father. Women had no authority except within

---

Greek Architecture

Greek architecture has influenced styles of building in the West right up to the present day. There were three styles of architecture based on the different types of column.

The Doric and Ionic styles emerged in the late seventh and early sixth centuries B.C. The Doric style, with its sturdy columns and undecorated capitals (the top of the column), was predominant on the Greek mainland and in the Greek colonies in Italy and Sicily. The more elaborate Ionic style had thinner columns and capitals with spirals. The Ionic style was used on more massive projects, designed to show off the power and wealth of the eastern Greek cities of Ionia (in present-day Turkey). The Mixed style, sometimes called the Corinthian, was a combination of Doric and Ionic. Its capitals resemble the leaves of the acanthus plant, and it was to become the main style of Roman architecture.

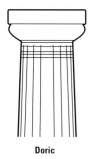

Doric   **Ionic**   **Mixed/Corinthian**

The three different styles of Greek columns. The Doric column was simple in design and may have been a stone imitation of a wooden column. The Ionic was more decorative, while the Mixed style with its leafy capitals was extravagantly ornate.

the home, where they were responsible for domestic duties. Men and women usually lived in separate sections of the house. Upper-class women hardly ever left their homes and had to be escorted by a slave when they did. Poorer women had more freedom because they had to work.

━ CLOTHES AND POTTERY ━

The sculpture, pottery, and jewelry of the Greeks tell us quite a lot about what they wore. On the Greek mainland women wore a *peplos*, which was a length of woolen cloth wrapped around the body, belted at the waist, and fastened by pins at the shoulders. In Ionia women tended to wear the *chiton*, a tunic usually made from linen, which sometimes had long sleeves with buttons. Fashion swung between embroidered, colorful fabrics to plain garments and then back to patterned clothes with gold ornaments. Men wore a simple tunic fastened at the shoulder and a rectangular cloth called a *himation*, which was wrapped around the body with one end thrown over a shoulder.

People generally went barefoot for much of the time, particularly indoors. Leather sandals were the common form of footwear, but shoes were also worn. Horsemen wore calf-length boots. Hats protected both men and women from the sun. Wealthy people wore gold, silver, and ivory jewelry.

Although Greek pottery was intended for everyday use, it was nearly always beautifully decorated. Several centers produced figure-decorated pottery.

At Corinth during the seventh and sixth centuries B.C. pots in a range of shapes were produced, all decorated with bands showing exotic animals from the east such as lions or mythical beasts such as sphinxes. Pots made at Athens in the sixth, fifth, and fourth centuries B.C. provide important information about Greek

Greek Literature

Two famous epic poems have come down to us from the ancient Greeks— the *Iliad* and the *Odyssey*. Until recent times it was believed that they had been written by the blind poet Homer in the ninth century B.C., but scholars now think that they may have been written by a number of poets over a long period of time. At first the poems would have been passed on by word of mouth, but by 700 B.C. they had been written down in their present form. The epic poems are long accounts of events during and after the Trojan War—fought between Greece and the city of Troy (located in present-day Turkey). The poems tell of the beauty of Helen of Sparta (the cause of the war), the heroic deeds of men, and the plots and counterplots of the gods (who took sides). They also give us one of the few vivid pictures of life in Greece during the Dark Ages (about 1100–800 B.C.). The stories in the *Iliad* and the *Odyssey* have inspired and influenced many writers through the centuries.

Alexander the Great

One of the greatest military commanders of the ancient world was Alexander the Great of Macedonia. He was also, by virtue of his extraordinary campaign of conquest that took him overland as far as India, one of the greatest explorers of the ancient world.

Alexander was born in Macedonia in northeastern Greece in 356 B.C., the son of its king, Philip II. When Alexander became king himself, at age 20, he began a military campaign to conquer the might of Persia. In a series of victories he defeated the armies of Darius, the Persian king, and conquered Anatolia and Egypt. In Egypt he was recognized as pharaoh (king), and he traveled far into the African desert to the oracle of Amun at the Siwah Oasis.

Alexander then turned to the east, marching on Mesopotamia and Persia and capturing the cities of Babylon and Persepolis. Even after the death of King Darius of Persia, Alexander determined to continue east, toward the lands that lay beyond the vast mountains of the Hindu Kush. He was not sure what he would find there besides "dense forests and vast deserts," but he rather thought it might be the end of the world (which at that time was believed to be flat). In 329 B.C. he tackled the mountains anyway. When his men ran out of food, they were forced to eat their pack animals raw because there was no firewood. In spite of this, his army was victorious when they reached the other side—the land of the Bactrians and Scythians.

Alexander then crossed the Indus River with an army of 75,000 men and defeated the Indian king Poros. He believed that India was the last province of Asia, and with it his conquests would be complete. But as he led his army farther to the north and east, he realized that India was very much bigger than he had been led to believe.

This great campaign had lasted eight years and had covered a distance very nearly equal to going halfway around the world. Alexander's Greek foot soldiers had marched every step of the way. Tired and homesick, his army refused to march any farther.

On the return journey Alexander sent one of his admirals, Nearchus, to find out if Mesopotamia and India could be linked by sea. Nearchus sailed down the Indus River and then up the Persian Gulf to be reunited with Alexander's army near the mouth of the Tigris River (in present-day Iraq).

Alexander sent out another three expeditions to explore the Persian Gulf, and he even thought about sending an expedition around Africa. But after returning to Babylon in 323 B.C., he died, possibly from malaria, age 32.

ABOVE: A cutaway drawing of a typical Greek house built around a central courtyard. The artist has shown some of the furniture and activities that would have taken place in each room.

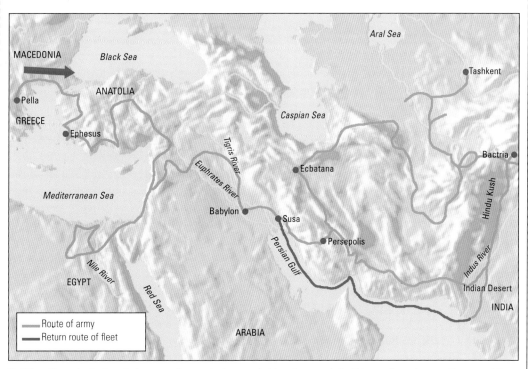

By 323 B.C. Alexander the Great had conquered an empire that stretched from Greece to India. This map shows the route his army took from Greece on its eight-year campaign—through much territory that was quite unknown to the Macedonians. In addition, on the return journey Alexander sent out a fleet that sailed from the mouth of the Indus River along the coast and up the Persian Gulf to the Tigris River.

social life because they were decorated with scenes of everyday life as well as pictures illustrating stories about the gods.

There were two main techniques for decorating pots. One was called black-figure, in which "glazed" figures were painted onto the natural orange of the clay pot. The other was red-figure, in which figures were outlined in black and then left as red against the "glazed" black background. The Greeks were very fond of holding drinking parties, and many of the pots were made for this purpose—amphoras to contain water and wine, *kraters* for mixing the water and wine, jugs (*oinochoai*) for pouring, and cups for drinking.

➤ SCULPTURE ➤

The ancient Greeks are famous for their sculptures of the human form. The Greeks created statues for several reasons. Often a statue of a god or a goddess was placed in a temple as a focus for worship. One of the most famous was the gold and ivory statue of Zeus on his throne at Olympia. People coming to worship at a temple might place a statue of the god or even of themselves in the sanctuary around the temple to mark their devotion.

Athletes who won victories in the games held at sanctuaries sometimes put up a victory monument. Cities might erect portrait statues of their prominent citizens in public places. Finally, sculptures could be used as markers over graves.

Cemeteries were usually outside the city walls. Because personal belongings were generally buried with the dead for use in the afterlife, much of what we know about the Greeks comes from excavating burial sites. At Athens in the eighth century B.C. large amphoras were placed on tombs and were decorated with scenes of people in mourning standing around the corpse, which was laid on a couch. Greeks believed that souls had to pay a coin to Charon, the ferryman, to row them across the Styx River into the underworld. There they were judged according to the way they had lived their earthly lives.

Celts

The Celts were a collection of fierce, warlike tribes that lived in central and western Europe between the eighth century B.C. and the first century A.D. They were all skilled horsemen, spoke similar languages, and shared many religious and artistic customs.

Although the Celts themselves were illiterate and left no written records, a good deal of Celtic history can be gathered from Roman writers. From them we learn that in the fourth century B.C. Celtic settlers and raiders from north of the Alps thrust into Italy and the Balkans. Celtic warriors sacked Rome in 390 B.C. and in 279 B.C. they reached almost as far as Delphi in Greece. In the third century B.C. the Celts could be found as far east as the Balkans and Anatolia.

The Roman army fought back strenuously against these invading "barbarians" and defeated them at the Battle of Telemon in northern Italy in 225 B.C. After that the Romans gradually engulfed Celtic lands in Italy, Iberia (present-day Spain and Portugal), and Anatolia.

The Roman commander Julius Caesar began conquering Gaul (present-day France) in 50 B.C. As the Romans pushed into Celtic areas, they killed and took prisoners on a massive scale. Of a population of between six and seven million Celts, one million were killed and another million sold into slavery. By the end of the first century A.D. the Romans had conquered much of England and Wales, and all central Europe south of the Rhine and Danube rivers had fallen under Roman control. The Celts who lived outside these regions had been defeated by Germanic tribes from the north and Dacians from the east.

All traces of Celtic civilization in Britain and Gaul were finally destroyed in the fifth century A.D., when Germanic invasions followed the collapse of the Roman Empire. Today, Celtic languages survive only on the western fringes of Europe—in Scotland, Ireland, Wales, Brittany in France, and Galicia in Spain.

➤ CELTIC CULTURE ➤

There were two main periods in Celtic culture. One was the Hallstatt, which lasted from about 800 B.C. to 500 B.C., and the other was La Tène— from 500 B.C. to A.D. 50. The Hallstatt culture

LEFT: This silver bowl, decorated with mythological figures and scenes, was made to be used in Celtic rituals. It was placed in a bog in Gundestrup in Denmark as part of a sacred ceremony. A repeated scene on the inside of the bowl shows a hunter about to slay a bull with a sword.

RIGHT: A map showing the sites of some of the towns, hill forts, and burial mounds of Celtic and Iron Age Europe. Celtic culture flourished first in the Hallstatt region (colored brown on the map), and then in the La Tène region (gray). In the third century B.C. the Celts spread over most of Europe and as far as the Balkans (as shown by the green area).

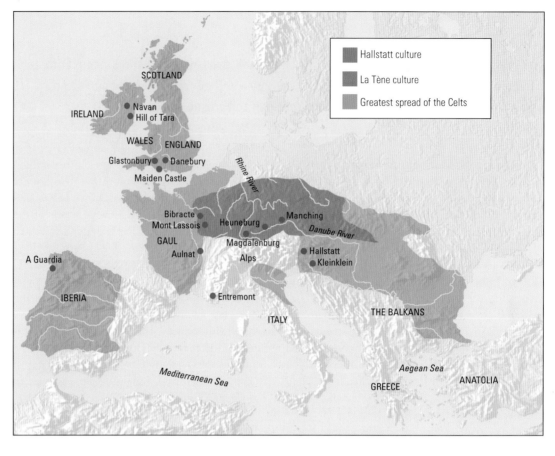

■	Hallstatt culture
■	La Tène culture
■	Greatest spread of the Celts

BELOW: A gold torc (neckpiece) that would have been worn in battle by a Celtic warrior. The Celts believed the decoration on the torc had magical qualities.

was named after a cemetery in Hallstatt, Austria, in central Europe. Its people were skilled iron-workers and were good horsemen. They established a salt-mining industry and a trading empire. A wealthy elite of chieftains lived in fortified hilltop settlements and were buried with many of their possessions—weapons, jewelry, wagons, and other luxury goods.

After the mid-fifth century B.C., wealthy burials ceased and Hallstatt declined rapidly. The culture that followed, named La Tène after a lakeside village in Switzerland, had centers of power in an area north of the Hallstatt zone. The Celtic warriors who crossed the Alps in the fourth century B.C. came from the La Tène culture. The La Tène region was also the home of the decorative art style that would become known as Celtic.

The Greeks and Romans saw the Celts as dangerous but vulnerable opponents. The fury of the Celts in war was legendary, and their bravery and expert horsemanship much admired. They were, however, seen as lacking the discipline of Greek and Roman soldiers. Some of the Celtic practices, such as preserving the severed heads of distinguished enemies and displaying them to guests, were considered horrific by the Mediterranean peoples.

The Celtic warrior looked completely different from the Roman legionaries. He had long hair, bleached with lime, and wore trousers instead of a tunic. He also wore jewelry and a colorful checkered cloak. Typically he would have

A Celtic Village

The drawing below is of an Iceni village in Britain. It housed about 100 people and was built near a spring to provide the villagers with drinking water. The village was surrounded by a palisade of timber stakes and a moat, and the only entrance was guarded by a watchtower. A drawbridge across the moat was worked by a system of weights hung in baskets at the ends of long poles—this enabled the drawbridge to be raised when an enemy approached. On top of the watchtower the Iceni would often display the severed heads of their enemies.

Inside the village there were several different kinds of houses, all built of timber stakes and thatched with reeds. The round house belonged to the chief and his family, and here on winter evenings the warriors of the village gathered to feast and drink. These warriors lived in the long house with their families—it had a cooking section with a fire where the women prepared meals. In the winter the cattle may also have been brought into the long house. Around the inside of the palisade there were much smaller dwellings that housed the old people and the infirm. Other buildings included a chariot house, a corn bin, and the smokehouse, where the villagers smoked meat and fish in order to preserve them through the winter. In the center of the village was a deep hole with poisonous snakes at the bottom. This was the snake pit. The villagers threw enemy captives and wrongdoers down it and left them there to die.

carried a long iron sword, a spear, and a large leather shield. Additional protection was provided by a helmet and chainmail—although there are many reports of Celtic warriors going into battle naked apart from their torcs (decorated gold or bronze neckpieces).

Warfare was extremely important in Celtic society. Tribes were governed by warrior elites for whom a reputation for bravery in battle was an important source of power and status. Failure, particularly in a leader, was just not acceptable, and Celtic chieftains sometimes committed suicide rather than submit to the shame of defeat. The power of a Celtic warrior was also determined by the number of his followers, so the ability to distribute wealth gained through raiding or conquest was of great importance.

Farming was the principal activity for a Celtic community. Although practices varied depending on the nature of the land, in general the Celts used mixed agriculture, working with both livestock and crops. The countryside was covered with small farmsteads and villages, with fortified hilltop settlements serving as markets, craft centers, and tribal capitals.

— CELTIC WOMEN —

Women occupied a more prominent position in Celtic society than they did in the Greek and Roman worlds. Their fighting ability is mentioned by many writers, and they enjoyed legal rights over property in marriage. The existence of important female leaders such as Queen Boudicca of the Iceni tribe—the Romans' most feared

The Spread of Iron

Smelting iron ores was much more complicated than smelting copper. The method for extracting iron from iron ore was first discovered by the Hittites in Anatolia around the middle of the second millennium B.C. For centuries the method was a closely guarded secret, but after the breakdown of the Hittite Empire in the 12th century B.C. the technology spread, first to the Aegean and then to the rest of Europe. By the eighth century B.C. iron was being extensively worked in the region of the Hallstatt Celtic culture.

Although ironworking was more complex and laborious than bronzeworking, the new metal had two major advantages. First, it occurred naturally in greater quantities and over a far wider area than tin and copper, the two elements that go into making bronze, and was therefore cheaper. Second, it was a far stronger metal than bronze and could be honed to a sharper cutting edge. This gave the Celts an advantage in battle and also enabled them to clear forests and plow the land more efficiently.

opponents in Britain—show that it was possible for women to occupy the very highest offices.

Even while they were conquering Celtic lands in Italy, Iberia, and Anatolia, the Romans were developing trading links with unconquered Celtic lands in Gaul and central Europe. Rome required raw materials and slaves. Local Celtic chiefs needed luxury goods to give to their followers, and opportunities to obtain these things through raiding had diminished. So a flourishing trade was established, and as the volume of trade increased, coinage became more widespread. Many of the villages and hill forts developed into complex trading settlements known as *oppida*.

RIGHT: A decorated bronze shield found in the Thames River in London, England, where it may have been placed as part of a religious ceremony.

LEFT: Although the Celts fought with iron swords, their helmets and shields were often made of bronze. This decorated bronze helmet was found in northern Britain.

Only in northwestern Europe did life continue in much the same way as it had for centuries.

➤ CELTIC BARDS ➤

Although the Celts had no written literature, they did have a professional class of poets, storytellers, and musicians known as bards. Bards were required to train for 12 years, learning by heart a vast oral tradition of story-poems. They also composed songs to honor or mock living people, and were thus treated with great respect by chieftains and warriors, for whom reputation was all-important.

The Celts used a calendar much like the present-day one, and their festivals fell at significant points in the agricultural year. The greatest festival took place on November 1 and marked the end of the old year and the start of the new. Known in Ireland as Samain, it was a time when the spirits of the dead could roam free. It survives to this day as the festival of Halloween.

Celtic Art

The La Tène civilization of the fifth century B.C. is renowned for its style of decorative art, which became known as Celtic art. Specialized and highly skilled craftsmen made mirrors, shields, and sword handles in gold and bronze. Influenced by both Mediterranean and eastern European art, they developed an original style characterized by swirling lines and irregular patterns. Certain animals and motifs used in Celtic art had religious significance. For example, boars and crows, which often appear on weaponry and armor, are thought to have represented war gods in animal form. However, much of the hidden meaning of Celtic art is no longer understood.

The back of a bronze mirror that was found at Desborough in Britain. It is richly engraved with decorations of swirling patterns that are typical of the La Tène culture. The circles in the design were probably made with a compass.

The Celts believed in a great number of gods rather than one all-powerful deity. Although these gods varied from region to region, three central figures can be identified: a god of the tribe, who was associated with war, a god of the sky and the earth, and a god who was associated with crafts and industries. The number three had particular significance for the Celts—there are many three-headed statues and three-sided motifs in Celtic art.

Religious ceremonies involved the ritual of placing valuable items in pits, rivers, springs, bogs, and lakes. Religious specialists, known as Druids, acted as the intermediaries between man and the gods. In addition to overseeing all sacrifices, Druids acted as judges in criminal cases and had the power to exclude all those found guilty from the religious life of the community. The Druids also had the power to start rebellions and unify warring tribes against Rome.

BELOW: The Celts were constantly at war, and they built hill forts to shelter large communities. This hill fort in Wales is protected by a double rampart of drystone walls.

Danebury Hill Fort

Danebury hill fort was one of many hilltop forts that were built in southern Britain between 1000 and 500 B.C. The forts were the community centers of their day, serving as a market place and venue for religious festivals as well as being a secure haven in times of danger.

Hill forts were enclosed with high banks of soil and deep ditches. The only way in was through an entrance gate set in the defensive ramparts. Inside were clusters of roundhouses, rows of granaries, workshops, storage pits, and trackways. The forts were the centers of local life, where the surrounding farming community stored its harvest, where traders conducted their business, and where religious festivals may have been held. In times of trouble the forts served as safe havens, sheltering people, animals, and possessions until the threat of danger had passed.

Hundreds of hill forts are known in Britain, and many have been partially excavated. From the information they yielded we know a great deal about everyday life in Iron Age Britain before the Roman invasion.

For three weeks in the summer of 1969 the British archaeologist Barry Cunliffe excavated trial trenches at Danebury hill fort in the English county of Hampshire. He quickly realized that a clump of 100-year-old trees growing on top of the hill was damaging the 2,500-year-old prehistoric fort. Since a bark-eating fungus was killing the trees, the local authority agreed that they could be felled—and so it was possible for the archaeologists to move in and excavate the area before new trees were planted. The Danebury "dig" lasted 20 years. Each summer the secrets of Danebury were gradually uncovered until more than half the fort's 12-acre (5-ha) interior had been excavated.

➤ THE DEFENSES ➤

Danebury's transformation from hill to hill fort began about 600 B.C., when a large area of the hilltop was enclosed by a timber wall about 13 ft (4m) in height. This was supported by a rampart of earth behind it. In front of the wall was a ditch to give extra protection against invaders. About 400 B.C. this arrangement was changed dramatically. In place of the timber wall a huge rampart was built leading down to a V-shaped ditch. The distance from the bottom of the "V" to the top of the rampart was about 53 ft (16m). This would have been very difficult for an attacking force to

scale, particularly if the attackers were being pelted with missiles.

Hill forts were most vulnerable at their entrances. At the main east entrance to Danebury the builders constructed an elaborate system of ramparts and ditches to make it exceedingly difficult for invaders to gain entry. Even if an enemy were able to break through the outer gate, they would have to pass through a passageway flanked by flint ramparts, from the top of which the defending soldiers would use slings to pelt the invaders with stones.

The hill fort was used for 500 years by the farming community of the surrounding lowlands.

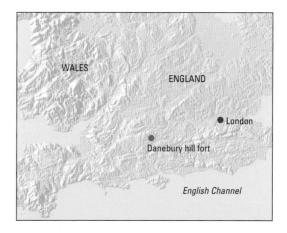

LEFT: Danebury hill fort is in the county of Hampshire, in the south of England.

BELOW: The top of the fort's inner rampart as it is today. Danebury was protected by a formidable system of ditches and ramparts.

The Mystery of the Pits

More than 1,000 large pits were excavated at Danebury out of an estimated total of 5,000. They came in a wide variety of shapes and were cut deep into the chalk bedrock, to a depth of up to 6 ft (2m). Research has shown they were used mainly to store wheat and barley, preserving surplus grain from the summer's harvest so that it could be used to sustain the hilltop's inhabitants through the winter months.

It might seem strange that a damp underground pit could act as a silo for perishable grain, but experiments have shown it was possible. Once a pit was filled with grain, it was sealed with a layer of clay to make it airtight and watertight. Inside the pit grain in contact with the damp walls began to germinate, for which it needed oxygen. But since the pit was sealed tight, fresh oxygen could not enter. The germinating grain quickly used up what little oxygen there was and released carbon dioxide in the process. With no more oxygen the grain stopped growing, forming a layer or skin around the inner walls. Starved of oxygen, the bulk of the grain went into a kind of suspended animation, which is how it remained until the pit was opened weeks or months later.

A pit's useful life was short—perhaps no more than two years—by which time fungi would have made it unsuitable for storing food. At Danebury abandoned pits had rubbish and animal carcasses dumped in them. Some became burial pits for the dead, while others contained severed arms and skulls, hinting that they may have been used for some kind of ritual ceremony. The mystery of the pits is yet to be solved.

While some people lived in the hill fort itself, many more lived in scattered farmsteads on the gentle, rolling chalkland that lay all around it. The number of people living at the hill village at any one time may have been no more than 200.

The buildings of the village were of two main types: houses and granaries. Circular houses, about 20 ft (6m) across, snuggled close to the ramparts where they were sheltered from the wind. Inside them were hearths, ovens, and pits where food and personal property were stored. Square-built granaries, propped up on stout wooden legs, stored grain above ground level, Then, as now, people went to great lengths to safeguard their food reserves from pests.

The major occupation of the local people was agriculture. Farmers raised sheep, cattle, and pigs, and grew wheat and barley in fields around the hill. Droveways indicate that animals were herded up to the hill village, where they were killed (thousands of bones were found there).

People lived on a diet of animal- and cereal-based products. Farm animals gave meat, milk, and cheese, while grain was made into flour for bread or stewed to make porridge. Wild fruits, berries, plants, and nuts were also on the Iron Age menu. Sea salt was used at Danebury, indicated by the remains of baked clay containers with traces of salt. Salt was an essential part of the diet and was also used to preserve meat.

Spinning and weaving were common household crafts at Danebury. Combs made from antler and bone were used to pluck the coarse wool from sheep. The wool was then spun into yarn using hand-held spindles weighted with stone or clay weights. Cloth was woven on upright looms and was probably colored with vegetable dyes.

Metalworkers made objects such as tools and items of jewelry from iron and bronze. Shale from the south coast found its way to Danebury, where it was worked into bracelets.

There seems to be evidence that the inhabitants of Danebury carried out some kind of ritual or magic. A number of skulls from horses and cows were found at the bottom of pits where they had been carefully placed. In other pits were found the remains of pottery vessels, apparently deliberately smashed. It may be that the inhabitants were giving gifts of food to the gods in return for good harvests.

⭢ LAST DAYS OF DANEBURY ⭠

For about 300 years there was little change for the community at Danebury. Daily life went on as usual, tied to the changing seasons and the agricultural cycle. The ramparts were maintained in good condition, the ditch was cleaned out, new buildings replaced old ones, and so on.

But then, around 100 B.C., the hill fort was abandoned. Its wooden gateway was burned down, and the defensive ditches began to fill up with silt washed down from the earthen banks. For unknown reasons the community moved away from their hilltop village, leaving it to be reclaimed by nature.

BELOW: A cross-section of the main rampart. The figure is kneeling at the original ground level.

Thule People

The Thule people were the ancestors of the present-day Inuit who live within the Arctic Circle. The Danish scholar Therkel Mathiassen, who studied sites in Canada in the 1920s, suggested they had migrated eastward from the Bering Strait across the Arctic roughly 1,000 years ago.

Archaeological studies in Alaska and the Bering Strait region soon confirmed this proposed origin and spread of the Thule people. These studies revealed that the Inuit's ancestors had come originally from northeast Asia. Approximately 2,000 years ago they developed a new way of life along the coasts and islands of the Bering Sea. During this period they started to hunt sea mammals—including some whales—to provide food and clothing, and many of the basic elements of Thule technology appeared. By A.D. 700 they had spread northward to the shores of the Chukchi Sea, including northwestern Alaska.

Climates became warmer around A.D. 1000, and this may have triggered an expansion across the Arctic. Pacific bowhead whales spread into northern Canadian waters, and sea-ice cover was reduced at this time. The Thule people took advantage of the new opportunities for whale hunting with their sophisticated technology and moved eastward into new lands. Inuit legends tell of a vanished people (called the Tunit) who were living in these lands at the time. By around A.D. 1200 the Thule had reached Greenland, where they met and traded with the Vikings.

Although some driftwood carried north by ocean currents was available, many Thule tools and weapons were created from animal skin and bone. Whales and walrus were hunted from

ABOVE: The remains of a stone Thule house in northern Greenland. Thule houses were often built semisubmerged in the ground for protection against the icy elements.

umiaks—large boats made of a wood frame covered with skin. Smaller boats or kayaks, also with hulls of skin, were used for hunting seals.

The Thule were the first Arctic people to use dogs for transportation. They had ladderlike dog sleds constructed of wood, with some pieces made of bone, ivory, and baleen (whalebone). Ivory or bone swivels or trace buckles were attached to the harnesses of the dogs.

Ways of combating the deadly cold were fundamentally important. Clothes made from animal skins and fur, including hoods, trousers, mittens, and boots, were sewn tightly together with

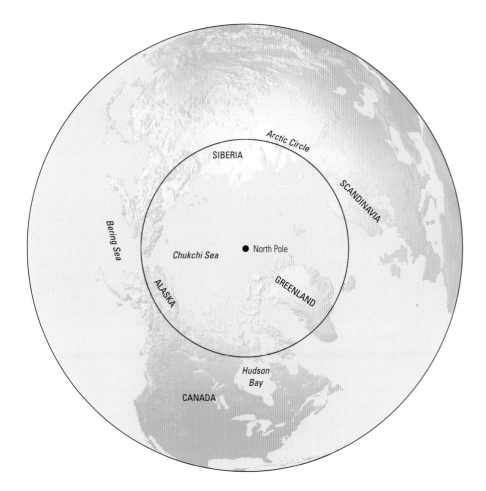

RIGHT: The ancestors of the Thule people came originally from Siberia in northeast Asia. They moved eastward first to the islands of the Bering Sea before moving on into Alaska and spreading throughout the whole of the Arctic region.

BELOW: This picture on a piece of seal-gut skin was found in eastern Greenland in the 19th century. The figures of men and women and the umiak (boat) were sewn on. The umiak was a large open boat, used for transport and whaling, that held many people and was known as "the women's boat." The smaller kayak, or "men's boat," was used for fishing and hunting seals.

needles and awls. Clothing was designed in two layers to provide the added insulation of a pocket of air between inner and outer garments. The Thule people also wore visors and carved ivory goggles to deflect the glare of the snow during summer months.

Winter houses were cleverly designed to protect against the cold. They were either round or rectangular in shape and always constructed with a sunken entrance tunnel. Cold air remained trapped in the lower tunnel, keeping the living quarters comfortably warm. The foundations were formed of blocks of stone, while the frame was built either from driftwood or giant whalebones. Added warmth and light were provided by blubber lamps of stone or clay. Although archaeologists have yet to discover a preserved snow house or igloo, large "snow knives" of whalebone—like those formerly used by the modern Inuit to cut building blocks of snow—have been found at Thule sites.

Whaling brought about great changes in Thule society. Hunting the largest animals on earth required a large and organized team. At the same time, the enormous quantity of meat and other products provided by a single whale supported many people—so some Thule villages became very large, with many houses.

After A.D. 1400 the climate became colder in the northern hemisphere. Sea ice made whale hunting difficult in the Canadian Arctic, and people reverted to winter seal hunting and built igloos from blocks of frozen snow for permanent winter houses. New Arctic cultures were emerging, marking the end of the Thule period.

Hunting Technology

In order to kill larger sea mammals, the Thule used an ingenious toggle-head harpoon. This was fashioned with a detachable head (carved from ivory) designed to catch in the wound. Secured by a sinew line and often attached to a drag float (made from seal skin or bladder and inflated with an ivory nozzle), it allowed the hunter to exhaust and retrieve his wounded prey from icy waters.

The Thule made a variety of other weapons, including bone darts, propelled with throwing boards, for hunting seals. Lances and sinew-backed bows with antler arrows were used for hunting Arctic land mammals such as caribou, muskox, and polar bear. Birds were hunted with pronged darts, and a variety of intricate hooks, sinkers, and nets were designed for fishing.

Rome

At its height the Roman Empire covered most of Europe and the countries bordering the Mediterranean Sea. The empire was ruled by provincial governors answerable to the emperor, and linked to Rome by the empire's fabulous network of roads.

The story of Rome began about 1000 B.C., when people first started living on a hill overlooking the Tiber River in central Italy. The settlers belonged to a people called Latins, who inhabited a region around the Tiber called Latium. They were farmers and herders, and made their villages on hills so that they were easy to defend against neighboring tribes. The Palatine Hill, where the Latins first settled, was just one of seven hills that were later to provide

the setting for the magnificent city of Rome, the center of one of the greatest empires that the world has ever known.

The first kings of Rome came from the Latins and two other peoples, the Etruscans and the Sabines. The Etruscans were a highly civilized people who built roads, temples, and public buildings in the growing city. They had a great influence on the people of the city, and their ruler Lucius Tarquinius, or Tarquin the Proud, became

ABOVE: The remains of the main forum in Rome. The forum was a large open space used as a market place and a venue for political meetings.

elephants over the Alps into Italy, but he and Carthage were eventually defeated. Romans were proud of their military power and their growing republic, but the gap between rich and poor was widening. This led to conflicts among political leaders, and in the confusion one of the greatest Romans—Julius Caesar—rose to power.

Born about 100 B.C. into a wealthy family of the patrician class, Julius Caesar began his career in the Roman army before becoming a consul. In 58 B.C. he took command of the Roman armies in Gaul (present-day France) and soon conquered the whole of that territory. Three years later he raided Britain.

Caesar's growing power and popularity worried many Roman politicians, especially a rival general named Pompey, who was particularly jealous of Caesar. In 49 B.C. Pompey persuaded

king of Rome in 534 B.C. Tarquin was an arrogant man, and in time the citizens of Rome came to hate him. In 509 B.C. they threw him out and decided that they would be better off without an all-powerful king. Rome became a democratic republic, run by representatives of the people elected by the citizens.

ABOVE: The Roman aqueduct at Nerja in Spain. The Romans built many aqueducts—some over great distances—to bring water to their cities.

➤ THE ROMAN DEMOCRACY ➤

The new Roman Republic was headed by two consuls, who were voted in each year, and they were helped by other officials and a state council called the Senate. Not everyone could vote, however, and women and slaves were excluded. Ordinary working people, called plebeians, were not allowed to become consuls or hold a high office in the republic. These positions were held by patricians, noblemen who owned land and traced their origins back to early Rome. Since officials were not paid, only the rich could afford to become politicians. However, over the centuries the plebeians gained more rights, and soon after 300 B.C. they gained equality under Roman law. By that time there was also a third, middle class, the *equites* or knights, made up of rich businessmen who did not come from a noble family.

The Roman Republic built up a strong, well-trained army and expanded rapidly. By the end of the third century B.C. Rome had conquered the whole of Italy. Between 264 and 146 B.C. the Romans fought three long wars against Carthage, a powerful city on the north coast of Africa. In the second of the wars the brilliant Carthaginian general Hannibal led his army of 40,000 men and 37

RIGHT: A bronze statue of Julius Caesar. Caesar was a successful general, and his military power combined with his popularity with the people enabled him to seize political control of Rome.

Roman Clothes

Romans wore simple clothes made of wool or linen. Men, women, boys, and girls all wore tunics, which were gowns that hung to the knees or lower. Men who were full Roman citizens wore a *toga*, which was a large, loose piece of woolen cloth worn over a tunic and wrapped around the body. *Togas* were usually white, although black versions were worn at funerals. Boys became citizens and put on the *toga* at age 14.

Women wore a long dress called a *stola* over their tunic, and this came in a variety of colors. A large shawl called a *palla* was draped over the dress for outdoor wear.

Women also dyed their hair—blonde and red were favorite shades—or wore wigs. Their personal slaves helped them put on makeup, using chalk for whitening the skin and ocher for red lips and cheeks. Both men and women wore comfortable leather sandals on their feet.

A mosaic from the fifth century A.D. showing a wealthy Roman woman being dressed by her slaves. One of her servants is shown holding up a mirror so that she can see her hair and makeup.

the Senate to order Caesar to disband his army. Caesar refused, and civil war broke out.

During the many battles that followed, Caesar showed his brilliance as a general. After an easy victory near the Black Sea he sent a message to the Senate saying, "*Veni, vidi, vici*" ("I came, I saw, I conquered"). The civil war ended four years later when Caesar defeated an army led by Pompey's sons in Spain. Caesar was now ruler of the Roman world, and he declared himself "dictator for life." At a public festival the general Marcus Antonius (Mark Antony) offered him a king's crown, but Caesar refused it, aware of the unpopularity of kings among the Roman people.

In the two years that followed, Caesar made many reforms that were to have a major impact on Roman life. He drew up a new legal code, reformed the calendar, created a police force, and took steps to reduce overcrowding in Rome.

Despite these achievements, however, many patricians were unhappy at having a single ruler, and two noblemen began to plot against Caesar. On the Ides (the 15th) of March 44 B.C., the very day on which a fortune-teller had warned Caesar to be careful, the conspirators stabbed him to death outside the Senate house.

⟶ THE FIRST EMPEROR ⟵

A period of confusion and intermittent civil war followed the death of Caesar as Marcus Antonius and Caesar's adopted son and heir Octavian tried to share power. Seventeen years after the death of Caesar, Octavian became the first Roman emperor. He took the name Augustus, meaning "revered" or "respected." The Senate and consuls remained in office, but all real power rested with Augustus. He made sure that the boundaries of his empire were well defended and that the

Roman provinces around Europe were under control. Before he died, in A.D. 14, Augustus had groomed his stepson Tiberius to take over as the second emperor. This move prepared the way for a succession of emperors who would rule the Roman Empire for a total of almost 500 years.

Augustus and Tiberius were both highly capable politicians and ruled the empire well. However, the third emperor, Caligula, quickly built up a reputation for cruelty and eccentric behavior. He is famous for making his favorite horse a consul and building a special palace for it. The Senate could not control the bizarre behavior of their leader, and Caligula was assassinated in A.D. 41. His uncle, Claudius, replaced him.

Claudius was a scholarly man who wrote histories of the Etruscans and Carthaginians. His armies invaded Britain in A.D. 43, and he added other provinces to the empire. Claudius did much to improve the Roman civil service, the body of officials who managed the nonmilitary activities of the government, such as collecting taxes and constructing public buildings.

Claudius's adopted son Nero was only 16 when he became the next emperor in A.D. 54, and he was more interested in acting, music, and chariot-racing than ruling the empire. Nero was another emperor famed for his cruel behavior. He was suspected of being responsible for starting a great fire that in A.D. 64 almost destroyed Rome. Nero himself blamed it on the Christians and tortured many of them to death. He eventually committed suicide in A.D. 68.

⊶ ROADS AND RELIGION ⊷

In order to be able to move quickly throughout the empire, the Romans built first-class roads. They chopped down woods, cut into hillsides, built bridges, and drained marshes so that their roads could be as straight as possible. These roads replaced the winding tracks that they found in many of the provinces of their new empire.

Roman roads were made by digging a ditch, filling it with rubble, and laying flat stone slabs on top. The roads were slightly arched in the middle, so that water drained off. Many modern roads throughout Europe still follow the direct routes of the Roman roads, which covered about 50,000 miles (80,000km).

As the Romans traveled throughout their empire, they began to adopt gods and goddesses worshiped in other regions. In Egypt, for example, they adopted the goddess Isis. In Persia there was Mithras, and in Britain the Celtic sun-goddess Sul. Since early times the Romans had

The Roman Army

In order to rule their huge empire, the Romans needed a well-trained, well-equipped army. By the middle of the first century A.D. the army was made up of 28 legions, each containing about 5,500 men (legionaries). Each legion was commanded by an officer called a *legatus*, who was usually appointed by the emperor, and was divided into 10 groups called cohorts. The cohorts were further split up into centuries, which were units of about 100 soldiers under the command of a centurion. Centurions were responsible for training and discipline, which was important because the army had to put up with harsh conditions both in camp and on the march.

The soldiers in the Roman army were Roman citizens, but other men from the empire could join auxiliary forces and be granted citizenship if they fought well. When a new legionary joined the army, he was issued with a uniform and equipment (that he had to pay for). A Roman soldier wore a helmet of leather or metal, a woolen tunic covered by a chainmail vest, and sandals. He carried a shield made of wood or leather, two javelins, and a sword about 2 ft (60cm) long. In cold climates he might wear trousers and boots.

When the Roman legions were on the move, they had to make a new camp every night. They were expert at doing this quickly and efficiently, and the next day they would take the camp down and move on. A Roman soldier would cover about 20 miles (30km) in a five-hour march before stopping to build another camp.

A relief from Trajan's column, a stone monument that celebrates the emperor's military conquests. It shows Roman legionaries fighting Dacian soldiers.

believed that gods and goddesses were everywhere and controlled human actions. They made offerings and prayed to these gods, so that they would be friendly and helpful. Most important was the god of the sky, Jupiter. His wife, Juno, was thought to look after women. Other deities included Mars, god of war; Venus, goddess of beauty and fertility; Janus, guardian of the door;

The Colosseum

Roman emperors, patricians, and plebeians all loved spectacular, bloodthirsty events, and one of the most important buildings in a Roman town was the amphitheater. In A.D. 70 the emperor Vespasian ordered the building of the most famous Roman amphitheater of all, the Colosseum in Rome.

The huge oval Colosseum took 10 years to build and was completed in A.D. 80 by Vespasian's son, Titus. It could hold 50,000 people and was built for gladiator contests, animal displays, and even mock sea battles, for which the whole arena was flooded.

The Colosseum had 75 rows of marble and wooden seats in four separate tiers. The emperor and his guests sat at the front. Behind and above him sat patricians, then plebeians, foreigners, and slaves. Women sat right at the top, where they were protected from the weather by a huge awning.

Underneath the wooden floor of the arena, which was covered with sand to absorb blood, was a network of passages. Here there were rooms for the gladiators and other performers, and dens for wild animals. The Romans enjoyed watching gladiators kill animals and considered this great sport. On the Colosseum's opening day 5,000 animals were slaughtered, including lions, tigers, leopards, and elephants. Criminals were also killed by being thrown into the arena to be attacked by lions.

Most of the gladiators were slaves captured in war, and they were trained to fight in schools paid for by patricians. There were many different kinds of gladiator. Some, such as the *samnite*, wore heavy armor, while others fought with just a sword and shield. The popular *retiarius*, meanwhile, carried a three-pronged spear and used a net to trap his opponent. According to the Roman poet Statius, women sometimes took part as well.

A wounded gladiator raised his forefinger to ask the crowd for mercy. Spectators waved handkerchiefs or pressed their thumb against their forefinger if they wanted to spare him, or turned the thumb toward the chest if they wanted him killed. If a gladiator showed great bravery, he was sometimes given a wooden sword, which signified that he was now a free man.

The remains of the Colosseum, which was probably the most spectacular of all the buildings in ancient Rome. The amphitheater could hold 50,000 spectators who enjoyed watching gruesome gladiatorial contests.

Ceres, goddess of the harvest; Mercury, messenger of the gods; and Vesta, goddess of fire. Many Roman emperors were also worshiped as gods, especially after their death.

Every Roman home contained a shrine with small images of the household gods. These were guardian spirits who looked after the family and to whom the family prayed. Roman children were brought every morning to worship Vesta at the hearth with the rest of the household, and this was an important part of family life.

In Rome itself only rich patricians could afford their own separate house. Most people lived in an apartment block called an *insula*

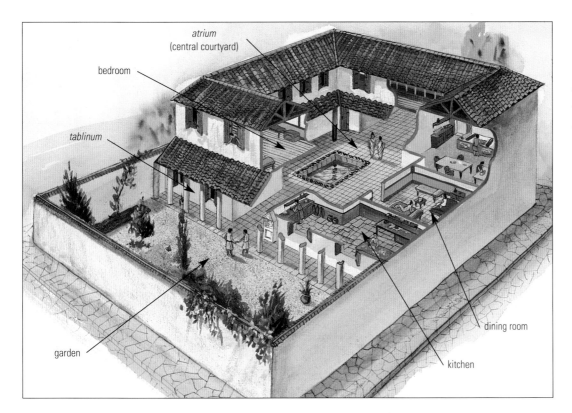

atrium
(central courtyard)

bedroom

tablinum

garden

dining room

kitchen

LEFT: A cutaway drawing of a Roman town house, showing the various rooms grouped round the central *atrium*. Even town houses usually had a small garden.

(meaning "island"). Some blocks were five or six stories high. The lower floors had large, comfortable rooms, but higher up the rooms became smaller and more basic. On the ground floor there were usually shops or businesses opening onto the street. Richer houses were built around an *atrium*, or inner courtyard, and included a kitchen, dining room, and bedrooms. The most important room in the house was the *tablinum*, the main living room.

The water supply in the city of Rome was very good, as it was in all Roman towns. The Romans built aqueducts to bring water from nearby rivers or springs, and many patricians had water supplied directly to their homes. For everyone else there were public lavatories' and baths—larger towns had several of each.

⇥ HOUSEHOLD SLAVES ⇤

Better-off Romans led a comfortable life, which was only possible because they had slaves. The mistress of the house ran the household, and was in charge of the slaves. Household slaves were usually treated well, but they were not protected by the law, and their mistress could work them as hard as she wanted. A rich family could own dozens of slaves, and even poorer families usually had at least one. Slaves could be tortured if they behaved badly, and the Roman poet Juvenal wrote of slave girls being beaten for not doing their mistress's hair properly. Sometimes slaves were set

free for good service. A freed man or woman did not have the same rights as other people, but their children became full Roman citizens.

At the height of the empire the city of Rome had about a million inhabitants, and in the rest of Italy there were a further five million people. Up

---

Roman Baths

Roman emperors built luxurious public baths, which were decorated in marble and gold, and were popular not only for bathing but as a place for exercising and simply meeting friends. The larger baths had separate pools for men and women, while others might have special times set aside for each sex. The baths had cold pools, warm pools, hot steam rooms, and warm fountains for washing.

The Romans believed that it was good to sweat out dirt. They had no soap, so instead they made slaves rub oil into their perspiring skin and then scrape it clean with a special curved instrument that was made of metal, bone, or wood.

The baths were available to everyone, and they usually cost one

quadrans (a "quarter"), the smallest Roman coin. Sometimes even this cost was met by the emperor or a rich city sponsor. Large numbers of slaves kept the baths working properly. Heat was produced in a wood-burning furnace that blew hot air under the floors and up through the walls. This system was also used for central heating in richer people's houses.

Some Romans also brought their own slaves to the baths, to carry their towels, rub them down, and scrape their skin, while others hired these services at the baths. The public baths were used in a similar way to today's leisure centers and health clubs. As well as pools, there were usually sitting rooms, gardens, a gymnasium, an exercise field, and a library.

to 70 million people were scattered throughout the Roman Empire, and the majority in the Roman world lived by farming. Some rich city-dwellers grew even richer by owning farms, where they built large country villas. In the fertile valleys near Rome itself farmers grew wheat, rye, and barley. On hillsides they planted olive groves and vineyards, for olive oil and wine, and grazed sheep and goats. The second largest city in the empire, Alexandria in Egypt, also shipped vast quantities of grain to Rome.

➤ THE FALL OF ROME ➤

The enormous size of the empire made it difficult to administer properly from Rome, and eventually some of the provinces were invaded. In the third century A.D. a Germanic people known as the Goths invaded Roman territory in Greece, while the Persians overran Mesopotamia and Syria. In 330 Emperor Constantine moved his capital to the city of Byzantium and named it Constantinople (it is now Istanbul, in Turkey). Sixty-five years later the empire was split in two—the Western Empire, which remained under the jurisdiction of Rome, and the Eastern Empire which was administered from Constantinople.

The Western part of the empire was increasingly invaded by Vandals, Visigoths, and other Germanic tribes whom the Romans called barbarians. The Roman army suffered a series of devastating defeats, and its generals were forced to make a succession of humiliating treaties with

German chiefs which involved losing vast amounts of land. The empire became so weakened that in 410 the Visigoths sacked Rome itself. Then in 476 the Germanic chieftain Odoacer overthrew the last emperor of Rome, Romulus Augustulus, and declared himself to be king of Italy. Odoacer agreed to accept the emperor in the East as his overlord, and the Eastern, or Byzantine, Empire survived until 1453. But the great empire built by the Romans had come to an end almost 1,000 years earlier.

Rome and Christianity

For hundreds of years the religion of Christianity existed alongside traditional Roman beliefs. However, the followers of Christianity were persecuted right from its beginnings in the first century A.D. Because Christians usually lived in close-knit communities, they were regarded suspiciously by other Roman citizens. Magistrates could order suspected Christians to carry out pagan rituals, and if they refused, they could be put to death.

Despite this treatment, Christianity flourished, and by the third century A.D. there were many large Christian communities throughout the Roman world. By this time Christians could be found at every level of Roman society. In A.D. 312 the emperor Constantine dreamed that if he painted the Christian symbol of a cross on the shields of his soldiers, he would win a decisive battle. The dream came true. After this Constantine became more and more closely involved with the Christian church, surrounding himself with Christian advisers and putting the religion's symbol on the empire's coins. He was eventually baptized on his deathbed in A.D. 337, making him the first Christian emperor.

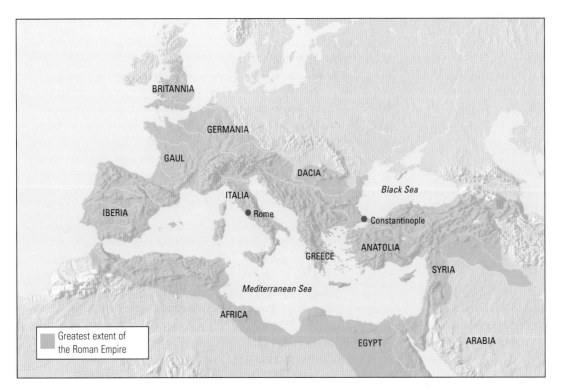

LEFT: The extent of the Roman Empire at its height, after the death of the emperor Trajan in A.D. 116. Later Roman emperors found it increasingly difficult to administer and defend the lands conquered by their predecessors.

Pompeii

Pompeii was a city in southern Italy that flourished during the Roman Empire. In A.D. 79 a nearby volcano erupted and buried the city in lava and ash, preserving it for the next 2,000 years. It is now one of the most famous archaeological sites in the world.

LEFT: The ruins of Pompeii as they are today. Pompeii was a walled city with long, straight roads leading to seven gates in the outer wall. This view from the north wall shows the central paved street leading to the forum.

Pompeii was just an ordinary city of no particular importance. It became a Roman community in 91 B.C., and over the next 150 years many wealthy Romans built houses there, enjoying its beautiful climate on the shores of the Mediterranean Sea. There was one drawback to the city's location: it was overlooked by the volcano of Mount Vesuvius. However, this did not cause its citizens any particular concern—they had never known a volcanic eruption. In A.D. 62 Vesuvius rumbled, and Pompeii was shaken and damaged by a severe earthquake. Seventeen years later there were more earth tremors in the region, but the people of Pompeii ignored them and went on with their daily lives.

On August 24, A.D. 79, Mount Vesuvius erupted. A violent explosion of hot volcanic ash and dust, small pumice stones, and larger chunks

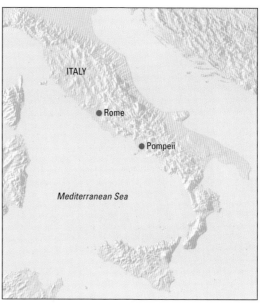

LEFT: In Roman times Pompeii was a pleasant Mediterranean resort on the Bay of Naples.

The Plaster People of Pompeii

Giuseppe Fiorelli found many skeletons during his excavations in the lava at Pompeii. He also quickly realized that the victims' bodies had made hollows in the ash and pumice, which had then hardened before the bodies and clothing decayed over the years. These hollows, or spaces, were like the molds that sculptors use, and Fiorelli devised an ingenious method of filling them to make copies of the bodies.

He poured liquid plaster into a hollow, and when the plaster set and hardened, he chipped away the surrounding lava to reveal the plaster cast. This cast was a detailed copy of the individual, sometimes even including an expression of fear or agony on the victim's face. Casts were made of people and animals, including a dog that had been chained up and was unable to run away. Many of the victims were trying to cover their faces with their hands or clothing as they suffocated. Casts were also made of doors, shutters, and even tree roots.

Altogether, about 2,000 bodies have been found at Pompeii out of a total population of about 20,000. Many citizens must have managed to escape from the catastrophe into the surrounding countryside, but there may also be many more bodies still to be discovered.

---

of lava suddenly rained down on Pompeii. In the streets the air was filled with poisonous fumes as the sky turned dark. Some people tried to take shelter, others ran for their lives as the city was buried under about 16 ft (5m) of ash and lava. When this volcanic debris hardened, it sealed up much of the city. Survivors fled as further eruptions shook the region, and the nearby city of Herculaneum was also smothered by lava.

Pompeii was gone. It was buried and then totally forgotten, though in later centuries local farmers spoke of a "lost city" and found pieces of pottery and other ancient traces. In 1594 workmen building an aqueduct in the region uncovered ruined buildings. Then in 1709 a local farmer found large slabs of marble while digging a well. This started a hunt for buried treasure, and many valuable items must have been unearthed and taken away. Thirty years later an engineer named Rocco Alcubierre used strong tools and gunpowder to tunnel through the solid lava. He immediately discovered wall paintings and the steps of an amphitheater.

→ KEEPING RECORDS ←

For more than 100 years most of the people who visited the site were only interested in finding valuable pieces of treasure. Then in 1860 Giuseppe Fiorelli took control of the excavations. He began investigating the city block by block, keeping accurate records of all the finds at the site. He numbered every doorway, so that each house and shop could be identified. Whenever possible, he left things where they were found, so that it became easier to build up a picture of the whole community. Excavations have continued steadily since then, with occasional breaks.

A great deal about the events of August A.D. 79 has been learned from the writings of Pliny the Younger, who was staying at the nearby town of Misenum. His uncle, Pliny the Elder, commanded a fleet of ships that rushed to rescue survivors from the sea and get a closer view of the volcanic eruption. Pliny the Elder was himself overcome by fumes on the shore and died.

About three-quarters of the city has been uncovered and today's visitors to the site can get a good idea of what daily life was like in Pompeii. Buildings have been restored, with reconstructed roofs, and scientists have identified the preserved seeds of many plants and regrown the gardens that Pompeians enjoyed.

At the time of the eruption there were three public baths in Pompeii where men and women could bathe and relax. Some wealthy citizens had their own luxurious bathroom at home. There were two theaters—a large open building for plays that held about 5,000 spectators, and a smaller, enclosed building for concerts and recitals. The amphitheater, where gladiators fought and killed each other as well as wild animals, has also been fully excavated.

In A.D. 79 the Harbor Gate of the walled city of Pompeii was only 1,650 ft (500m) from the Bay of Naples. The eruption flung ash and lava into the bay, raising the level of the seabed, and Pompeii is now a mile and a half (2km) inland. This shows the force of the disaster that buried a city and created a unique archaeological site.

BELOW: This house in Pompeii, like other Roman town houses, was built around an *atrium*—a central pillared hall open to the sky.

Anglo-Saxons

From the beginning of the fifth century A.D. Britain began to be invaded by fierce tribespeople from Norway, Denmark, and northwest Germany. They were the Angles and Saxons, and they were eventually to establish a culture in Britain that would last for over 400 years.

The invaders began arriving in Britain after the Roman legions had left the province. They came in narrow longboats, each manned by 28 powerful oarsmen. The boats had no sails and were not suitable for an ocean crossing, but the invaders rowed along the coast of Holland before making the short crossing to Britain.

These warriors were tall, strong fighters with blue eyes and long blond hair. At first the Anglo-Saxons were hired as mercenary troops to defend the British from their northern enemies—the Picts, who lived in what is now Scotland. But by A.D. 600 the Anglo-Saxons had settled in the east and south of England and conquered the British who had hired them.

Anglo-Saxon England was divided into seven kingdoms—Northumbria in the north, Mercia and Wessex in the west, East Anglia in the east, and Essex, Kent, and Sussex in the southeast. Although some of the British were driven west into Wales and Cornwall, many of them stayed and probably intermarried with the Anglo-Saxons. However, the British were treated as second-class citizens and were forced to become farm laborers or slaves.

The Anglo-Saxons had a hierarchical society, with the king and his nobles at the top, free farmers in the middle, below them farm laborers—who were not allowed to leave the place where they worked—and slaves. The nobles

ABOVE: A reconstruction of an Anglo-Saxon village at West Stow in East Anglia. Anglo-Saxon farmers lived in one-roomed houses built with timber walls and thatched roofs.

BELOW: A drawing of an Anglo-Saxon longboat, which was powered by 28 oarsmen.

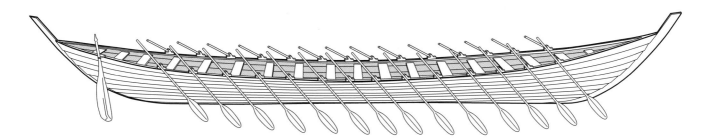

owned large amounts of land given to them by the king, and the free farmers, or *ceorls* (pronounced "churls"), were given less land and had to serve in the king's army. The lowest group of people were slaves—people who had been captured in war, broken the law, or were simply so poor they had sold themselves in return for food.

Most of the people living in Anglo-Saxon England were farmers. They lived in individual farms or hamlets (small villages) of between two and 10 farm units. Each farm had a principal house made of thatch and wood in which the family lived and slept. Other buildings surrounding the house were used as workshops or storehouses. Sometimes there would be a fenced yard attached to the farmhouse, and the other buildings would be within the yard. Toward the end of the Anglo-Saxon period, between the ninth and 11th centuries A.D., the development of a new type of large open field meant that farmers needed to work with each other in teams. So farmers began to live together in large villages instead.

← ANGLO-SAXON NOBILITY →

The nobles lived in halls built of oak with thatched roofs. Often the wooden walls and doors were carved, and under the wooden floors there was space where goods could be stored. There were no bedrooms in these feasting halls, as they were called, so the nobles ate and slept with their retainers. Sometimes these large halls acted as royal centers, such as those discovered at Yeavering in the kingdom of Northumberland and at Cheddar in Somerset. Yeavering is known to have been visited by King Edwin in the 620s and Cheddar by Alfred the Great in the ninth and 10th centuries.

Anglo-Saxon nobles were buried with their weapons beside them to signify their status, and their wives were buried wearing dresses fastened by decorated brooches. In the sixth and seventh centuries A.D. the graves of kings and noblemen and their families were covered by earth mounds, called barrows.

In Anglo-Saxon society if somebody injured or killed someone else, they had to pay money, known as *wergeld* or blood money, to their victim or their victim's family. The amount paid depended on who had been hurt and how severely. So a small injury to an unimportant person required a small payment, while an injury to a noble required a large payment.

Women could be rich and powerful in Anglo-Saxon society. Ethelfled, the daughter of King Alfred, was known as "the Lady of the Mercians"

and was one of the most powerful people in England. Marriages were prearranged, but the woman could decide not to marry her chosen husband. She was also able to leave her husband and keep her children to help support her. Marriages involved "Morning Gifts"—the husband gave his wife money and lands. Poorer

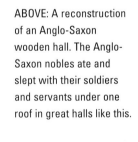

ABOVE: A reconstruction of an Anglo-Saxon wooden hall. The Anglo-Saxon nobles ate and slept with their soldiers and servants under one roof in great halls like this.

LEFT: A reconstructed scene showing women in Anglo-Saxon dress spinning and weaving.

Sutton Hoo

In 1939 several extraordinary Anglo-Saxon burial mounds were dug up at Sutton Hoo near the Suffolk coast in East Anglia. In one of the mounds were the remains of a wooden ship 100 ft (30m) long that had been dragged up from the nearby Deben River. A burial site had been laid out in a cabin in the center of the ship. There was no body, but the burial site contained some of the most beautiful Anglo-Saxon arms, armor, and jewelry ever found. The finds included a helmet and parade shield, gold and garnet jewelry, drinking horns with silver fittings, a lyre, a scepter, and numerous gold and silver objects, including gold coins. Clearly Sutton Hoo was the grave of a great warlord. Some historians believe that it was the grave of Raedwald, the king of East Anglia, who died in about A.D. 625.

BELOW: A map showing the seven Anglo-Saxon kingdoms and the location of important towns, ports, and burial sites.

A reconstruction of the helmet found in the tomb at Sutton Hoo.

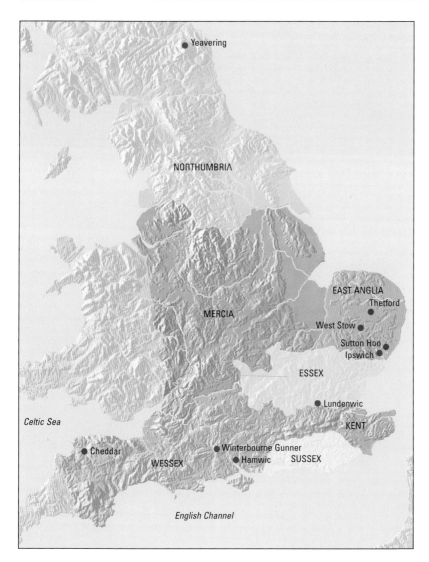

women were given jewelry for their wedding. However, most women were farmers' wives and spent their time weaving cloth, making clothes, and working in the fields.

⬩ ANGLO-SAXON TRADE ⬩

Towns developed slowly out of centers of trade. Here nobles sold slaves, animals, skins, leather, and wool cloth in exchange for goods and jewelry from other countries—millstones from Germany, pots from Egypt, wine from northern France, and precious stones from the Middle East. The ports at Lundenwic, Ipswich, and Hamwic became important centers of trade between the seventh and ninth centuries. However, these ports were not fortified and they were attacked by Viking raiders from Scandinavia. In response the Anglo-Saxons started building fortified towns to replace the trading ports, and many of these towns still exist today.

Viking raids in the ninth century destroyed all the Anglo-Saxon kingdoms except Wessex. In the 10th century the Wessex kings fought back, conquered the Danish Vikings, and created a single kingdom of England. This united kingdom even survived the invasion by the Danish king Cnut.

However, after the English king Edward the Confessor died childless, William, Duke of Normandy (known as the Conqueror), invaded England from Normandy and defeated the Anglo-Saxons at the Battle of Hastings in 1066. From then on he ruled England as William I.

Vikings

From the late eighth century A.D. the Vikings became known throughout Europe as bold, ruthless raiders. These fierce adventurers, also known as the Norsemen, sailed from their homeland in Scandinavia to terrorize a large area of western Europe.

For over 400 years the Vikings made a succession of violent raids on European coastal towns and villages, building up a fearsome reputation that has lived on to the present day.

The Vikings were the descendants of Germanic peoples who started moving to the northern region of Europe about 4,000 years ago. They settled in Scandinavia, the region that includes Denmark, Norway, and Sweden. By the end of the eighth century A.D. their population was growing quickly, and there may no longer have been enough good farmland at home to support their increasing numbers. This may have been the reason why they turned to raiding—and it is probable also that many young Vikings regarded raiding as a quick and easy way of gaining wealth and honor.

Norwegian Vikings began their raids in the 790s, attacking the coasts of England, Ireland, and Scotland. The warriors usually appeared suddenly in a small group of ships, swarming ashore with their spears, swords, and battleaxes. They plundered villages, churches, and monasteries, and then just as quickly sailed away again. They were soon joined by Danish Vikings, who invaded England in 865. They conquered much of the country but were forced by King Alfred the Great to settle in the eastern region, which became known as the Danelaw.

By this time Norwegians and Danes had also looted and burned towns in France, Belgium, the Netherlands, Italy, and Spain, although they did not settle there permanently in any great numbers, as they had done in Britain.

However, Swedish Vikings did travel along the rivers of eastern Europe to set up trading centers, and by the late 800s the Slavic towns of Novgorod and Kiev were Viking strongholds. The main Viking people involved in these explorations were the Rus, and it is from them that we get the name of the modern country of Russia.

➤ THE LONGSHIPS ➤

In order to carry out their raids, the Vikings developed fast and sturdy warships. In ancient times the Scandinavians had used fragile canoes

and boats made of animal skins stretched over a timber frame. Now, however, the Vikings built the powerful boats for which they became famous—their longships. These narrow boats were made from planks of oak rather than animal hide and had a steadying keel and a large central sail. A team of specialized craftsmen was needed to build each boat.

ABOVE: An artist's impression of a Viking longship containing a raiding party about to land. The Vikings were ruthless raiders and were greatly feared throughout northern Europe.

RIGHT: The Vikings spread out from Scandinavia to colonize Britain, France, Russia, Iceland, and Greenland. Viking explorers are thought to have crossed the Atlantic as early as A.D. 1000. They probably landed at Baffin Island, although they may have sailed as far south as Labrador or even Maine.

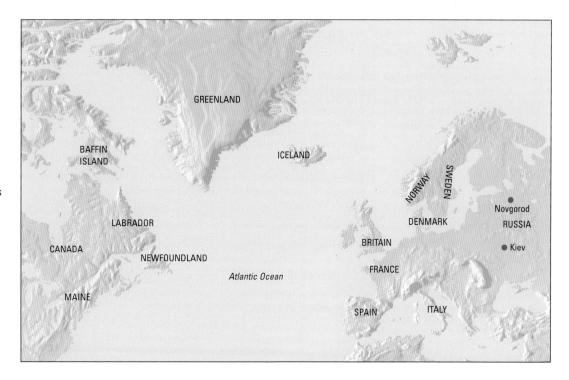

The Viking longship had up to 30 oars, each powered by one oarsman, on each side of the ship. The oars were used near land, when extra speed was needed, or when there was little wind. Each longship also had a single sail, made of tough woolen cloth strengthened by strips of leather, and this was generally used on the open sea. Viking ships could sail in shallow water, which made them useful for traveling along rivers and near coasts. They were also light enough to be hauled or carried over land when necessary. Modern archaeologists know a great deal about longships because the Vikings sometimes buried them with famous warriors.

Most Vikings were freemen, and many were farmers, growing cereals, fruit, and vegetables,

RIGHT: A reconstruction of a Viking longhouse. A longhouse consisted of a single large communal room that housed several families living together. It was usually built from wood and the roof was tiled, thatched with reeds, or covered with turf.

Viking Explorations

The Vikings were expert navigators and sailors, so it is not surprising that they were responsible for some of the greatest feats of exploration in the ancient world.

One of the great Viking explorers was Erik the Red. In about 980 he was exiled from his home in Iceland and decided to sail west. He made landfall on an icy, inhospitable place that he named Greenland (hoping to encourage others to follow him). He settled there, and when the term of his exile was over, he returned to Iceland and persuaded a group of adventurers to go back with him and set up a large colony. The Viking settlements on Greenland lasted for several centuries.

Perhaps the greatest Viking explorer of them all was Erik's second son, Leif Eriksson, also known as Leif the Lucky. Sometime after 1000 he sailed west from Greenland across the Atlantic Ocean. He made landfall at a place he named Helluland, meaning "land of flat stones." It was probably Baffin Island in present-day Canada. The explorers then sailed on to Markland ("forest land"), which was probably the Canadian mainland of Labrador.

Finally, the Vikings reached Vinland ("wine land"), where wild grapes grew. This may have been the island of Newfoundland, where Viking remains have been found, though some historians believe that Vinland was in modern-day Maine. This great voyage of discovery took place nearly 400 years before Christopher Columbus crossed the Atlantic.

The remains of Brattahlid, the settlement that Erik the Red established in Greenland in the 10th century A.D. It was from Greenland that Erik's son, Leif Eriksson, crossed the Atlantic in one of the greatest voyages of discovery ever known.

and raising cattle, pigs, sheep, and goats. Merchants and others also made settlements near the coast, both at home in Scandinavia and when they traveled. Their wooden houses had roofs covered in turf. Early towns had markets, where people traded furs, textiles, and iron. The freemen also traded in slaves, who were mainly prisoners who had been captured in raids. Slaves often worked as laborers and servants on farms and in workshops. They had few rights, and their children were born slaves as well.

Above the ordinary freemen and downtrodden slaves there was a class of Viking nobles. These nobles included those who had great

RIGHT: This Viking buckle clasp from Norway is made of gold and inlaid with precious stones. The Vikings were expert metalworkers.

wealth or those who were descended from honored warriors. The most powerful were chieftains who controlled large areas of countryside. By about 890 Harold Finehair had defeated many local kings and chieftains and had become the first king of Norway.

By the ninth century Norwegian Vikings had started settling in Iceland, where they led a more independent life and escaped the growing power of the king. Viking Iceland was a form of republic, where laws were passed by an assembly, called the *althing*, which met on a rocky plain each midsummer. In other parts of the Viking world communities had a governing council called a *thing*. This council was made up only of freemen; women and slaves had no right to speak. The *thing* had such great power that it could even decide who should be king. It made laws, held trials to judge criminals, and decided whether the community should go to war.

Viking Gods

The Vikings believed in a great number of gods. The most important was Odin. He was king of all the Norse gods and goddesses, and was thought to live in a place called Asgard, the home of the gods. He was the god of war and death, and he inspired ferocious Viking warriors called Berserkers, who worked themselves up into a frenzy of rage before throwing themselves into battle without armor.

Odin's oldest and most powerful son was red-bearded Thor, the god of thunder, lightning, and wind. He was the most popular Viking god because his supposed power over the weather had a great effect on people's daily lives. Thursday is named after Thor, and Friday after Frigg, his mother.

By the end of the 10th century contact with European Christians had put an end to most of the earlier Norse beliefs. In about 960 King Harold Bluetooth of Denmark became a Christian, and soon after the colonists of Iceland voted to do the same.

This picture stone is believed to illustrate a story from Norse myth in which Odin, king of the gods, tricks the king Ermaneric into killing his son.

→ VIKING HOUSES ←

The Vikings built different kinds of houses depending on the materials that were available in the region. Most of their houses were single-story structures, and many of them had just one room. The walls were generally constructed of wood, and there was usually just one doorway and no windows, to keep in the heat from the hearth. The pitched roof was sometimes made of wooden tiles or thatch if reeds were available locally. The houses in Iceland and elsewhere had roofs made of a thick layer of turf.

In the farming settlements there was often a large longhouse at the center, where a family and farmworkers all lived together. Inside the dark, smoky house there were wooden benches along the walls, where people sat during the day and slept at night. Women were in charge of the home and also of the farm if their husbands were away raiding or trading.

Over 300 years the Vikings had an enormous influence throughout Europe, and especially on England and France. Their last invasion of England took place in 1066, just weeks before it was conquered by the Normans, who themselves were descendants of Viking settlers in northern France. William the Conqueror, who became king of England after defeating King Harold at the Battle of Hastings, was a descendant of the Danish Viking chieftain Rollo, who had raided northern France and founded the Duchy of Normandy in 911.

The Viking settlements also had a lasting effect on Iceland, and this northern island still retains some elements of Viking culture today. In Scandinavia the three Viking kingdoms eventually became the present-day nations of Denmark, Norway, and Sweden.

Chapter 3:

India and the Far East

As in the Middle East, the early civilizations of India and the Far East developed in the valleys of great rivers—the Indus and Ganges in India, the Yellow and Yangtze in China, and the Mekong in Southeast Asia. It was from the farming communities who had settled in these fertile river valleys to grow their crops that the first cultures and cities in these regions arose.

BELOW: Rice was the staple crop throughout the ancient Far East, grown in flooded paddy fields like the ones shown here.

Indus Civilization

Thousands of years ago a civilization emerged in the fertile valley of the great Indus River in the region that is now India and Pakistan. This was the Indus civilization, which archaeologists also call the Harappan civilization, after one of its major cities.

Until around 2600 B.C. people from several different but related societies lived in villages and small towns in various parts of the Indus region. Around 2600 B.C. these peoples came together to create a single society that built large, sophisticated cities and developed an advanced civilization with a culture that included a form of writing. This civilization lasted until about 2000 B.C.

The Indus River is one of the world's great rivers, flowing from the Himalaya Mountains through Pakistan and into the Arabian Sea. After leaving the mountains in the north, the river's five main contributory branches flow through a plain called Punjab (which means "five rivers" in the local language). Further south the branches join up into the Indus River, which then continues on its way to the sea. The southern part of the plain is called Sind, an old name for India that gave Sindbad the sailor his name.

⤙ NATURAL RESOURCES ⤚

The people of the Indus civilization lived in Punjab and Sind, and depended on the Indus River (and another river that has long since dried up) for water to irrigate their farms. They also lived along the coast of the Arabian Sea, where they built ports for sea trade. Rugged hills and mountains form the western boundary of the Indus Valley, and here the Indus people found many useful materials such as colorful stones and copper that their craftsmen could use to make tools and ornaments. They also found flint (which they used for making stone tools) in the low hills near the coast. In order to obtain these materials, people in most parts of the valley had to rely on traders and merchants for their supply.

Farmers had been living in the hills around the Indus Valley since 6500 B.C. or even earlier. These people lived in simple village houses made of mud bricks. They made jewelry from sea shells and stones like lapis lazuli and turquoise. They buried many objects with their dead, so that their loved ones would be well-supplied in the afterlife.

In about 5000 B.C. these early farmers began to make ceramic pots and soon developed other remarkable skills. Craftspeople started making fancy jewelry from rare stones and shell, and tools and weapons from copper. They even learned how to make artificial materials like faience—made from partly melted sand, faience looks almost like glass. As people spent more time making things, they had less time for farming, and so they began to exchange their products for food. This change was an important step toward a new kind of society, one in which there were different occupations, different ranks, and different levels of power.

By about 3000 B.C. several different societies of this new kind occupied the Indus Valley. Archaeologists call this time, between 3200 and 2600 B.C., the Early Harappan period. Most of the people in Early Harappan societies continued to live in farming villages.

These villages often had walls around them or were built on clay platforms, so that the yearly floods of the rivers would not wash away the houses. People also started to gather in towns containing as many as 5,000 inhabitants. These places attracted many craftspeople, and towns became the centers for special crafts. The towns

ABOVE: The upper reaches of the Indus Valley with mountains behind. The fertile valley of the Indus River enabled early farmers to produce enough food to support city populations.

Stone Stamps

The people of the Indus civilization made a large number of stone stamps—over 2,000 have been discovered. Each stamp was square, with a small, round handle on one side and an engraved picture on the other flat surface. The picture on the stamps was usually of an animal—most often it was a bull, but it could be a rhinoceros, elephant, water buffalo, unicorn, or some other beast. A line of writing, which was probably a person's name, title, or occupation, appeared above the animal picture. It seems the stamps were used as marks of ownership. For example, a merchant could mark his ownership of merchandise by tying up the goods with string, attaching a lump of wet clay over the knot, and then pressing his stamp into the clay. When the clay had dried, the only way to untie the knot would be to break the seal.

Because the stamps were used to make impressions, the writing engraved on the stamps had to be in reverse (like mirror writing) so that people could read the result.

Three stone stamps engraved with animal pictures and showing inscriptions in the writing of the Indus people.

were also the places where merchants lived, the traders who carried the craft goods from place to place around the region. As some people became richer, they started to surround themselves with expensive things and to build large houses. Some of the towns even had different neighborhoods separated by walls, the rich and powerful in one neighborhood and the poorer folk in another. These changes suggest that Early Harappan societies were turning into complicated cultures.

During the century between 2600 and 2500 B.C. society went through a massive upheaval that

RIGHT: Part of the remains of the Indus city of Harappa. The city was laid out on a grid system, with broad streets separating the buildings, which were constructed of baked mud bricks of a uniform size.

produced what archaeologists call the Mature Harappan culture. This culture was based on city life, and archaeologists have discovered five major cities in the Indus region. Mohenjodaro in Sind was the largest of them, while the city of Harappa in Punjab was nearly as large—each city held as many as 50,000 or more people. The other three cities were about half this size. In many ways these cities were larger versions of Early Harappan towns. Each city had several sections— each section was surrounded by a wall, and some were built on huge brick platforms. Some city sections contained residential neighborhoods, and others held government buildings.

The public buildings at Harappa and Mohenjodaro seem to be of several types. The original excavators identified what they thought were enormous granaries for storing the public grain supply, a great bath or sacred pool, and a college or assembly hall. However, archaeologists today are not at all sure what purposes these large and well-planned buildings served. Unlike other early civilizations, it has not been possible yet to identify the palaces of rulers or the main temples.

The cities' residential areas were planned out in a very logical way, with a regular grid of wide streets running north–south and east–west to make blocks. Peoples' houses were of more or less the same design, with rooms around a central open space. Stairs led to upper stories or to the roof, and the windows had attachments for wooden screens. This arrangement meant that families could live and work indoors or outside according to the weather and sleep on the roof during hot weather. Some houses were larger than others and had smaller residences attached to them, perhaps for servants.

The rulers of these cities took great care to provide for drinking water and sanitation. They built a public well in each city block (some houses also had private wells) and constructed an elaborate system of drains to carry away sewage and excess rainwater.

⌐ CITY LIFE ⌐

Most craftspeople lived and worked in the cities and towns. These skilled workers made many special goods like metal tools and weapons, shell bangles, beads, stoneware (a special pottery almost as hard as rock), bracelets, cotton cloth, stone seals, and pottery. Some of their skills were so sophisticated that we still do not really understand how they made their artifacts.

Many products required enormous amounts of work. For example, a bead-maker needed to

work for two weeks to produce a single long bead of carnelian (a red stone similar to quartz). These long carnelian beads were a valued and expensive item in Harappan times, and rich people wore necklaces and belts that had taken over a year to make. Poorer people wore imitation beads made from clay and then painted red. Foreigners also valued these carnelian beads and other Harappan products, and traders took them to Sumer (in present-day southern Iraq) and other lands.

ABOVE: This model of a two-wheeled cart, bullocks, and driver is made from terracotta and was found in the city of Harappa. The wooden bits are modern additions.

Efficient Drainage

The people who built the towns of the Indus civilization understood that it was necessary to devise a method of disposing of sewage and excess rainwater. So they equipped their cities, and even their villages, with a sophisticated system of sewers and drains that allowed unwanted waste to flow under the city walls and out onto the plain around the settlement.

Drains from each house carried waste and bath water into gutters that ran along the residential streets. Many of these street drains were open to collect excess rainwater that otherwise would flood the roads. The drains flowed into sewers that ran below the main streets.

Even by modern standards the drainage system the town planners created was an impressive piece of engineering. The drains were made of baked brick, which lasted a long time, and had tanks at various points so that solid waste would settle and not clog

the drains. Archaeologists excavated one drain in the city of Harappa that had an arched roof 5 ft (1.5m) high. The Indus drainage system was very advanced—few other civilizations had anything similar—and it was not equaled until modern times.

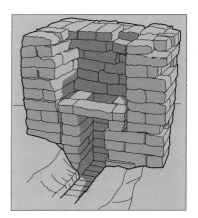

The drainage and sanitation system of the Indus Valley civilization was far in advance of its time. Many houses had brick privies, like this one, connected by drains to covered sewers that ran beneath the streets and out of the city.

Despite the high status of cities in the Mature Harappan civilization, country life also remained extremely important. Archaeologists know of over 1,500 Mature Harappan settlements, and almost all of these were villages. Even these villages contained solidly built houses, and the villagers enjoyed the same variety of goods as the town-dwellers. The farmers relied on irrigation canals to carry river water to their fields, where they grew mainly wheat and barley, along with legumes, sesame, and vegetables. In some areas the farmers also grew rice and cotton. Animals such as sheep, zebu (humped cattle), and water buffalo provided milk and meat. These villagers must have worked very hard to feed not only themselves but also the inhabitants of the cities.

The Harappans were one of the early peoples who invented a type of writing. This mysterious script was not an alphabet, like the present-day one, but used over 400 different signs to represent syllables (such as "ba," "bi," "ta," "ti," and so on) and some entire words. Other early writing in different parts of the world also used a complicated mix of syllables and words, but none is related to the Harappan script.

Although archaeologists have found hundreds of inscriptions, all of them are very short, and no one as yet has been able to decipher them. The inscriptions appeared on pots and copper tools, and on a variety of objects made of stone, shell, or ivory, and their purpose was perhaps to name the makers or owners of the items.

⇥ THE END OF AN ERA ⇤

Sometime around 2000 B.C. the Indus civilization began to change again. People left the cities for life in the countryside and craftspeople stopped making their more laborious and expensive products, while merchants no longer used stamps to mark their property. The Indus people also abandoned their writing. Instead of the uniform Mature Harappan style, many different ways of making pottery and other items arose in various parts of the Indus Valley. It appears that in many ways, people had returned to the style of life that had prevailed many centuries before. No one knows what happened to bring this about, although some people think that climate change may have played a part. Farmers may not have been able to supply the large cities with enough produce, and so people had to migrate.

Part of the reason may have been the appearance of a new people, called Vedic Aryans, who moved into the Indus Valley from Central Asia. But they did not come as destroying conquerors.

Instead, aspects of the Indus culture gradually changed and spread to other parts of northern India. These Late Harappan cultures formed part of the cultural setting from which the cities of the Ganges plain arose over a thousand years later.

BELOW: The extent of the Indus civilization in 2500 B.C. and its five major cities (marked in red).

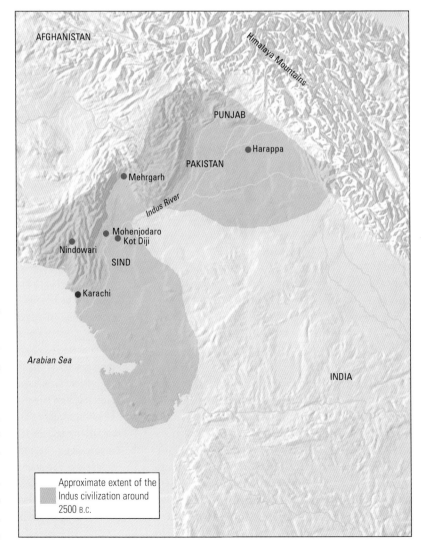

Approximate extent of the Indus civilization around 2500 B.C.

Mohenjodaro

Mohenjodaro was the largest of the five cities of the Indus Valley civilization. When these great cities were discovered in the 1920s, the Indus Valley civilization was recognized as one of the major civilizations of the ancient world along with Egypt and Mesopotamia. A team of British archaeologists, led by John Marshall, started digging at Mohenjodaro in 1922. A decade of excavation uncovered large areas of the city and gave us an exceptional picture of life in this ancient Indian town.

Mohenjodaro sits on the right bank of the Indus River in the region known as Sind, now within the present-day country of Pakistan. By ancient standards the city was enormous, covering an area of one square mile (2.6 sq. km) and containing about 50,000 residents. A city of this size had to rely on farmers and animal herders to supply its food. Some of the people who lived in the city may have tended gardens and fields, but many of the citizens followed other trades.

Craftsmen labored in workshops to make fine pottery, metal tools, stone beads, stone seals, flint tools, and other products typical of the Indus Valley civilization. Other city-dwellers ran shops selling these goods or organized trade expeditions to other places in the Indus Valley and beyond. Some wealthy families would have owned country estates or invested in business firms or workshops. And no doubt government officials and priests lived in the city, but excavations so far have uncovered few traces of their presence.

The city contained several distinct mounds separated by lower stretches of land. The mounds had been formed by people building houses on top of earlier dwellings that had crumbled away over time. By carefully digging through the different levels of buildings, archaeologists have discovered how the city changed over the centuries. Marshall uncovered about 500 years of rebuilding. He also discovered how the city-dwellers had arranged their lives.

Mohenjodaro shows every sign of having been built according to a plan. The place has two main parts—a small high mound to the west and a much larger group of mounds to the east, separated by several hundred yards

The ruins of Mohenjodaro, showing the western mound in the distance. Narrow streets between the houses connected with the regular grid of main streets.

(meters) of open space. The larger, eastern area held all the residential neighborhoods, where most people worked and lived. In this section of the city wide avenues formed a regular grid running north–south and east–west. The avenues connected to a regular network of smaller streets and lanes between the houses.

The residents of Mohenjodaro seemed to have liked privacy—their front doors and windows faced side roads and alleys, and blank walls ran along the larger streets. Houses came in several different models and sizes. The smallest ones were simple terraced houses, each with only a single room. Most houses, however, had several rooms and a courtyard where the family could do their chores outdoors. The largest houses had more rooms and several courtyards, and some of them even had semidetached servants' quarters. The houses often had staircases that led to an upper floor or to a flat roof where the family could sleep on hot summer nights. Many of the houses had baths and privies, which were connected to an elaborate sewer system running beneath the streets.

The high mound to the west had a very different character. This sector of Mohenjodaro was basically a massive brick

platform 1,200 by 600 ft (366 by 183m) and about 40 ft (12m) high. There were several buildings on this platform that may have had religious or civic purposes.

One of these buildings had a large water tank 8 ft (2.4m) deep, almost like a deep swimming pool, at its center. The tank was carefully built of mud bricks and plaster, and sealed with asphalt to make it watertight. Two staircases led down into the tank from opposite ends. A porch with columns to hold up a roof ran around the tank, and suites of rooms surrounded the entire structure. The building, which archaeologists have called "the great bath," probably had a religious purpose and may have been used in rituals that needed the purifying effects of water.

Next to the great bath stood another building that archaeologists have called the granary. This structure survives only as closely spaced rows of square blocks, with narrow ventilation passages between them. The blocks clearly served as the foundation for a building that once stood on this spot, but no one knows if it actually was a granary.

A third building at the other end of the platform has been named the assembly hall. This building was a big open hall with rows of pillars holding up the roof, a design suited to large gatherings of people.

China

People were living in the vast region that is now called China long before the beginning of written history. Ancestors of the Chinese people formed farming settlements near two mighty rivers, the Huang He (Yellow) and the Chang Jiang (Yangtze), over 9,000 years ago.

Near the more northern Huang He, or Yellow River, the early farming settlements consisted of wooden houses plastered with mud and thatched with reeds. The farmers grew a cereal plant called millet, as well as hunting game and fishing in the river.

Further south people built houses on stilts on the marshy land next to the Chang Jiang, or "Long River." They grew rice in the flooded marshes, and archaeologists have discovered an early settlement there dating from about 6000–5000 B.C. Evidence from the site has shown that these early Chinese people used stone tools and kept buffalo, pigs, and dogs.

⬦ THE SHANG DYNASTY ⬦

By about 3000 B.C. villagers were starting to protect their settlements with earth walls. Communities grew larger under the leadership of strong rulers, many of whom figure in Chinese legends. Rulers passed power on to their brothers or sons, and the first dynasty, or ruling family, to leave a historical record was the Shang.

The Shang dynasty, which governed a large region around the Huang He River, dates from 1766 B.C. Around this time the Chinese learned how to make bronze and the people of the Shang period used this knowledge to make bronze tools, weapons, and vessels.

People of the Shang period were ruled by a priest-king, who was called the "Son of Heaven." The spirits of royal ancestors were worshiped and consulted on important decisions, and there were also many gods, especially those of the sun—who was seen as a father-figure—and earth, who was a mother-figure. The Shang kings and their nobles hunted deer, wild boar, tigers, and wolves. It is thought that they had several capitals, one after the other, and it is known that in about 1400 B.C. they made their capital at Anyang.

Anyang grew into a symmetrically laid out city with palaces and temples for the king and his nobles, who traveled in style in horse-drawn chariots. The houses of ordinary people were made of wattle and daub (a mixture of clay and twigs), with roofs thatched with straw.

Many Shang relics have been found at Anyang, including more than 10,000 pieces of bone and tortoise shells inscribed with Shang writing. This had more than 3,000 symbols and was an early form of Chinese pictographic writing. These bone and tortoise-shell fragments are called oracle bones—because they had been used as a way of contacting the gods. Questions were written on the bone or shell, which was then heated until it cracked. The cracks were examined by priests, and supposedly the shape of the cracks gave answers to the questions.

ABOVE: A painting from the 13th century showing Chinese farmers threshing and sifting rice. Rice farming is thought to have begun in China as long ago as 7000 B.C.

LEFT: A decorated bronze cooking vessel from the Shang period (1766–1100 B.C.). To make pots like this, the Chinese used the "lost-wax" technique. A wax model of the object was covered in clay and fired. Then the liquid wax was poured out, and hot, molten bronze poured into the clay mold and left to cool. The clay mold was then broken to expose the bronze pot. Several molds would have been needed to make a pot like this one.

To the west, the territory was ruled by another dynasty, called the Chou, who were thought of as barbarians by the Shang. Nevertheless, for many years the two peoples lived peacefully alongside each other. Then Chou tribal warriors fought a long, hard battle against the Shang and eventually defeated them.

➤ THE CHOU DYNASTY ➤

The Chou became the overall ruling dynasty in about 1050 B.C., and the ruler divided his kingdom into more than 100 states, each headed by a local chief. To control their new lands, the Chou ruler set up a feudal system about 2,000 years before a similar system was established in Europe. Below the ruler the top class of Chou society was made up of five ranks of noblemen. Each rank rented land from the nobles immediately above them in status, and all the land was farmed by commoners. These ordinary people also looked after their own plots of land, helped by the lowest class of Chou society—the slaves.

The ruler set up his capital at Hao, near present-day Chi'an, which was close to the banks of the Huang He River. Each Chou ruler was succeeded by his eldest son, and they worked hard to keep all the different states together.

In the eighth century B.C., however, a weak Chou ruler caused problems. He was called Yu, and he was not a very good leader. Yu spent a great deal of time with his mistress, and his behavior greatly angered his nobles, particularly those related to his wife. Eventually, they lost patience with him and overthrew him.

One Chinese legend gives a colorful account of Yu's downfall. According to the story, Yu decided one day to play a practical joke to amuse his mistress. He ordered that beacons be lit on the hills surrounding the capital, which was a signal to his nobles that the city was under threat of attack. The nobles immediately sent out their armies, only to find that there was no threat, and it was all a trick. While Yu and his mistress found the soldiers' anger funny, others were less amused. Yu's father-in-law was particularly angry. He gathered forces from tribes in the west and led a real invasion. Once again Yu ordered the beacons to be lit. However, this time the nobles

The Discovery of Silk

According to a Chinese legend, silk was discovered in about 2700 B.C.—a thousand years before the beginning of the Shang dynasty—in the palace gardens of a ruler named Huangdi. The ruler asked his wife Xilingshi to find out what was damaging his mulberry trees. Xilingshi discovered that little worms were eating the mulberry leaves and spinning shiny white cocoons. She took some of the cocoons into the palace to study them and dropped one into hot water. To her amazement a delicate, gauzy tangle came away from the cocoon, which she found was made of one long slender thread.

Xilingshi was so pleased with the fine thread that she gathered many more cocoons and used their silk to weave a special robe for her husband. She then persuaded him to give her a grove of mulberry trees so that she could have a constant supply of cocoons and silk. It is also said that Xilingshi invented the silk reel, for winding the threads together, and the silk loom, for weaving the threads into material.

It is not known if this legend is based on truth, but the Chinese were certainly the first

to discover how to make silk, and for about 3,000 years they were the only people who knew how to produce the material.

A 17th-century painting showing the traditional method of making silk. Silk was one of ancient China's most important exports.

ignored the signal. Yu was killed, and his mistress was carried off by the tribesmen.

In 771 B.C. Yu's son—the new ruler—moved the Chou capital farther east to Luoyang. The individual states within the Chou kingdom now began to build more territorial walls, since they were more and more at war with each other. Ambitious local lords fought for power, which led to growing disorder. In these unstable conditions many thinkers tried to find ways of bringing people together in harmony. Among them were two men whose ideas were to have a lasting impact on Chinese life—Laozi and Confucius.

➤ THE AGE OF PHILOSOPHY ➤

Laozi (a name that means "Old Philosopher") lived in the sixth century B.C. Little is known about him apart from legends, but we do know that he believed the most important thing was for people to live their lives as simply as possible and in harmony with nature. His Tao, or "Way," reflected nature's patterns, and his later followers, who were called Taoists, tried to live by his teachings. According to legend, Laozi tried to leave his home state of Honan when he was an old man. But the border guard, who was a great admirer of the Tao, would not let him pass until he had written down his teachings, which were only known by word of mouth. Laozi agreed and wrote 81 short poems, which have been studied ever since.

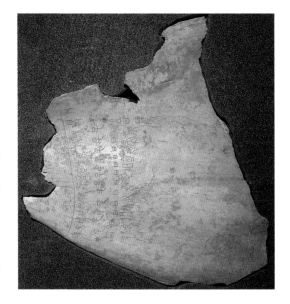

LEFT: An oracle bone dating from the Shang dynasty (1766–1100 B.C.). Oracle bones were used by priests to predict the future and obtain guidance from the gods. The bones were engraved with questions, after which they were heated until they cracked. The priests then examined the shapes of the cracks carefully to discover the answers to their questions.

Experts now believe that this book, called the *Tao Te Ching* ("The Classic of the Way and the Virtue"), was probably written by Taoist followers hundreds of years later.

Confucius (551–479 B.C.) is a Latin version of the Chinese title Kongfuzi, which means "Great Master Kong." This was the title given to Confucius, who was born Kong Qui, in the Chou state of Lu. Confucius's father died when he was very young, and he worked hard to help his mother. He spent his time studying, as well as practicing archery and music. When he was 22,

---

Confucianism

An 18th-century painting of the two philosophers Confucius (right) and Laozi.

In the sixth and fifth centuries B.C. the Chinese philosopher Confucius introduced a new way of thinking. Confucius believed that every person should be truthful, brave, and courteous to others. If families behaved in this way, governments and rulers would be well ordered too, so the well-being of an entire kingdom began in ordinary people's homes. Children should obey their parents, and in just the same way ordinary people should obey their rulers. Confucius included many of his rules in sayings. One example of his sayings is, "A gentleman takes as much trouble to discover what is right as lesser men take to discover what will pay."

However, while Confucius believed that people had a duty to obey their rulers and governments, he also believed that these governments had a duty to their subjects. He believed that good behavior by rulers would have a more beneficial effect on ordinary people's lives than laws and punishment. Confucius even went as far as to say that corrupt governments should be overthrown by their subjects.

Today, Confucianism is often called a religion, but it has no priests and does not advocate worshiping gods. Confucianism is really a philosophy, a guide to morality and good government. The teachings of Confucius proved to be remarkably enduring and had a huge influence on Chinese society for much of the following 2,500 years.

RIGHT: A painting showing
the first emperor Ch'in
Shihuangdi overseeing the
burning of books and the
execution of dissident
scholars by throwing
them into a pit.

Confucius became a teacher of history and poetry. In addition to these subjects, he taught his students to think about their lives and the way in which they should live. It is for these teachings that he is still followed 2,500 years later.

Confucius was afraid that squabbles and wars between the different Chou states would lead to the destruction of civilization. He believed that society could be saved if it concentrated on sincerity and honesty. Confucius was given some minor official appointments in Lu, but the ruler of the state ignored his advice, and Confucius resigned in about 496 B.C. He went into exile with a number of followers and wandered the courts of the kingdom for 13 years.

BELOW: A lacquer box from the days of the Han dynasty. The technique of lacquering, using a varnish obtained from the sap of the lacquer tree, was invented by the Chinese in about 1200 B.C.

Toward the end of his life Confucius spent his time teaching and writing, but it is not clear if any of his writings survived. However, his disciples wrote down his sayings in a book called *The Analects*. When Confucius died, he was not very well known. His followers spread his ideas, and by about 200 B.C. his teachings began to have a great influence on the way China was governed.

By the time he died, Confucius had seen many of the things that he had been worried about come true. By 479 B.C. the Chou dynasty was finding it difficult to control its territory of seven warring states. There were devastating battles between huge armies using horse-drawn chariots, bronze swords, and deadly crossbows (which had just been invented in China). The armies had a total of more than six million soldiers, and in one battle in 260 B.C. more than half a million men were killed. The long reign of the Chou rulers ended just four years later, as the warring states went on fighting.

Among these provinces the northwest state of Ch'in showed both the greatest ferocity and the best military discipline. In 221 B.C. the Ch'in ruler, Cheng, was able to declare total victory over his rivals and call himself Ch'in Shihuangdi —the First Emperor of Ch'in.

‑ CHINA'S FIRST EMPEROR ‑

Shihuangdi became the first emperor of a unified China (our name for the country comes from the word Ch'in). Shihuangdi established central control of his empire, taking all control away from the local chiefs, who were forced to move to the new capital at Chanyang. He divided China into new districts—the officials who ran the districts were responsible directly to him. He also ordered the building of a network of roads, canals, and bridges throughout the empire. Then he sent huge numbers of workers to build a great wall across the north of the empire to keep out possible invading armies.

The "First Emperor" tried to make everything standard throughout the land. He introduced standard weights and measures, and ensured that the characters of the written Chinese language were made the same everywhere. Then he ordered a series of bonfires so that all existing writings could be burned, except those on such useful subjects as medicine, farming, and fortune-telling. His reason for doing this was to destroy books written by people criticizing his rule, and to destroy all knowledge of the past. Scholars who objected were thrown into a deep pit, and hundreds were killed.

The Great Wall of China

China's Great Wall was part of the building program of the first emperor, Ch'in Shihuangdi. Although stretches of earth wall had been built by different northern states as early as 300 B.C., it was Shihuangdi who ordered that these short lengths should be repaired, strengthened, and made into a continuous stone wall to keep out invaders from the north.

A force of 300,000 peasants, ex-soldiers, and slaves took 20 years to complete the task. They worked in harsh and cruel conditions, especially in the bitterly cold winter. Men who fell ill were simply thrown into the foundations of the Great Wall, and building went on over their bodies.

When it was completed in about 200 B.C., the wall was about 2,100 miles (3,400km) long. It was about 30 ft (9m) high and the outside of it was covered with stone slabs. Along the top was a roadway that was wide enough for chariots to use. Soldiers were posted in watchtowers that were placed every 300–600 ft (90–180m). In times of danger a chain of beacons would be lit to warn soldiers further along the wall.

Later, other Chinese emperors strengthened Shihuangdi's wall and extended it, and the last major renovation took place over 1,500 years later. During the Ming dynasty, which controlled China from 1368 to 1644, the Great Wall was gradually rebuilt to a length of more than 3,700 miles (6,000km), from the mountains of northwest China to the Gulf of Bo Hai. Many parts of the wall still exist today.

The Great Wall of China was originally built by the emperor Ch'in Shihuangdi in order to keep out invaders from the north. It has since been rebuilt many times.

Shihuangdi was nicknamed the "Tiger of Ch'in." He was a tough politician and a strong general, but he was afraid of death. In his great palace there were more than 1,000 bedrooms so he could spend each night in a different one in case someone tried to kill him. He also had a special tomb built so that he would be protected after his death. His tomb contained a model army of more than 7,000 life-size soldiers, chariots, and horses made of terracotta. This terracotta army originally carried real bronze weapons, but they were stolen by grave-robbers.

◄ RISE OF THE HAN ►

Shihuangdi died in 210 B.C. after being emperor for just 11 years, and his son proved to be a weak leader. There were rebellions, and a new dynasty—the Han—gained control in 202 B.C.

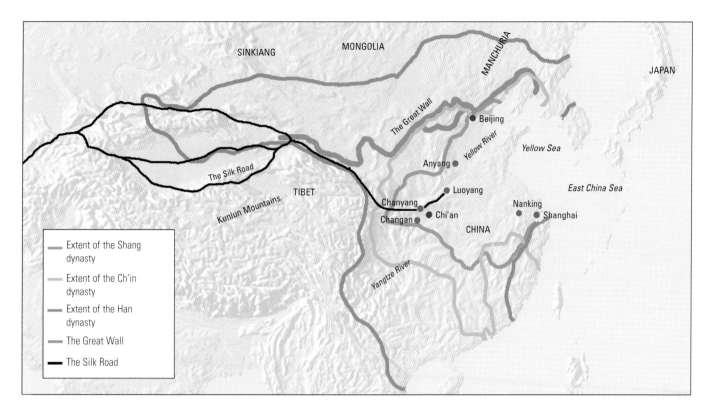

Map labels: SINKIANG, MONGOLIA, MANCHURIA, JAPAN, The Great Wall, Beijing, Yellow River, Yellow Sea, Anyang, TIBET, Luoyang, East China Sea, Chanyang, Nanking, Changan, Chi'an, Shanghai, CHINA, Kunlun Mountains, The Silk Road, Yangtze River

ABOVE: This map shows the boundaries of the Shang, Ch'in, and Han dynasties. It also shows the Silk Road and the Great Wall. The Silk Road was the route used from the second century A.D. to transport silk and other luxury goods to the West.

RIGHT: A Chinese jade necklace. Jade was considered by the Chinese to be the most valuable of all materials, and they called it the "stone of heaven." It is a very hard stone and difficult to work—despite this, jade jewelry was being made in China as early as 3000 B.C.

The first Han emperor was Liu Bang, a simple farmer's son. Liu set up regional provinces similar to those during Chou times and made peace with the tribes that had threatened to invade China from Mongolia. Liu was an uneducated man, but he did away with the harsh laws brought in by the "First Emperor." The Han dynasty went on to rule the Chinese Empire for more than 400 years, and the majority of today's Chinese population still call themselves Han.

The Han emperors believed in a strong central government. Emperor Wu Ti, who ruled from 140 to 87 B.C., was determined to improve the quality of his bureaucracy, and he introduced a civil service examination to select officials. He also founded an imperial university where students learned the Confucian classics, and eventually Confucianism became the state philosophy. Under Wu Ti's rule the arts flourished. Han poets wrote in a particularly clear style that is still famous in Chinese literature, while artists produced beautiful glazed pottery, and stone carvings. Most of these artists, teachers, philosophers, and civil servants lived in the Han capital, Changan, which, like all ancient Chinese towns, was laid out in an orderly, symmetrical style.

➤ MEDICINE ➤

By the time of the Han dynasty medical knowledge was already highly advanced. Ancient Chinese medicine was based on the idea that in a healthy person there was harmony between opposing forces, and this was the basis of the ancient technique of acupuncture, which is still in use today. Doctors found paths in the body that responded to stimulation by needles and restored the balance between the two main forces of nature, called yin and yang. Yin was the female force, associated with earth and darkness, while yang was the male force, associated with heaven and light. Acupuncturists inserted needles at points on the body to bring these two forces into line with each other and so relieve pain.

The Invention of Paper

Ancient Chinese scholars wrote on strips of bamboo (which were then tied together to form books) or on wood or cloth made from silk. In A.D. 105 this all changed when Cai Lun, an official at the court of the Han emperor Hoti, invented paper.

The first paper was made from silk rags. Then other fibrous materials were used, such as bamboo, mulberry bark, or hemp. The raw material was soaked in water to soften it. Then it was boiled and pounded until it formed a pulp. To make a sheet of paper, a fine bamboo mesh was dipped into the pulpy mixture and lifted out covered with a thin layer of fibers. The mesh was pressed to drain the water off and then left to dry on a heated wall. The finished sheet of paper was then taken off the mesh and brushed flat on a hard surface.

Later, Chinese paper-makers used rags, rope, and old fishnets for the raw material. The paper they made was used for wrapping things and for clothing, as well as for writing. The Chinese managed to keep the art of paper-making a secret from the rest of the world for hundreds of years.

In A.D. 25 the Han capital was moved to Luoyang. Around A.D. 105 the Han wish to keep order was helped by the invention of paper, which made record-keeping much easier. The Han empire continued to grow for a time, but it eventually collapsed because of rivalries between generals, imperial advisers, and officials. The dynasty ended in A.D. 220, and for the next 400 years China was again divided into warring states.

China was reunified during the short rule of the Sui dynasty, from 581 to 618. At this time the canal system that had been started hundreds of years before was rebuilt and extended. By 610 Chinese engineers had planned and built the Grand Canal to link the Huang He River with rivers farther south. This enormous canal made it easier to transport rice and other food from the south to the north of the empire, where the greater part of the population lived. The Grand Canal of the Sui dynasty was extended even farther in later years and is still in use today.

⇀ THE TANG DYNASTY ⇀

In 618 a powerful new dynasty took control of the empire. The Tang dynasty was to last for almost 300 years, and this proved to be a golden age for China. Under the Tang emperors the imperial capital at Changan grew to become the largest city in the world, with more than a million people living there. Many foreign traders and scholars visited Changan from the rest of Asia. Buddhism had been brought to China from India some centuries earlier, and now it began to flourish.

In this prosperous age wealthy people led a very comfortable life. They lived in brick and wooden houses with two or three floors and beautiful gardens and courtyards, wore luxurious silk clothes, and had plenty of leisure time. They liked to listen to music and poetry, as well as playing games such as chess and cards. They bought goods made of gold, silver, and jade, and were especially fond of bowls, cups, and other vessels made of porcelain (also called china—from chinaware—because it was developed in China). The finest porcelain was kept for the emperor's use; the second grade was for the emperor to give as gifts; and the third grade was for everyone's use.

During the Tang period, China expanded its borders and traded with other lands. Many merchants traveled to and from Central Asia, Persia, and the Mediterranean Sea along the Silk Road, a trade route that was more than 3,700 miles (6,000km) long. The goods that the Chinese merchants took eastward were silk, paper, and porcelain, while foreign merchants brought wool and precious metals to China. The markets of Changan would have always been full of activity, and this increased trade brought more wealth to the empire's craftsmen and farmers. The lot of ordinary people also improved under the Tang— it was possible for intelligent people to raise their status by passing exams and getting a position in the civil service.

But once again upheaval shook China. In 868 there was a military revolt against the Tang dynasty, and 13 years later rebels captured Changan. Provincial governors declared their independence from the central government, and in 907 the last Tang emperor was toppled.

RIGHT: Two pottery figurines of princesses from the Tang period (A.D. 618–907), showing the clothes and hairstyles fashionable at the time.

Ch'in Shihuangdi's Tomb

In March 1974 a small group of Chinese peasants went out to dig some wells in the countryside near the city of Chi'an in north-central China. Instead of water they found an extraordinary treasure trove—an underground chamber containing a terracotta army.

As Chinese archaeologists began to excavate the site—which became known as Pit 1—they counted more than 6,000 figures, all standing ready for battle. The soldiers were larger than lifesize, and every man had a different face—as if each had been modeled on a real individual. Two years later in 1976 there was further excitement when two smaller pits were discovered nearby. They revealed yet more clay warriors with weapons, horses, and chariots. What was the explanation for this great army hidden beneath the ground?

The answer to this riddle lay in a gently sloping hill some 4,600 ft (1,400m) in diameter about one mile (1.6km) west of Pit 1. This hill was actually a burial mound concealing the tomb of Cheng, king of the state of Ch'in, who as Shihuangdi ("First Emperor") ruled China from 221 to 210 B.C. Scholars believe that the clay soldiers were buried in the pits to provide magical or symbolic protection for the emperor's tomb. It may well be significant that they face east—the direction from which the emperor's enemies advanced when he was alive.

The terracotta soldiers appear to replicate Shihuangdi's actual army and so shed fascinating light on the way that an ancient Chinese military force was organized. In Pit 1, a rectangular chamber measuring about 690 by 200 ft (210 x 60m), the infantry are drawn up in 11 long rows in battle formation. Their bodies are made from

LEFT: Each soldier in the tomb has different features, making it seem as if the figures were modeled from a real-life army.

local clay. It seems that the craftsmen used molds for the basic shapes, then sculpted and painted individual details by hand. Heads and arms were made separately and attached to the bodies later.

➤ THE CHINESE ARMY ➤

The soldiers stand four abreast in nine main columns and two abreast in the two columns on either side. Although the three pits were raided for weapons by enemy soldiers in 206 B.C., considerable numbers of bronze arrowheads, razor-sharp swords, crossbow triggers, and daggers have remained to show the range of deadly arms at the disposal of the imperial army. The soldiers did not, however, have shields or, apart from officers, helmets. This suggests that the army relied on aggression and speed. In fact historical accounts contrast the mobility of Ch'in troops with the slowness of their enemies, who

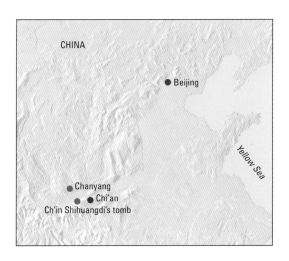

CHINA

Beijing

Yellow Sea

Chanyang
Chi'an
Ch'in Shihuangdi's tomb

LEFT: The tomb of Shihuangdi is located in north-central China near the modern-day city of Chi'an.

The Treasures of the Tomb

While the terracotta soldiers that guard Shihuangdi's tomb have now been seen by millions of tourists, the contents of the tomb itself remain hidden from the eyes of the modern world. However, despite the fact that it has yet to be excavated, it is still possible to imagine the treasures the tomb may hold thanks to the work of the ancient Chinese historian Sima Chian (about 145–90 B.C.).

Chian's description of the tomb makes it sound like a place of wonder. Beneath a ceiling painted with stars, Chian recorded, a huge, sculpted model landscape, complete with palaces and towers, was created to represent the emperor's lands. Rivers and seas were formed from flowing streams of mercury. Tests carried out by present-day scientists have indeed shown large quantities of mercury in the area of the tomb, so backing up Chian's account.

However, anyone tempted to break into the tomb to view these wonders for themselves would be well advised to read Chian's description of its defenses. It seems that the tomb is protected by an elaborate system of booby traps, with loaded crossbows, ready to fire, aimed at its entrances.

were weighed down by heavy armor. This theory is supported by the clay warriors, most of whom wear light mail coats, made of small overlapping pieces of metal. The crossbowmen and archers wear even lighter clothes, made out of cotton, which would have allowed them freedom of movement to get quickly into position and maneuver their weapons more effectively.

As well as bowmen, the pit revealed the presence of spearmen in the army, each with a menacing spear 7ft (2m) long, and six chariots drawn by four clay horses. Two of the chariots carried drums and bells, which would have been struck by officers to sound out orders to the troops above the din of battle.

In Pit 2, which lies only 65 ft (20m) north of Pit 1, a further 1,410 soldiers, horses, and chariots were uncovered. Although smaller still, Pit 3 is highly important because it contains the army's command unit. This has been deduced from the presence of 68 taller-than-average armored warriors who surround an empty chariot. Archaeologists believe this select bodyguard protected the chariot-borne commander of the army, whose statue has not survived.

➤ THE FIRST EMPEROR ➤

It was with fierce, mobile, disciplined men such as these that Cheng defeated his enemies to become the first emperor. He was born in about 258 B.C. and crowned king of Ch'in in 246, at the age of only 12. At this time the seven states of China were fighting each other for supremacy. But as the clay soldiers suggest, Cheng used his massed formations of infantry to rout the other states. Cheng managed to destroy his enemies and by 221 had unified China.

Practical and energetic, Cheng—now called Shihuangdi—quickly stamped his mark on his country and people. Ruling from his capital of Chanyang, he strengthened the role of the central government. He had a countrywide·network of canals and roads built and created the 3,000-mile-long defensive barrier that became known as the Great Wall.

However, while the emperor could be progressive in some ways, he was ruthless and intolerant in others. He was also highly superstitious and dreaded the thought of dying. His fear of death encouraged him to start the building of his tomb as soon as he became king of Ch'in.

Shihuangdi finally died of illness in 210 B.C., and only four years later the empire that he had hoped would last forever was replaced by the Han dynasty. The first emperor was duly buried in his tomb along with some of his wives and those unfortunate craftsmen who knew its secrets. More than 22 centuries after his death his tomb remains unplundered and, under the watchful eyes of the terracotta warriors, its secrets are still waiting to be brought to light.

RIGHT: Most of the vast army of terracotta soldiers guarding the tomb of Ch'in Shihuangdi was discovered in 1974 in what is called Pit 1, shown here.

Southeast Asia

The mainland of Southeast Asia is a vast region that includes the present-day countries of Cambodia, Laos, Myanmar, Thailand, Vietnam, Malaysia, and Singapore. Despite the diversity of the region, the languages and cultures of its peoples share many common features.

The history of the region has been shaped by three major river systems: the Chao Phraya, the Mekong, and the Red rivers. Each had a fertile delta and flooded every year, producing ideal conditions for growing rice—the staple food crop of ancient Southeast Asia.

The first peoples of Southeast Asia were hunter-gatherers, but by around 5000 B.C. groups of them had settled and begun farming. Historians are uncertain exactly when rice-growing spread to the area, but it is probable that it was introduced by people who had come from the basin of the Yangtze River in southern China. Whatever its origins, rice agriculture was certainly widespread by 3000 B.C.

The next important development was the discovery of how to work metal. Production of bronze objects in Southeast Asia began about 2000 B.C., while ironworking appeared later, around 500 B.C. At first historians thought metal-working technology had been introduced from China, but it is thought that the local inhabitants evolved their own methods. This indicated that more complex societies were developing.

━ THE DONG SON ━

The Dong Son culture of the Red River Valley is one of the best-known of these early societies because of the fine bronze objects found in its graves. In particular, by 500 B.C. the Dong Son were producing enormous bronze drums decorated with incised and modeled geometric shapes and scenes from daily life. One of these drums weighed 150 lb. (70kg), and to make it, over one ton of copper ore needed to be smelted. Drums have been found over a large area of Southeast Asia, which indicates that the Dong Son had a flourishing trade with other cultures. Little more is known about the Dong Son except that they were ruled by chieftains, and their society was structured into classes. In A.D. 43 the areas ruled by the Dong Son warrior-lords were incorporated into China.

Toward the end of the first millennium B.C. many Southeast Asian kingdoms were ruled by an overlord and a noble class based on hereditary

ABOVE: Rice was the staple crop of ancient Southeast Asia and was grown in flat paddy fields or on terraces like these.

power. Because these kingdoms had no fixed boundaries, and their political power depended on the ability of their ruler to tackle enemies and make alliances, they were not kingdoms or states in the usual sense. Historians sometimes use the Sanskrit word *mandala* to describe such a "state." Each society was focused on its own center and its own ruler, and its boundaries constantly expanded and contracted as different rulers made alliances. *Mandalas* grew up in river valleys and at places where trade routes crossed. Some of these

BELOW: The Moon of Pejeng, a bronze drum made by the Dong Son people around 300 B.C.

Vietnam—A Rebel Colony

A strong local culture existed in the Red River Valley before Chinese occupation in about 100 B.C. Power was held by tribal chiefs, who were large landowners with many peasant farmers under their control. When the Chinese extended their rule over this area, they divided it into military districts headed by Chinese governors. The Chinese built roads, waterways, and harbors, introduced plows and draft animals to pull them, and brought with them new tools and weapons, and advanced methods of mining. For about a century they allowed local rulers to retain some power, but in the first century A.D. local lords were replaced by Chinese officials, and China began to exploit Vietnam's vast resources of wood, precious metals, pearls, and ivory, as well as taxing the peasants.

The Han dynasty (202 B.C.–A.D. 220) tried to make the local people more Chinese by suppressing traditional customs and beliefs and imposing Confucian teachings, the Chinese language, and even Chinese clothing and hairstyles. Some of these changes were beneficial and were accepted, but others were deeply resented. The first major rebellion against the Chinese took place in A.D. 40 and was led by a noblewoman called Trung Trac, whose husband had been executed by the Chinese. She and her sister and the armed followers of local chiefs succeeded in overthrowing a number of Chinese strongholds and set up an independent kingdom. Three years later it was crushed by a large Han army, and the sisters were put to death. Vietnam was subjected to renewed attempts to make it fully Chinese. Further rebellions were quickly put down. However, in A.D. 939 Vietnamese forces led by the general Ngo Quyen finally overthrew Chinese rule and declared the country independent.

societies built settlements with walls and moats; others created trading centers, which were often linked by canals.

During the first millennium A.D. the cultures of Southeast Asia were heavily influenced by their contacts with two major powers—China and India—but in very different ways. The Chinese contact was mainly political and military. Some parts of the region, such as what is now northern Vietnam, were annexed and ruled as provinces, while other *mandalas* were made to pay tribute to the Chinese court. India, however, did not attempt to conquer or colonize Southeast Asia. Initial contacts were probably made by Indian merchants. Roman demand for Oriental products, such as gold, spices, and silks, combined with Indian advances in shipbuilding, encouraged Indian merchants to sail with the monsoon winds to the coastal areas of Southeast Asia to trade. Gradually, settlements grew up around the ports. It is likely that some traders married local women and that Indian ideas and beliefs slowly turned these ports into Hindu-Buddhist kingdoms.

BELOW: Key sites in Southeast Asia.

⬥ OC EO AND FUNAN ⬥

Excavations at Oc Eo in modern South Vietnam have revealed the remains of a large port that flourished between the first and sixth centuries A.D. and was connected by canals to a number of other settlements. Oc Eo obtained its food supplies from the rice farmers of the Mekong Delta. Its citizens made glass jewelry, tin ornaments, and pottery, and imported goods from as far away as Rome. The Chinese called the region around Oc Eo "Funan" (the Port of a Thousand Rivers), and according to their records the ports of the delta handled bronze, silver, gold, and spices.

The peoples of Southeast Asia seem to have adopted aspects of Indian and Chinese culture that were in harmony with their own societies. Sanskrit is the language of the earliest inscriptions found in the region, and it also strongly influenced many of the local languages. The Hindu and Buddhist religions, together with their familiar styles of art and architecture, were also readily accepted by most of the peoples of Southeast Asia.

Anuradhapura

Anuradhapura is a vast ancient city on the island of Sri Lanka. Its ruins—among the finest in Southeast Asia—spread out over 20 square miles (52 sq. km). For 1,400 years, from the fourth century B.C. to the 10th century A.D., Anuradhapura was the capital of the Sri Lankan kings.

Anuradhapura lies in the dry northern part of Sri Lanka. In ancient times it was hard to grow crops there, but the Sri Lankan kings solved this problem by building a network of lakes, ponds, and canals, which transformed the region into a lush paradise.

The site of Anuradhapura has been occupied since around 700 B.C., but the city still seen there today in ruins was not begun until about 350 B.C. At that time a rampart and an enormously wide moat were constructed around the existing settlement of wattle and daub houses. Over the next 200 years buildings of brick and tile gradually replaced the earlier ones. Throughout the next millennium Anuradhapura became increasingly wealthy through trade, and successive kings built beautiful palaces, temples, and monasteries there. The fame of the city spread far and wide, attracting travelers and pilgrims.

➤ THE COMING OF BUDDHISM ➤

In the third century B.C. the Sri Lankan king Devanampiyatissa was converted to Buddhism by Prince Mahinda, the son of Emperor Ashoka of India. Devanampiyatissa built several Buddhist monasteries in Anuradhapura and also monuments to house Buddhist relics that were sent by the emperor—the collar bone of the Buddha and a sapling from the tree under which he had received enlightenment.

In the second century B.C. Sri Lanka was invaded by Elara, a king from south India, who took Anuradhapura. King Dutugemunu eventually recaptured the city and defeated Elara in a duel fought on elephants. After his victory, King Dutugemunu built several monasteries as a memorial to those he had killed in battle to regain the throne.

During the first century A.D. the city's network of canals and reservoirs was extended to bring water to the surrounding region. Many large lakes and small ponds were built to store water. Anuradhapura grew prosperous by trading in rice, spices, elephants, and precious stones.

In India, Hinduism took over from Buddhism as the main religion, and Anuradhapura became an important center of the Buddhist faith. Many new monasteries were built in the city, and thousands of monks lived there.

Over the centuries a succession of great kings ruled Sri Lanka from Anuradhapura, but in 993

ABOVE: One of the carved guardstones that were placed next to steps and doorways at Anuradhapura.

King Rajaraja I of south India invaded the island and overran the capital. In 1070 Sri Lanka's independence was restored, but the capital was moved to a safer site.

⇀ THE *DAGOBAS* ⇀

The most impressive buildings of Anuradhapura are its domed monuments, called *dagobas*. They are the largest in the world and were built to house holy Buddhist relics. They were once the centerpieces of fine monasteries, and while many of the monasteries have crumbled, the *dagobas* were built of more enduring materials, and remain. They were built in the shape of bells or bubbles and have steeples on top with rock crystals at the very peak. The crystals would have glittered in the sun and been visible for miles.

Surrounding Anuradhapura are statues of the Buddha and many carved stones. Semicircular stone "doormats" called moonstones were placed at the foot of stairways. They are carved with symbols that represent the Buddhist path to enlightenment. Upright stones called guardstones also flank steps and doorways, decorated with images of dwarfs or serpent kings.

The Mahavihara, or Great Monastery, lies at the heart of the city. It is home to one of the world's most sacred Buddhist shrines, that of the Bo tree. According to Buddhist tradition, Buddha gained enlightenment while he was sitting under the Bo tree. A sapling from the tree was brought from India, and it has been cared for every day and night for over 2,000 years. Each year its many heart-shaped leaves shade more than a million pilgrims who come to pray at the Buddhist shrine.

Opposite the Bo tree are the ruins of the Brazen Palace, built by King Dutugemunu in the second century B.C. to house the monks of the

ABOVE: The Great Dagoba of Anuradhapura, which stands on a platform guarded by over 300 carved elephants.

Great Monastery. This once magnificent building had nine stories with 1,000 rooms and a roof of copper plates that gleamed in the sun. Nothing remains of it today but its 1,600 columns, some of them carved with reliefs of dwarfs.

Another of King Dutugemunu's monuments was the Mahathupa, or Great Dagoba, which stands on a platform supported by 338 carved elephants. On top of it is a crystal 2 ft (60cm) high. According to a legend, King Dutugemunu fell ill before this monument was finished. His brother had it covered with white cloths and topped with a fake bamboo steeple, so that when the king was carried to inspect it, he would believe it had been completed. He died before it was finished.

In woodlands to the north lies the Thuparama, the oldest Buddhist monument in Sri Lanka. It was built by King Devanampiyatissa around 244 B.C. to house the Buddha's collar bone. A legend relates how the sacred relic gave off fire and streams of water as it arrived on the back of an elephant, and an earthquake shook the island when it was placed inside the monument.

To the east lie the ruins of the Jetavana Monastery, founded in the fourth century A.D. Its *dagoba* is 400 ft (120m) tall—taller than most of the Egyptian pyramids. In the grounds of the monastery there is a ruined dining hall with two giant stone troughs, which could hold enough curry and rice to feed 3,000 monks.

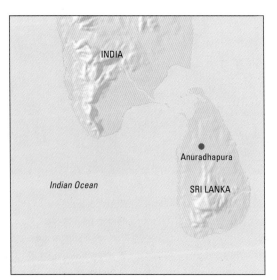

INDIA

Anuradhapura

Indian Ocean

SRI LANKA

LEFT: The ruins of the ancient city of Anuradhapura lie in the north of Sri Lanka.

India

After the Bronze Age civilization of the Indus Valley, another great civilization arose in northern India that was to become India's first empire. Just as the earlier Indus civilization was shaped by the Indus River, so the later Indian civilization was shaped by the mighty Ganges.

For more than a thousand years after the end of the Indus Valley civilization in about 2000 B.C. the ancient peoples of India lived in villages and small towns. Some significant changes occurred during this time. A new people entered India from the north, bringing with them a new way of life and a new language—Sanskrit. These Vedic tribes (which called themselves Aryans) were a cattle-herding people who gradually conquered the native inhabitants of the Ganges plain and began to settle down in small towns.

According to the *Vedas* (the sacred texts that gave these people their name) the people of the Vedic tribes divided themselves into three classes or castes (*varnas*): the priests (*brahmans*) came first, then the warriors, with the landowners and merchants third. The conquered natives became the fourth class, the peasants. The Vedic tribes constantly fought among themselves.

Gradually, cities began to form again, and by 600 B.C. there were many of them in northern India. They were often the center of small kingdoms or republics—Kausambi was a typical example. About 10,000 people lived in Kausambi, with more people in small towns and villages around the city.

The city of Kausambi was protected by a large earthen wall that surrounded it. Inside the walls the Kausambians followed many different occupations. Potters made a special pottery with a glossy black surface, using methods that are still not understood. Metalworkers made craft goods from copper or tools and weapons of iron. Jewelers turned out fancy beads made of expensive stones and shell. Merchants traded from shops or with merchants in other cities. Government officials collected taxes and supervised public works, and policemen kept order. Most villagers around Kausambi were farmers.

Around the same time as the rise of the cities some local governments started manufacturing silver coins to make buying and selling easier. These first coins were small, elongated bars with a bend at one end.

Writing probably appeared in the fifth century B.C. The oldest Indian writing known comes

LEFT: The Mauryan king Ashoka erected carved pillars in many parts of his kingdom. This one at Sarnath, with its four outward-facing lions, has become the symbol of modern India.

from Sri Lanka, the island country at the southern tip of India. Here archaeologists have found pot fragments with letters scratched on them that date to around 400 B.C. Although no examples have been found, it is likely that the

---

Southern India

Southern India was separated from the north by the Vindhya Mountains and the Narmada River, and developed in isolation from the north. Little is known about its early history. But while the civilizations of the north were based around the great rivers, the south was influenced by the sea. Ancient records tell of trade in pearls, gold, and precious stones. In the third century B.C. contacts were made with the Mauryan Empire, and the powerful southern families, or clans, gained an insight into new and different political systems. This was to have an influence on the development of the early southern states of the Cholas, Pandyas, and Cheras. But it was not until the sixth century A.D. that the first major kingdom of south India emerged.

merchants of northern India were using the same script to keep their accounts, and that these may date to an earlier time than the Sri Lankan pottery. It seems that writing began as a way of recording business details. Later, officials started to record the affairs of government, and other people wrote down the stories and myths that up to then had been memorized and passed on orally.

↠ LOCAL WARS ↞

This Vedic period seems to have been prosperous but not peaceful. The many princes fought among themselves, and the successful princes began to conquer their neighbors. Soon four kingdoms had come to dominate northern India, and they continued to struggle with one another

RIGHT: The vast Ganges River is the sacred river of India and represents fertility and rebirth. Bathing in the Ganges is regarded as a purifying ritual.

BELOW: The extent of the Mauryan Empire during the rule of King Ashoka (around 273–232 B.C.). The capital of the empire was at Pataliputra.

for supremacy. By about 330 B.C. the kingdom of Magadha had emerged victorious and had begun to try to control other parts of India.

In addition to these wars, society was undergoing great changes. Kings and governments were becoming more powerful, and some people, such as merchants, grew very wealthy even though most of the population remained village farmers. Because the religion of the *brahmans* came from simpler times, it soon became less suitable for the new ways of life in cities and large kingdoms. Several thinkers proposed new religions to meet the new needs. One was Gautama, who established a way of life known as Buddhism. Another was Mahavira, who believed in non-violence. His followers, called Jains, so dreaded killing any living thing that they covered their mouths with masks to avoid inhaling insects.

At the same time that the Ganges kingdoms were forming, the Persians were conquering almost all of the Middle East from modern Afghanistan to Egypt and northern Greece. The Persian Empire also included part of India, in an area that today belongs to northern Pakistan.

The might of the Persian Empire was toppled by the young Macedonian leader Alexander the Great. By the time he died in 323 B.C., age 33, Alexander had conquered all the Persian lands, pushed down as far as the Indus River, and had considered invading the powerful Magadha kingdom. But after a hard-won battle against Porus, king of the Punjab, near the Jhelum River, Alexander's army turned for home. After Alexander's death his generals fought for pieces of the Macedonian Empire, but none of them was able to hold on to northeast India. During this confusion the first Indian Empire took shape.

↠ THE MAURYAN EMPIRE ↞

In 320 B.C. a young Indian named Chandragupta Maurya overthrew the ruler of Magadha and placed himself on the throne. Some stories say that Chandragupta helped fight Alexander's army

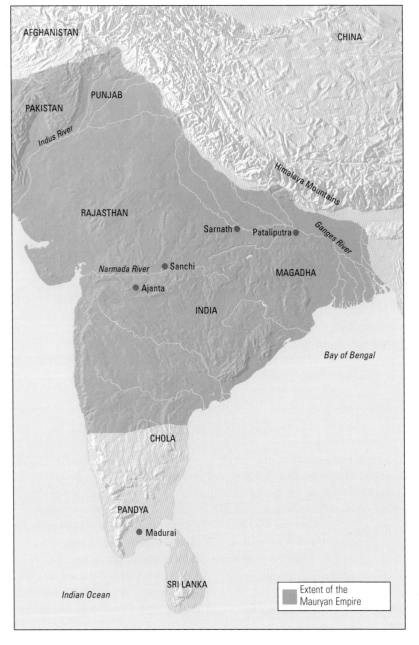

AFGHANISTAN

CHINA

PAKISTAN

PUNJAB

Indus River

RAJASTHAN

Himalaya Mountains

Sarnath

Pataliputra

Ganges River

Narmada River ● Sanchi

● Ajanta

MAGADHA

INDIA

Bay of Bengal

CHOLA

PANDYA

● Madurai

SRI LANKA

Indian Ocean

Extent of the Mauryan Empire

when the Greeks invaded India. If so, maybe that experience gave Chandragupta the ambition to rule his own empire. Within a year of Alexander's death Chandragupta had seized northwest India and Afghanistan from the Greek generals.

When Chandragupta's son, Bindusara, came to the throne, he conquered large areas south of the Ganges. By about 250 B.C., under the rule of his son, Ashoka (about 273–232 B.C.), the Mauryan Empire covered most of north India. Ashoka was a powerful and just king, and India enjoyed peace and prosperity during his reign.

The Mauryan rulers built a huge capital city at Pataliputra (modern Patna). Pataliputra stretched for about nine miles (14km) along the bank of the Ganges River and was one of the biggest cities in the ancient world. A wall made of thick timbers circled the city, and an enormous moat ran around the outside of the wall, which had 570 towers and 64 gates. Not a great deal of the city has been excavated, so little is known about it. However, one dig found the remains of a palace—an immense platform with 80 stone pillars to support a wooden roof 20 ft (6m) high.

The Mauryans built many other cities. Archaeologists have excavated several cities with square walls and straight streets. People lived in spacious houses (some of which had a second floor) with up to 15 rooms. In the middle of the house was a courtyard where the family could bake bread, cook, and do other tasks in the open air. We can imagine windows with fancy wooden shutters to keep out the strong sunlight of northern India, balconies over the courtyard, and maybe even scented trees and flowering vines.

The Mauryan kings also constructed many religious buildings outside the cities. Buddhists built several kinds of monuments. *Stupas* were domes of earth and brick built to protect a sacred

object. At first the *stupas* were simple mounds of earth, but they were soon enlarged and decorated. Later *stupas* contained relics (objects or remains) from holy people or sacred texts. There was a path around the *stupa* so that people could walk and meditate. The Buddhists also constructed large worshiping halls with a domed ceiling. Some were round, and others were long, with a rounded end for a small indoor *stupa*. Many of the early halls were cut into living rock, like the rock-cut monasteries and temples at Ajanta, the first of which were created in the second and first century B.C.

The *brahmans* also built temples, which were mainly for the god Vishnu, although we know less about them. Both *stupas* and temples were the beginnings of the Buddhist and Hindu traditions of spectacular and beautiful buildings that flourished during the centuries after the Mauryans.

Ashoka was the first Indian king to write down his orders and also to record his deeds. These writings were carved on rocks and on tall stone pillars in public places. Ashoka's pillars are among the most famous of India's ancient monuments.

The Caste System

The *varnas* (social classes) of Vedic times were the beginning of the traditional Indian caste system in which people were born into a particular group called a *jati* and had to marry someone of the same *jati*. The *varnas* were groups of *jatis*. The caste system was closely connected to religious ideas about ritual purity and pollution, and the *jatis* and *varnas* were ranked according to how pure they were. Not surprisingly, the *brahmans*, or priests, were the most pure, and the *shudra*, peasants, were the least pure. To prevent the purer people from being contaminated by less pure people, there were many rules governing proper behavior. Those outside the caste system were considered outcasts, and so "untouchable."

The Changing Role of Women

Before the rise of the Mauryan Empire, Indian society, especially in the south, was matriarchal—so this meant that women had a high status, and the family name and property often descended through the female line. However, as Vedic influence increased in the north, women there came under the control of the men in their family but they still retained some rights over property; and high-ranking women were well educated.

During the Mauryan Empire women's roles became focused on marriage and care of the family, but upper-class women were still well educated. By the Gupta period most women were completely restricted to a domestic life. And in some parts of India an upper-class widow was expected to throw herself onto the funeral pyre of her dead husband, killing herself to become a *sati* (a virtuous woman). Some high-ranking women were still educated, but only so they could talk intelligently with their husbands. The restrictive rules on women applied mostly to high-ranking families however— peasant women had to work with their families in the fields.

BELOW: The Great Stupa at Sanchi, which has four carved stone gateways. The *stupas* were great mounds of earth and brick built during the Mauryan period to hold sacred objects. This one was begun by King Ashoka but was only completed after his death.

They are made of a special sandstone that occurs near modern Banaras on the eastern Ganges plain. Each pillar is a single piece of stone about 40 ft (12m) long, polished to a fine finish. At the top is a decorated cap and a figure of an animal—often a lion, but sometimes a bull or horse. The pillar at Sarnath has four lions, a piece of art that modern India adopted as its symbol.

Most of Ashoka's pillars were erected in the Magadhan heart of the Mauryan Empire, but others were placed in central India and far to the northwest. This meant that these massive pieces of stone had to be hauled, probably using elephant power, for nearly 1,000 miles (1,600km) across plains and hills.

Later Mauryan kings faced problems that they could not solve, and the empire fell apart when the last Mauryan ruler died in 185 B.C. After this India split again into many kingdoms. Foreigners, including Greeks from Afghanistan, ruled some of the kingdoms in northeast India.

— THE KUSHANS —

Around A.D. 100 the Kushans, from Central Asia, invaded northern India, creating an empire that stretched from Central Asia down to the basin of the Ganges River and included lands along the Silk Road, the caravan route that connected China with India and Europe.

The Kushans restored much of the grandeur of the Mauryan Empire and embraced Buddhism.

Under their protection the religion spread across Asia into China, and many magnificent pieces of Buddhist sculpture were produced. Their empire lasted around three centuries before breaking up into small states again.

Despite the political breakup of the Mauryan Empire, sea trade through the Indian Ocean began to flourish. Roman ships, laden with the products of the Mediterranean civilizations, sailed into the Indian Ocean to trade for Indian goods, such as spices, ivory, and jewels. They also voyaged down the western coast of India, and some even ventured northward along the eastern coast. The kings controlling central India promoted Indian trade by sea both westward to Arabia and Africa, and eastward to Southeast Asia. Trading connections also carried colonists into Central Asia and Southeast Asia.

Although India had lost the political unity of the Mauryan Empire, people continued to prosper under the many kingdoms that followed. More spacious cities were built. Craftspeople like potters, carpenters, and metalworkers formed guilds that established work rules, inspected the quality of products, and set prices. The guilds had close links with the caste system and helped ensure that children entered their parents' occupation and stayed within their own caste. The guilds grew so rich that they could afford to donate money to build Buddhist monuments.

Buddhist worshiping halls, *stupas*, and monasteries grew bigger and more ornate as they were decorated with sculptures, stone rails, and elegant gateways. Some Buddhist caves also had very elaborate images painted on their walls. Buddhist artists in northwestern India borrowed many Greek ideas and created a graceful style of sculpture that had an enduring influence on later Indian art. However, Buddhism was not the only religion. The *brahmans* continued to offer sacrifices to their gods. The gods of Persia and Greece had worshipers in northwestern India. And, according to tradition, the apostle St. Thomas established Christian churches in the south.

⤙ THE GUPTA EMPIRE ⤚

In A.D. 320 a family of rich landowners called the Guptas gained power in Magadha. The first king, Chandragupta I, only ruled over the eastern Ganges area. However, the second king, Samudra, began to build a large empire by conquering neighboring lands. The Guptas' power reached its height during the reign of Chandragupta II (375–413), when the family controlled all of northern India from the mouth of

LEFT: This red sandstone statue of the Buddha is typical of the fine sculptures produced during the period of the Kushan Empire.

the Ganges River as far as the Indus River and into north Pakistan.

The Gupta kings favored the Hindu religion and revived many *brahman* rituals. At the same time, Hinduism itself was changing. People began to worship gods in a more personal way, instead of only sacrificing to them, and the priests became less important than before. Statues of gods became the focus of Hindu devotion. These statues were symbols of the god, and many had four or eight arms, with each hand holding an object that represented a different aspect of the god. However, Hindu temples remained fairly small, simple buildings; the impressive temples with towers and elaborate sculpture that we see today belong to a later age.

Hindu philosophers began to write down their thoughts, and several different schools of Hindu philosophy that developed at this time have continued to the present day. The philosophers and priests of the Gupta period wrote many of the most sacred books of Hinduism.

The Guptas were tolerant of other faiths, and Buddhist beliefs remained widespread. The kings and other wealthy people gave large amounts of money to both Hindu temples and Buddhist monasteries, but gradually Buddhism became less popular. Today Buddhism is not common in India, its birthplace, but is still the faith of many people in China, Japan, and Southeast Asia.

The Gupta period was the golden age of classic Indian literature and art. Mathematics and astronomy also made great advances. Scientists declared that the earth was a spinning globe and that lunar eclipses were caused by the shadow of the earth covering the moon. One Buddhist university was so famous that students came from China and Southeast Asia to take classes.

Religions of India

There have been many different religions in India since the Vedic people arrived 3,000 years ago. The ancient sacred texts, the *Vedas*, describe a religion in which the *brahmans*, or priests, performed rituals for different occasions and different gods. The *brahmans* were the keepers of tradition, and the only people who could rightfully make sacrifices and perform other activities for the gods. The role of the *brahmans* gave this religion its modern name, brahmanism.

Over time brahmanism changed slowly into Hinduism. An early kind of Hinduism formed during the centuries after the Mauryan Empire (after 200 B.C.). The many separate gods were combined into Vishnu, Shiva, and their wives. Although Hindus did not believe in one all-powerful god, they did believe in the oneness of creation.

By the time of the Guptas and their successors (A.D. 300–700) people were offering their devotion (*bhakti*) directly to Vishnu or Shiva, and the *brahmans* gradually lost their key role as priests. Moral teachings emphasized the importance of living by the rules that the *brahmans* continued to develop. Thinkers created six philosophies of

religion, the world, and life, and even today Hinduism embraces many different ways of worshiping.

Buddhism, however, is a very different kind of religion. It was founded by Siddartha Gautama (born around 563 B.C.). He came from a noble family and grew up in luxury. But he was unhappy with his privileged existence, and when he was 29 years old, he left his family to seek the meaning of life. After many years of wandering he began preaching. He became known as the Buddha (the enlightened one), and he taught that the way for people to avoid suffering was to stop wanting material things. He also offered eight rules for living that would bring peace and calm.

Buddhism was popular with the lower castes and in cities, since the new religion was a way for people to avoid the rigid control of the *brahmans*. Buddhism quickly became popular throughout India when King Ashoka converted to it. It then spread to Sri Lanka and Southeast Asia and later to China, Japan, and Korea. However, Buddhism virtually disappeared from India in the 12th century when the Muslims invaded.

This stone carving from the temple of Dasavatara dates from about A.D. 500. It shows the god Vishnu reclining on the coils of a sleeping snake, while waiting for the beginning of the next golden age. Like other Hindu gods, Vishnu is shown with several arms.

The Hindu schools mostly taught subjects that were useful for religious debates, such as grammar, composition, logic, poetry, and public speaking. The schools had plenty of money, and education was free. However, most children did not go to school but obtained a practical education from the professional guilds of their parents.

The Gupta kings believed in letting local people solve local problems, and so the chamber of commerce and the guilds were responsible for administering many of the cities. Crafts flourished, and India became famous for its fine cloth, carved ivory, pearls, and other special products. Trade with other countries became increasingly important. Cities grew prosperous, although many poor people still lived in shanty towns.

➤ INVADING HUNS ➤

This period of peace and prosperity started coming to an end when the Huns from Central Asia invaded India around A.D. 460. The Indians resisted them for a while, but trade was disrupted, reducing the revenues of the Gupta Empire. The Gupta kings grew weaker. Parts of the empire declared their independence—and then the Huns invaded again.

In the chaos that followed, city life disappeared entirely from parts of India, and the Buddhist monasteries fell on hard times. Gupta kings continued to rule for another five decades, but only over their Magadha homeland.

In about 515 most of northwest India became part of the Huns' Central Asian empire. Little is known about the rule of the Huns in India apart from the fact that they were cruel conquerors who oppressed the local peoples. Fortunately, they did not rule India for long—their empire collapsed when they were defeated by the Turks in the middle of the sixth century.

In 606, about a hundred years after the last Gupta, a brilliant, dynamic chief named Harsha became king of Kanauj, a city in the central Ganges plain. Harsha created a north Indian empire, but it was much smaller than those of the Mauryans and Guptas. He failed to defeat the now powerful kingdoms in southern India, so he contented himself with ruling the Ganges plain. Like the Guptas before him, Harsha lavished money and gifts on Hindu and Buddhist organizations. He also promoted the arts. One of the masterpieces of Sanskrit literature is a biography of Harsha, written to glorify his deeds. However, when he died after 40 years on the throne, his empire fell apart. India would have to wait nearly a thousand years for another empire to form.

Korea

According to Korean legend, the founder and first ruler of the ancient state of Korea was called Tangun. Today's Korean calendar is based on the year Tangun is supposed to have been born, which corresponds to the year 2333 B.C.

According to the ancient legend, a god named Hwanung came down to earth, where a bear and a tiger asked him to transform them into humans. Hwanung gave them bundles of garlic and a herb called mugwort, and told them to eat the herbs and stay in their cave for a hundred days. The tiger failed the test, but the bear came out of the cave as a young woman. Hwanung married her, and she gave birth to a son, Tangun. Historians believe that a real-life leader named Tangun might have ruled over an ancient tribal state called Choson from a city near Pyongyang, the capital of modern North Korea.

The ancient people of the Korean peninsula were greatly influenced by the powerful Chinese Empire. A Chinese nobleman and scholar named Kija is said to have moved to Choson in about 1028 B.C. after the Chinese Shang dynasty had been overthrown. It is known for certain that by 400 B.C. a league of tribes lived around the area of the Taedong and Liao rivers. The tribespeople knew how to use iron to make farming tools, horseriding equipment, and weapons. They lived in wooden houses and developed a method of heating their floors called *ondol*, which worked by burning fuel in an oven under the clay floor. This

ABOVE: The Pulguk-sa temple in Kyongju was built around A.D. 751. It is one of the finest examples of Buddhist architecture from the Silla kingdom.

Korea in the Stone Age

About 5,000 years ago wandering tribes from the Mongolian plains and the northern part of present-day China moved into the Korean peninsula, which stretches between the Yellow Sea and the Sea of Japan. These tribal people hunted and fished along the coasts and rivers, while some went inland and settled as farmers.

Archaeologists have found stone spears and flint arrowheads used by these Stone Age people, as well as bone hooks and stone weights used for fishing. The farming people made plows and sickles from stone. They lived in dugout shelters covered with thatched roofs, which were huddled together in small groups.

ABOVE: A silver crown made in the sixth century A.D. and worn by the Silla kings. It was originally encrusted with many semiprecious stones.

is why Koreans traditionally sleep on the floor, especially in winter, though today the *ondol* system works by pumping hot water through underfloor pipes.

The recorded history of ancient Korea begins with the capture of Choson by a general named Wiman in 194 B.C. Wiman may have come from China, and in 108 B.C. Choson was taken over by the warriors of the Han dynasty that ruled China at that time. Four Chinese colonies were established in the northern half of the peninsula. Korean tribes quickly won back three of them, but the fourth colony, called Lolang, managed to last for over 400 years. During that time Korean tribes came together to form the kingdoms of Koguryo, Paekche, and Silla.

This period in Korean history is known as the Three Kingdoms. The king of Koguryo built a strong army that defeated and drove out the Lolang Chinese from northern Korea in A.D. 313. Chinese influences remained strong in this region, however. Later, in the fourth century the Buddhist religion reached Koguryo in a form that encouraged its followers to pray for the protection and welfare of the kingdom.

The teachings of the Chinese philosopher Confucius were introduced soon afterward. Confucius had taught people to follow their true nature and develop sincerity, fearlessness, compassion, and wisdom. This philosophy was taught to the sons of the kingdom's nobles in Chinese-style schools.

The kingdom of Paekche was also heavily influenced by China and in its turn passed some of its culture on to Japan.

THE KINGDOM OF SILLA

In the kingdom of Silla the nobles who served the king were strictly divided into different social classes according to their ancestry, under a system called *kolpum* or "bone rank." The Hwabaek (state conference), composed of men of "true bone" (royal origin), made important state decisions. Sons of Silla nobles joined special training schools where they learned to be soldiers and leaders. One of the most important parts of their training was the martial arts, especially the Korean form of kickboxing called taekwondo.

During this time the three kingdoms were always looking for ways to defeat each other. Finally, King Muyol of Silla gained the support of the Chinese Tang emperor Gaozong, who sent an army to help defeat Paekche and Koguryo. Eight years later, in A.D. 676, Silla drove the Chinese back to their own empire. For the first time in its history the peninsula of Korea was united.

The kings of Silla ruled from their capital, Kyongju, which was built in the style of the Chinese capital of Changan. As the kings began to increase their power over the people, they drastically reduced the power of the Hwabaek. They also gave money and land to their nobles—to retain their support—and built luxurious palaces and tombs.

Buddhism continued to increase its influence, and this gave rise to many beautiful temples and great works of art. At the same time, a national school, named Kukhak, was founded, where the Confucian classics were taught.

Taekwondo

The most popular martial art in Korea is an ancient form of Korean fighting called taekwondo, "the art of hand and foot fighting." It combines the movements of karate and kung fu with its own spectacular jumping and spinning kicks.

During the sixth century, the young sons of nobles in the kingdom of Silla were taught to become strong warriors and members of a group called *hwarang*. They were trained as military leaders, and taekwondo was an important part of their training. When weapons became more common, young men continued to practice taekwondo, to build their physical strength, and to challenge others. So the martial arts that were once the "arts of war" became disciplined sports and a means of self-defense.

In ancient times taekwondo kickboxers wore no protection at all. Today, they wear headguards and chest protectors, and there are strict rules to avoid injury.

Korean Tombs

During the Three Kingdoms period the Korean ruling classes lived lives of great luxury. We can gain glimpses of this luxury from the impressive tombs left by the rulers. Each of the three kingdoms—Koguryo, Paekche, and Silla—had central cemeteries that contained large numbers of huge royal tombs.

The style of these tombs varied from place to place. Early Koguryo and Paekche tombs were generally made in the shape of stone pyramids. They were usually about 165 ft (50m) wide and about 16ft (5m) high. Later tombs took the form of stone chambers covered by earth mounds. Silla tombs of this period often consisted of a wooden chamber covered in earth.

Whatever form they took, these royal tombs tended to house great riches: gold and silver ornaments, ceramics, lacquerwork, and ornate weapons. The so-called Great Tomb at Hwangnamdong in Silla contained over 2,500 such items. Many of these stone tombs also featured elaborate murals on their walls. These artworks depicted scenes from both Korean myth and everyday life, and the paintings have helped historians recreate the lives that these Korean kings led.

One of the great Korean mound tombs. This style of tomb originated in China but spread throughout the Korean peninsula during the Three Kingdoms period. The tombs were repositories not only of the dead king and his family, but also of a hoard of treasure. Their walls might also be painted with scenes from the life of the dead king.

LEFT: A map of Korea showing the three ancient kingdoms of Koguryo, Silla, and Paekche.

During the eighth century the strict system of status began to break down. Perhaps the king of Silla had become too powerful in the eyes of his nobles and ordinary subjects. New, powerful families emerged in the provinces, and some constructed military fortresses, supposedly to fight Chinese pirates. Village leaders gained in power, and many farmers found themselves paying tax to both a local lord and the central government. This meant that many left their farms to become rebels or robbers.

Silla broke apart as the kingdom lost control over former Koguryo and Paekche territories to the rebels. The Koguryo military general Wang Kon united the rebels and in 918 founded a new kingdom, called Koryo, with its capital at Songak. This kingdom was to last for over 450 years.

Khmer Empire

The Mekong River rises in the mountains of Tibet and flows southeast through present-day Laos, Cambodia, and Vietnam to its delta at the South China Sea. The fertile land of its delta was the early site of a civilization that grew to control a vast area of Southeast Asia.

ABOVE: A relief from the Bayon temple at Angkor Thom showing two female dancers. Khmer temples were often decorated with elaborate wall carvings that showed scenes from the Khmer way of life.

The story of the Khmer Empire begins in the first century A.D. when a kingdom called Funan was established in the Mekong Delta. According to legend, a foreign nobleman married a local queen named Willow Leaf and set Funan on the path to success. Whatever truth lay in the legend, Funan was fortunately placed, for the Mekong region lay on a trade route between India and China. We still use the term Indochina for the region because it was influenced by both the Indian and Chinese cultures.

Funan reached the height of its power in the fourth and fifth centuries A.D. The Funan king lived in a luxurious palace, and his rich courtiers wore gold and silver jewelry and kept many slaves. At about the same time, 310 miles (500km) north of the delta region in the southern part of modern Laos, another people were settling on the banks of the Mekong. They were the Khmers, who were starting to move south along the river. By the start of the sixth century rivalries and wars among the Funan rulers had begun to weaken their kingdom. The Khmers continued south and quickly conquered Funan. The power of the Khmer king soon extended over a large area of land that stretched from the mountains in the far north to the Mekong Delta in the south.

➤ THE KHMERS ➤

Unlike the earlier Funan people, the Khmers had no great wish to trade overseas, and by the seventh century there was much less direct contact with India. The Khmers were farmers, and their main crop was rice. In their hilly northern lands they had developed techniques to divert water from main rivers into smaller, man-made canals to irrigate the land and make it fertile.

The Khmer brought these skills with them to the flat plains of present-day Cambodia. Here the Mekong floods the land during the rainy season from May to October. The Khmers made the most of the flood by storing its waters in huge reservoirs. As the years passed, they learned which were the best times to release water along man-made canals to flood the paddy fields where they grew rice. In this way they managed to harvest up to four crops of rice every year, instead of just one, and this fed their growing population.

About 125 miles (200km) north of the delta region the Mekong is fed by a smaller river that flows from a lake called Tonle Sap (which means "Great Lake"). At the height of the floods each year water flows back from the Mekong, and the lake swells to three or four times its normal size during the dry season.

King Jayavarman II made the region around the lake the center of his Khmer kingdom at the beginning of the ninth century. The land was ideal for rice-growing with Khmer irrigation; the

By the year 1200 the Khmer people had built about 600 temples around the region of Angkor. They had also built many roads to link the capital with other parts of the empire, with rest houses for travelers to shelter in at night. Hospitals were built at Angkor and along the roads. All this building work needed a great deal of manpower, and the growing population of up to a million was fed mainly on the good harvests of rice made possible by the Khmers' clever irrigation system.

There were several strict classes within Khmer society that were seen as quite separate from each other. Beneath the king was a class of learned Hindu priests and military leaders, some of whom were members of the royal family. Although only the king could order the building of a temple, these nobles sometimes founded their own shrines in villages outside the capital. Beneath the officials there were landowners and teachers who lived in provincial areas. Then came soldiers, craftsmen, and farmers. All of these people were free citizens, but beneath them all was a class of slaves.

lake was a great source of fish; there was plenty of good timber in the jungle forests; and sandstone and other rocks could be quarried in the Dangrek Mountains to the north. Jayavarman's reign, which lasted from 802 to 850, signaled the beginning of a long period of wealth and power for the Khmer Empire.

At the end of the ninth century King Yasovarman founded a new Khmer capital just to the north of the Great Lake. This was Angkor, which means "city" in the Khmer language, and it was to become the center of the expanding empire. Over the next 200 years the Khmer Empire stretched as far north as China and as far south as the Malay peninsula, covering much of the land that is now Laos, Thailand, and Vietnam, as well as Cambodia.

► WAR AND CONQUEST ◄

By the start of the 12th century Khmer civilization had reached its zenith. The most powerful of all the Khmer kings, Suryavarman II, was crowned in 1113. Suryavarman waged war against neighboring peoples, such as the Mons, Thai, Vietnamese, and Chams. These wars were not always successful, however, and in 1177 the Chams, who lived in the kingdom of Champa on the South China Sea coast, sailed ships up the Mekong and destroyed Angkor. The Khmers soon rebuilt the city and then attacked and conquered Champa 26 years later.

ABOVE: The ruins of Ta Promh, one of the 600 temples built around the Khmer capital of Angkor.

RIGHT: A carved Khmer figurine of the Buddha being watched over by the cobra god Naga.

Hindus and Buddhists

In its early days the Khmer Empire was influenced by both Hindu and Buddhist ideas brought back from India by visitors from that land. In return many Khmer pilgrims traveled to India to study sacred texts. One pilgrim who studied the Hindu religion abroad was the king Jayavarman II, who was particularly influenced by the idea of the *devaraja*, or god-king. When he returned to his kingdom, Jayavarman had himself made god-king in a special ceremony. According to this strand of Hinduism, power was bestowed on the king personally by the god Shiva.

Jayavarman's descendants continued this tradition, and this gave them enormous power over their subjects. The Khmer citizens believed that their spiritual well-being depended on the prestige of their king: by contributing to such communal projects as the great temples, they were guaranteeing themselves eternal happiness. Things changed with King Jayavarman VII, who ruled from 1181 to 1219. While he shared his predecessors' obsession with building spectacular temples, this Jayavarman was a devout Buddhist, so his Bayon temple is full of Buddhist images.

From this time Buddhism became more popular in the Khmer Empire, and followers of Theravada Buddhism began to arrive in Angkor. They did not believe in worshiping their kings as a god, and these Buddhist beliefs may have weakened the empire.

Units of about a hundred villages made up large provinces, each controlled by a governor. Ordinary people lived in wooden houses, which were built on stilts to avoid flooding. The walls were made of wood, bamboo, or palm leaves, and they had thatched roofs. Villagers cooked in clay pots over open fires and served food in ladles made from coconuts and cups made from large leaves. Nobles' homes usually had tiled roofs and were richly furnished inside. The Khmer used elephants for carrying loads and hunting.

Khmer scholars, who were highly respected, used palm leaves and animal skins to write on, but none of them have survived. All we know about Khmer daily life has been gained from inscriptions on temple walls, as well as from the writings of a 13th-century Chinese envoy.

➤ A CHINESE REPORT ➤

The envoy described a royal procession through the bustling city: the Khmer king rode on an elephant, whose tusks were sheathed in gold, and he held the precious sword of state in his hand; he was barefoot, and the soles of his feet and palms of his hands were dyed red. The Chinese visitor also recorded that the royal palace was richly decorated and had long covered corridors and verandas. When the king wished to give an audience, he would appear at a golden window.

The king had five royal wives who, like other women in Angkor, went barebreasted and barefoot. Important people were carried through the streets on litters, with attendants holding a golden parasol over them. The common people were very humble and at the sight of a foreigner would fall face down on the ground.

During the 13th and 14th centuries no important building took place at Angkor, and the Khmer Empire began to decline. There were quarrels within the royal family, and the ordinary workers may have found it difficult to keep up the vast irrigation projects. When Angkor was attacked by Thai forces from the north, vital reservoirs were damaged.

In 1431 the Thais finally captured the city after a long siege. The weakened Khmer court was forced to move south to Phnom Penh, and for this reason many people in modern Phnom Penh, now the capital of Cambodia, are descended from the ancient Khmers.

BELOW: By the end of the 11th century the Khmer Empire covered a vast area of Southeast Asia.

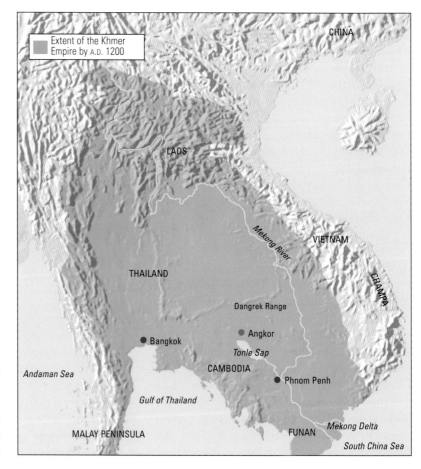

Extent of the Khmer Empire by A.D. 1200

CHINA
LAOS
Mekong River
VIETNAM
CHAMPA
THAILAND
Dangrek Range
Angkor
Bangkok
Tonle Sap
Andaman Sea
CAMBODIA
Phnom Penh
Gulf of Thailand
Mekong Delta
MALAY PENINSULA
FUNAN
South China Sea

Angkor Wat

In November 1859 a French scientist called Henri Mouhot was hacking his way through dense jungle in Cambodia, Southeast Asia, in search of new plants when he was suddenly confronted by the ruins of huge stone towers and terraces. He had stumbled on the long-abandoned ancient city of Angkor and the magnificent Hindu temple of Angkor Wat.

Mouhot was amazed by the city's size and splendor, and wrote in his diary, "What strikes the observer is the immense size and prodigious number of blocks of stone of which the buildings are made. . . . What means of transport, what a multitude of workmen, must this have required, seeing that the mountain out of which the stone was hewn is 30 miles distant!"

Angkor had been built by a succession of kings of the ancient Khmer Empire. The first city of Angkor was built in the ninth century by King Yasovarman. When Suryavarman II became king in 1113, he embarked on an ambitious building program, which included Angkor's most spectacular construction, a massive temple that took 30 years to build. This was the temple of Angkor Wat, which means "temple of the capital."

Angkor Wat was built to a set plan. The Khmer people had adopted Hinduism, a religion that came from India and which has many gods. So Khmer temples were designed to express aspects of the Hindu religion, with each part intended to symbolize the world of the Hindu gods.

The temple compound covers an area measuring 5,000 by 4,300 ft (1,500 by 1,300m) and consists of a pyramid of stone terraces in three diminishing stories. On the top terrace are five lotus-shaped towers that represent the five peaks of Mount Meru, which, according to Hindu belief, is the home of their gods. The terraces themselves represent the mountains that Hindus believe encircle the world. Around the whole of the temple is a moat 600 ft (180m) wide—this represents the ocean that lies beyond the mountains at the edge of the world.

Along the walls of the temple are more than 4,000 ft (1,212m) of relief sandstone sculptures. These sculptures show scenes from the life of Suryavarman II, the sun-king.

The five lotus-shaped towers on top of the temple of Angkor Wat represent the five peaks of Mount Meru, home of the Hindu gods. The moat around the temple represents the ocean at the edge of the world.

Some of the scenes show Suryavarman inspecting his soldiers and granting audiences. Others show warriors fighting from chariots or mounted on elephants, and fleets of ships sailing off to war. In others there are armies of monkeys and victory marches with flags and banners. Other reliefs spread over hundreds of feet of walls, galleries, and pillars show more than 200 temple dancers, naked to the waist and with strings of pearls around their necks.

The city of Angkor was built on the Cambodian floodplain, a vast area of fertile land. To make the land even better for growing crops, the Khmer built canals and irrigation channels to divert water from the rivers. They also built storage lakes to act as reservoirs from which water was fed into the waterways. It was a civil engineering program on a massive scale, designed to give the land and the Khmer people a constant supply of water. As a result the land was very productive. The main crop was rice, which was grown in flooded paddy fields.

KHMER SOCIETY

The Khmer Empire was very well organized. At the top of Khmer society was the king, who was believed to have magical powers. He rarely left his palace, and when he did so, he carried a sacred sword and rode out on an elephant with gold-encased tusks accompanied by many courtiers. The king surrounded himself with his relatives and other aristocratic families. They controlled all the land and had armies ready to keep order. Thousands of servants and slaves labored to build the defensive walls and the temples, and the waterways and reservoirs.

To maintain the king and the lavish court, villages in the countryside had to pay taxes. Because the Khmer did not use money, the people had to pay their taxes in kind, bringing their goods to the city themselves, either on their backs or by cart. The taxes were usually paid in rice, but the people might also pay in cloth they had woven or animals, rhinoceros horn, salt, honey, or wax.

Angkor reached its greatest size about 800 years ago, when its buildings occupied a vast area of about 40 sq. miles (104 sq. km). It was one of the world's largest urban centers, with a population of perhaps as many as one million people. The monumental size of Angkor Wat may have caused the downfall of the Khmer Empire. The expense and effort needed to build and maintain the temple complex was so great that Angkor's life-giving waterways were neglected. As the wealth of the city and temple declined, Angkor came under attack from its aggressive neighbors.

This was the start of Angkor's downfall. In the 1400s the Khmer abandoned the city and moved south to build a new capital. Angkor was left to the jungle. Its waterways silted up and its temples disappeared beneath the dense undergrowth.

Japan

Japan consists of a group of islands off the coast of Korea in the north Pacific Ocean. Its recorded history does not go back very far—the first history of Japan, called the *Kojiki*, or "Record of Ancient Matters," was written in A.D. 712.

LEFT: The Todai-ji temple at Nara is an imposing example of a Japanese Buddhist temple. It was built originally in the eighth century A.D. and has since been reconstructed.

The *Kojiki* was a retelling of myths and legends passed down by followers of the ancient Japanese religion of Shinto. The legends traced the origin of the Japanese islands back to divine beings and especially to the sun-goddess, Amaterasu. According to the *Kojiki*, a descendant of Amaterasu named Jimmu founded the Japanese Empire in 660 B.C. The Japanese people believed that Jimmu and all the emperors who came after him were divine beings. In later centuries when an emperor appeared outside his palace walls, people bowed low and did not dare look at his face. If the divine emperor passed in the street, people kept their windows and doors shut.

The early Japanese lived by hunting and fishing. By 200 B.C. many had become farmers, growing rice and other crops and living in villages. In later years taxes were paid in rice, measured in *koku*—the amount of rice eaten by an adult in a year.

Different regions were controlled by clans, who were constantly at war. One of the most important was the Yamato clan, descendants of Emperor Jimmu. They lived in the area around present-day Nara. The Yamato family became so powerful that they took over the other regions, and from A.D. 400 Japanese emperors ruled from the Nara area. At that time the Japanese began to build burial mounds to cover tombs, and more than 10,000 of them have been discovered in recent times. The slopes of the mounds were covered with rows of clay models of warriors, priests, dancers, houses, and other objects. The models acted as guards and servants for the dead.

⇀ CHINESE INFLUENCE ↽

In A.D. 57 Japanese messengers traveled to China, and over the next few hundred years Japan adopted many new ideas from the powerful Chinese Empire. The Japanese borrowed the Chinese system of writing, which used symbols, and adapted it to suit their own spoken language. They also learned many arts and crafts from China: how to cast bronze, make fine porcelain, and weave silk. In 552 Buddhism came to Japan from China and Korea. Buddhists believe in a duty of kindness to all living things, and they were able to live alongside those who followed the ancient Shinto beliefs and showed great respect for nature.

In 593 Japan's first empress, Suiko, gave power to her nephew, Prince Shotoku, and he

RIGHT: The Great Buddha at the Todai-ji temple. This eighth-century statue is one of ancient Japan's most famous monuments.

BELOW: Heijo (present-day Nara) became the capital of Japan in A.D. 710. It was succeeded by Heian (now Kyoto) 84 years later.

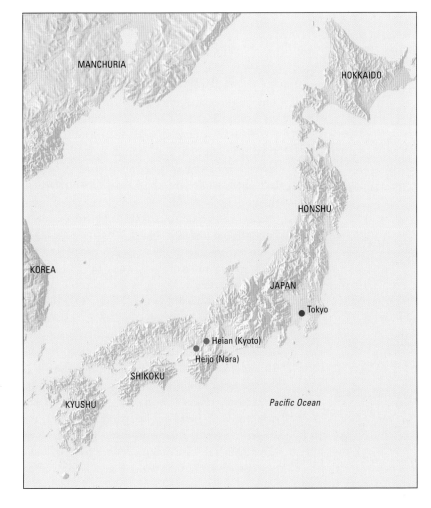

encouraged the further spread of Chinese ideas. Buddhists began to decorate their temples with flowers, and these simple and beautiful arrangements developed into a Japanese art form. This art of flower arranging, called *ikebana* (living flowers), still forms an important part of Japanese life today. The Chinese also introduced paper to Japan, and the Japanese developed new methods of folding paper into artistic shapes and objects. They called this creative art origami, which means "paper folding." At the important Shinto shrine at Ise, gods were represented by figures made out of special paper.

CAPITAL CITIES

Heijo (present-day Nara) was made the capital of Japan in 710, and the city became the center of government. It was also the focus of Japanese Buddhism—the Horyu-ji temple had been built there a century earlier. This famous temple may be the oldest wooden structure in the world still in use. Another important Buddhist temple was dedicated there in 752: the Todai-ji temple, which contains a bronze statue of the Great Buddha that is 53 ft (16m) high. By 794 many in the imperial court thought that Buddhist priests had too much influence on state affairs, and Emperor Kammu moved the capital 25 miles (40km) north to Heian (modern Kyoto).

Like Heijo before it, the city of Heian was laid out in a grid pattern—both cities were modeled on the then Chinese capital of Changan. The city of Heian soon grew to a population of 100,000, of whom about 10,000 were aristocrats or officials.

The courtiers who surrounded the emperor became known as "dwellers among the clouds." They lived in luxury, filling their days by walking in beautifully designed gardens, writing letters and poems, and attending court ceremonies. At these ceremonies noblemen wore a robe over wide pants, with a trailing panel of cloth, and a cap. Ladies of the Heian court wore a silk kimono,

The Samurai

The warrior class of samurai lived by a strict code of honor known as *bushido*, or "way of the warrior," and they showed unquestioning loyalty and obedience to their lord. The samurai prized honor above health, happiness, or even life itself.

At the beginning of a battle a samurai proudly shouted out his name and those of his ancestors, challenging opponents to come and fight. To be defeated in battle was the greatest dishonor, and rather than suffer such a disgrace a samurai would sometimes commit suicide in a ritual act called *seppuku*. The method of death was *harakiri*, or "belly cutting": the warrior would slit open his own abdomen, and then another warrior would cut off his head.

The bow and arrow formed the chief weapon of the early samurai, who usually fought on horseback. Later, they carried two large, curved swords. They wore armor made from heavy strips of leather and plates of metal tied together with silk threads.

Samurai received rigorous military training, and their methods of fighting were passed on from one generation to the next. Martial arts such as kendo began as samurai fighting skills. In kendo, contestants score points by calling out and striking a target area with a two-handed bamboo sword. Special rules and protective clothing prevent injuries, and all the strikes and defensive actions are performed in a traditional, formal way.

LEFT: A terracotta figurine of a Japanese soldier from around A.D. 500. It shows the type of armor and weapons used at this time.

with 12 layers of trailing robes in different colors. At court a formal dance called *bugaku* was performed for the emperor and his courtiers. All the dancers were men. They dressed in ceremonial costumes and often wore masks. They danced to special music, called *gagaku*, which was played on flutes, oboes, zithers, drums, and gongs. Those who spent their lives at the Heian court thought all other people were barbarians.

During this period the emperors gave away a great deal of land to noble families, and some of the clans became extremely powerful. In 858 the important Fujiwara clan took over effective control of the country, though they still respected the importance of the divine emperor. Emperors married daughters of the Fujiwara family, which gave the family even more influence.

At this time official contacts with China were broken off, and Japanese traditions flourished. New artforms were developed: noblewomen invented a beautiful form of writing, called calligraphy, using brushes and ink on fine paper. The Japanese also contributed to the history of literature. Around A.D. 1000 a lady of the court named Murasaki Shikibu wrote a long story called *The Tale of Genji*, which many historians call the world's first novel. The story's main character, Genji (the Shining Prince), is a handsome nobleman, and the tale tells of his adventures at court.

→ AGE OF THE SAMURAI ←

The Fujiwara and other great families established vast private estates. The lords who controlled the estates were called *daimyo*, and many of them were rich and powerful enough to keep and pay for their own armies. They hired warriors to protect their lands and the peasants who farmed them. The warriors were known as samurai ("those who serve") and followed a strict code of honor called *bushido*.

In the middle of the 12th century two of the most powerful families, the Taira and the Minamoto, began to fight for control of the Fujiwaras' imperial court at Heian. In 1160 the Taira clan seized power, but their supremacy lasted just 25 years. Then they, in their turn, were defeated in a sea battle off the coast by the Minamoto clan. This left the Minamoto family as the strongest in Japan. Yoritomo, the chief of the Minamoto, claimed to be the protector of the emperor and ruled in his name. In 1192 the emperor gave Yoritomo the title of shogun, or "great general." Yoritomo set up a form of military government that was to rule Japan in the name of the emperor for the next 700 years.

Chapter 4:

The Americas

The earliest known culture of the Americas was that of the Olmecs, which developed in Mesoamerica around 1200 B.C. It was followed in about 900 B.C. by the culture that developed in South America around the Andean village of Chavín de Huantar. In North America the Hohokam culture first appeared around 300 B.C. at much the same time that the Maya in Mesoamerica started building their temples. Other cultures followed, culminating in the great empires of the Aztecs in Mesoamerica and the Incas in the Andes.

BELOW: The ancient city of Teotihuacán in Mexico, thought to have been built before A.D. 100. The main avenue aligns with the point where the star Sirius rises.

Olmecs

The Olmec civilization was the earliest in Mesoamerica, emerging from farming communities in the fertile Gulf Coast region around 1200 B.C. Few Olmec settlements survive, and most of what we know about the civilization has been learned from its ceremonial centers.

There were three main ceremonial centers—San Lorenzo, La Venta, and Tres Zapotes. The first of them, San Lorenzo, was built during the 12th century B.C. It took the form of a vast man-made mound built over a natural plateau, apparently in the form of a huge bird in flight. On it were set pyramids and courtyards, sprinkled with ponds and canals to provide water for ritual bathing. Eight gigantic stone heads were also put up in the complex. They were made from basalt, which was brought from the Tuxtla Mountains 50 miles (80km) away. It is thought that the stone heads were probably portraits of the Olmec rulers. They and the elite of Olmec society lived here, directing the efforts of the vast peasant labor force who constructed the monuments.

The complex at San Lorenzo was systematically destroyed around 900 B.C. and replaced by La Venta, which lay to the northeast. La Venta was located on a large island surrounded by swamp. The huge central complex here was laid out along a straight line running approximately north to south. It included colossal heads and large sculpted slabs and statues as well as pyramids and courtyards. Mosaic floors were constructed in the courtyards and immediately covered by soil. Precious objects such as jade figurines and iron-ore mirrors were also buried as offerings. One collection of precious objects included 16 human figures carved in jade and arranged in a circle, along with six polished stone axes—the axes may have been included to represent the standing stones that featured within the complex. La Venta remained the major Olmec

ABOVE: One of the eight gigantic stone heads found at the ceremonial center of San Lorenzo. The sculptures are carved out of basalt and are 10 ft (3m) high.

LEFT: This group of 16 jade figures and six celts (stone axes) was found buried at La Venta and was intended as an offering to the gods. The figures are 7 in. (18cm) high and were arranged to depict a ritual scene.

religious center until it was destroyed and replaced by Tres Zapotes around 400 B.C., when the Olmecs were in decline.

➤ VAST TRADING NETWORK ➤

The Olmecs seem to have dominated or at least heavily influenced most of Mesoamerica for many centuries. It is not known whether they conquered and ruled the surrounding lands or whether they were just the most successful and best organized traders of the time. However, it is certain that the Olmecs built up a vast trading network. This was partly due to their need to obtain certain raw materials. Iron ore was needed to make mirrors for the elite to wear to show their status, while jade and stingray spines were used to make ceremonial needles for bloodletting rituals. The iron ore was brought from Oaxaca, the jade from Guerrero, and the stingray spines from the waters of the Gulf of Mexico.

In order to consolidate this large trading network, the Olmecs established a system of outposts. One example was Teopantecuanitlan in Guerrero. Here archaeologists have found Olmec-style monumental buildings and typical Olmec carvings. Such outposts controlled the supply of raw materials from their sources, and Olmec people based in these outposts ensured the smooth running of the trade networks. The Olmecs also controlled or influenced other key centers, such as Tlatilco in the Valley of Mexico and Chiapa de Corzo in the Chiapas region.

Olmec-style architecture and distinctive Olmec objects such as pottery and figurines appear in such sites alongside local structures and objects. Olmec pottery and carvings were also placed as offerings in local graves. Olmec pottery featured many recurrent motifs—one mythical animal that crops up frequently in Olmec art is the so-called "were-jaguar," a creature that was half-human and half-jaguar. Images of this creature also often occur in later Mayan artworks.

Apart from writing, almost every aspect of later Mesoamerican culture was first seen among the Olmecs and the groups that they dominated. Olmec ceremonial centers like La Venta and San Lorenzo were made up of pyramids laid out around courtyards (or plazas). These sites were the forerunners of the ceremonial complexes of the Maya, Toltecs, and Aztecs, whose temples were generally constructed on the top of various forms of pyramids.

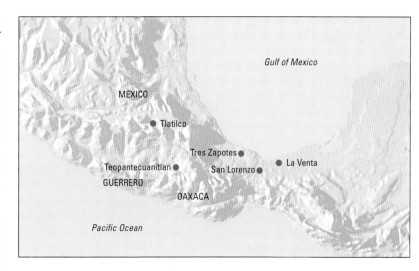

ABOVE: The main Olmec centers lay in the north near the Gulf of Mexico, but the Olmecs' trading empire stretched south to Guerrero and Oaxaca.

Olmec Religion

The religious practices of the Olmecs contained many elements that were also found in later Mesoamerican civilizations. For example, human sacrifice played an important part in Olmec religion, as it did in that of the later Aztecs. Many Olmec relief carvings show naked captives being sacrificed, while at San Lorenzo charred and butchered human bones suggest that the Olmecs may also have practiced cannibalism. Among the ritual offerings and other finds at Olmec sites were many stingray spines and needles made of highly prized jade. They were used by the Olmec people to make personal sacrifices of their own blood, a practice that occurred in other Mesoamerican civilizations.

The Olmecs also shared with later Mesoamericans a strong interest in astronomy—Olmec ceremonial centers were laid out in alignment with the constellations and other features of the heavens.

An Olmec altar found at La Venta on which ritual sacrifices would have been performed. The seated figure wears a jaguar mask—the jaguar was a motif that appeared frequently in Olmec art.

Chavín Culture

Chavín de Huantar was a village in the Andes Mountains that flourished between 900 and 200 B.C. At its height, between 2,000 and 3,000 people lived in Chavín de Huantar and it became the most important civilization to exist in South America up to that time.

Chavín de Huantar was situated in a valley high up in the mountains—over 10,000 ft (3,100m) above sea level. Even at that high altitude the land around the village was good for growing crops and herding animals. The Chavín people grew the native highland crops of the Andes, including tubers such as the potato and grains such as quinoa. They grazed animals on the surrounding mountain highlands.

Herds of South American camelids—llamas and alpacas—provided meat for the Chavín peoples, and the llama was also important for trade. Although no animal native to the Americas can be ridden, the llama was used as a pack animal, and large caravans of llamas probably brought many desired products to Chavín that were unavailable locally, such as fruits, chili, cocoa, and fish.

Chavín de Huantar became a vital center for trade, which helped to make the village powerful. It was located at a river crossing between the Huachesa and Mosna rivers along an important set of trade routes through the steep and rough terrain of highland Peru. This location probably allowed the Chavín people to carry out and control trade in the many items that came from the different zones of the Andean region—the deserts along the coast, the steep mountains of the Andes, and the jungles in the east.

Many of the food crops, minerals, and raw materials that are found in each specific area cannot be found anywhere else. Because of their location, the Chavín people were able to accumulate a number of exotic items from other areas, such as sea shells and pottery.

ABOVE: This rectangular sunken court lay at the center of the temple complex at Chavín de Huantar. The temple attracted many pilgrims from the surrounding towns and villages.

Chavín Art

Chavín art was greatly influenced by the surrounding environment, in particular the lush jungles lying to the east of the mountains. Jungle animals are a common motif, with jaguars, snakes, and caimans (a type of alligator) appearing frequently. These animals were often combined with human figures to create strange creatures that were half-human and half-animal.

One of the most famous sculptures at Chavín is the Lanzón monolith (or standing stone). Made out of white granite and built into the floor and ceiling of the temple at Chavín de Huantar, it depicts a wild creature with a cat's mouth with fangs, massive eyes, a head full of snakes, and human hands and feet. Some believe that the figure linked the heavens with the underworld.

⤙ THE CHAVIN TEMPLE ⤚

Around 900 B.C. the Chavín people began to build a stone temple at Chavín de Huantar. It was to become the most important temple pyramid in the Andean area. The fearsome-looking gods of Chavín were to be worshiped for hundreds of miles, from coastal villages to towns high up in the Andes Mountains, and pilgrims came from miles around to worship the gods at the temple. These Chavín gods, along with many other aspects of the Chavín culture, were to have a lasting influence on the art and religion of the surrounding region.

When the site of Chavín de Huantar was excavated, archaeologists found the remains of a monumental temple enclosing a rectangular court. They also discovered an extraordinary network of underground passages and rooms, known as galleries, underneath the temple.

The architecture of the temple was elaborate. It was built of large cut stone blocks and pieces of shaped rock of different sizes, all carefully fitted together. The walls were decorated with many large carved stone heads that were built right into the walls.

There were also spectacular stone friezes and carvings that showed a wide range of supernatural figures. These figures were a mixture of animal and human—they had animal features such as fangs and claws but stood upright like men. Some of the creatures were birdlike or catlike. These carvings suggest that the Chavín people worshiped a group of strange and brutal gods.

War—at least ritual warfare—was extremely important to the Chavín people. Some of the carved and painted figures found in the temple show weapons, including spears, shields, knives, and clubs. A few of the carvings indicate that some people—possibly those defeated in a war—suffered a gruesome fate. These carvings show creatures carrying decapitated human heads.

By around 200 B.C. the importance of Chavín had begun to diminish, and no more buildings were built. The influence of the Chavín culture, however, lived on. New civilizations, including those of the Nazca and Moche, were to produce decorative motifs, pottery, textiles, and metalwork that had clear similarities to Chavín. These and later Andean civilizations also developed the extensive trade networks that had been the foundation of the prosperity of Chavín de Huantar and the Chavín culture.

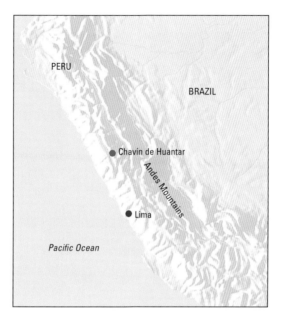

LEFT: A map showing the site of Chavín de Huantar high up in the Andes Mountains, where it was well placed to become an important center for trade.

BELOW: The Lanzón monolith in one of the underground galleries beneath the temple.

Southwestern Peoples of North America

The Southwest region of North America includes the present-day states of Arizona, New Mexico, southern Utah, and Colorado. Between the third century B.C. and the 15th century A.D. three distinct farming cultures developed here—the Hohokam, the Mogollon, and the Anasazi.

LEFT: The ruins of Cliff Palace, Mesa Verde, a spectacular town built into the cliffs of Colorado by the Anasazi people. Cliff Palace had around 220 rooms and 23 ceremonial rooms (kivas). It was one of the most complex structures in the Southwest.

Although much of the Southwest region is desert, there is enough rain to grow crops in some parts, and the Hohokam, Mogollon, and Anasazi cultures were all based on corn.

All three cultures prospered and expanded between A.D. 700 and 1200, which coincided with a period of good rainfall over the entire region. By the 14th century, however, most of their towns and villages had been abandoned. The most likely explanation for this is a combination of prolonged drought, crop failure, and fighting over scarce resources. Although these prehistoric cultures faded away, their descendants—the Pueblo peoples—continue to live in the region today, numbering around 50,000.

➤ THE HOHOKAM ➤

Hohokam culture first appeared in the Salt and Gila river valleys of southern Arizona around 300 B.C. The early Hohokam (300 B.C.–A.D. 500) lived in wattle-and-daub houses made of interwoven sticks covered in mud, set in shallow pits dug in the sand to keep them cool. Because the desert was very dry, they dug channels from the rivers to irrigate their crops. Extra food came from hunting and gathering.

Between A.D. 500 and 1100 the Hohokam expanded southward and established links with Mexico. Evidence for this comes from the discovery of ball courts (similar to those used by the Maya) and rare objects like mirrors made of pyrite (a shiny brass-colored mineral) and shells. They began to grow cotton as well as corn, and a large network of irrigation canals was constructed, which required extensive cooperation among villages. This allowed the Hohokam to grow two crops a year—one in spring and one in summer—and support a growing population.

Between A.D. 1100 and 1400 the Hohokam began to incorporate aspects of Anasazi style into their architecture. They built compact settlements surrounded by thick adobe walls made of stone, clay, and sand. Within these compounds they built large multistoried community houses. Snaketown, the main Hohokam settlement, covered more than 300 acres (120ha) and had over 100 kivas—underground rooms used for meetings and religious ceremonies. When the valleys were eventually abandoned, the Hohokam left behind a complex network of irrigation canals that are a testament to their engineering skill; there were over 150 miles (240km) of canals in the Salt River Valley alone.

➤ THE MOGOLLON ➤

Mogollon culture emerged in the Mogollon Mountains of Arizona and New Mexico (east of the Hohokam) around 200 B.C. Like the Hohokam, the Mogollon people lived in small villages of sunken pit houses. But instead of irrigating the land with canals, they relied on rainfall and river floods to water their crops. They were the first people to make pottery in the region, probably having imported the craft from Mexico. The first pots they made were plain brown, but later they started to add simple decoration.

After A.D. 700 the Mogollon started building rectangular pit houses out of stone with separate underground rooms. Around A.D. 1050 Anasazi people spread into the region and began to live peacefully alongside the Mogollon. The Mogollon abandoned their pit houses in favor of the newcomers' multistoried apartments.

Based in the "Four Corners" area where the modern boundaries of Arizona, New Mexico, Colorado, and Utah meet, the Anasazi—sometimes called the "Ancient Ones"—were the most

advanced of the three prehistoric Southwestern cultures. Archaeologists divide Anasazi culture into several periods from A.D. 100 to the present.

➤ THE ANASAZI ➤

Their history begins with the Basketmaker people (A.D. 100–500) of the Rio Grande Valley, who lived in caves and rough adobe shelters. They are named after their fine yucca-leaf baskets, which were woven so tightly they could hold water. Pumpkins and corn supplemented food from hunting (deer and rabbits) and gathering. Food was stored in underground pits.

Around A.D. 600 the Basketmakers became more settled and began growing beans and

ABOVE: Examples of Anasazi pottery found at Cliff Palace, Mesa Verde. The black-and-white geometric patterns are typical Anasazi designs.

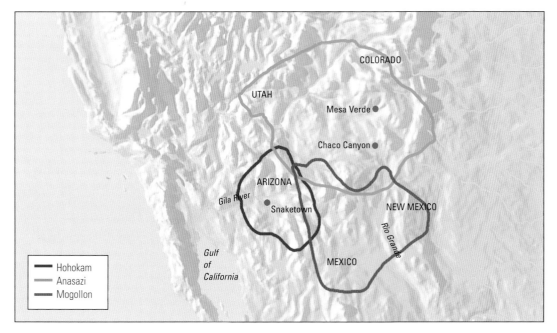

LEFT: The cultures of the Hohokam, Mogollon, and Anasazi existed at the same time in regions that overlapped each other slightly.

keeping turkeys. The underground storage pits evolved into sunken houses with connecting rooms and ceremonial chambers.

The change from the Basketmaker to the Pueblo culture occurred around A.D. 700. At this time stone buildings began to replace the adobe shelters, and houses were built above ground and were larger. Farming flourished, and the growing population soon expanded outward into Utah, Colorado, and New Mexico. These Pueblo people lived in small villages of around 100 people. They began to trade with Mexico, exchanging turquoise for shells, macaw (parrot) feathers, and copper bells.

➤ CHACO CANYON ➤

The Classic Pueblo period (A.D. 1050–1300) saw both the height of Anasazi culture and its decline. The northern sites were abandoned, leading to the concentration of a large population of up to 30,000 in vast multistoried pueblos (towns). They included Pueblo Bonito in Chaco Canyon, which had a population of 1,200, and Cliff Palace at Mesa Verde.

The pueblos of Chaco Canyon ruled over 150 Anasazi villages, which formed a network stretching some 250 miles (400km) from north to south. This network was important because Chaco Canyon could only grow enough food for half its population, so a large amount of food had to be imported. Pueblo Bonito (A.D. 900–1200) was the largest of the Chaco pueblos and was probably the administrative and religious center. Designed in a characteristic "D" shape with its straight back to the canyon wall, it had three stories of terraces containing nearly 800 interconnecting rooms and 40 kivas arranged in a semicircle around a large central plaza. The roof of each tier provided an open terrace for cooking and craftwork. There were no outer doors, so access to the rooms was by ladder through the roof.

One of the most puzzling features of the Chaco area is its network of "roads." They are up to 30 ft (9m) wide, follow a straight course, extend for over 200 miles (320km), and link the outlying pueblos to Pueblo Bonito. Without wheeled vehicles or pack animals there seems to be no good reason for their construction, which would have required a large amount of labor and organization.

When Chaco Canyon culture collapsed in 1150, the Anasazi moved on, regrouping into smaller pueblos. Around 1250 land-level sites were abandoned in favor of heavily protected clifftop sites, as widespread crop failure led to

Mimbres Pottery

The finest pottery in the Southwest was made by the Mimbres—Mogollon people who lived by the Mimbres and Gila rivers—from about A.D. 1000 to 1130. Their shallow bowls have distinctive black-white or orange-red geometric and figurative designs, showing people, animals, and mythical beings. They are beautifully painted and reveal a sense of pattern and movement unequaled in any other pottery of the period. The meaning of many of the designs is not known, but some of the fish designs represent species from the Gulf of California, which was hundreds of miles away.

Many of the bowls found in burial tombs have holes. Archaeologists believe that before the bowls were placed in the grave, they were ritually "killed" by having a hole punched through the bottom. This released the soul of the bowl's maker.

A Mimbres bowl showing a woman giving birth. The bowl has been ritually "killed."

fighting over the remaining resources. At the same time, many Anasazi moved eastward toward the Rocky Mountains. They may have been lured by a new religion—the Kachina religion, still practiced in today's pueblos, which involves elaborate ritual dances. The religion's large-scale ceremonies provided a focus for community life and may have taught the Anasazi descendants to live together again in large pueblos.

LEFT: Chaco Canyon in New Mexico, where some of the largest Anasazi pueblos are found. The remains of the underground ceremonial rooms of the Chetro Ketl pueblo can be seen in the foreground.

Hopewell

When European explorers set out across North America during the 16th and 17th centuries, they found no traces of prehistoric culture outside Mexico. But when they reached the Ohio and Mississippi valleys in the 18th century they found signs of an ancient American culture.

These signs came in the form of thousands of earth mounds dotted across the Woodlands region of southeastern North America. These earthworks, which varied in size, shape, and function, were built over a period of 2,500 years by three different peoples—the Adena, the Hopewell, and the Mississippians.

Even when faced with this evidence, many settlers still considered these structures beyond the abilities of Native Americans. So they invented a mythical, long-vanished race of people called Mound Builders. Eventually, however, historians realized that the Mound Builders could not have come from somewhere else—the earth mounds had indeed been built by prehistoric Native Americans.

The Hopewell people were based around the Mississippi basin (in present-day Illinois, Indiana, and Ohio) from about 100 B.C. onward. They succeeded the Adena people (see box on page 167) and did everything on a far grander scale. The Hopewell people adopted the agricultural techniques and burial practices of their Adena predecessors before replacing them and spreading out in all directions across the eastern half of North America.

To the east the Hopewell culture stretched as far as the Appalachian Mountains; to the south it reached the Gulf of Mexico; to the west it covered the eastern side of the Great Plains (from Oklahoma to North Dakota); and to the north it swept around the top of the Great Lakes.

The Hopewell combined the cultivation of corn and other crops (like squash and sunflowers) with the hunting and gathering of their ancestors. The cultivation of corn allowed for a settled village life and a regular food supply, which led in turn to a gradual increase in population. Food surpluses were stored for hard times ahead and were controlled by the group's leaders. But the storage of wealth also created social divisions, allowing the leaders to become richer and display their differences in the way in which they were buried and the quality of their grave goods.

By A.D. 500 the Hopewell culture was in decline—nobody knows why. Possibly a change

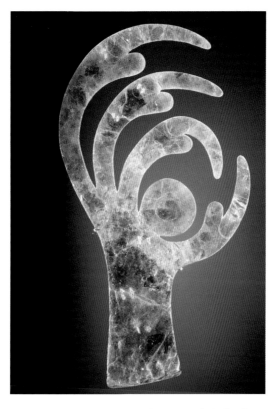

LEFT: A piece of mica fashioned into the shape of a bird's foot. Mined in the Appalachian Mountains, mica was a popular choice of material for Hopewell jewelry.

in climate (which might have spoiled the harvests), or overpopulation, or a combination of the two led to a breakdown in the trading networks and the breaking up of the settlements.

➤ BURIAL MOUNDS ➤

Much of what we know about Hopewell life comes from our study of their burial mounds and earthworks. The graves underneath these mounds were of two types: simple clay basins containing the cremated remains of ordinary people, and more elaborate log tombs built for the wealthy, who were often buried along with their servants and rich funeral offerings. The tombs were then burned and covered by earth or stones. Burial mounds were often built on top of each other, sometimes to a height of 140 ft (40m).

The densest collection of Hopewell sites is in the Ohio Valley. These complexes are much larger than those of the Adena, and the surrounding embankments often extend for many miles in geometric patterns. While some of the

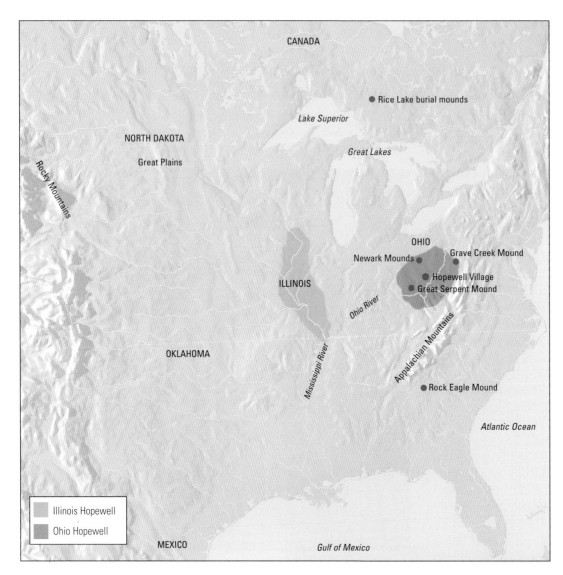

embankments may have been used for defense, historians believe that most were used for ceremonial purposes. The shapes were precisely built and connected to each other by straight causeways thousands of feet long.

While the farmers lived outside these complexes in mud and thatch huts, the clan leaders and priests would have had their houses inside. The sheer size of these burial complexes suggests the existence of a powerful and extremely well-organized ruling class with the authority to mobilize the large numbers of people needed for their construction.

Some earthworks took the form of huge effigies, mainly in the shape of winged humans, birds, reptiles, and other animals. They are unique to the American continent and can only be properly seen from the air. It is most likely that the form of these effigy mounds was intended to represent the local deities. Among the most famous are the Rock Eagle Mound in Georgia,

which was built from tons of broken boulders and depicts a huge bird with a wingspan of around 120 ft (37m), and the Great Serpent Mound in Brush Creek, Ohio.

➤ GRAVE GOODS AND TRADE ➤

Excavations in the Hopewell burial mounds have revealed a dazzling selection of beautifully crafted objects made from rare materials. These grave goods provide evidence of a system of trading links that stretched across a huge area.

Copper, which was used to make ornaments and axes, was obtained from around Lake Superior; the volcanic rock obsidian, which was used for knives and spearheads, came from the Rocky Mountains, over 1,000 miles (1,600km) away to the west; conch shells and shark teeth came from the Gulf of Mexico; and clay came from the Appalachian Mountains to the east. Also from the Appalachian Mountains came the sought-after mineral mica, which could be split into thin transparent sheets and cut into shapes. Minnesota stone came from the northwest; and silver and gold from Canada.

These raw materials were turned into jewelry, mica and copper cut-outs, carved pipes, musical instruments, figurines, and carved shell necklaces. These objects were buried with the dead person to reflect their status, while practical items such as axes, conch drinking horns and pearls (for money) helped them in the next life.

Merchants from Ohio who traveled to distant places to obtain these raw materials would prob-ably have exchanged copper, which was available locally, or finished manufactured goods for them. The rapid spread of Hopewell culture has led some historians to compare it to a religious cult rather than a single culture. According to this theory, as more groups came to trade with the Hopewell, they adopted the Hopewell cult of the dead and started to build their own burial mounds, many of which are found along the natural trading routes of the Ohio, Illinois, and Mississippi rivers.

BELOW: Examples of Hopewell jewelry. The necklace is made from pearl beads, while the earrings and pendants are of beaten copper.

From the objects found in the burial mounds we know that the Hopewell wore jewelry, along with ornaments that were sewn into clothing or inserted into headdresses. They also smoked tobacco in stone pipes. With their delicate animal and human carvings, these pipes represent some of the finest examples of ancient art found on the North American continent.

The figures on these pipes and the clay figurines made by the Hopewell give us important clues to what the Hopewell people might have looked like. They show barebreasted women wearing belted skirts and men wearing "G-strings," made of thin pieces of material worn between the legs and tied at the waist, and breast ornaments made of shell. The men have the crowns of their heads shaved.

The Great Serpent Mound

Probably the most famous Native American earthwork is the Great Serpent Mound in Ohio. This remarkable construction is about 2,000 years old, and it dominates a narrow strip of land in a fork of Brush Creek near Cincinnati. Archaeologists are still not sure whether this mound was built by the Adena or Hopewell people.

Made from yellow clay on a base of stones, the grassy mound takes the form of a slithering snake that curls along a natural ridge. At one end, its tail is tightly coiled, while at the other, its jaws appear to be closing around an egg. It is 1,330 ft (405m) long, 20 ft (7m) wide, and about 3 ft (1m) high.

With steep wooded slopes on one side and a sheer cliff on the other, the site dominates the surrounding landscape. It was carefully chosen to inspire awe in those who saw it. But just why it was built remains a mystery. In the mythology of some Native American tribes a divinity known as Horned Serpent, or Water Monster, is regarded as the guardian of all sources of life, especially water. The "egg" in the jaws of the serpent originally contained a small circle of burned stones. A fire lit there could have been seen for miles, showing perhaps that the serpent spirit of the waters was alive and watchful. Another possibility is that the mound was built to celebrate a solar eclipse, with the egg (about to be swallowed) representing the sun.

Best seen from the air, the Great Serpent Mound is the most spectacular earthwork in North America. To preserve the mound, it is now surrounded by a walkway built for tourists.

Moche

The Moche (or Mochica) civilization was one of the great ancient Andean civilizations. It originated in the Moche and Chicama valleys of what is now Peru and flourished along the northern coast of the country between the first and eighth centuries A.D.

LEFT: The Moche were highly skilled metalworkers and left behind many stunning examples of their art. This sculpture of a human head is made out of gold—a Moche specialty—and is decorated with turquoise.

Although the Moche left no written records, a vivid picture of their culture can be gleaned from their pottery decorations and murals. Vast pyramids, burial tombs, and depictions of human sacrifice also tell us much about the Moche and their well-organized, class-based society.

Moche society was ruled by an elite class of priests and warriors, supported by the labor of craftworkers and farmers. The largest city of the civilization was itself called Moche. From here the warlike Moche people conquered the weaker groups living in the surrounding lands, establishing Peru's first major kingdom. At the height of the civilization (between A.D. 200 and 600) Moche settlements extended over 215 miles (350km) along the hot, dry coast.

The Moche grew corn, beans, and other crops. To water their fields, the Moche built earthen aqueducts to channel streams down from the surrounding Andes Mountains into an extensive system of irrigation canals. Some of these aqueducts are still in use today. Where steep slopes made farming difficult, the Moche built terraces to increase the amount of fertile land available. These intensive farming methods allowed the Moche to expand their territory along the coast. Because there was no central government, each river valley formed a self-contained, self-governing social unit.

The Moche built cities containing large plazas (squares) and flat-topped pyramids. The pyramid walls were made of adobe bricks and built up in layers. To make the bricks, soil and water were mixed with straw and trodden into a mulch. The mulch was molded in wooden frames and baked in the sun. The dried bricks were then carried to the site and laid by specialist bricklayers.

THE TEMPLE OF THE SUN

The most impressive temples in Moche are the Temple of the Sun (Huaca del Sol) and the Temple of the Moon (Huaca de la Luna). The Temple of the Sun was the largest adobe structure in pre-Hispanic America. Built from over 140 million adobe bricks, the pyramid now measures around 1,100 by 525 ft (340 by 160m) around the base and over 130 ft (40m) high. Originally it was much larger, but the sides have been damaged by the weather and by treasure hunters. Facing the pyramid, at the foot of a large white hill, stands the smaller Temple of the Moon on whose platform courts and rooms once stood. Smaller pyramids were built all along the north coast.

The Moche decorated important public buildings such as the Temple of the Moon with spectacular painted murals. Many murals celebrated their success in war, showing gruesome scenes of naked prisoners being captured and beheaded. Scenes on Moche pots also show prisoners being sacrificed to fanged gods seated on top of the pyramids.

The large plaza between the two temples in Moche was used as a cemetery, and the tombs found here and elsewhere provide strong evidence of a class-based society. One of the most spectacular archaeological finds of recent years was the Lords of Sipán tomb in the Lambayeque region of northern Peru. In 1987 archaeologists excavated the multilayered grave dating from around A.D. 300 and found a hoard of grave goods that demonstrated the enormous wealth of the Moche ruling class.

Two of the tombs belonged to local rulers. All the corpses were laid to rest on their backs, and were dressed in elaborate tunics and adorned with gold and silver jewelry that included ear plugs, nose ornaments, bracelets, necklaces, and breastplates. Specially sacrificed male and female servants were also found.

➤ MOCHE POTTERY ➤

Ceramic pots and bottles were also buried in Moche graves, giving us vital clues to the Moche way of life. Mass-produced in molds, the red-and-

LEFT: The huge Temple of the Sun at Moche is one of the largest ancient monuments found in the Americas.

Nazca Lines

The Nazca lines cover over 200 square miles (520 sq. km) of desert in southern Peru. It is thought that they were probably made by the Nazca Indians. The Nazca were contemporaries of the Moche and lived to the south of them between about 350 B.C. and A.D. 600. The lines were made by removing the dark surface stones to expose the lighter rock below and they portray well over 100 designs, including huge figures and geometric forms. These include a hummingbird (a common design on Nazca pottery), a monkey with a spiraling tail, and a killer whale, and the designs vary from 1,650 ft to five miles (500m to 8km) in length. Many of the lines cross to form squares and triangles. They owe their preservation to a very dry climate.

The designs can only be seen properly from the air, leading to much speculation as to how and why they were made. One of the mysteries is how the builders kept the lines so straight considering the distances involved. The most widely accepted explanation for their creation is that they represent the largest astronomy book in the world. Many of the figures predict the positions of stars and constellations at different times of the year—for instance, the beak of the hummingbird aligns with the position of sunrise at the summer solstice. This may have helped farmers decide the best time for sowing and harvesting their crops.

This hummingbird is one of the most spectacular of the Nazca line drawings.

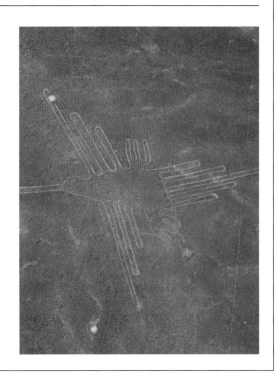

LEFT: This elaborate ceramic figure, typical of the Moche culture, shows a creature that is part-deer and part-human. It may represent a shaman undergoing a transformation process.

and weaving The extraordinarily graphic nature of these designs makes these objects remarkable not only as art, but also as a record of the culture from which they came.

The collapse of this great Moche culture was probably caused by a series of natural disasters. A prolonged drought in the sixth century was followed 100 years later by a great earthquake, extensive flooding, and sandstorms, which ruined the once-fertile fields. As if this was not enough, the Moche were finally attacked and conquered by the aggressive, neighboring Huari.

white pots took the form of human heads, human and demonic figures, animals, fish, birds, plants, religious scenes, and buildings. Famous for its realistic detail, Moche pottery includes some of the finest sculpture in the history of ceramics. Many of the pots are painted with vivid scenes from ceremonial and everyday life, showing warriors with prisoners, human sacrifice, hunting,

RIGHT: By A.D. 600 the Moche had built up an empire that stretched 215 miles (350km) along the coast of Peru.

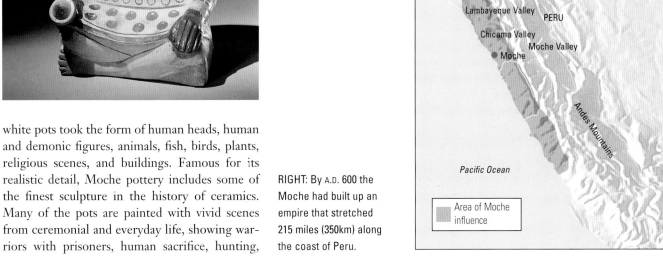

Maya

Centuries before the time of the Aztecs and the Incas, a Native American people called the Maya established a civilization in southern Mexico and Central America. This civilization flourished for over 600 years, and left a legacy of magnificent buildings and sculptures.

The Maya were descended from the original hunter-gatherer inhabitants of the region, who settled on the Yucatán Peninsula of Mexico and part of present-day Guatemala about 3,000 years ago. The settlers lived in small villages made up of simple thatched houses, and they grew crops of corn, beans, and squash.

Around 400 B.C. these Mayan settlers started to build temples where they could worship their many gods. As their population grew, separate city-states developed, each with its own godlike king. There was no single capital city and no overall king or central administration, but the Mayan civilization flourished and became very powerful between A.D. 250 and 900, which historians call its classic period. During those years each Mayan king had complete control over the villages and farmlands surrounding his city. When a king died, power passed to his eldest son.

Most Mayan people were farmers. They lived in small villages in the hot, humid rainforest, cutting down and burning trees and bushes to make clearings. The ashes that were left behind were good for the soil, and this kind of farming—called slash-and-burn—is still used in Central America today. The farmers planted their crops in May, ready for the rainy season. Sometimes, in low-lying swampy areas Mayan farmers built up raised plots of land that were surrounded by water channels that could be used to irrigate the soil. This system of agriculture was the forerunner of the *chinampas* method that was used more extensively by the later Aztec civilization.

→ FOOD AND DRINK →

Corn was the most important crop, and it formed the main part of most meals. The Maya used corn to make a kind of porridge spiced with chili

ABOVE: The imposing ruins of the pyramid, palace, watchtower, and temples of the Mayan city of Palenque.

peppers. They also ate tamales—corn husks filled with a mixture of meat and corn dough—and the flat corn pancakes that the Spanish later called tortillas. The Maya used corn to make an alcoholic drink called *balche*, which was sweetened with honey and spiced with tree bark.

The Maya had no horses or cattle to carry heavy loads, so farmers had a lot of hard work to do. Many farmers had their own plot of land, and in each village there was communal land that everyone helped look after. They dug canals to bring water from nearby rivers and swamps to help their crops grow. On sloping land they built flat terraces for their fields, surrounded by walls. The men and older sons did most of the farmwork, clearing the fields, planting seeds, and harvesting the crops. They also went hunting and fishing, using bows and arrows to kill deer, rabbits, and large rodents called agoutis. They set traps to catch animals such as iguanas and shot birds with blowpipes. Some families kept dogs to help with hunting, and they raised turkeys and honey bees on their farms.

LEFT: A clay vase depicting the Mayan deity Vucub Caquix, who took the form of a giant macaw (a parrot). Vucub Caquix was one of the most important Mayan gods.

➤ RURAL AND URBAN LIFE ➤

Farming families, including parents, children, and grandparents, lived together in small, simple houses near their fields. The family's house was made of wooden poles lashed together. Its roof was thatched with palm leaves or grass, and it was usually steeply angled so that rainwater ran off easily. One half of the house was used for cooking

and eating, with a firepit in the middle of the plastered floor. The family slept in the other half of the house on raised beds made from wood and woven bark. While the men were out in the fields, the women and older daughters cooked, looked after the young children, and collected firewood and water for the house.

Women also made the family's clothes. Since it was usually warm in the Mayan homelands, they had simple, comfortable clothes. Men wore a loincloth, a strip of material wound around the waist and between the legs. Women wore a long, loose, short-sleeved dress that they wove from cotton and other material. If the weather turned cold, both men and women put on a cloak, which they also used as a blanket at night. The Maya wore leather sandals or moccasins on their feet. All their work was done with stone and wooden

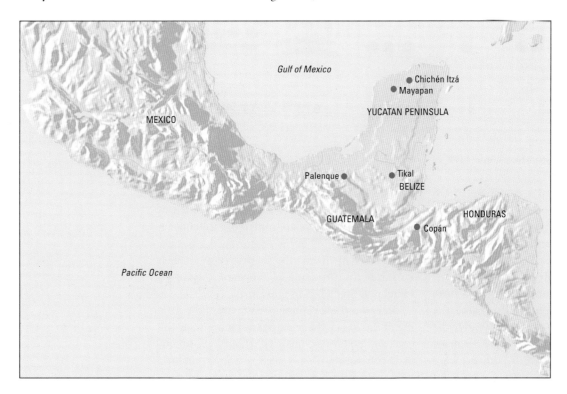

LEFT: The Maya were based on and around the Yucatán Peninsula, in present-day Mexico, Belize, Guatemala, and Honduras.

Mayan Numbers

To write numbers, the Maya used a system of dots and bars. One dot stood for 1; two dots for 2; three dots for 3; and four dots for 4. A horizontal bar stood for 5. The numbers up to 19 were written by combining dots and bars, like this:

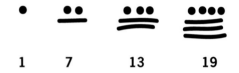

| 1 | 7 | 13 | 19 |

The Maya used a base-20 number system (ours is base-10). Every time a dot or line moved up a row it represented a new multiple of 20. In our system the numbers move to the left, from units, to 10s, then 100s, and then 1,000s.

In the Mayan system the rows from the bottom were: units, 20s, 400s, and 8,000s. To make this easier to follow the Maya invented a number zero, which they usually represented with a shell symbol. So in order to write the number 20 they put a shell (a zero) in the bottom units row, and a single dot in the next row up, which was the 20s row.

Some examples of larger numbers are shown below.

This system of counting was used by merchants and traders. Confusingly, the Mayans used a slightly different system when working out dates, although the principles were the same. For representing dates the figures in the third row from the bottom represented multiples of 360—the number of days in the Mayan year. The figures in the top row represented units of 7,200 (360 x 20), and so on.

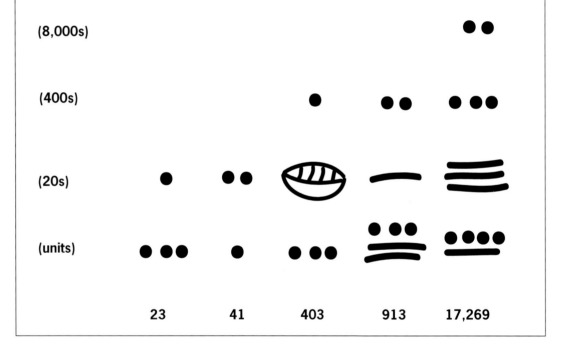

| | 23 | 41 | 403 | 913 | 17,269 |

tools, since the Maya had not discovered how to use any metal.

Life in a Mayan city was very different from life in the villages. At the heart of each separate kingdom was a city containing magnificent stone palaces, temples, and pyramids, all grouped around a large central plaza. They were an amazing feat of building, especially without metal tools. Mayan workmen used cutters made from the glassy volcanic rock obsidian to carve the limestone blocks for the buildings. Some of the buildings were covered with white plaster made from ground limestone, while others were painted bright red or blue.

The king and his relatives lived in a stone palace in the center of their city. They were surrounded by courtiers and servants. Nobles and priests also lived in the city, the largest of which may have had a population of up to 100,000. A great deal about life in the great Mayan cities has been learned from the ruins excavated at Palenque in present-day Mexico, Copán in Honduras, and Tikal in Guatemala.

Religion played an important part in the daily life of the Maya. They worshiped more than 160 gods and goddesses, many of whom were identified with natural forces such as wind, rain, and lightning. They believed that the four rain gods,

The Ball Game

An important feature of the ceremonial center of a Mayan city was the ball court. It was shaped like a large capital "I" and was surrounded by high, sloping walls. The largest ball court, at Chichén Itzá in modern Mexico, was 480 ft (146m) long and 118 ft (36m) wide—several times larger than most Mayan ball courts. The game was played by two teams of players who tried to hit a solid rubber ball, about 8 in. (20cm) in diameter, through a stone ring set high in the wall. At the Chichén Itzá ball court the wall was 26 ft (8m) high. The players wore protective padding, including a large belt that was probably made of leather, and they were not allowed to use their hands or feet to hit the ball. It must have been very difficult to propel the heavy ball with the forearm, elbow, or hip, and games may have gone on for a long time. Historians believe that the "game" was more of a religious event or sacred ritual, practiced as part of a complex ceremony. After some games, the losing players had their heads cut off by priests, and their blood and bodies were sacrificed to the gods. Some ball courts were surrounded by rows of skulls, and some balls had a human skull inside them.

The ball court at Copán, the most perfectly preserved example in existence today. Ball courts are found at almost all major Mayan sites, although they vary enormously in size.

each called Chac, controlled rainfall, so they prayed to them constantly to send enough rain for their crops, but not so much that their farms and villages would be washed away.

The sun-god was called Kinich Ahau; and the moon goddess, who was also identified with medicine and weaving, was Ix Chel. The Maya believed that each evening the sun-god, after crossing the sky, descended to the underworld, the land of death. When he rose again next morning, he was like a skeleton himself.

━ BLOOD AND SACRIFICE ━

The Maya prayed and sacrificed to their gods to maintain the natural balance of the earth's forces. Religious festivals in honor of certain gods took place on special days throughout the year. To obtain the help of their gods, the Maya also held ceremonies, fasted, sacrificed animals, and offered gifts. They made offerings of precious stones, beads, and prized feathers by throwing them into wells.

The Maya also practiced human sacrifice. They did this because they believed that the gods would give them what they wanted in return for food and blood, which the gods needed to sustain them. For instance, the sun-god needed human blood to help him make his journey across the sky each day. The sacrificial victims were often enemies captured in war. Many of them had their hearts cut out with a flint knife. Some were tied to a stake and shot with arrows, while others were rolled down the steps of a pyramid or hurled from a great height onto a pile of stones.

The Maya carried out a ceremony in which they offered their own blood to strengthen the gods. At important events such as the dedication of new buildings, the beginning or end of a war, or the planting of crops, the city's king led a special bloodletting ritual. Crowds gathered in

RIGHT: This pottery model of a human figure is almost 2 ft (60cm) high and served as the top of an incense burner. The Maya were expert craftsmen and produced many intricate ceramic items.

RIGHT: A stone carving showing a Mayan lord and his wife performing a bloodletting ritual. The man holds a flaming torch, while the woman draws blood by pulling a thorn rope through her tongue.

the central plaza to watch dancers move to the music of flutes, wooden trumpets, and turtle-shell drums. Then the king and queen arrived, and pierced themselves with spines or sharp obsidian blades. Their royal blood spattered onto pieces of bark paper, which were then burned in a ceremonial fire. The priests who conducted these religious ceremonies were so important that they also sat with a group of nobles on a city's council of state, which advised the king and helped him rule his city-state.

Special ceremonies were also held at funerals. Dead bodies were painted red and then wrapped up in straw mats with a few personal belongings. Farmers and ordinary people were buried under the floor of their house. Kings and some nobles were laid to rest in their finest clothes in tombs inside the city pyramids. Sometimes servants were sacrificed and buried with them, along with jewelry and other precious items, for use in the next world.

At Palenque, for example, the king Pacal was buried in A.D. 683 in a tomb inside the base of the pyramid that is called the Temple of the Inscriptions. A narrow shaft led from the tomb to the top of the nine-step pyramid, where there was a rectangular temple. The shaft was blocked up after Pacal was buried in the tomb.

➤ READING AND WRITING ➤

We have been able to learn a lot about the Maya because they developed their own system of writing. They were one of the few ancient civilizations to create an original system of their own, rather than simply adopt that of another culture. The Mayan system was made up of picture symbols, called hieroglyphs. Some of these represented whole words, while others represented phonetic sounds. It is probable that only scribes, priests, and nobles could read all the hieroglyphs, and the scribes were held in very high regard.

The scribes used quills made from turkey feathers to write on the bark of fig trees. They sometimes wrote on one long strip of bark and then folded it over to make pages—these Mayan books are called codices. Unfortunately, however, only four of them still survive. The Maya also covered their cities with hieroglyphs carved into the stone of buildings. They also kept records on large, upright stone monuments called stelae. They used the stelae to record important dates and great events in the lives of important people. They often recorded the life of a king, as well as the events of his reign.

The Mayan Calendars

The Maya had two different types of calendar. The first calendar was based on the time taken by the earth to orbit the sun and was made up of 365 days. This Mayan year was divided into 18 "months" of 20 days each (making 360 days in the year), with an extra five days at the end of the year to make up the full 365. These extra days were believed to be a period of extreme danger, when all sorts of things could go wrong, so people made extra sacrifices, fasted, and avoided any kind of unnecessary work at this time.

The second calendar was a sacred almanac of 260 days. There were a total of 20 differently named days—such as Ahau, Ik, and Imix—and each was combined with a number from 1 to 13. Each day would be represented by the combination of a name and a number—5 Ahau, for example—and would be associated with particular gods and goddesses. Priests used this sacred calendar to look both back into the past and forward into the future, so people would consult it before any important occasion.

The starting points of these two Mayan calendars only coincided once every 52 calendar years (or 18,980 days), and these cycles have become known as the Calendar Round. Later Mesoamerican civilizations such as the Aztecs also used the 52-year cycle as the basis of their calendar.

According to Mayan tradition, the world was already near the end of its fifth sun. Historians believe Mayan priests predicted the fifth world would be destroyed by a massive earthquake on a date equivalent to December 23, 2012.

Mayan priests also acted as astronomers. They observed the positions of the sun, moon, and stars in the night sky, and calculated exactly how long it took for the moon to go around the earth and the earth to go around the sun. They made accurate tables of solar eclipses, so that they could predict them for the future. Priests also made detailed studies of the movements of the planet Venus, which they considered very important. Modern observatories and computers tell us that the Mayan astronomical tables were accurate to within one day over the course of 6,000 years.

— TRADE AND WAR —

During the classic period Mayan cities traded with each other. The people of the lowlands traded such things as handicrafts and jaguar skins with people in the highlands. In return, the highlanders traded jade, obsidian, and cacao beans, which were used to make chocolate. The cities also made war on each other, perhaps to gain prisoners whom they could sacrifice to the gods.

Some historians believe that these wars helped weaken the Mayan city-states. There may also have been a series of bad harvests. During the ninth century, after about 600 years of what is called the classic period, the Maya abandoned their centers in the lowlands of Guatemala; some moved north to cities in the lowlands of the Yucatán Peninsula of Mexico, while others moved to the southern Guatemalan highlands. The Mayan kings and priests lost their power, and the largest remaining city, Chichén Itzá, was then governed by a council of nobles.

After several centuries of decline, the Mayan civilization ended completely when Spanish conquerors overran Guatemala in 1525 and the Yucatán Peninsula of Mexico in 1541.

LEFT: A Mayan palace at Kabah, on the Yucatán Peninsula. Impressive stone buildings like this were found not only in the major Mayan centers but in smaller towns as well.

Tikal

The Mayan civilization was made up of a number of separate city-states spread across a large area of Central America. Tikal, in the swampy lowlands of what is now Guatemala, was one of the most important and possibly the largest of the Mayan cities.

Tikal flourished for over 1,000 years and at its height had a population of more than 60,000 people and covered an area of 50 sq. miles (130 sq. km). A series of 29 kings from a single family ruled Tikal from before A.D. 300 until the ninth century.

Tikal was abandoned by the Maya around A.D. 900, hundreds of years before the Spanish conquerors took over the surrounding region. The ruins at Tikal remained largely untouched for centuries, until 19th-century explorers and archaeologists began to rediscover and study Mayan sites in Guatemala, Honduras, and Mexico.

When explorers first visited these sites, the ruins were covered with the creepers, trees, and undergrowth of the jungle. It is easy to imagine their amazement when they cut their way through the rainforest to find huge stone pyramids covered in engraved pictures and hieroglyphics.

Tikal began as a small farming village in about 800 B.C. Around 500 years later the Maya started building a ceremonial center where the people could worship their many gods. The buildings were put up around a Great Plaza, about 400 ft (120m) long and 250 ft (75m) wide.

THE GREAT PLAZA

Like almost all Mayan ceremonial buildings of the period, the plaza was built of limestone, which was available in large quantities locally. In the city's heyday this huge plaza would have been the setting for magnificent ceremonial processions.

On one side of the plaza the North Acropolis became a place of burial monuments for the kings who ruled Tikal. We have learned a great deal about the city and its people from the tombs of these kings, which were often decorated with elaborate and richly detailed wall paintings. We can tell from the riches contained in these tombs that the kings of Tikal lived lives of great luxury. To commemorate their achievements the kings put up upright stone monuments, or stelae, which are an extremely important source of information. These monuments were decorated with carvings that contained not only images of the rulers themselves but also the dates of their reigns. The earliest stela found at Tikal dates from A.D. 292.

New limestone buildings and monuments were constantly being built at Tikal, some on top of those already in existence. Those that excite most interest today were constructed in the eighth century, when the city was at the height of its power. Around 727 a king called Ah Cacao was buried in the pyramid known as Temple I at the east end of the Great Plaza. This magnificent structure was built over the royal tomb after the king's body had been placed inside. It is a stepped pyramid, with nine levels. The Maya believed that the underworld was made up of nine layers, and the pyramid represents this. A single set of steps leads to the temple at the top of the pyramid, which is 155 ft (47m) high.

At the west end of the Great Plaza is Temple II, which was probably built for Ah Cacao's wife. But the largest structure of all at Tikal is Temple IV, which rises to 215 ft (65m) and can be seen from a distance of 12 miles (20km). Other, smaller pyramids were also built in the eighth century. Some were put up in pairs, and experts believe they were built to celebrate the end of periods of time that the Maya called *katuns*. A *katun* was made up of 20 *tuns*, or years. A twin-pyramid complex was put up at the end of each 20-year period in order to honor the passage of time. These structures are unique to Tikal.

More than 3,000 separate structures have been found at Tikal, and many more buildings lie beneath them. Strangely, the city was not surrounded by any defenses or fortifications, apart from a dry moat to the north.

Tikal's power began to decline in the ninth century, probably because of destructive wars with other city-states, perhaps combined with crop failures in the surrounding farmland. Eventually the rulers, nobles, and ordinary people of Tikal abandoned their ceremonial city to the jungle.

The ruins of the Mayan city of Tikal in present-day Guatemala. Tikal was probably the largest of the great Mayan cities, and its temples and pyramids are some of the most spectacular found in Central America.

Mississippians

The Mississippian culture was the last major prehistoric culture to develop in North America. It lasted from about A.D. 700 to the arrival of the Spanish conquistador Hernando de Soto and the first European explorers in 1540, reaching its peak in the 13th and 14th centuries.

The Mississippians are probably best remembered for their pyramid-shaped mounds. However, the jewel of Mississippian achievement was without doubt the 12th-century city of Cahokia, which was America's first metropolis north of the Rio Grande.

The Mississippians' highly developed towns and intensive style of agriculture marked an important cultural advance over the earlier Woodland tribes (like the Hopewell) and matched the growth and expansion of the southwestern Anasazi culture, which took place from about A.D. 700 to 1200.

For the 300 years after the decline of the Hopewell culture (from around A.D. 400) there was no alternative unifying tradition, so different groups of people in the eastern Woodlands followed their own local ways of life. Then, around 700 a powerful new group emerged from northern Mexico and settled in the southeast.

They brought with them protein-rich beans and a new and very successful strain of corn. In some areas the new corn could be planted and harvested twice in the same season, greatly increasing the yield. This dramatic increase in the food supply helped to stimulate the initial growth of Mississippian culture between present-day St. Louis and Vicksburg, and was almost certainly the most important factor in the expansion of the culture. By A.D. 1000 there were large concentrations of people in towns throughout the southern and central Mississippi Valley.

Towns appeared first on the banks of the Mississippi and its major tributaries, the Tennessee and Cumberland rivers. Later towns also grew up in the fertile surrounding lands. Mississippian settlements have been found in the present-day states of Mississippi, Alabama, Georgia, Arkansas, Missouri, Kentucky, Illinois, Indiana, and Ohio, with other scattered settlements extending northward into Wisconsin and Minnesota and westward onto the Great Plains.

Mississippian settlements were larger than any built before in the Americas. With thousands of inhabitants, they were the first real towns, in North America. A typical town consisted of up to

LEFT: A pottery vase from around A.D. 1000 made in the shape of a weeping human figure. Weeping eyes were a recurring motif in Mississippian artworks and are believed to have had symbolic significance.

20 large, flat-topped mounds grouped around a ceremonial square. The mounds were made from earth, with a ramp or stairway of logs leading to the summit. The size of the squares varied from 10 to 100 acres (4–40ha). Temples, mortuaries, a meeting house, and the homes of religious and political leaders were built on top of the mounds. They overlooked the townspeople, who lived in long houses made from mud, wattle (interlaced branches), and thatch.

A defensive stockade separated the town from the farming villages scattered over the fertile river plain. Each large town or village dominated a satellite of lesser villages, with government in the hands of the chiefs and priests. This system was imported from Mexico, where it had been used from around 850 B.C. onward.

◄ CAHOKIA ►

The largest and most powerful Mississippian town was Cahokia, founded on the site of present-day East St. Louis, Illinois, in around A.D. 700. The town yields clear evidence of a

LEFT: This stone pipe found at Spiro shows a woman grinding corn. Corn was a central part of the Mississippians' diet.

Until its decline around 1450 Cahokia was probably the seat of government for the entire surrounding area. It was also an important trading center for grave goods, including copper from the Great Lakes, and mica, which was found in the Appalachian Mountains.

Another important town, Emerald Mound, lay in the lower Mississippi Valley near the present-day city of Natchez and was one of at least nine towns inhabited by the Natchez tribe. They were still living there when French explorers visited them in the 18th century. These explorers provided valuable descriptions of the tribe's way of life. They were ruled by a powerful chief called the Great Sun, who wore elaborate feather crowns and cloaks, and was carried everywhere in a litter. Anyone who displeased him was instantly put to death. When the Great Sun died, his wife, servants, and pipebearer were killed and buried with him. The smoking of a pipe played an important role in many ceremonies, and the Great Sun's pipebearer was one of his most important servants.

sophisticated culture that existed there around 1100 or 1200, at least 300 years before the European discovery of North America. Today, Monk's Mound is all that survives of a city that sheltered 10,000 people and spread out over five sq. miles (13 sq. km) at the height of its prosperity between 1050 and 1250.

The mound itself has a 16-acre (6ha) rectangular base, which makes it larger than the Great Pyramid of Giza. It is 1,000 ft (300m) long, 700 ft (200m) wide, and rises in four terraces to a height of 100 ft (30m). Unlike their counterparts in other cultures, the mound's builders had no pack animals to help them and must have carried the earth themselves in baskets.

A further 100 earth mounds, supporting official residences and temples and housing the dead, were once visible from the summit of Monk's Mound. Less important sites were placed farther away from the center. Important people were often buried under the floors of temples, while others were buried in cemeteries outside the towns. Grave goods such as pottery and shell or copper gorgets (neck ornaments) were placed around the bodies.

The scale of such public works and the distribution of temples suggest that the Mississippians had a dominant religious cult with a body of priest-rulers who could command the services of a large, stable, and docile population, as well as several artist-craftsman guilds.

➤ SOCIAL ORGANIZATION ➤

Mississippian settlements were organized into specialized social hierarchies, with peace chiefs, war chiefs, mortuary priests, and clan heads. These leaders supervised the production, collection, and distribution of food and materials. War chiefs tended to be more active and at least a generation younger than peace chiefs.

While the peace chief held sway in the village, the war chief was in charge of the areas outside

BELOW: Mississippian settlements could be found across the eastern states.

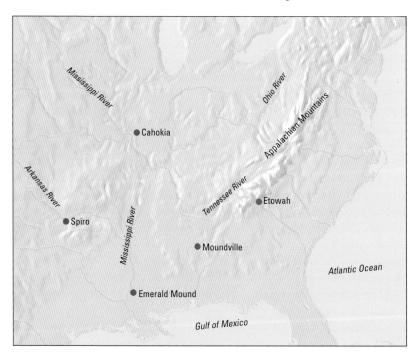

the village, except when the village was under threat of imminent attack. The degree of chiefly power and authority varied considerably across the region. While chiefs such as the Natchez Great Sun were seen as gods, the leaders of other tribes, such as the Choctaws, Creeks, and Cherokees, were simply treated as respected elder members of the community.

Warfare was quite common and often led to the formation of alliances between different groups. Such alliances later turned into tribal confederacies. These conflicts were usually fought for the purpose of gaining prestige or revenge for an injury, rather than territorial expansion or economic control.

➤ ARTS AND CRAFTS ➤

Besides grave ornaments and body decorations (such as earrings and bracelets) the Mississippians also produced many different items for everyday domestic use, such as baskets, clay vessels, and clothing (made from animal skin). Mississippian potters crafted highly decorative pots that were distinguished by having crushed shells incorporated within the clay.

Most of the craftwork of the Mississippians was executed in copper, shell, stone, and wood, which were turned into elaborate headdresses, ritual weapons, sculptured tobacco pipes, and copper-covered wooden masks. Designs were engraved, embossed, carved, or molded and included feathered serpents, birds, skulls, and spiders, plus human figures and geometric motifs.

By the mid 15th century Cahokia and the other cities of the central Mississippian region had fallen into decline. This may have been because of the spread of diseases like tuberculosis, or because farmers could no longer grow enough crops to feed the population. Whatever the reason, many city-dwellers moved away and built smaller villages. Some still grew crops, but many returned to the old hunting-and-gathering ways.

Between 1500 and 1700 the Great Plains were gradually taken over by semiagricultural peoples like the Apache and Comanche, who now had the use of horses, which had been introduced by the Spaniards. These Great Plains peoples came to dominate the existing Mississippian peoples, who by this time had evolved into tribes such as the Pawnee and Crow. Farther south the first European explorers found the Mississippi culture still flourishing, but not for long. The last remnants of this ancient culture were finally broken up and forced to mix with other tribes by the French at the beginning of the 18th century.

The Southern Cult

Religious ceremonies were very important to the Mississippians. Rites were performed to honor ancestors, accompany the burial of important leaders, and celebrate successful harvests, hunts, and battles. In much of the region dominated by the Mississippians, but especially in the south, people followed a religion known as the Southern Cult. The religion was mainly concentrated in three towns: Moundville (Alabama), Etowah (Georgia), and Spiro (Oklahoma), but the distribution of cult objects extended beyond the limits of any single Mississippian town.

Exact details of the cult's beliefs are not known, but death and burial played an important part in its rituals. Many Southern Cult objects have been discovered, including shells and copper sheets carved with symbolic designs such as weeping eyes and hands holding an eye. Some towns specialized in the production of ceremonial costumes and ornaments.

A shell neck ornament showing a winged shaman holding a severed human head, one of the many cult objects found at Etowah, Georgia.

RIGHT: A soapstone pipe found at Spiro, showing a warrior beheading an enemy. Smoking had a religious significance for the Mississippians, and pipes like this would have been used for ceremonial purposes only.

Toltecs

In the sixth and seventh centuries A.D. the northern and central highlands of Mexico were populated by nomadic tribes. By A.D. 700 some of them had settled in and around a village about 45 miles (70km) north of modern Mexico City. They came to be known as the Toltecs.

The village grew into a small town and then a large city called Tollan, which meant "Place of Reeds." Today the ancient city is usually referred to as Tula, and between about 900 and 1200 it was the capital of the Toltec Empire.

The Toltec Empire is shrouded in mystery, and even today we know comparatively little about its size and organization. However, we do know that the Toltecs were farmers, and that like other peoples of Central America, they irrigated their fields with water from local rivers and streams to produce crops such as corn and beans. The people of Tula also made and traded a wide variety of goods, especially tools made of obsidian, which they obtained from mines near the city of Pachuca, about 40 miles (60km) away. Control of the mines attracted new settlers and helped Tula grow. At its height in the 11th century the city probably had up to 50,000 inhabitants.

➤ TOLTEC ARCHITECTURE ➤

Much of Tula has been uncovered by archaeologists in the past 60 years, so we know a good deal about it. Most of the houses were single-story with many separate rooms, and the houses were grouped around central courtyards. The houses had flat roofs and thick walls of sun-dried bricks held together with mud, which kept the occupants cool in the day and warm at night.

The city was laid out in a rough grid and had a ceremonial center that included a large plaza, pyramids, a palace complex, temples, and two ball courts similar to those found at Mayan sites. Historians believe that the same ceremonial ball game was played throughout Central America.

One of Tula's two main pyramids, which is called Pyramid B by archaeologists, has four levels, a single staircase, and rows of columns on the top. These columns are carved from basalt in the shape of giant Toltec warriors, and are almost 15 ft (5m) tall. The columns once served as pillars to support the roof of a temple that stood on top of the pyramid. The group of stone warriors must have been an impressive and frightening sight to the people who mounted the steps of the pyramid 1,000 years ago. Alongside the pyramid there are several rows of smaller pillars, which once held up

the roof of a covered area that archaeologists think may have served as a royal residence.

➤ TOLTEC ARCHITECTURE ➤

The Toltecs were an extremely warlike people. The temples and palaces at Tula are covered with carvings that show battle scenes involving Toltec soldiers. The fact that such scenes vastly outnumber all others indicates the huge importance of

ABOVE: These four statues of Toltec warriors still stand on the top of Pyramid B. They were built as pillars to support the roof of a temple.

The Feathered Serpent

The great god Quetzalcoatl ("the snake with feathers of the quetzal bird") was honored by the Toltecs as the son of the earth goddess, and he was also associated with the morning star. Many Toltec rulers identified themselves with him, and his image appeared frequently at Tula, as it did at Teotihuacán and later Aztec sites. One Toltec king particularly closely associated with him was Topiltzin.

According to legend, toward the end of the 10th century the king Topiltzin took the name Quetzalcoatl. Topiltzin was a good ruler who discouraged the practice of human sacrifice, but he was persecuted by Tezcatlipoca, the god of the night sky. Tezcatlipoca taunted and humiliated Topiltzin-Quetzalcoatl so much that he finally left his capital, Tula, in shame. As he headed toward the coast, still pursued by

the night god, most of his companions died. When he reached the sea, according to the legend, Topiltzin-Quetzalcoatl built a raft of snakes and sailed away to a safer place.

Several Mayan myths tell of the arrival of Quetzalcoatl, whom they called Kukulcan, at Chichén Itzá at about that time. Historians certainly believe that some of these legends may be based on fact.

---

warfare in Toltec society. One image that appears again and again is that of a Toltec warrior wearing an elaborate feathered headdress and clutching a handful of spears. Coyotes, jaguars, and eagles also feature prominently, and it seems likely that the Toltecs named warrior orders after these animals in the same way as the later Aztecs.

Toltec invaders may have been responsible for the destruction of the great city of Teotihuacán, which was not far to the south. Toltec influence certainly reached at least as far as the Mayan city of Chichén Itzá, which lay more than 700 miles (1100km) away on the Yucatán Peninsula. Many of the buildings at Chichén Itzá are designed in a recognizably Toltec style and are decorated with sculptures and carvings showing Toltec soldiers. Historians are undecided as to whether the Toltecs actually conquered Chichén Itzá or whether they simply traded with the city. However, it is certain that in one way or another the Toltecs greatly influenced its development.

➤ FALL OF THE TOLTECS ➤

The last Toltec ruler was a king called Huemac, who ruled in the 12th century. By that time the Toltecs were losing their power and influence. This may have been due to disagreements among the leading people of the city of Tula, or to drought and poor harvests in the region, or the threat of attack from outsiders. Whatever the reason, Huemac was forced to leave his capital city and went south to the Valley of Mexico. Tula itself was overrun by invading tribes, and it soon lay in ruins—the invaders hurled columns from the top of the pyramid temple and then buried them. They also dug into the pyramid, looking for hidden treasure.

Despite this, however, the fearsome reputation of Tula and its warlike inhabitants lived on, and the later Aztecs were proud to see themselves as the Toltecs' spiritual descendants.

LEFT: A column of basalt carved into the shape of a Toltec warrior. A military theme ran through much of Toltec art, reflecting their aggressive character.

BELOW: The Toltecs' capital Tula lay in the highlands of present-day Mexico, north of the modern Mexico City. However, the Toltecs' influence was felt as far away as Chichén Itzá on the Yucatán Peninsula.

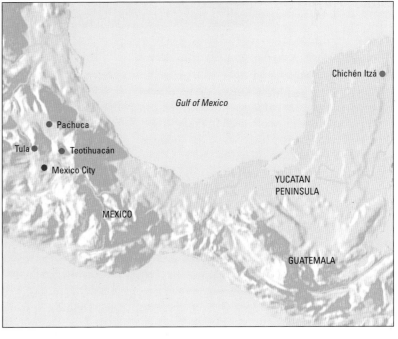

Aztecs

The Aztec Empire flourished in Mesoamerica between the 14th and 16th centuries. The Aztecs were a brutal people who built their extensive empire through warfare. They took many prisoners who they then sacrificed to their gods in a grisly ceremony.

Despite their extreme brutality, the Aztecs were in other ways a highly civilized people, with impressive cities, art forms, and a special form of pictographic writing.

The early Aztec people lived in the northern region of the country that we know today as Mexico. They were wandering hunters who spoke a language called *Nahuatl* and called themselves *Mexica*. In the 1100s these nomadic people moved south to the Valley of Mexico, but they were not welcome among the other peoples who already lived in the fertile areas. The settled peoples must have thought of these warlike nomads as barbarians. However, the *Mexica* were very highly skilled warriors, and so several of the city-states hired the Aztecs to fight for them as mercenary soldiers.

The Aztecs showed little respect for other people and were not popular. Around the year 1300 they asked the people of Culhuacán, who lived near the southern shores of Lake Texcoco, for a special bride so that they could start their own royal family. The Culhuacán ruler made a gift of his own daughter, but instead of marrying her, the Aztec leader had her beaten to death. An Aztec priest wore the dead girl's skin at a ceremony, and the outraged Culhuacáños drove the Aztecs from their territory. They then fled to an uninhabited island in the lake, where they founded their first settlement.

Aztec legend tells of them arriving at this spot in a different way. When they were still wandering around a mythical place called Atzlán, in northwest Mexico, without a permanent home,

ABOVE: Santa Cecilia Acatitlán, the only Aztec pyramid of its type to have been fully restored. A comparatively small building, the pyramid was probably only used by its local community.

Huitzilopochtli, god of sun and war, told the Aztecs to look for a special sign and settle where they found it. The sign was an eagle perched on a cactus grasping a snake. According to the legend, in about 1325 the wandering tribe found what they were looking for on a marshy island in Lake Texcoco. They settled there and built a new village, which they called Tenochtitlán. Translated, this means "the place of the prickly-pear cactus."

Life was not easy on the small swampy islands that the Aztecs had chosen for their homeland. The early settlers caught fish in the lake and trapped water birds with nets. But they had to pay tribute to the Tepánecs, who controlled the shores of the lake. The Aztecs needed to grow more food, and this meant having more land. They achieved this by making what they called *chinampas*, or "floating gardens," on the lake itself. To do this they sank reed rafts filled with mud on top of each other, until the mud rose above the surface of the water.

Gradually, the Aztecs filled in the spaces between their floating gardens to make room for houses. They constructed highly complex drainage systems and piped fresh water from one zone to another. They transported rocks and earth to the main island to make a level surface for the growing town of Tenochtitlán. Then they built a 10-mile (16-km) long dike across the lake to prevent salt water from the north of the lake contaminating the fresh water surrounding their farms and houses. Finally, they built causeways to connect the rapidly growing city to the mainland and to the other islands.

By 1400 Tenochtitlán had become an important, powerful city, and the Aztecs were ready to expand on the mainland. Their leader, Itzcoatl ("Obsidian Serpent"), formed an alliance with two other city-states, Texcoco and Tlacopán, and together they fought and defeated the Tepánecs in 1428. Tenochtitlán's warriors were feared throughout the region, and the city quickly became the most powerful member of the triple alliance. The Aztecs and their allies soon conquered other city-states in the Valley of Mexico. The new empire expanded considerably under Montezuma I, who ruled the Aztecs from 1440 to 1469 and conquered large areas to the east and south, including the lands of the Mixtecs. Conquered cities were forced to pay heavy taxes to their Aztec overlords.

The leader, or emperor, of the Aztecs was called the *huey tlatoani*, or "great speaker." He was chosen from the members of a royal family by a council of nobles. The emperor had great power but consulted the council of nobles before making important decisions. He rarely appeared in public and was treated like a god.

➤ WARFARE ➤

One of the most important roles of the emperor was to act as commander of the army. Unlike most empire-builders, the Aztecs did not have a permanent army, but all male citizens were expected to leave their fields and fight when they were needed.

Boys were trained at school to use weapons, and from the age of 15 they went to war.

ABOVE: A scene from an Aztec codex showing two of the civilization's many gods—the farming deity Xipe Totec (left), and the storm god Quetzalcoatl ("the serpent").

BELOW: By the early 16th century the Aztecs had conquered a large empire.

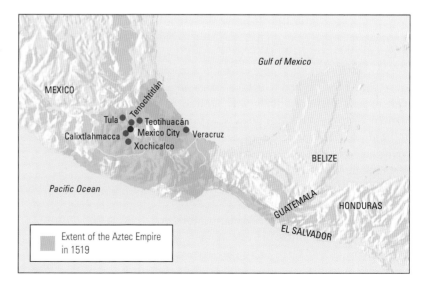

Human Sacrifice

The Aztecs needed a constant supply of prisoners to be sacrificed. They did not sacrifice people as a punishment or to celebrate their victory in war, but as part of a ritual to feed and please their gods. Human sacrifice played an important part in all major religious ceremonies. The Aztecs worshiped hundreds of gods and goddesses, and they believed these deities needed human blood to remain strong.

The sacrifices took place at temples, of which the most important was in the ceremonial center of Tenochtitlán. The Great Pyramid there was a stepped stone pyramid rising to a height of almost 200 ft (60m). At the top of the pyramid were two temples, each reached by a long flight of steps. To the left was the Temple of Tlaloc, god of rain and fertility, and to the right, that of Huitzilopochtli, god of the sun and war and a special guardian of the people of Tenochtitlán. The Aztecs believed that if they did not feed the gods, they would destroy the world. According to tradition this was already the fifth world, which would itself eventually be destroyed by a great earthquake.

Victims, both men and women, were lined up on the pyramid steps and shuffled upward until they reached one of the altars. Then they were seized by priests and stretched across a sacrificial stone. A priest slashed open the victim's chest with a knife and tore out the heart, which was the most precious thing that could be offered to the gods. The heart was placed in a bowl, and the dead victim's body was thrown down the temple steps. Sometimes part of the body was given as a reward to the victim's captor, and pieces were eaten as a ritual.

Successful warriors were rewarded with gifts of land or slaves, and those wounded in battle won the right to wear a long cloak of honor to hide their scars. The Aztecs had no iron, so most of their weapons were made of wood. They used the glassy volcanic rock obsidian to make spikes and blades. They had slings, bows and arrows, and spears that were thrown with a wooden spearthrower called an *atlatl*. At close quarters they wielded wooden clublike swords spiked with obsidian blades. Warriors wore quilted cotton suits, which were soaked in salt water to make them stiff and so act as armor. They also wore feathered headdresses and carried wicker shields covered in leather.

There were two special groups of fighting soldiers—eagle warriors and jaguar warriors. They wore battledress made partly from the animals whose names they took. They also wore headdresses with an eagle's beak or jaguar's jaws. When they fought, these knights and other warriors tried to wound and capture their enemies rather than kill them. This was because they wanted as many captives as possible to take back to Tenochtitlán in order to sacrifice them. Whenever the Aztecs conquered a city, they usually took thousands of prisoners.

➤ THE AZTEC CALENDAR ➤

Aztec priests used a sacred calendar to work out lucky days on which to hold celebrations, go to war, or sow crops. There were 260 days in this calendar's year, made up of 20 named days that were combined with the numbers 1 to 13. The Aztecs also used a solar calendar made up of 18 "months" of 20 days, with an extra five unlucky days at the end of each year—making a year of 365 days. The two calendars worked together,

BELOW: A stone figure of Ometecuhtli ("Two Lord"), who was the supreme god of the Aztecs.

and the first day of each occurred at the same time only once every 52 years. The end of each of these 52-year periods was considered to be a time of great danger. Women and children were kept indoors for fear that outside they would turn into animals. At a special ceremony a priest lit a fire on a piece of wood on a sacrificial victim's chest and tore out the heart. From this flame torches were lit that would light new fires that would protect the Aztecs for the next 52 years.

⊸ AZTEC SOCIETY ⊷

Aztec society was made up of four main classes: nobles, commoners, serfs, and slaves. Individual families of nobles and commoners belonged to larger clans. Each clan owned an area of land that was divided up among the families according to their needs. Commoners farmed their own land, while nobles' land was worked by serfs. Many slaves were people who had fallen on hard times—people could be sold into slavery if they had large debts they could not repay.

Nobles lived in large, two-story houses made of stone or sun-dried mud bricks. The houses had flat roofs, some with gardens on top, and were built around a patio. There were separate living rooms, bedrooms, kitchens, and servants' quarters. Commoners' houses were much simpler and were often made of reeds plastered with clay.

While the houses of the nobles were highly sophisticated, the most stunning examples of Aztec architecture were the pyramids built to honor their gods. The largest of these was the Great Pyramid at Tenochtitlán, which was set in a spectacular ritual center of stone monuments, plazas, and stairways.

For clothing, Aztec men generally wore a loincloth and a cloak knotted over one shoulder. Women wore a sleeveless blouse and a wrap-around skirt. Nobles' clothes were made of embroidered cotton, while ordinary people wore plain garments woven from fiber called agave.

The Aztecs' main food was a thin corn pancake called a *tlaxcalli*, which in Spanish is called a tortilla and is still eaten in Mexico today. The Aztecs scooped up other food with their tortillas or wrapped them around spicy meat or vegetables. Their sauces were flavored with chili peppers. Although corn was the main crop, farmers also grew beans, squash, avocados, and tomatoes. The Aztecs crushed cacao beans and whipped the mixture into a cold, frothy chocolate drink flavored with vanilla or spices. They also used cacao beans as small change when they were bartering in the market place.

The Aztecs used pictographic writing, which was mainly made up of small pictures. Some stood for ideas, while others represented the sounds of syllables. Writing was mainly used for business records, tax lists, censuses, and religious documents. Paper was made from the bark of wild fig trees, and sheets were stuck together to make a long, folded book called a codex. However, only a very small number of skilled scribes, who were usually priests, could read and write. Priests also acted as astronomers and kept detailed records of the movements of the stars and planets.

At the end of the 15th century, the Aztec Empire was at the height of its power. It was made up of about 15 million people in 38 provinces, and the capital city of Tenochtitlán had a population of up to 250,000. In 1502

ABOVE: The Calendar Stone, thought to have once formed part of the Great Pyramid at Tenochtitlán. At the center is the face of the sun-god Tonatiuh. It is surrounded by symbols representing the days of the Aztec year.

BELOW: The feet of eagles' heads on this Aztec bowl suggest its owner was a member of the warrior class.

Montezuma II became emperor, and he continued to extend the empire into south-central Mexico. Many of the city-states conquered by the Aztecs hated their overlords and disliked paying so much tribute.

By 1519, however, Montezuma II had become seriously worried by several ill omens that threatened to make the year—called "One Reed" in the Aztec calendar—a disastrous one. A comet had appeared in the sky, and the temple of Huitzilopochtli had burst into flames. Most importantly, One Reed was the year when legends said that the god-king Quetzalcoatl, lord of the winds, who had been driven out of the Toltec capital of Tula hundreds of years before, would return from the east to seek revenge. Aztec priests demanded thousands of human sacrifices to counteract these evil omens, and this greatly upset the cities that had to supply the victims. When Montezuma was told that strangers with white faces and beards had arrived on the east coast, he thought that one of them might be the god-king Quetzalcoatl himself. If he fought the god-king, the gods might be so angry that they would destroy the whole empire. Montezuma decided to welcome the strangers.

➤ THE FALL OF THE EMPIRE ➤

In reality the strangers were a body of Spanish conquistadors, under the command of Hernán Cortés. As the small Spanish army of 500 soldiers headed inland, many subjugated Native-American warriors joined the Spanish side and agreed to fight their hated Aztec rulers. When Cortés reached Tenochtitlán, he and his soldiers were amazed by the size and beauty of the city. Though full of mistrust, Montezuma greeted the Spaniard as a friend.

However, when a Spanish commander killed some Aztec nobles, who were holding a religious ceremony, the Aztecs rebelled and fought the Spaniards. They stoned Montezuma as a traitor and forced the Spaniards from Tenochtitlán. But Cortés soon made more local allies, regrouped his troops, and attacked the city again with full force. The Aztecs held out for 10 weeks before they surrendered on August 13, 1521. With the fall of Tenochtitlán all Aztec resistance ended. Their great empire had come to an end.

The remaining Aztecs became the slaves of the Spanish conquerors. Tenochtitlán was completely destroyed, and Mexico City was later built on its ruins. When archaeologists excavated the site of the Great Temple there they found about 6,000 Aztec objects.

LEFT: Part of a strip from an Aztec codex showing scenes from daily life. The picture at the top shows nobles playing *patolli*, a game of dice. Other pictures show animals, prisoners undergoing punishment, and a band of musicians. Much of what we know about Aztec life is derived from the codices—or picture books—that were left by their scribes.

Teotihuacán

The site of one of the largest ancient cities of the Americas lies about 30 miles (50km) to the northeast of modern Mexico City. Although it was built many centuries before the Aztecs ever saw it, we still use their name for it—Teotihuacán, which in their language meant "place of the gods."

When the Aztecs found the city in the 14th century, it was overgrown and in ruins. Nevertheless, they saw that it had once been a great city, and they came to believe that it had been built by the gods. For them Teotihuacán became a place of pilgrimage.

After the Spanish conquered Mexico in 1521 the ruins at Teotihuacán were once again forgotten. Then, at the end of the 19th century explorers and archaeologists started investigating ancient Mexican sites and excavation of Teotihuacán has continued to this day. Even now much of the city remains unexplored, and we still have a lot to learn about the people who originally built it and lived there. We do not know what language they spoke or even what they called themselves. Archaeologists, however, like to call the people of the city Teotihuacános.

The city of Teotihuacán was founded as a small settlement some time around 200 B.C. Experts are not certain of the exact date, but at that time about 2,000 people were living there, and 300 years later the population had increased to around 60,000. While there is no evidence that Teotihuacán was the center of an empire in the conventional sense, we do know that it was the heart of a huge trading network. The city thus had a great cultural influence over a very wide area of present-day Mexico and Guatemala.

STREET OF THE DEAD

By A.D. 100 there were already many fine buildings in the city, all laid out in an organized way on a grid pattern. A wide avenue ran through the city in roughly a north-to-south direction. The Aztecs called this avenue the Street of the Dead. They probably thought that many of the buildings along the avenue were tombs, although actually they were not.

At the south end of the Street of the Dead were two large areas. One was a complex of

The Pyramid of the Sun, which was the largest building at Teotihuacán. A broad stairway leads to the top of the pyramid, which was originally the site of a small wooden temple.

religious and other important buildings, which archaeologists call the Citadel. It includes a temple called the Pyramid of the Feathered Serpent, which contains images of the Mesoamerican god Quetzalcoatl. The other rectangular area is called the Great Compound, and it was probably the city's main market place.

To the east of the Street of the Dead lies the largest and most famous building of Teotihuacán—the Pyramid of the Sun. At the very top of the avenue, about one and a half miles (2km) from the Citadel, lies the Pyramid of the Moon. This pyramid is smaller than that of the Sun, but it stands on higher ground and so reaches the same height. It is now 140 ft (43m) tall and originally had a temple on top. Looking from the Street this pyramid lines up exactly with Cerro Gordo, which was a sacred mountain in ancient times. Walking up the Street of the Dead, Teotihuacáno worshipers would have seen the pyramid slowly obscure the mountain, as if taking its place. It may be that the building was meant to represent the holy peak.

URBAN HOUSING

The Street of the Dead and the great pyramids, temples, and market were surrounded by the residential parts of the city. By A.D. 500 about 200,000 people were living in Teotihuacán, making it the largest city in Mesoamerica. There was a neighborhood for craftworkers, as well as a special quarter for foreign visitors. There were also about 2,000 apartment compounds where ordinary Teotihuacános lived. These were single-story buildings with many rooms, but probably just one entrance, so that people could live quietly and privately. Related families probably lived together in each compound, and the largest had room for about 100 people. The compounds had flat roofs made of thin poles laid across beams, and there were narrow alleyways between the buildings. At its peak in the sixth century A.D. the city covered an area of about eight sq. miles (20 sq. km).

Teotihuacán flourished from about A.D. 200—by which time all the major buildings had been constructed—to A.D. 600. From that time the city began to decline in wealth and influence. There may have been struggles for power within the city, or it could be that there were farming problems due to overuse of the surrounding land or poor harvests. Around 650 to 700 much of the city was burned to the ground, which leads archaeologists to believe it may have been attacked, either by invaders from the nearby city of Cholula to the south, or by Toltecs from the north. Whatever happened, the city was abandoned and lay in ruins until it was discovered by the Aztecs hundreds of years later.

Incas

The Inca Empire was the largest and most powerful civilization in ancient South America. The Incas ruled much of what is now Ecuador, Peru, and Bolivia, plus parts of Chile and Argentina, encompassing areas of coastal desert, mountains, windswept plains, forests, and jungles.

LEFT: The Incas built their empire in the mountainous terrain of the Andes, terracing the slopes to grow crops.

Until the beginning of the 15th century A.D. the Incas were one of a number of small warring tribes that lived in the highlands of what is now southern Peru. Then a highly skilled Inca general by the name of Inka Yupanki won a decisive battle against a neighboring tribe called the Chanka. Assuming the name Pachacutec, Yupanki took the Inca throne and began to assert his authority over the surrounding lands. According to Inca historians, Pachacutec began his reign in 1438, and this date is traditionally seen as the start of the Inca Empire.

As their strength and power grew, the Incas began expanding their territory. They made treaties with cooperative local chiefs and attacked and subdued chiefs who refused to cooperate willingly. The Incas used a variety of strategies to rule their new lands. In cases in which the local chiefs accepted Inca domination, the Incas often left them in power and just imposed new rules and taxes on the people. However, they also took

the sons of the local rulers to the capital city, Cuzco, to attend school and learn Inca ways. These boys served as hostages to keep their fathers from rebelling. When local chiefs proved rebellious or incapable of carrying out their tasks, the Incas appointed their own governors to oversee newly conquered territories. The governors were men loyal to the Inca emperor, and they were given many privileges. They collected tribute (tax paid to the Inca overlords in the form of goods), controlled land and large herds of animals, wore special clothing reserved for the elite, and lived in luxurious palaces.

➤ KEEPING THE PEACE ➤

In areas where the local people proved especially troublesome, the Incas resorted to large-scale movement of the population. They moved whole communities of cooperative people into the areas where the inhabitants were causing problems. They also took some of the troublesome people and moved them to other parts of the empire. Since people from different parts of the empire spoke different languages and had different customs, they often distrusted and disliked one another. The Incas turned this distrust to their advantage, counting on the members of each group to spy on the other groups and to inform the Inca governors of any talk of rebellion.

➤ RELIGION ➤

Religion under the Incas was based on the worship of many gods. The most important god for the Incas was the sun-god Inti, whom the ruling Inca considered to be his own father. The Coricancha, the main temple dedicated to the worship of Inti, was one of the most magnificent buildings in the empire. Built from the finest cut stone, its walls were covered with sheets of gold. Beautiful terraces surrounded the temple, planted not with ordinary crops but with small figures of corn and other plants made of gold and silver.

Other Inca gods were usually associated either with heavenly bodies, such as the moon, planets, and stars, or natural phenomena, such as thunder or the sea. The Incas also worshiped local shrines known as *huacas*. *Huacas* were supernatural powers located either in special places, such as mountain peaks or springs, or in objects such as large boulders or statues. The gods were thought to have universal powers, while the *huacas* had mostly local significance. The goodwill of both the gods and *huacas* was needed to ensure success in all endeavors, from agriculture to war.

The Incas did not discourage people from worshiping these local *huacas*. Whenever possible, however, the Incas moved the more important *huacas* to Cuzco. This practice forced people to make pilgrimages to Cuzco in order to worship and so reinforced the city's role as the center of the empire.

Some religious activities were directed by the Inca emperor, or by priests or priestesses, or even by healers and other specialists. Other religious activities were carried out by individuals. The worship of Inca gods and *huacas* often involved making offerings. It was customary to offer the first sip of a drink of *chicha*—a beerlike drink made from corn or other plants—to Pachamama, the earth-mother goddess. People buried small offerings at or near shrines as well. These could be small carved llama figurines or packets that might include stones, coca, food, and other items wrapped up together before being buried. Offerings also included portions of slaughtered animals, and sometimes entire animals were

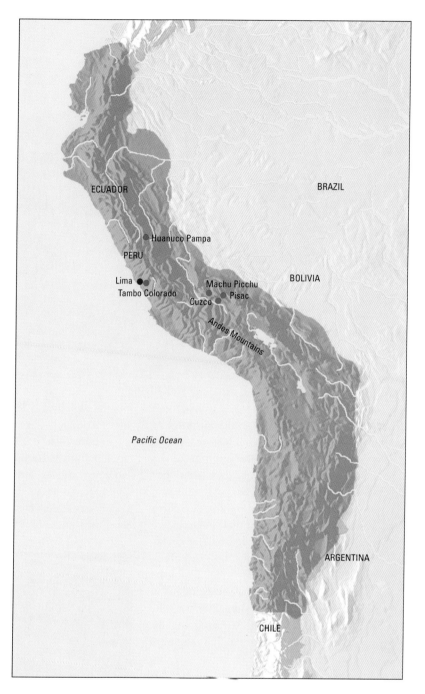

sacrificed to specific gods. On very rare occasions human sacrifice occurred.

The center of the Inca Empire was the city of Cuzco. This contained the most important of the Inca temples, the Coricancha, known today as the Temple of the Sun. Also located in Cuzco were the major administrative buildings, and the starting point of the Inca road system. All roads really did lead to Cuzco, and the Incas did everything that they could to ensure that Cuzco was the most important point in the empire.

The Inca Empire was called *Tawantinsuyo*, the "Land of the Four Quarters." The empire was divided into four regions by lines that ran from

ABOVE: The Incas built a huge empire that stretched over a vast area of South America. This map shows the extent of the empire at its height as well as the location of key Inca towns and cities (indicated by red dots).

the center of Cuzco, so that the city itself was divided into four quarters. For the purposes of administration each of the four quarters of the empire was considered equal to any one of the others, although modern maps show that they covered very different-sized areas.

Many historians have been puzzled as to how the Incas could keep control of their huge empire without the benefit of either the wheel or of any animal capable of carrying heavy loads or pulling wagons. The largest animals that could be domesticated in the Andes were South American members of the camel family—the llama and the alpaca. These animals became important for food, wool, and for transportation, but they were too small to be ridden. A llama could carry no more than about 40 lb. (20kg) of goods. This meant that large numbers of llamas were needed to carry goods across the empire.

Transportation under the Incas did not just rely on the llama, however. Llama caravans carried some food and other items across long distances to where the Incas needed them, but it was men who carried most of the loads. Men also carried the litters that the Inca rulers rode on, while during the harvest farmers collected their produce into bundles that they carried to storehouses on their backs. In a similar way babies were carried everywhere on the backs of their mothers or older sisters. It was human labor that fueled the Inca Empire, and it may have been a need for an increasingly bigger workforce that

spurred the Incas' desire to constantly expand their territory.

The Inca Empire covered a vast area of land ranging from barren deserts to steep mountains and dense jungles. Transportation and communication across these huge distances and varied terrain was a great challenge. However, the Incas developed an impressive network of roads and

LEFT: A silver figurine of an Inca nobleman. The figure's earlobes have been stretched by metal discs, a fashion that was restricted to Inca nobility.

Chaski—Relay Messengers of the Incas

At the height of the Inca Empire runners known as *chaski* carried messages and small goods along the road systems across the Andes. Along the routes runners were stationed every one to five miles (1.6 to 8km), depending on the terrain and altitude, and verbal messages were transferred from one runner to the next in relay style. An early Spanish chronicler recorded that Inca runners could carry letters from Lima to Cuzco—a distance of 400 miles (650km)—in three days, a task that required 12 days on horseback. *Chaski* were an incredibly fast and efficient way of sending messages, and the roads they traveled were the arteries that kept goods, information, and services flowing through the realm.

BELOW: A rope bridge made from mountain grasses in the traditional Inca way. At 150 ft (45m), the original version of this bridge over the Apurimac River was the longest in the Inca Empire.

efficient methods of transporting information, food, and other goods that were not surpassed until the second half of the 20th century.

Inca roads were built across all kinds of terrain. Wide roads with mud sidewalls ran across the coastal deserts, while stone stairways wound through the most mountainous regions. Stone walls lined huge roads on the high plains, while raised earth causeways crossed marshy lands. Other types of Inca roads and paths were devised to suit various other types of terrain.

➤ INCA BRIDGES ➤

In the mountains good bridges were needed to span rivers and gorges. Narrow spans could be crossed using simple bridges made of logs or planks on masonry foundations. The wider and deeper canyons of important rivers required more elaborate engineering, however. The Incas built strong rope suspension bridges across such canyons, so allowing the uninterrupted movement of people and goods along the roads of the empire.

The Incas were famous for their architecture. Inca stonemasons and builders cut individual stones that fitted together exactly to form stately structures for palaces, temples, and public buildings. Many Inca buildings in the highlands of Peru are still standing, while modern buildings have been destroyed by the frequent strong earthquakes that shake the Andean region.

The hallmarks of the best Inca architecture are perfect siting in the landscape, well-crafted and carefully placed stone blocks, and ingenious and efficient use of human labor, levers, and ropes to move the huge stones into place. Inca buildings are thus renowned not just for their beauty but also for the remarkable engineering skills of those who built them.

Domestic buildings were much simpler. The average citizen of the Inca Empire was a farmer who lived in a small house with one or two rooms made of stone or mud. Men worked on their own

lands and contributed labor to communal projects, including the construction and maintenance of irrigation canals. Women helped with the farming, tended small children, spun wool, and wove, as well as cooking and brewing *chicha*. Children also worked, tending herds of llamas and alpacas, and learning the skills of their fathers and mothers. People who were not farmers might be fishermen or herders. Everyone participated in religious life, communal labor parties, and carried out any special work required by the Inca emperor or by religious leaders.

→ THE TAX SYSTEM →

Land and goods were divided into those products owed to the Inca emperor himself, those reserved for the gods, and lands and products that could be used by the common people. All families and towns owed some of their labor to the Inca emperor. Often they had to pay items of tribute such as textiles and food goods as well. There was no money in the Inca Empire, and value was measured by goods and units of labor. People and the things they produced were what was valuable to the Inca emperor, and human labor and products were what was owed to him as "tax."

It is often said that the Incas had no real system of writing—that is to say, they never used any system of symbols to represent their spoken language. They did, however, have a very important and very powerful system for keeping records, known as quipu. Quipu were groups of knotted string used to keep track of important official information. Trained scribes and quipu readers recorded such things as the number of goods and soldiers sent with an army, and perhaps set down historical events as well. No Spaniard ever learned to read or understand the quipu properly, and the use of quipu died out as Spanish writing took over the task of record-keeping after the conquest. However, it is clear that quipu were an effective and important tool for keeping records.

LEFT: An Inca female figurine made of gold. It is wrapped in a piece of brightly colored woven woolen textile, fastened with a gold pin. The statuette is of one of the "virgins of the sun," handmaidens of the Inca emperor who lived with him in his palace.

→ THE END OF AN EMPIRE →

The Inca Empire was one of the greatest civilizations ever to develop, but its end came about very quickly. In the late 1520s and early 1530s the empire fell into disarray because of a vicious civil war between two half-brothers, Huascar and Atahualpa. Atahualpa finally won in 1532 but was quickly captured by a Spanish adventurer called Francisco Pizarro. Although Pizarro was in charge of only 168 men, he managed by treachery to take control of the Inca Empire, killing Atahualpa and putting an emperor loyal to the Spanish in his place.

Hundreds of years later, however, the influence of the Incas and their ancestors is still seen in Peru, and many of the achievements of the empire have never been equaled.

Inca Weapons and Armor

The Inca soldiers who conquered vast stretches of South America had a wide range of weapons at their disposal. The main hand weapons were the mace, the club, and the battleaxe. To attack from a distance, the Inca armies used slings, bows and arrows, and darts. They also used *bolas*—lengths of rope with weights on the end that were whirled around the head and then flung at the opposing troops. The Inca emperor himself carried a large club with a star-shaped head made of stone, copper, gold, or silver.

Inca armor suited close combat. Protective headgear included cloth, wooden, or cane helmets. To protect their bodies Inca warriors either wrapped themselves in layers of fabric or wore quilted cotton shirts or tunics. Soldiers carried shields made of wooden frames covered with deer skin, fabric, or even feathers. They might also use cloth around their arms to protect them against clubs. Inca armies were a colorful sight, but they were also well-fed and disciplined, and were a highly efficient fighting force.

Machu Picchu

The Inca town of Machu Picchu was apparently abandoned by its citizens sometime in the 16th century. What makes it unique is the fact that it was never discovered and destroyed by the Spanish—so its remains give us an excellent idea of what an Inca city was like.

LEFT: The spectacular ruins of Machu Picchu. The town was built around a large open space, called the Great Plaza, where public meetings were held. The great stone stairway can be seen in the foreground.

In July 1911 an American explorer and archaeologist named Hiram Bingham left the city of Cuzco in Peru on an expedition to find the old Inca city of Vilcabamba. Bingham knew that Vilcabamba had fallen to the Spanish invaders of Peru in 1572. But the actual site of the city had never been found, and Bingham was determined to discover it. With several mules to carry their baggage, Bingham and his team set off toward the northwest, along the Urubamba River. Five days and about 60 miles (100km) later, Bingham met a local farmer who claimed there were old ruins on a nearby mountain. After a steep climb Bingham and his companions reached some stone walls covered in creeper and moss. They then saw buildings made of white granite, partially hidden by vegetation. Bingham had found the remains of an Inca town that were, as he later wrote, "as wonderful ruins as ever found in Peru."

However, what Bingham had found was not Vilcabamba—the ruins were those of a small fortified Inca town that had once held about 1,000 inhabitants. It lay on a ridge between two mountain peaks, one called Huayna Picchu, the other Machu Picchu—and it was after this mountain that the ruins were named.

⇀ WELL-PLANNED TOWN ↽

Machu Picchu was built in the 15th century. It was probably part of the royal estate of the Inca king Pachacutec (who ruled between 1438 and 1471). Among the town's buildings were houses for both the local ruling class and the resident workers who tended the surrounding farmland.

The town was carefully planned, and the Inca architects who designed it probably used clay or stone models to guide them. The buildings were set on different levels and reached by stairways. The town's center was the Great Plaza. This was an open space where large meetings were held and public announcements made. On all sides of the plaza were large, well-constructed buildings made of stone where the nobles lived.

Around the town terraced fields for farmers were cut into the sides of the mountains and surrounded with drystone walls to prevent the soil being washed away. Numerous channels supplied the terraces with water.

Craftsmen and workers had small houses located away from the town center. These humble homes had roofs thatched with grass and usually only one room to house the entire family. Families who were related to each other lived in a group of between two to eight small houses clustered around a courtyard. In this shared open space the women of the households cooked food on small clay stoves.

Bingham also discovered two temples. They were small and simple, and probably roofless so that the Incas could observe the sun, stars, and moon—which they believed to be gods. The sun was the most important god and was thought to be the divine father of the Inca kings. At Machu Picchu it seems that the sun was worshiped on a small hill near the two temples. Here stands a low stone platform that supports a short pillar. It is called Intihuatana, the "hitching post of the sun." In winter, on the shortest day of the year, Inca priests symbolically "tied" the sun to this post to make sure that it would return the following year to warm the earth and ripen the crops.

➤ CRAFTS AND METALWORK ➤

Archaeological finds at Machu Picchu show that Inca craftsmen were skilled in working metals and stone. By mixing tin with copper, they created bronze. With this they made axes, chisels, and knives. They also made hammers and knives from a dark hard rock called diorite. And they made strings of beads from a stone called green schist. However, much to his disappointment, Bingham did not find any great artistic treasures or any gold. This is surprising since the Incas were famous for their goldwork.

Many of the objects Bingham found were buried in graves. More than 100 burials were uncovered, revealing 173 skeletons, most of them women. The most interesting burial was that of a middle-aged woman. From examining her bones

ABOVE: Machu Picchu is set on a ridge between two peaks 2,000 ft (610m) above the river valley, making it one of the most dramatic archaeological sites in the world.

it was possible to tell that she had died from a disease. Buried with her were a bronze mirror, a knife with a handle in the shape of a flying bird, and a few woolen fibers from some sort of cloth. In other burials Bingham found drinking bowls, pins for fastening clothes, bronze tweezers, and ornamental knives.

It is not known why Machu Picchu was abandoned. Disease or a civil war may have been to blame. But because the town was so well hidden, its ruins have survived to tell their story.

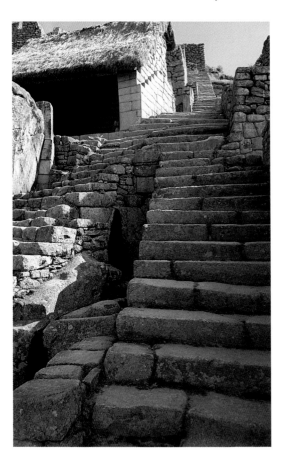

RIGHT: One of the many long stone stairways used as streets in Machu Picchu.

Chapter 5:

Oceania

The colonization of Australia, the Pacific islands, and New Zealand is one of the most extraordinary feats of ancient peoples. The Aborigines arrived in Australia by sea from Southeast Asia more than 40,000 years ago. Thousands of years later, around 1500 B.C., the ancient Polynesians started their own migration from Southeast Asia, sailing in double-hulled canoes to colonize a multitude of islands spread across the vast Pacific Ocean. One of their final landfalls was on New Zealand, about A.D. 1000. These were epic voyages, without maps or navigational aids, by some of history's greatest sailors.

BELOW: An 18th-century illustration of Polynesian double-hulled canoes—the vessels in which the ancient Polynesians made their epic voyages across the Pacific Ocean.

Aborigines of Australia

For at least 40,000 years the Australian Aborigines lived as hunter-gatherers in almost complete isolation from the rest of the world. During this time they developed a society with a complex system of beliefs and social relationships.

The ancestors of the present-day Aborigines arrived in Australia from Southeast Asia more than 40,000 years ago during the last Ice Age. At that time the level of the sea was lower, so Australia, Tasmania, and New Guinea formed a single landmass. This landmass was still separated by water from Southeast Asia, however, so the first Australians must have arrived by sea. This sea crossing to Australia is one of the first examples ever of people using boats. At the end of the Ice Age—about 10,000 years ago—the ice melted and the level of the sea rose, cutting Australia off from New Guinea and leaving the Aborigines isolated on the Australian continent.

The ancient Aborigines lived a wandering life, hunting wild animals and gathering whatever food they could find. However, they did not wander aimlessly in search of food but within clearly defined tribal territories. They also knew where certain plants would be growing and when they would be ready to gather, so they visited these places regularly at the right time to find food.

The Aborigines hunted large land animals such as kangaroos, wallabies, and emus and caught sea mammals such as seal, turtle, and dugong (a sea cow with flippers and tusks). They also ate small creatures, including possums, kangaroo rats, lizards, and snakes. Witchetty grubs were a favorite food, since they were one of the very few sources of fat. The Aborigines speared fish or caught them in nets. Sometimes they built traps to catch fish or eels.

The Aborigines normally lived in small groups of a few families. Occasionally the whole tribe, or even several tribes, would gather together in one place. This might be because a lot of a certain kind of food was to be found there at that time. At these gatherings, people would take the opportunity to perform ceremonies, exchange goods, arrange marriages, and settle quarrels.

ABOVE: A present-day Aborigine making a traditional spear for hunting. Spears usually had pointed heads made of flint, and the ancient Aborigines used them to kill kangaroos, wallabies, and other animals.

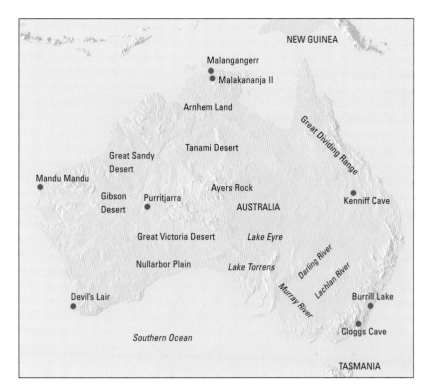

ABOVE: The red dots on this map of Australia show the sites of some of the caves and rock shelters used by the Aborigines from between 40,000 and 17,000 years ago.

ancestors created both the land and the social order. This meant that the Aborigines believed they had a spiritual relationship with their territory, and that the land, the animals, plants, human beings, and the spiritual ancestors were all one. The ancestors had not simply created the world in the past but were continually present in the land, filling it with their life-giving creative powers. Many Dreamtime ancestors had been transformed into features of the landscape—rocks, rivers, and waterholes, and these were considered to be sacred places.

The close relationship the Aborigines had with the land carried with it the obligation to take care of it. They did this by performing ceremonies and by taking an active part in managing it. The main tool they used for this was fire. Some plants in Australia grow better after the land has been burned off because there is less competition from other plants. By burning the land and so clearing it, the Aborigines could encourage the plants they needed for food to grow there.

Aboriginal society was based on a complex kinship system, in which complicated rules about relationships determined people's responsibilities and how they behaved to each other. The exchange of gifts was important in strengthening social relationships. As a result, trading networks developed between tribes, and valuable items might be sent hundreds of miles.

Because they were constantly on the move, the Aborigines usually built temporary shelters of wood or bark. Sometimes these were little more than a brush windbreak. In the southwest of what is now the state of Victoria, however, winter huts were substantial wooden structures with turf roofs. These huts were often reused every year.

The Aborigines' mobile lifestyle meant that their tools and weapons had to be easy to carry. Most of their tools and weapons were made of wood and stone—a typical tool-kit varied from region to region, but it usually included spears, shields, clubs, knives, hatchets, digging sticks, and grinding stones. This equipment was carried in a bag made of basketry or animal skin. The Aborigines also used dishes made of wood or bark. In cooler regions they wore cloaks made out of kangaroo and possum skins.

Many tools were multipurpose; the spearthrower used in western Australia is a good example. It was used for throwing spears but it also had a stone flake fixed in the handle for carving wood. In northern Australia some groups built seagoing canoes, while in the southeast people built canoes of bark to use on rivers.

⇀ THE DREAMTIME ⇀

Although there were about 500 different tribal groups, speaking at least 250 separate languages, all Aborigines shared the same set of beliefs. They believed in something they called the Dreamtime—the time of creation, when their

Aboriginal Art

The Aborigines have been decorating rock surfaces for thousands of years, by painting or engraving pictures on them, or sometimes by using stencils. Some of the rock paintings are at least 20,000 years old and may be much older. The Aborigines also decorated their tools and weapons, and drawings were made on skin cloaks and on sheets of bark. For ceremonies people would make elaborate soil and sand sculptures and paint their bodies.

Rock art was part of the Aborigines' spiritual life. The meaning of the images was often hidden from outsiders who had not been initiated.

With the coming of the Europeans and the disruption of Aboriginal society the meanings of many of the paintings and decorations have been lost.

This recent rock painting in Kakadu in northern Australia is part of an Aboriginal art tradition that goes back over 20,000 years.

Polynesians

The ancient Polynesians first set out across the Pacific from the coasts of Southeast Asia about 1500 B.C. and gradually spread throughout the Pacific islands. These voyages of settlement represented a spectacular achievement by ancient peoples sailing in canoes.

LEFT: These carved wooden statues were found at a temple site on the west coast of Hawaii and depict traditional Polynesian gods. The Hawaiian islands were settled sometime around A.D. 400.

Today the Polynesians are scattered over an area that forms an immense triangle, with the Hawaiian islands, New Zealand, and Easter Island at its corners. Although they are spread over such a large area, genetically the Polynesians form a single group. They speak dialects of the same language, and share many cultural features.

The exact origins of the Polynesians are uncertain. Expansion of human settlement into the remote Pacific began in about 1600 B.C. with the appearance of a distinctive culture called Lapita. Evidence for this is found in the pottery at Lapita sites, which is usually elaborately decorated with stamped designs. There are many of these sites spread over Melanesia and western Polynesia from New Guinea to Samoa. Some archaeologists believe that the Lapita culture originated in Southeast Asia, while others think that it developed locally in Melanesia. It is generally agreed, however, that the Lapita people were the ancestors of the Polynesians.

The Lapita way of life seems to have been very much focused on the sea. Most Lapita sites were coastal villages, and in some cases people even seem to have built their houses on pillars over the water. The sea provided a good deal of food—fish and shellfish—and shell was used to make fishhooks and adzes (axes) as well as

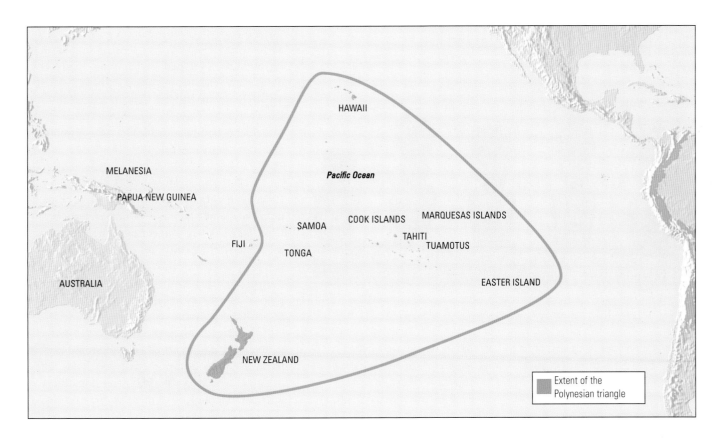

ABOVE: The so-called
Polynesian triangle,
which was formed by
Hawaii, New Zealand,
and Easter Island.

Amazing Voyages

The settlement of the remote islands of the Pacific is all the more impressive when we realize that it was achieved without navigational instruments or charts. Polynesian double-hulled canoes were large and fast, and were capable of voyaging thousands of miles. The canoes were sailed by skilled navigators who used their detailed knowledge of the stars, cloud patterns, winds and swells, and the habits of seabirds to keep track of their position and locate land. In 1976 the skill of these navigators was demonstrated when the *Hokulea*, a replica of a traditional Polynesian canoe, was sailed from Tahiti to Hawaii using age-old navigation techniques.

A present-day Polynesian boatbuilder making a canoe from a hollowed-out tree trunk, using traditional techniques.

ornaments, such as armbands, beads, and other decorative and valuable objects. The Lapita colonists also brought domestic animals and plants with them to the islands they settled.

The expansion of the Lapita people seems to have been rapid, suggesting that they had sophisticated boatbuilding and navigation techniques. It is likely that the development of the large double-hulled sailing canoe was a key factor in their success. The Lapita migrations must have been deliberate, since they carried with them sufficient equipment, plants, and animals, as well as enough people, to establish successful settlements. Their voyages were certainly not one-way; there is evidence of long-distance trading networks for obsidian and other items linking Lapita communities. The Lapita culture seems to have lasted for about 1,000 years.

➤ COLONIZING THE PACIFIC ➤

The main features of Polynesian culture seem to have developed on the islands of Samoa and Tonga. Like their Lapita ancestors, the Polynesians were seafarers. About 300 B.C. voyagers from Samoa and Tonga began another eastward migration. They discovered and settled the Cook Islands, Tahiti, the Tuamotus, and the Marquesas Islands. By A.D. 400 both Hawaii and Easter Island—two points of the Polynesian triangle—had been colonized. New Zealand—the

Easter Island

These stone statues (or moai*) were erected at Ahu Nau Nau, where the original inhabitants of Easter Island first landed. Over 800 such statues have been found on the island.*

One of the most amazing feats of the Polynesian navigators was to reach and colonize Rapa Nui, or Easter Island. This tiny speck of land, only 64 sq. miles (166 sq. km) in area, is one of the most remote of the Polynesian islands. The difficulty of the voyage probably meant that only one lot of settlers reached it—in the early centuries A.D. The people then developed in isolation, building great stone platforms (*ahu*) all around the shoreline and carving hundreds of huge stone statues (*moai*) of their ancestors, many of which were placed on these platforms, facing away from the sea.

The islanders may have brought about their own downfall by destroying the forests of huge palm trees that covered the island, even though the trees were the foundation of their society. The resulting lack of timber stopped the production of statues, since there were no more rollers, levers, or rope. The inhabitants could no longer build canoes, so no more deep-sea fish could be caught. There was no more fuel for cremations, and burial became the new method of disposing of the dead. Food became scarce, and violence erupted after centuries of peace. Clans raided each other, toppling their rivals' statues.

The ancestor worship of the past was replaced by a new social system based on a warrior elite. Every year a new leader, or "Birdman," was elected by means of an endurance race. Each candidate's representative had to go down a cliff, swim out to an islet, and bring back intact the first egg of the sooty tern. By the time the first Europeans arrived on Easter Sunday 1722, the population had declined catastrophically, and there were virtually no trees left on the island.

divided into chiefs and commoners, and there was also a form of slavery. The most elaborate social hierarchies developed in Hawaii, Tonga, and Tahiti. The Polynesians shared a broadly similar set of religious beliefs. Ceremonial enclosures, known as *marae*, were a prominent feature of the settlements and provided a focus for ceremonies and community meetings.

⇀ FARMING TECHNIQUES ⇀

Polynesian agriculture was based on a range of crops, including yams, sweet potato, taro, breadfruit, bananas, and sugarcane. The Polynesians practiced shifting cultivation, which meant that a patch of land was cleared, the vegetation was burned, and then crops were planted. Later, the plot was allowed to lie fallow and gradually return to natural vegetation.

On some islands very complex systems of irrigation were used to bring water to crops. Taro, in particular, was grown in irrigated fields. Pigs, dogs, and chickens were the main domestic animals, although not all of them were introduced to all islands. Most domesticated plants used by the settlers originated in Southeast Asia. The sweet potato, however, came from the Americas, which indicates that at some point the Polynesians reached South America and brought it back.

Over time the tradition of making pottery, which the Polynesians had inherited from the Lapita culture, seems to have declined, and complex decoration was simplified or abandoned completely. Finally, the Polynesians seem to have stopped making pottery entirely.

third point of the triangle, and the hardest to reach, was settled about A.D. 1000.

There is no doubt that the Polynesian colonizing voyages were deliberate and that exploration to find new islands preceded colonization. Like their Lapita ancestors, they took with them everything necessary to establish successful settlements. In a few cases the colonies were not successful and were abandoned.

Polynesian societies were organized into tribes and clans. Normally they were further

RIGHT: A stonewalled ceremonial enclosure on Tahiti. Such enclosures were used for meetings and religious rituals and are found throughout Polynesia. The British explorer James Cook saw human sacrifices being made here during his visit in 1769.

Maoris

The arrival of the Maoris in New Zealand around 1000 A.D. was among the last of the island explorations of the Polynesians. The New Zealand group of islands was one of the farthest lands the Polynesians reached and involved a hazardous journey into the unknown.

ABOVE: Present-day Maoris wearing traditional dress. The Maori people arrived in New Zealand 1,000 years ago, and soon colonized both islands.

We do not know exactly where the Maoris came from, or why they left their original homes. Culturally they resemble the peoples who lived to the northeast, in areas such as Tahiti. The winds and currents in the South Pacific meant that sailing to New Zealand was easier from this direction, even though the islands of Fiji, Tonga, and Samoa were actually closer. Return voyages would have been extremely difficult, so it is not surprising that there was little contact between the Maoris and the rest of Polynesia after the first settlers reached New Zealand.

Maori oral traditions tell of the arrival of double-hulled canoes (*pahi*) at several landing sites on North Island. The canoes would have carried everything the new settlers needed to survive, including animals and food plants. The settlers came from tiny tropical islands, and New Zealand—or Aoteoroa (the land of the long white cloud) as they called it—would have been quite unlike any place they had ever known. It was very large—much larger than all the other Polynesian islands put together—and had a cool temperate climate. There were great forests in which grew plants they had never seen before, many species of unknown birds, volcanoes, and high mountains capped with snow in winter. To survive in this unfamiliar environment, the new arrivals had to be both adaptable and resourceful.

⤙ EARLY SETTLEMENTS ⤚

The settlers quickly spread through both islands. The earliest settlements were small, mainly on the coast, and were occupied seasonally.

An important source of food for these early settlers were marine creatures, such as seals, dolphins, whales, seabirds, and shellfish. Many of the tropical food plants the Maori had brought with them could not be grown in the temperate climate of this new country. Only the sweet potato could be cultivated—and even that would not grow successfully on South Island. However, new local food plants were soon discovered, including the roots of the native bracken and the cabbage tree. Fiber from native flax plants was used to make clothing. On South Island, where the climate was much cooler and so sweet potato could not be grown, people lived by hunting, fishing, and gathering foods.

Tools and weapons were made from stone. Greenstone, or nephrite (a kind of jade) was one of the new types of stone discovered by the Maori settlers. It is mainly found on South Island and was traded to North Island. Greenstone was used to make weapons, personal ornaments, and other precious and beautiful objects.

Like other Polynesian societies, Maori society was divided into classes—commoners and families of the chief. The people were also organized into tribes (called *iwi*) and subtribes or clans (*hapu*). A group of *iwi* claimed descent from the crew of a single founding canoe. Daily life was organized around villages where members of a single *hapu* lived.

Maori Tattooing

Tattooing was a widely practiced form of skin decoration in the Pacific, and the word itself is Polynesian in origin. Maori tattooing was particularly elaborate and distinctive in style. The ornate curving designs are similar to those used in their woodcarving. Both men and women wore tattoos, but those of the men usually covered more of the body. The color was applied by dipping small bone tattooing chisels in pigment and then tapping them into the skin. The process was painful, and complicated tattoos might take years to complete. Tattooing was a skilled art done by specialists who were highly respected in Maori society.

A 19th-century illustration of a Maori chief's complex spiral tattoos.

At the center of each village were the *marae* (a ceremonial open space) and the meeting house. The meeting house was often richly decorated with carved designs and is still an important center for present-day Maori communities. Houses were mostly rectangular and built of wood. Warmth and light were provided by fires in stone-edged or scoop hearths, and cooking took

The Extinction of the Moa

When the first Maori settlers arrived in New Zealand, they found many new species of birds. These included about eight species of flightless birds known as moa, relatives of emus and ostriches. The largest moa were taller than a human being. Because the moa had not been hunted by any native New Zealand animals, they were unafraid of the newcomers and so were easily killed. By the 17th century A.D. the moa and several other species of birds were extinct.

Hunting probably contributed to the extinction of the moa, but another reason may have been the loss of their natural habitat caused by the Maori habit of clearing large areas of forest land with fire. Changes in the climate and the introduction by the Maoris of dogs and rats to the island may also have played a part.

RIGHT: A greenstone breast pendant. Such items were precious and were passed down through generations.

BELOW: This map of New Zealand shows the sites of some of the larger *pa*, or fortified settlements.

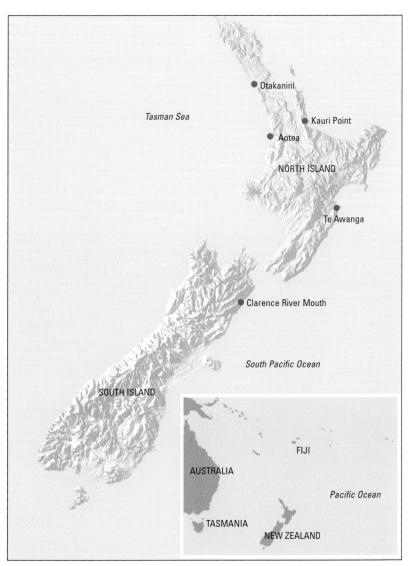

place outside in earth ovens. Underground storage pits were used to store sweet potatoes. Although people lived more or less permanently in villages, they would move seasonally to temporary camps to hunt or fish or tend crops.

⟶ WARRING *HAPU* ⟵

From about A.D. 1300 there seems to have been a marked increase in warfare in Maori society. People began to build numerous fortified settlements known as *pa*. Most of them were on North Island, where over 5,000 have been found. *Pa* were built of packed earth and timber, and had complicated arrangements of banks, ditches, and palisades. Some *pa* were cut into hillsides, while others were built on easily defended ridges, promontories, or the cones of extinct volcanoes. *Pa* were also built on the edges of lakes and swamps. Some *pa* seem to have been used mainly in times of war, while others were more permanent and acted as major tribal centers.

This rise of fortified settlements indicates an increase in hostilities between *hapu*. This may have been because the Maori were now competing for dwindling resources. A cooling climate, forest clearance, and overhunting made the living less easy. Certainly the population on South Island seems to have fallen at this time. By the time the Europeans arrived in the 19th century, conflicts between *hapu* had become very fierce.

Chapter 6:

Across the Cultures

Even though ancient cultures might be separated from each other by great distances, and the means of travel were primitive, there was plenty of cross-fertilization of ideas and information in the distant past. Trade was the internet of the ancient world. Traders carrying goods from city to city also spread news and unwittingly acted as purveyors of ideas and knowledge of other cultures. This chapter looks at some aspects of ancient life and examines their differences and similarities in various societies.

BELOW: Caravans of camels like this transported goods along ancient desert trade routes such as the Silk Road, providing a link between widely separated peoples.

Agriculture

The change from hunting and gathering to farming started in about 9000 B.C. in the Fertile Crescent, an arc of land stretching from the Persian Gulf to the Mediterranean Sea. This profound change in lifestyle led to the early settlements, and eventually to the rise of cities.

LEFT: Farming started in the Middle East about 11,000 years ago. Because early farmers had no domesticated animals, they had to carry the harvested crops themselves, like these present-day farmers in Afghanistan.

The end of the last Ice Age created unusually moist conditions in which wild grains flourished. They were gathered by nomadic peoples, who gradually began to experiment by scattering the grain so that it would grow again. In this way they eventually transplanted the wild grains from their natural habitat—the mountains that fringe the region—to the fertile valleys of the Euphrates and the Tigris rivers. When people started to plant crops deliberately in one place, they had to stay in the same place (or return to it) to harvest the crop. So over time wandering hunter-gatherers became settled people.

These early farmers started to try to improve their crops by selecting and growing the best plants. In this way they were able to adapt grains for the benefit of humans—a process that is called domestication. By 7000 B.C. wheat and barley were being cultivated over a vast area, from Anatolia (today's Turkey) to present-day Pakistan.

The practice of keeping animals—mainly goats and sheep—for the benefit of humans also began at this time. By about 4500 B.C. farmers in Mesopotamia were using animals to pull simple wooden plows. Farmers in the two great valleys of the Euphrates and Tigris rivers also began to experiment with irrigation by digging channels that transported water from the rivers to nearby fields. Both these innovations the plow and irrigation—helped increase the yield of crops.

The Yellow River Valley of China was an area where agriculture developed separately. Millet was grown in China from about 6000 B.C. Millet is resistant to drought and so was an ideal crop for this region, which is rich in fertile soil but very dry. In the more humid conditions of south China wet rice farming was started around 5000 B.C. People also started growing other water-loving plants, such as water-chestnuts, yams, and other tubers. Rice, which was to become the most widely grown grain in the world, was soon being cultivated over an immense area, from the Ganges Valley in India to the islands of the Philippines in the Pacific.

As farming became the main way of life, people started to grow more crops than they needed.

Surplus food supplies were kept in storage for times when little was produced, and this meant that fewer people had to spend all their time producing food. For the first time people were able to live in large, settled communities. They could now develop craft skills and take part in long-distance trade. This led to new activities such as developing new tools, making pottery, and working with metals such as gold and copper.

→ THE NILE VALLEY ←

The Nile Valley was the center of one of the world's earliest urban civilizations. The power of ancient Egypt was supported by its agriculture, which had flourished since about 4500 B.C. Every year the Nile River flooded, and when the floodwaters receded, they left a layer of fertile silt spread over the land, which was immediately planted with wheat and barley. Egyptian farmers also grew other crops like onions, garlic, leeks, beans, lentils, lettuce, cucumbers, dates, figs, melons, and grapes. Government tax collectors inspected the produce every year and set production targets for the farmers to meet.

Egypt's prosperity depended on the Nile River, and when the floods were unusually low, the consequences were disastrous. Around 2150 B.C. a series of low floods resulted in very poor harvests and led to widespread famine.

All the earliest urban civilizations were supported by agriculture. The cities that developed around 2500 B.C. in the valley of the Indus River in present-day Pakistan were supplied by a rich agricultural region. The Indus River flooded every winter and in the spring, when the floodwaters receded, farmers planted wheat and barley, which grew easily in the soil that had been made fertile by the flood. At the ancient city of Mohenjodaro in Pakistan a fragment of woven cotton was found, the earliest evidence from the ancient world of cotton cultivation.

As new areas of the world were colonized, new crops were cultivated. From about 1500 B.C. an extraordinary movement of people took place from the islands of Southeast Asia. By around A.D. 1000 these Polynesian colonists had crossed the vast expanse of the Pacific Ocean, settling in scattered island communities from New Zealand to Easter Island. They grew local crops such as yams, taro, breadfruits, bananas, and coconuts. With limited land available they were forced to expand the areas of cultivable land by building terraced fields into the hillsides, a practice common in many mountainous areas, such as Greece, South America, and Southeast Asia.

From the fifth millennium B.C. agriculture began to develop in eastern North America. Corn soon became the staple crop, and settlements appeared. The first North American towns developed in the middle Mississippi Valley around A.D. 700. These towns had large populations of up to 10,000 people and therefore depended on plenty of food being grown by farmers.

Until A.D. 700 corn could only be grown in the south of the region, because it needed about 200 frost-free days for ripening. When a new type of corn was developed that ripened in just 120 days, it was grown more widely. In the rich lands of the Ohio, Tennessee, Arkansas, Red, and Mississippi rivers two crops of corn were harvested a year, plus sunflowers, beans, and squash. This output could support big urban populations.

ABOVE: The Chinese were the first people to grow rice, from about 5000 B.C. Rice needs a great deal of water to grow, and early Chinese farmers soon found ways of irrigating their fields, as shown in this Chinese painting.

BELOW: A map showing the Fertile Crescent (green) in the Middle East, where farming first began.

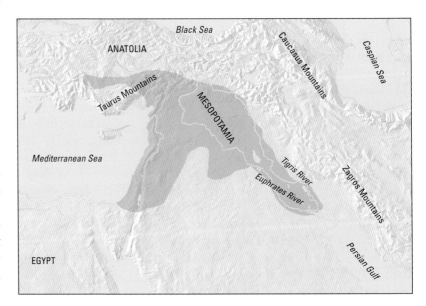

Calendars and Clocks

When hunter-gatherers started to become farmers in Neolithic times, they found that they needed to record the changes in the seasons so that they would know when to plant and when to harvest their crops. To do this they had to devise calendars.

LEFT: The Aztecs used both a solar calendar and a 260-day ritual calendar, in which each day was associated with a particular god. In this illustration from an Aztec codex, each rectangle represents a different day in the ritual calendar and contains a picture of the associated god.

The first calendars may have been simple bone implements with sequences of notches or holes carved in them. The Blanchard Bone, found in southwestern France, dates to 30,000 years ago and some archaeologists believe that the marks on it show the phases of the moon over a two-month period.

The ancient Egyptians were the first to use a dating system in around 3000 B.C. They used both a lunar and solar calendar. To keep their lunar calendar accurate, they also followed the movements of the stars. The particular star they followed was Sirius, the brightest star in the sky, which reappears in the night sky every year just before dawn in July. Egyptian astronomers were able to calculate that the star appeared once every 365 and a quarter days. We now know that this is the amount of time it takes for the earth to revolve around the sun. The Egyptians used this figure as the basis for their solar calendar.

The Egyptian solar calendar divided the year into 12 months, each of 30 days. At the end of the year there was a special five-day month to make up the 365 days of the year. An extra day was then added every fourth year to even things up. A similar system was used in ancient Mesopotamia.

The Babylonians, however, had a slightly different system. They used 29- and 30-day months alternately, and divided up the week into seven days—probably because there were seven known planets, and seven was their sacred number.

The ancient Chinese used a lunar calendar, but it was very complicated. Their calculations were related to the place where the sun rose on the horizon. The system was based on a 19-year cycle, and the emperors decided when a month should be added to the year. They had to add seven months over every 19-year cycle, with one day taken away from every fourth 19-year cycle. The new month was added about halfway

Lunar and Solar Years

Months are measured by the time between one full moon and the next (in other words, the time it takes for the moon to orbit the earth). Years, on the other hand, are measured by the time it takes the earth to orbit the sun. The moon keeps a very regular cycle of 29 and a half days between one full moon and the next. However, in a 365-day solar year there are only 12 complete moon cycles between one winter solstice (midwinter's day) and the next. This means that a lunar calendar will be about 11 days too short. So, to maintain a calendar that keeps in step with the seasons and the moon's cycles, extra days have to be added to the 29-day lunar month.

ABOVE: The vessel on the right is part of an ancient Egyptian water clock dating from around 1415 B.C. The water would have drained into another vessel, represented by the modern glass container on the left. Unlike sundials, water clocks were able to measure time during the night as well as during the day.

between the shortest day and the first day of spring. This was a highly accurate lunar calendar—but complicated to operate.

The calendar of Republican Rome was made up of 12 months and 355 days. The year was short by about 11 days because the calendar was based on the lunar year. So an additional month was supposed to be added when necessary between February 24 and 25. This was rarely done, however, because an extra month on the calendar would mean that state officials, who might be opponents of the politicians in power, would stay in office a month longer. By 46 B.C. the calendar had become so distorted that New Year's Day fell on the solar date of October 14, 77 days early.

For this reason Julius Caesar, who had become the dominant political leader, added 90 extra days in 46 B.C. and introduced the Julian calendar, based on the one used in Egypt. The Egyptian calendar was a lunar calendar that had four months of 31 days, one month of 28 days, and the remaining seven months had 29 days.

Caesar ordered that four months should be increased to 30 days and three to 31 days, with February still kept at 28 days. An extra day was added every fourth year. With minor adjustments, this is basically the calendar used today.

The people of ancient Mesoamerica saw time as cyclical. They used a ritual calendar, called the *tzolkin*, based on 260 days. It consisted of combinations of 20 different day names and 13 numbers. Each combination, or day, had its own god. A solar calendar of 365 days, called the *haab*, was also used to measure the seasons and for state affairs. The two calendars were interconnected and every 52 years complete cycles of both calendars coincided.

➤ CLOCKS ➤

Besides keeping track of months and days, ancient peoples tried to find ways of measuring the length of a day. The Babylonians and Greeks measured the day from sunset to sunset, the ancient Egyptians from dawn to dawn, and the Romans from midnight to midnight.

It was the Babylonians who introduced the 24-hour day. The Babylonian counting system was based on the number 12, so they divided the periods of light and dark into 12 sections each. One of the first ways of measuring these units was to stick a wooden or stone post in the ground or on a wall and then to follow the shadow it cast.

Toward the end of the fourth century B.C. a Mesopotamian named Berosos improved on this system by placing the post, now known as a gnomon, at a slant. This cast a more accurate shadow over the different seasons than a straight post.

To measure time at night or on cloudy days, water clocks were developed. In these water is allowed to drain slowly from one container into another. People were able to tell the time by looking at the water level in the second container.

However, the rate of the water's flow out of a container is not constant. The more water in the container, the faster it flows out. An ancient Greek named Ctesibius, who lived during the third century B.C., invented a way to make the flow constant. He used three containers. One, always kept full, flowed into a second. The second had two holes, one halfway up and the other at the bottom—the hole halfway up ensured that the amount of water in the second container remained more or less constant. The third contained a float with a central post. At the top of the post was a statue holding a pointer. The pointer, when aligned with a pillar marked with the hours like a sundial, allowed one to tell the time.

Jewelry

Jewelry is one of the most ancient crafts, and the skills of jewelers in the ancient world were often highly developed. When we look at some of the beautiful and intricate jewelry from early civilizations, it is hard to believe that it was produced so long ago.

We know a good deal about the jewelry of the past because people were often buried with their most precious jewels for use in the afterlife. Very early jewelry may have been worn for protective reasons—amulets (lucky charms), for example. However, it was soon being worn for purely decorative purposes. Elaborate, expensive jewelry was also a status symbol that indicated its owner was wealthy or had a high position in society. For this reason, in some societies jewelry could only be worn by the ruling classes.

In ancient times, like today, jewelry was made from a wide variety of materials, such as metals, gems, amber, animal teeth and bone, glass, pottery, and shell. Jewelry design in different cultures depended on the materials available and the beliefs and customs of the people concerned.

➤ SUMERIAN JEWELRY ➤

Some of the ancient world's most spectacular pieces of jewelry come from Sumer, in the southern region of Mesopotamia (present-day Iraq). In the 1920s and 1930s the British archaeologist Leonard Woolley excavated the Sumerian city of Ur. He uncovered an extraordinary quantity of jewelry dating from about 2500 B.C. In a vast cemetery of more than 2,000 ordinary people Woolley came upon the graves of the Sumerian royal family. The kings, queens, and nobles had been buried with everyday goods needed for the afterlife and had been laid to rest in their court clothes. Both men and women were adorned with sumptuous jewelry (such as earrings, headdresses, and bracelets) made from precious metals and exotic gems.

Sumerian jewelers were highly skilled. They worked with four principal materials, each of which was brought to Sumer from far away. Gold and silver came from the regions that are now Iran and Turkey; lapis lazuli from Afghanistan; and from India came the red stone carnelian.

The Sumerians were the first to use two of the most important decorative techniques in the history of jewelry: filigree and granulation. Filigree is a pattern made of wires that is either soldered (using molten metal as a fastening) to a

LEFT: These hair ornaments, earrings, and necklaces date back to about 2500 B.C. They were found at Ur in the grave of a Sumerian queen.

backing or left as openwork. Granulation consists of tiny decorative balls or grains of metal attached to a piece of jewelry. The Sumerians also knew how to weld metals together, make alloys (mixtures of metal) and enamel, and cut stones.

The Egyptians were also skilled jewelers and produced many beautiful and elaborate pieces. They wore jewelry long before the first pharaohs ruled the land. From about 5500 B.C. people wore necklaces of stone beads, and bracelets and amulets of shell and ivory. The pharaohs, however, needed more sumptuous jewelry to proclaim their status. Egyptian jewelry-making was at its peak during the 400 years of the Middle Kingdom (2040–1650 B.C.), when jewelers worked in gold and silver using a variety of decorative techniques, including granulation and embossing. They also worked with gems, such as amethyst, carnelian, lapis lazuli, garnet, feldspar, and turquoise. The stones were cut, drilled, and polished by hand to make round, oval, conical, and tubular beads for bracelets and collars.

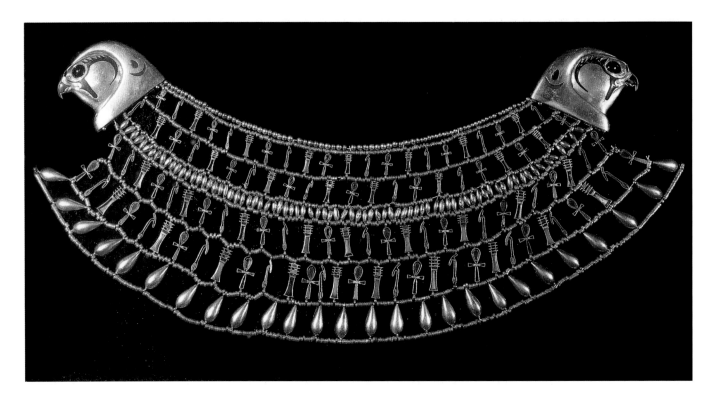

The jewelers' skills were most in demand for making gold funerary jewelry. The bodies of dead pharaohs were weighed down with great quantities of gold: masks covered their faces, breastplates were laid over their chests, and golden tips were added to their fingers and toes. All these were beautifully shaped and often inlaid with lapis lazuli and other semiprecious stones.

The Egyptians believed that gold was the metal of the gods, and to own it was to be nearer to them. However, few people could afford gold, so poorer people wore inferior-quality gems and a material called faience, a cheap imitation of lapis lazuli and turquoise.

Relatively few pieces of jewelry have survived from ancient Indian cultures. However, sculp-

ABOVE: A gold and turquoise ornamental collar that was worn by an Egyptian princess in around 1900 B.C. Gold was comparatively plentiful in ancient Egypt and was a favorite material for making jewelry.

tures have been found that give us some idea of what women wore. The left arm of a bronze statue of a dancer from the Indus Valley civilization (around 2500 B.C.), for example, shows that Indian women were already wearing masses of bangles. Other statues of women show them lavishly adorned with jewelry—hair ornaments, earrings, necklaces, chains, belts, ankle and arm bracelets—but wearing little else, suggesting that jewelry served as a form of clothing.

➤ CHINESE JADE ➤

Jade, the name given to the green mineral nephrite, had a special significance for the cultures of ancient China. It was not only valued as a precious and beautiful stone but was believed to have spiritual and magical properties. From about 1000 B.C. the Chinese carved pendants from jade in the form of creatures such as buffalo, fish, insects, birds, and stags. The pendants were attached to clothing to act as lucky charms that would protect the wearer from harm.

One of the most important pieces of jewelry for women, worn from as early as the Shang dynasty (about 1500 B.C.), was the hairpin. At first they were made from bone or jade, their ends carved into birds or abstract figures, but later they were made from gold. For men belt plaques were the main items of jewelry. These were made from a hard stone, such as jade or agate, and were fixed to a leather or silk belt. The most decorative belt plaques were carved with figures or scenes.

LEFT: A Celtic bracelet made from bronze, dating back to the first century A.D. The bracelet is decorated with disks of colored glass and enamel, and features the swirling lines characteristic of much Celtic art.

The Celts were a collection of tribes that lived in central and western Europe between the eighth century B.C. and the first century A.D. Both men and women wore jewelry. Bronze (a mixture of copper and tin) was made into bracelets, anklets, and fibulae (pins for fastening clothing together). Shale (a type of stone) and glass were also popular materials.

The principal piece of jewelry worn by the Celts was the torc, or neck ring. This was a broad loop of bronze, iron, or gold, which could be plain or decorated. A torc was a very prominent piece of jewelry that could not fail to be seen, so it was probably a sign of the wearer's wealth, rank, or position in society. Torcs may also have had a religious connection, since Celtic gods are generally shown wearing them, and some torcs were thrown into rivers, lakes, and bogs as offerings to the Celtic water gods. The Romans, who conquered many of the Celtic lands, were so impressed by the Celts' torcs that they copied them. The Romans awarded torcs to soldiers for acts of bravery.

In ancient Greece gold was difficult to acquire, so the early Greeks did not wear much jewelry. However, under the rule of Alexander the Great (356–323 B.C.) the art of jewelry-making flourished. Greek jewelers created some of the first cameos (a stone or shell carved in layers in relief). They also made earrings with pendants that were marvels of miniature detail. One of the best-known is a gold earring featuring a winged figure of a woman driving a two-horse chariot— although tiny, its detail is perfect.

Ancient Rome became renowned as a center for goldsmiths. Initially, their styles were influenced by the Greeks and Etruscans, but gradually the Romans developed a style of their own. Among the most popular items were massive gold rings. Originally reserved for noblemen and senators, they gradually began to appear on the fingers of those of lesser rank until even soldiers were wearing them. The Romans were the first to start using the harder gems such as emeralds (from the newly discovered Egyptian mines), sapphires, and diamonds. These gemstones were polished but were not cut.

➤ THE AMERICAS ➤

In South America gold was plentiful near the northern Andes Mountains, and the ancient peoples of South America became very skillful at working it. In particular, the Moche people of ancient Peru were highly skilled metalworkers and discovered how to plate copper objects with

gold or silver, a technique they used to good effect in their jewelry.

The Incas described gold as "the sweat of the sun." It was believed to have magical powers and to represent the sun's life-giving force. Gold was beaten into thin sheets, then formed into face masks, pendants, bracelets, and disks for pierced earlobes. Models of people and animals, such as the llama, were made from solid gold. Gold was also used to make religious objects, such as the crescent-shaped knife, called a *tumi*, used in sacrifices. The jewelry of the common people was made from metals like copper. Little Inca jewelry has survived, since much was looted and melted down by the conquering Spaniards in the 1500s.

ABOVE: A Chinese jade pendant from the Tang period (A.D. 618–907).

BELOW: A pair of turquoise and gold earrings made in about A.D. 400 by the Moche people of ancient Peru. The Moche used gold to make many pieces of jewelry and ceremonial objects.

Legal Codes

Early civilizations soon discovered that when people live together in a community, it is necessary to have a set of rules spelling out what people are allowed to do and what is forbidden. A set of penalties was also needed for when people broke the rules.

In the early small-scale societies, rules and punishments could be enforced by society as a whole or by representatives such as tribal elders. However, as societies got bigger, the task of drawing up and administering rules and penalties became much more complicated.

The need for a more sophisticated legal system first arose in Mesopotamia and Egypt about 5,000 years ago. Early Mesopotamian kings began to collect and record the laws and penalties that had evolved in their society and form them into official legal codes. The earliest surviving legal code was put together by King Shulgi of Ur (who ruled from 2094 to 2047 B.C.).

Mesopotamian kings took their task of administering justice very seriously and reformed laws that were no longer appropriate. Three centuries after Shulgi the Babylonian king Hammurabi (ruled 1792–1750 B.C.) had a new version of the laws inscribed on a huge slab of basalt, in order "to cause justice to prevail in the land, to destroy the wicked and the evil, so that the strong should not oppress the weak."

The king had the final say in any disputed issue, but most legal matters were dealt with by local judges and law courts. Many cases concerned property or family disputes. But there were also criminal cases such as robbery and murder to be tried. The judges hearing a case would call witnesses for both sides and would consider which side was in the right. Witnesses, accuser, and accused would all have to swear to tell the truth, taking an oath on a sacred object. A soldier of the court would deal with the penalties imposed—these would often be payments of money as compensation, but could also involve mutilation and, in extreme cases, execution. Prison did not exist. The principle familiar from the Bible of "an eye for an eye, a tooth for a tooth" was common in many ancient cultures, including Mesopotamia.

In ancient Egypt the tombs of kings and nobles, which were filled with gold and other luxury objects, were a great temptation to thieves and were often robbed. The ancient Egyptians believed that if tombs were robbed, then the dead would be deprived of the things that they needed for the afterlife. Tomb robbery was therefore a very serious crime. Transcripts of court proceedings show that the accused were beaten to extract their confessions. These confessions were extremely frank and detailed, giving us a fascinating picture of the activities of these robbers. Some were acquitted, but those found guilty were executed by being impaled on a stake, drowned, burned, or decapitated. For less serious crimes people could have their hands, ears, nose, or tongue cut off, be exiled, or sentenced to hard labor in the mines. People who were sent into exile would take their family with them.

The pharaoh was the highest legal and judicial authority in Egypt. Under him there were many levels of officials who acted as judges. Court proceedings were taken down at the time and placed in an archive for reference in future cases. Officials decided the penalties, but they could refer difficult cases to a higher authority and then ultimately to the pharaoh.

➤ GREEK JUSTICE ➤

In contrast, the administration of justice in Athens was a public matter in keeping with the city's democratic system of government. Cases were brought to court by any citizen who wanted to lodge an accusation: he could be given some of the fine paid if the accused was found guilty—but might be fined himself if the case collapsed. Large numbers of citizens acted as the jury—between 200 and 2,000 at a time. They had to listen to the speeches of the prosecution and defendants, vote on the case, and pass sentence. To aid them in their task, Athens, like other Greek city-states, had a codified set of laws. Those of Athens were written down in the seventh and early sixth centuries B.C. and displayed on wooden tablets in the market place. Part of the legal code of the city of Gortyn, carved on stone blocks around 450 B.C., still survives today.

In Rome laws were made by the Senate, various law-making assemblies, and magistrates. When the Roman state became an empire, the emperors made the laws. Emperor Theodosius collected all the laws into a legal code, which was published in A.D. 438. It was replaced by an exhaustively researched code published by Emperor Justinian in 534, accompanied by a digest giving all the sources used to compile it.

The death penalty was used in many ancient societies to punish those who had committed serious crimes, such as sacrilege, murder, treason, robbery, or arson. The Romans had their own

China and Legalism

In some ancient societies judges were allowed to use their discretion when trying and sentencing people. If a judge felt there were circumstances that merited dealing with the case leniently, he might reduce the sentence or dismiss the case altogether. Other societies had very strict legal codes in which every crime carried its own distinct punishment, and no exceptions were allowed. This way of dispensing justice is known as legalism, after a system used in the Ch'in period of ancient China (221–207 B.C.). Chinese legalism exerted strict control over all activities of citizens with a fixed set of punishments for wrongdoers. This system was administered by provincial magistrates. While systems like this were harsh, they were seen to be fair and prevented corruption, since a judge could not change the sentence once a criminal had been convicted.

Provincial magistrates in ancient China had to pass tough examinations before they could practice. This 18th-century painting shows candidates taking the test in a walled compound.

ways of dealing with serious offenders. Some were crucified, and some were killed in the amphitheaters as entertainment for the public. In the first half of the day, before the major entertainments, some criminals were thrown to wild beasts; others took part in fights to the death. In these fights only one person would be armed. When the armed man had slain his opponent, he became the unarmed combatant in the next fight.

Literature

Stories have been told or sung to an audience from earliest times, and with the advent of writing, these stories were soon to be written down. The earliest written literature dates from about 2600 B.C. when the Sumerians started to write down their long epic poems.

The modern meaning of the word literature is a body of writing by people who use the same language. For some people this means anything that is written down, while others believe that it should include only creative writing such as poetry, novels, plays, and short stories, and not writing such as journalism. The ancient Greeks, for example, viewed history as literature, whereas today most people would not agree with this.

The earliest form of literature in ancient societies was the long epic story chanted by a bard or minstrel to an assembled gathering, often with a musical accompaniment. These stories were usually in poetic form, which made them easier to remember. They told tales of gods and heroes, and it was in this way that the history and mythology of a people were handed down from one generation to the next. Later, when writing was invented, many of these long poems were written down, and so they survived to modern times.

The first epic stories to be written down were those of Mesopotamia, where writing began before 3300 B.C. At first writing was used solely for record-keeping, but by 2600 B.C. the Sumerians were writing epic poems. These early works are written in an obscure script that is difficult to understand, but later versions were written in more easily understood scripts and languages. One of these early epics was the *Epic of Gilgamesh*, which tells the story of the creation of the world, the legend of the first people and their destruction in a great flood. The epic focuses on the story of Gilgamesh, an early king of Uruk, who may have been a real person.

Gilgamesh was half-human, half-god, but he longed to live forever. A god who disliked Gilgamesh created a wild man called Enkidu who challenged Gilgamesh. They fought, Gilgamesh won, and they became friends. The two men set off on a journey and had a series of adventures. Enkidu finally died, and Gilgamesh went in search of a plant that would give him eternal youth. However, when he found the plant, it was snatched from him by a snake, and Gilgamesh sadly returned home.

ABOVE: This stone carving from the ninth century B.C. depicts a scene from the *Epic of Gilgamesh*. It shows the hero Gilgamesh flanked by two demigods.

In Egypt a special kind of literature developed based on notions of the afterlife and how to ensure the well-being of the soul. By the time of the Middle Kingdom (2040–1640 B.C.) people were often buried with a copy of the *Book of the Dead* beside them. This was a manual that told them in detail what would happen in the afterlife and instructed them on how to deal with the trials they would have to go through.

The Chinese also developed writing early. Detailed historical accounts date back to 2000 B.C., but the first poetry to survive is the *Shih Ching* (Book of Songs), dating from about 500 B.C., which contains over 300 folk songs and ritual psalms. These works have probably survived because in 26 B.C. the Han Chinese emperor ordered that the texts of all earlier literature should be collected and recorded for educational purposes. Poetry was seen to be one of the supreme accomplishments of the Chinese scholar. The first anthology of poems to survive is *Ch'u Tzu* (Songs of the South), which contains the poems of Ch'u Yuan and his followers (about 340–278 B.C.).

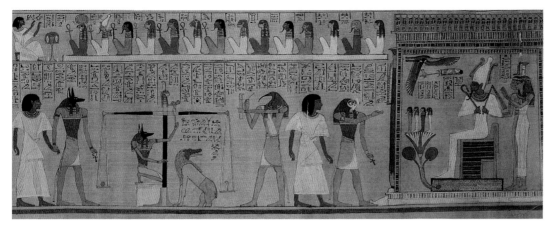

LEFT: A scene from an Egyptian *Book of the Dead* showing the heart of a man named Ani being weighed against the feather of truth. Osiris, god of the dead, views the proceedings from his throne on the right.

India's earliest surviving texts (apart from inscriptions from the Indus Valley civilization that are not yet understood) were the *Vedas*, religious literature that included rituals, hymns, philosophy, and myths. Composed around 1000 B.C., they were memorized and handed down word for word for generations. They were not written down until after 400 B.C. India's great epic poems are the *Mahabharata* and the *Ramayama*, which were probably composed around 800–500 B.C. but were not written down until a thousand years later. The *Mahabharata* contained 106,000 verses and described the struggle between cousins—the Pandavas and the Kauravas. It ended with a bloody war between gods and devils and all the heroes of the time—the Pandavas survived and established a prosperous reign.

⯈ GREEK LITERATURE ⯇

In ancient Greece music and poetry were closely linked. Poetry was usually performed in public, and the words were sung or chanted. Men called *rhapsodes* recited poetry at festivals or parties. The earliest surviving works of literature are two great epic poems—the *Iliad* and the *Odyssey*. They were originally believed to have been created by a blind ninth-century B.C. poet called Homer. Although Homer may have been the first author, scholars now think that a number of poets added to the poems as they told and retold them over the centuries. The poems were not written down until the seventh century B.C.

The *Iliad* tells of the last few weeks of the war between the Greeks and the city of Troy in Anatolia. The *Odyssey* tells the story of Odysseus's adventures during his journey home after the end of the Trojan War. It is thought that the *Epic of Gilgamesh* may have influenced Homer, since there are similarities between it and the *Odyssey*.

During the golden age of Greek art and literature in the fifth century B.C. all kinds of literature flourished in Athens, including drama, oratory, philosophy, history, and medical works. Three men in particular were important both in their own times and for future generations—Socrates, the philosopher; Herodotus, the historian; and Hippocrates, the doctor and medical writer.

The great epic of the Roman world was the *Aeneid*, written by Virgil (70–19 B.C.). It was strongly influenced by Homer—the story of the Trojan prince Aeneas's journey to Italy, where he founded the city of Rome, has many similarities with both the *Iliad* and the *Odyssey*. It took Virgil 11 years to write the *Aeneid*, and he died of a fever before he could make his final revisions.

Other famous Roman poets included Catullus, who adapted the forms of Greek poetry to write laments, love poems, and witty descriptions of daily life; Horace, who wrote the *Odes*—short poems on many subjects such as food, wine, and country life; and Ovid, who wrote *Metamorphoses*—15 books of poems, mostly on myths and legends.

The novel appeared at a much later date. The earliest known novel comes from Japan. The *Tale of Genji* was written by Lady Murasaki Shikibu in the early 11th century and tells of the life and loves of Prince Genji.

LEFT: This Greek vase from the fifth century B.C. depicts a scene from the *Iliad*. The Trojan king, Priam, asks the Greek hero, Achilles, to return the dead body of Hector, his son.

Metals

The discovery of how to extract and work metal was one of the keys to the development of human civilization. In fact, the discovery of metals was so important that historians use terms such as "Bronze Age" and "Iron Age" to label eras of history.

ABOVE: A gold Sumerian helmet from around 2600 B.C. Since gold is a soft metal, the helmet would have been of little practical use and would have been worn on ceremonial occasions.

The change from stone tools to metals ones made from bronze or iron had a huge impact on activities such as farming, since metal tools were much more efficient.

Metals such as gold, silver, and copper are usually found as ores—rocks and minerals that contain particles of pure metal. However, they also sometimes occur in a pure ("native") form as nuggets. When early people worked stone to make tools, they must sometimes have come across these nuggets—pieces of "stone" that behaved in a peculiar way, changing shape instead of breaking when hit.

By 8000 B.C. people in several parts of the world had learned enough about these strange materials to shape the nuggets into metal objects by hammering them. The first metals to be used in this way were copper and gold, and the first items made were simple objects like personal ornaments. Some early peoples in eastern North America produced knives, fishhooks, and ornaments by cold hammering the nuggets of pure copper that they found around Lake Superior between about 3000 and 1000 B.C.

Because the amount of metal that was available in a native state was very limited, it was not until people discovered the process of smelting that metal objects were produced in any great numbers. Smelting is the extraction of a pure metal from its ore by means of heating. For example, copper is extracted from ores such as malachite or cuprite. Historians believe that smelting was first carried out around 6000 B.C. in western Asia and southeastern Europe.

In order to smelt metallic ores, early metalworkers used the same kilns that they used to fire pottery. Although these kilns were very primitive, they were still capable of producing temperatures of around 2,000° F (1,100° C). This was hot enough to extract molten copper from its ore. The molten metal could then be poured into a mold to produce simple copper ornaments.

Eventually, some time during the third millennium B.C., more sophisticated ways of heating ores were developed. Bellows made of animal skin were used to blow air into a furnace through clay nozzles called tuyères. This technique allowed much greater temperatures to be reached.

⤙ MINING ⤚

People had been mining for flint from very earliest times, and now they discovered that metals could also be found deep in the ground. Copper was mined from around 4500 B.C. in the Balkans, in eastern Europe. The veins of copper ore did not run horizontally, so the tunnels in the mine often ran up or down, following them. The depth to which the shafts were sunk depended on the level at which the copper ore was found.

RIGHT: A bronze wine
vessel from the Shang
period of ancient China
(1766–1100 B.C.). Shang
bronzes are noted for
their intricate surface
detail, which was
achieved by casting the
molten metal in a
decorated mold.

The practice of mining for copper gradually spread westward from the Balkans, and certain areas began to specialize in the activity. For example, around 100 copper mines have been found in the Mitterburg region of Austria. It is estimated that about 13,000 tons of copper had been mined in this region by 800 B.C.

⯈ THE BRONZE AGE ⯇

Copper and gold are soft metals. They are suitable for making ornaments but not tools since they get blunt and bend. For this reason, the use of these metals had only a limited impact on the way that people lived. However, the discovery of the alloy bronze had a major effect on human development. Alloys are combinations of two or more metals. Bronze was made by mixing copper and tin, and the alloy produced was both strong and durable. So bronze was widely used to make tools and weapons, as well as vessels and jewelry.

Bronze was first made in the Middle East in around 3500 B.C., and the knowledge of how to make it gradually spread across Europe and Asia. Using various kinds of molds, ancient Chinese metalworkers were able to cast bronze ritual vessels in a range of elaborate shapes, all intricately decorated. Because the detail was present in the mold, little work was needed to finish off the cast pieces. In the Middle East, Europe, and South America, however, fine detail was added to decorative objects by using punches and hammers.

In some areas bronze was also used to make agricultural implements, and this development had a big impact on the way that people farmed. However, there were very few areas in the world where both tin and copper were in plentiful supply. In fact, tin was quite scarce, so extensive trade networks developed, bringing tin to areas where copper was mined and worked.

Ancient metalworkers also used other alloys. In the Aegean area and other parts of Europe, electrum, an alloy of gold and silver, was used to make jewelry. In the early Andean cultures of South America some elaborate masks, figurines, and ritual knives were made of *tumbaga*, which was an alloy of copper and gold. The Moche

RIGHT: Spearheads made
of copper from the Indus
Valley civilization, dating
from about 2500 B.C.

METALS | **219**

Molds

The earliest molds used for casting metal were very simple: a shape carved into a piece of stone into which the hot, molten metal was poured. Flat axes, daggers, and other simple shapes could be produced in this way.

By 3000 B.C. more complicated molds had come into use. A model of the object to be made was first carved in wood. Half of it was then coated in clay. When this was dry, the other half was also coated in clay and left to dry. The two pieces of clay were then removed and fired. Then the two pieces were fastened together to make a pottery mold and the molten metal was poured in. When it had cooled, the pieces of mold were removed, leaving a metal object in the shape of the original wooden design. Two-piece molds were used to produce objects in a variety of shapes. Even more complex shapes were created either in molds made in many pieces or by using the lost-wax technique.

This method involved making a model in wax of the object to be cast, sometimes with a clay core to save metal. The wax model was coated in clay that was then fired. This melted the wax so that it could be poured out, leaving a pottery mold. After the molten metal had been poured in and had cooled, the mold was smashed to reveal the finished metal object.

---

people of ancient Peru discovered how to coat copper objects with a thin, even layer of gold by using heat and dissolved corrosive minerals.

⟶ IRON ⟵

Unlike copper and tin, iron ores are abundant across the world, so once iron metallurgy got underway around 2000 to 1500 B.C., many people could have everyday tools and weapons of iron. Since only small quantities of pure iron occur—in meteorites—iron ores had to be heated to obtain the metal. Among the first people to do this were the Hittites of Anatolia. It is clear that iron was considered valuable, since iron objects are mentioned in letters as diplomatic gifts between Hittite and other rulers.

Very high temperatures, in excess of 2,800° F (1,540° C), are required to melt the iron in iron ore. Since such temperatures were not possible with the technology available in the West, iron ore was heated to reduce it to a hard, spongy mixture. This mixture was then hammered while red-hot in order to extract the metal. This method (forging) came into general use for making tools in Europe, the Middle East, and Southeast Asia during the first millennium B.C.

The Chinese also began working iron at this time. Because the type of iron ore available in China had a lower melting point than that available in the West, and because the Chinese had developed more sophisticated furnace technology, they were able to extract the iron as a molten metal. From the beginning, therefore, iron objects in China were cast in molds, a development that did not occur until much later in the Middle East, Europe, and Africa.

LEFT: This detail from an Egyptian tomb painting dates from around 1400 B.C. and shows craftsmen working on metal vessels. The Egyptians were highly skilled metalworkers and were renowned for their work with gold.

Numbers and Counting

The ability to count, calculate, and keep numerical records was probably more important to ancient peoples than the ability to write. Taxes and trade were two fundamental aspects of ancient life, and both needed accurate records of numbers and quantities of goods.

Different civilizations evolved different methods of counting and recording numbers. In order to handle large numbers, people used a base system. Today in the West we use a base system of 10. That means that when we start counting above 9, we put a "1" or a "2" in the left-hand column to signify "10" or "20," and so on. So when we see the number "15," we know it means 10 items plus another five.

At different times in various parts of the world other systems have been used. For instance, the Babylonians used a base-60 for their counting system, while the Maya worked with a base-20 system. We still preserve today some elements of the Babylonian system in the way we count time (60 seconds to the minute, 60 minutes to the hour) and in our measurement of angles (360 degrees in a circle).

➤ FINGERS AND TOES ➤

In prehistoric times, when human beings lived simple lives as hunter-gatherers, they probably used their fingers and toes to count on. In those distant days the ability to count up to 20 may have been enough. The use of larger numbers only became necessary when people started having many things to measure and count, probably when the first cities and civilizations developed. In particular, the ability to measure land became very important.

ABOVE: An Egyptian painting on a stone slab, showing a princess sitting at a table laden with offerings. The hieroglyphics behind her record the number of each kind of offering.

Babylonian Place Value

The Babylonians developed a highly sophisticated number system using a concept known as place value (which is also known as positional notation). It was a vital advance on earlier systems. Place value allows you to use the same symbol to represent the quantity of each power of your base units.

For example, in the system used in the Western world today the same numeral 5 is used in the number 555 to represent in turn the number of hundreds, of tens, and of units that make up the number. Which it is depends on where it is placed.

The Babylonians were working with a base-60 number system. So:
• their first place value (units) denoted 1–59 in our system
• their next place value represented the number of 60s
• and the third place value represented the number of 3,600s

The Babylonian symbol for 1 was ⅂ so 3 would be ⅂⅂⅂

They used the same symbol on its side for 10, so 11 would be written ◀⅂

Using place value, the number 191 would be written ⅂⅂⅂ ◀⅂ (3 x 60 plus 11 units).

The same symbols in the last example could also represent the number 11,460 (3 x 3,600 plus 11 x 60) or even the number 3.18 (three units plus 1/60 of 11), but it would usually be obvious which number was meant by looking at what it referred to.

Many of the early mathematical problems given to Mesopotamian schoolchildren were concerned with measuring land. These children were also asked to calculate problems like the rations needed by a team digging a canal of given length and depth, an important consideration for the authorities who had to commission this work. Temple and royal employees also had to be issued with rations. Taxes had to be calculated and recorded. Warfare was also important: some Mesopotamian school exercises concerned the volume of earth needed to create ramps up which siege engines could be dragged to bombard enemy cities. All these activities required the use of numbers—and often of large numbers—so more advanced methods of counting developed.

The most basic way of writing numbers was by using signs with particular numerical values, which were then added together. The ancient Greeks used modified letters from their alphabet,

BELOW: An ancient counting device, the abacus is still used in many countries today.

while the Romans used a selection of capital letters. We still use Roman numerals for things like the numbers on clock dials.

In Roman numerals the letter I represented 1, V represented 5, X represented 10, C represented 100, and so on. Numbers were written with a maximum of three of the same number symbols together (III for 3, CCC for 300, for example). The awkward cluster of four identical number symbols (IIII for instance) was replaced by a combination in which the next highest number symbol was preceded by one of these lower number symbols, which was then subtracted. So, IV denoted 4 (V minus I, that is, 5 – 1), and XC denoted 90 (C minus X, or 100 – 10). Numbers to be added came after the higher symbol—so IX is 9, while XI is 11.

Many other societies wrote numbers in a similar way—for example, the Egyptians had special signs for the numbers 1, 10, 100, 1,000, 10,000, 100,000, and 1,000,000. They wrote as many of the signs as were required by the number—so 9, for example, used nine strokes, arranged in two lines to make them easier to read. Calculations using such numerals were very cumbersome.

The numbers used in Europe and the Western world are generally known as "Arabic numerals." However, the Arabs themselves learned this system from the Indians, who had developed it and other complex mathematical ideas by the early centuries A.D.

— COUNTING DEVICES —

Many ancient peoples used a device known as an abacus to help them perform mathematical calculations. The device probably originated in Babylon and usually consisted of a board on

The Use of Zero

One vital concept, developed independently in India and China and by the Maya of Mesoamerica, was the use of a symbol—zero—to mark the absence of a value in the place-value system. The use of zero allows us to distinguish, for example, between the numbers 14, 104, and 140.

The Mayan system used only three symbols: a dot for 1, a bar for 5, and a shell for zero. So the number 4 would be represented by four dots, 9 by one bar and four dots, and 19 by three bars and four dots.

The Mayan system was a base-20 system, and place values were written one above the other. So the number 20 would be represented by a dot above a shell (one twenty, no units). The combination of four dots and a bar above a shell would represent 180 (nine twenties, no units), while two bars and three dots above a single bar and two dots would equal 267 (13 twenties, seven units).

These are examples of Mayan numbers, some of which use the shell symbol for zero:

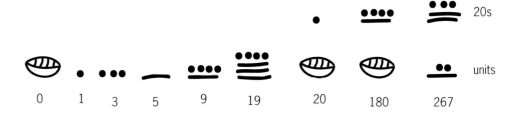

which pebbles were placed in columns. The pebbles represented different numbers depending on which column they were placed in—for example, counters in the right-hand column might represent units, while those in the next might represent 10s. The abacus acted as a memory aid and helped people make calculations involving large numbers. The abacus took different forms in different cultures—the type we are familiar with today is the Chinese variety in which the counters are strung on wires held in an open frame. Rather than an abacus, the Inca civilization in South America used a complicated arrangement of colored cords, known as quipu, for calculating and recording numbers.

The quipu worked in a similar way to the abacus and consisted of a long cord with a series of smaller pieces of cord attached to it. Knots were made in these smaller cords to represent different numbers and amounts.

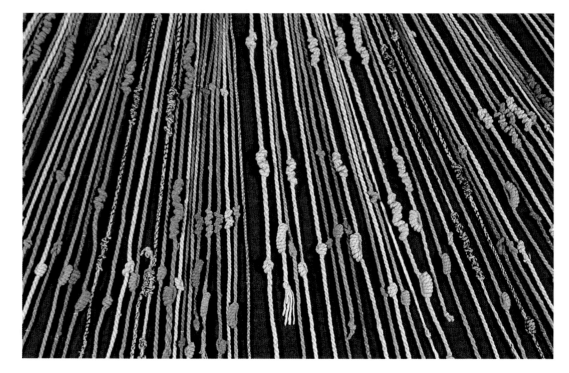

LEFT: The Incas of Peru used an elaborate system of knotted cords like these to record numbers. They were called quipu and were used by traders to record the amount of goods bought and sold.

Pottery

One of the earliest skills that people learned was how to make clay pots. Using clay they also learned to fashion figures of deities and animals. They learned techniques for decorating their pots and figures, creating some exquisite ceramics that have never been surpassed.

ABOVE: This powerful figure of a large, pregnant earth goddess seated on a throne of leopards comes from Çatal Höyük in Anatolia. The clay was molded and shaped by hand in about 6000 B.C.

When hunter-gathering people started to settle in one place, they found they needed vessels for cooking and serving food. The oldest pottery known was found at Shimomouchi in Japan—it is 12,000 years old. The pots were probably used to cook acorns; some still have soot on them from the ancient hearths. In China, pots of nearly the same age have been found and it is thought they were used for cooking seeds.

At Çatal Höyük in Anatolia, pottery has been found that is about 8,000 years old, making it the earliest known Middle Eastern pottery. The potters of Çatal Höyük shaped clay into models of animals and humans, to make seals and pendants, and into pottery vessels. To make a pot, they first mixed the clay with fine grit to strengthen it. Then they formed the mixture into coils, which were built up to form the pot on a round base. A paddle and anvil (round stone) were then used to shape the vessel. After a few days, when the clay had completely dried out, the potter used a bone or stone to polish the surface of the pot before firing it in a kiln.

The earliest potters used very simple techniques for decorating their pots. One was impressing—fingers were pressed into the wet clay to make marks, or, as in some early Japanese pottery, a rope was used to make the impressions. Another technique was incising—designs were scratched into the wet clay with a thumbnail or a pointed stick. This was the type of decoration used on Linear pottery, which was produced in Neolithic Europe in the sixth millennium B.C.

Later, slip (clay and water mix) and glazes were used to color pottery. The earliest form of decoration in Egypt, for example, was stylized animals and scenes from daily life painted in white slip on a red clay background.

The potter's wheel was invented at the beginning of the fourth millennium B.C. in Mesopotamia and was being used by potters in Egypt around 2500 B.C. Potters in the Americas never used the wheel—most of their pots were molded (shaped in or over an object such as a stone or a basket). The first pottery wheels were probably turned by hand, but eventually wheels with faster foot pedals were developed.

In the area around the Aegean Sea the potter's art seemed to flourish, producing outstanding examples of pottery from early Neolithic times to the Greek Attic pots of the sixth to fourth century B.C. Neolithic pottery from the island of Crete is particularly remarkable for its finely polished surface and incised patterns.

During the Bronze Age civilization of the Minoans (2500–1700 B.C.) the potters who worked in the palace at Knossos on Crete

RIGHT: A Mycenaean drinking cup found on the island of Rhodes. The Mycenaeans produced great quantities of elegant pottery decorated, like this goblet, with abstract designs.

produced some of the finest pottery ever made. It is called Kamares ware after the cave in which it was first found. The clay used to make this ware had to be very carefully chosen, then it was moistened and kneaded over many months before it

Earthenware and Stoneware

The first pots made were earthenware. People discovered that by molding clay into shapes and leaving them to dry in the sun, they could make vessels for holding dry goods. However, these pots could not be used for storing liquids since the clay absorbed the liquid and the pot eventually collapsed. Rather stronger pots could be made by baking the clay so that it hardened. At first the clay pots were just stacked in a hole in the ground, and wood was piled over them and set alight. Later potters invented the kiln. This was an oven in which the clay objects were stacked—the kiln was then heated by burning wood underneath it. Pots that had been fired were stronger than sun-dried ones, but they were still slightly porous and let liquids seep through slowly.

After the discovery of glass, glazes were used to make pots waterproof. The glaze was a coating made from powdered glass in water that was painted onto the earthenware. The pots were then fired a second time, and the heat fused the glass particles into a fine layer, making the pots waterproof and easy to clean. Glazes could also be used to color and decorate the pots.

Around 1400 B.C., people discovered how to make stoneware. This is pottery that is fired at such a high temperature that it vitrifies—a chemical change takes place, and the pots become glasslike and completely waterproof. Because stoneware is nonporous, it does not need to be glazed, except for decorative purposes. The first stoneware was made during the Shang dynasty in China and was being made in Korea by the time of the Silla dynasty (57 B.C.–A.D. 918). Stoneware was not produced in Europe until much later, in the 16th century A.D.

A Chinese earthenware pot dating from 5000–3000 B.C. The design was painted on with a brush.

was shaped. At some point Minoan potters discovered the wheel and started making their cups so thin that an ancient Greek source described them as being "light as the wind, as thin as skin."

One of the loveliest features of these delicate ceramics was the floral decoration painted onto the small, one-handled cups; the paint actually strengthened the eggshell-thin vessels. The red-and-yellow designs included plant motifs, fish, octopus, and frogs. The workshops at the palace of Phaestos on Crete used a great variety of patterns, with a profusion of spirals, rosettes, and lattices. These vessels were in great demand, and exports have been found in palaces on the mainland of Greece and south as far as Egypt.

The Mycenaeans (1600–1100 B.C.) also produced fine pottery that was heavily influenced in style by the Minoans. Mycenaean vases were exported to Egypt, the eastern Mediterranean area, and as far west as Italy and Sicily. With the end of the Dark Ages (about 1100–800 B.C.) and the rise of the Greek city-states simple geometric patterns were gradually replaced by decorative bands of animals and humans.

⟶ ATTIC WARE ⟵

From about 550 to 300 B.C. pottery made in Athens dominated the market. These pots, known as black-figure and red-figure ware, were

The Beaker Folk

Around 2800 B.C. a people whom archaeologists call Beaker Folk spread across western and central Europe, possibly from Spain. They are known from their individual round burial mounds that contained weapons and distinctive bell-shaped pottery beakers, decorated with horizontal rows of incised lines. The Beaker Folk were a warlike people, who carried bows, daggers, and spears. It is thought that they gradually spread through Europe as they searched for copper and gold. The beakers seem to have been used as drinking vessels, probably for social rather than ceremonial occasions. In central Europe the Beaker Folk came into contact with people of the Battle-Axe culture, who also produced beaker-shaped pottery, but in a different style. The two peoples gradually mixed and eventually spread to eastern England.

A bell-shaped beaker with a geometric design of incised lines.

beautifully proportioned and decorated. The clay was first colored red-orange by mixing it with red ocher. For the black-figure ware the figures were painted on the red clay with a shiny black pigment. For the red-figure vases the artist outlined the figures in black on the red background and then filled in the whole background with black paint, leaving the figures red.

The artists who painted the ware were highly skilled and produced vivid scenes of daily life and episodes from myths and legends. Attic potters did not use glaze or varnish, and the method they used to get such a high gloss on their pottery is still a total mystery today. Attic ware was highly valued and widely traded.

➤ SAMIAN WARE ➤

The Romans made a type of pottery known as Samian ware by pressing the clay into a mold with impressed designs. This produced red pottery with raised designs. Many potters put their own name into the mold, so we know exactly whose factory a pot came from. The early ones were molded in Italy, at Arezzo. But as the Roman Empire expanded, the pottery manufacturers followed and set up their molds and kilns in France, at Lezoux. Archaeologists excavating Arikamedu in India were surprised to find Samian ware there, proving the extent of Roman trade.

The Roman legionaries also had a taste for fine wine. So potters made a special storage vessel called an amphora. Filled with wine, amphoras were shipped all over the Roman Empire. Sometimes merchant ships were wrecked at sea,

and archaeologists have found the amphoras stacked in the hold at the bottom of the ocean.

As societies became larger with more people living in one place, many additional uses apart from cooking were found for pottery.

➤ CHINESE POTTERY ➤

In China, Japan, and Southeast Asia, for example, beautiful vessels were made to carry food and drink for the dead. They were decorated with

LEFT: A black-figure Attic amphora from the sixth century B.C. The black figures were painted in glossy black pigment on the orange-red polished surface. Details were added by incising lines or with small touches of white. Athens was the principal center of pottery manufacture in Greece, and the spectacular Attic vases were widely traded.

RIGHT: This Mayan ceramic whistle in the shape of a figure would originally have been brightly colored. It is a typical example of the Mayan potter's skill, with its expressive features, large earrings, and decorated robe.

painted scenes and were made in a wide variety of shapes. Some of the best examples come from a 3,000-year-old cemetery in Thailand called Ban Lum Khao. Dead children were placed in huge pots, together with miniature vessels and jewelry, then a lid was put in place. Men and women were buried with up to 50 red-painted vessels of unusual and attractive shape.

The Chinese invented a third type of pottery—porcelain—during the Tang Dynasty (A.D. 618–907). Porcelain is a thin, strong, translucent pottery made from kaolin (white china clay) and ground petuntse (a feldspar rock). Early examples were quite primitive, but by A.D. 851 an Islamic account of travels in the Far East tells of "vessels of clay as transparent as glass."

➤ NORTH AMERICA ➤

The most important early North American pottery was made in the southwest. All pots were made by coiling or modeling. In coiling, rolls of clay are added to a base and pinched together, while in modeling a pancake of clay is put over a form that serves as a mold. The first pottery was made by the Mogollon and Anasazi peoples, around A.D. 50. By A.D. 700 striking Anasazi pots with geometric black-and-white designs had appeared, forming the basis for the Pueblo pot style. The Mississippians (A.D. 700–1540) modeled clay head pots, hunch-backed women, and animals, often as bowls for tobacco pipes.

Central American civilizations may have begun making pottery earlier, in the second millennium B.C. Between about 600 B.C. and A.D. 1000 the Maya made simple pottery with red-and-black designs painted on a cream or orange slip. They also made elaborate models to attach to their pots—one pot had an abstract design on the lid, from the center of which emerged the model of a fierce jaguar with open jaws and sharp teeth.

The Maya used molds to mass-produce their figurines of gods and warrior priests. These figures give us a good idea of how the Maya people looked, what sort of clothes they wore, and the ornaments they preferred.

The Maya also created wonderful works of ceramic art that combined molded sections with hand-modeled details painted in reds, ochers, blue, and white after firing.

Pottery and Archaeology

Fired pots do not decay, which means that pieces of pottery are often found virtually unchanged after thousands of years, providing archaeologists with vital information about the past.

For instance, if two very similar styles of pottery are found a long way apart, it is likely that there is some connection between them. This might be because people have moved, but it might also be because the pots were exchanged as trade items. The Attic black-figure and red-figure ware from Greece, for example, is easily recognizable and examples have been found in widely spread locations. This has enabled archaeologists to build up a picture of trading links at that time.

New ways of studying ancient pottery have been developed in recent years. One is a technique that measures the amount of light heated pottery gives out. This can tell archaeologists when the pot was made. Another technique involves cutting a very thin slice through the pot, so thin that you can easily see through it. This is examined with a special microscope to find out which particular types of mineral or rock are present. In many cases it is then possible to determine where the pot was actually made, which in turn gives more information about trade routes.

Science

Science is the study of the laws governing the physical world. Practical science began more than two million years ago, when humans began making stone tools, showing they understood that if they hit a stone in a certain way, pieces would fall off to create a sharp cutting edge.

One of the first sciences to be studied systematically was astronomy. Because the movements of the sun, moon, stars, and planets were thought to reflect the actions of the gods and to predict important happenings on earth, accurate observations were essential. This combination of astronomy and religion was the basis of early science in Mesopotamia, Egypt, China, and Mesoamerica, and led to the study of mathematics and the development of calendars like those of the Maya and the Chinese.

Mathematical knowledge enabled ancient civilizations to carry out ambitious engineering projects. Stonehenge, the great megalithic stone circle built in England in the third to second millennium B.C., was a major engineering triumph, involving the transportation of huge blocks of stone from great distances away, and then erecting them on site. The same skills were needed to build the pyramids of ancient Egypt.

Warfare inspired the constant invention of better weapons and defenses. The Chinese devised crossbows, scale armor (bronze plates mounted on leather), armor of quilted paper so thick that arrows could not pierce it, gunpowder, and firelances (a primitive type of gun)—all before A.D. 1000. The Assyrians excelled in devising siege engines, while the Greeks and Carthaginians perfected warships.

The needs of trade between far-flung peoples spurred improvements in shipbuilding, vehicles, and roads. Bridges—such as the suspension bridges constructed by the Incas in the Andes Mountains—were often masterpieces of engineering. The study of astronomy, mathematics, and the calendar often resulted in improved aids to navigation.

Surprisingly, water power was not used until the closing centuries B.C., when watermills began to appear in various parts of the world. The largest mill known at this time was built by the Romans at Barbégal in France. A set of 16 waterwheels supplied power to a huge mill that could grind 27 tons (25 metric tons) of grain per day.

Some of the basic elements of modern science were known by ancient civilizations but not

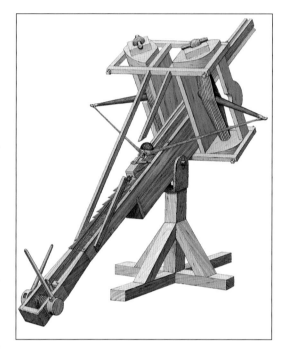

LEFT: The Greeks used their scientific knowledge to build highly destructive weapons. This stonethrowing catapult from around 300 B.C. was capable of throwing boulders 180 lb. (82kg) in weight. Its power came from the huge amount of energy that could be stored in the twisted rope springs that held the arms of the bow.

understood. The magnetic properties of lodestone (magnetic iron oxide) were known to both Chinese and Western civilizations. The tomb of the Chinese Emperor Ch'in Shihuangdi (258–210 B.C.) was said to be protected by magnetic doors that would capture any iron tools used against them. The Chinese also made bronze compasses using a lodestone ladle, while Greek and Roman priests used lodestone to make statues of the gods float in midair.

◄ ELECTRICITY ►

Natural electricity had also been observed. The Greeks, Romans, and Chinese knew that an attractive force (static electricity) could be created by stroking a piece of amber against fur. The Babylonians are said to have used electric fish as a means of anesthetizing patients. Some objects discovered in the cities of a Middle Eastern people called the Parthians may have been primitive electric batteries—these 2,000-year-old clay jars contained a copper cylinder sealed with asphalt into which an iron rod was inserted.

In about the sixth century B.C. some Greek philosophers developed a great curiosity about

The Amazing Archimedes

Archimedes (about 287–212 B.C.) was one of the greatest of the Greek mathematicians and inventors. He studied at the Museum in Alexandria and then lived in Syracuse, on the coast of Sicily. A practical application of his work was the spiral-shaped device for raising water called Archimedes' Screw, which is still used today in Egypt to draw water from the Nile.

One day when Archimedes got into a full bath of water, he saw that a quantity of water spilled out. He had discovered that an object displaces its own volume of water—and is supposed to have leaped out and run naked down the street shouting, "Eureka, eureka!" ("I've found it!") He also discovered that almost any weight could be moved with little effort by using a long lever and a fixed point, or fulcrum. He is reported to have launched the ship *Syracusa*—which had three masts and 20 banks of oars and carried 1,800 tons (1,633 metric tons) of cargo—single-handed, using a system of levers and pulleys.

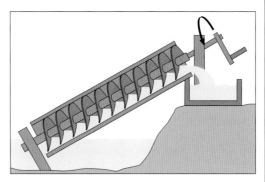

Archimedes' Screw, a device for raising water. When the handle was turned, water was forced upward by the spiral screw.

the way the world operated and why. Aristarchus proposed that the earth moved around the sun (rather than the sun moving around the earth); Archimedes worked out that an object always displaces its own volume of water; while Pythagoras figured out many basic rules of mathematics.

→ ATHENS AND ALEXANDRIA ←

Aristotle (384–322 B.C.) founded a school called the Lyceum in Athens that became the center of scientific inquiry of its day. Here the third century B.C. scholar Strato conducted many experiments into gases, some of which are still used to demonstrate that air occupies space. Later, the center of scientific investigation shifted to Alexandria in Egypt. Its ruler, Ptolemy II (308–246 B.C.), a pupil of Strato, was a great promoter of the study of engineering and science.

In Alexandria scholars conducted experiments in pure science—great names include Ctesibius, Philon, and Heron. Some of their inventions were of great practical value, such as the water pump devised by Ctesibius and Heron's diopter, a sophisticated surveying instrument. However, although the scientists of Alexandria became familiar with many mechanical devices and scientific principles—levers, pulleys, screws, siphons, springs, cogs, and valves; the knowledge that hot air expands; the use of wind and steam energy—they used them mainly to make entertaining novelties and gadgets. Heron, for example, created a mechanism that opened temple doors as if by magic when a fire was lit by the priest on the altar outside. In fact the fire heated air in a concealed metal globe, forcing water out of the globe along a siphon into a bucket. As it filled up, its weight operated a pulley that opened the doors.

The Romans later made practical use of many of these mechanisms, such as levers and pulleys in cranes. Modern scholars, however, have wondered why science did not develop further than it did at this time. One reason might have been that there were so many slaves that labor-saving devices were not considered important.

LEFT: A decorative seismoscope, a device for detecting the source of an earthquake, made by the Chinese scientist Zhang Heng in A.D. 132. It consists of a large barrel-shaped vessel decorated with eight dragon heads, each holding a brass ball in its mouth. Beneath each dragon is a model toad with its mouth open. When an earthquake occurred, an internal pendulum would swing in the appropriate direction, making the dragon on that side open its mouth and drop its ball into the mouth of the toad below.

Tithes and Taxes

As soon as ancient peoples started to live in communities with rulers and a nonworking elite, it became necessary to devise a means of diverting resources from the farmers and craftsmen to support the leisured classes. The universal solution was to impose tithes and taxes.

All ancient civilizations depended on the resources they produced, such as crops and livestock, valuable metals, and craft goods. The ordinary people who produced these resources supported themselves by their own labor, but the ruler and ruling class did not work and needed "unearned" income to support them. One way of raising this income was to tax the people who produced the resources.

To maintain their armies, to feed the slaves and others in their great palaces, and to live in luxury, the rulers of all the ancient civilizations taxed their people in one way or another—and often in many ways at once. Direct taxes were levied on individual citizens according to their wealth. Wealthier people were supposed to be taxed more than the poor, with each surrendering a proportion of their income. Indirect taxes were charged during the buying and selling of goods. Rulers might also charge taxes on imported goods, making them more expensive to buy, ask for "tributes" (payments) from conquered villages and peoples, and put taxes on such day-to-day essentials as salt.

➤ PAYMENT IN KIND ➤

Tax was not generally paid as money, except in the case of merchants or tradespeople, who were asked to hand over some of their gold or silver. For the mass of the population, most of whom worked in the fields and tended livestock, what their rulers demanded was a tithe. A tithe was a payment in kind—part of the farmer's harvest or some of his animals. There are records of kings becoming impatient for these goods and threatening fines for late payment.

Many ancient rulers and states had a highly organized system for calculating taxes. In civilizations where writing had developed—such as ancient Egypt, Greece, Rome, and China—very detailed records were kept. These set out who farmed what amount of land, the size of the harvests, and the numbers of merchants and traders, so that the amount of tax due from each

ABOVE: This ancient Egyptian wall painting from a royal tomb in Thebes shows court officials carrying out the annual census of livestock. The numbers of cattle, geese, and other farm animals in the country were counted every year to find out how much the farmers should pay in tax.

Tax and Corruption

Ancient tax systems were often haphazard and could change rapidly. For example, poor harvests might reduce the amount of tax a ruler could claim, or he might decide to impose heavier taxes to finance a war or a major building project. Equally, what a ruler might receive in taxes could be far less than the amount of tax actually paid by his subjects. This was most often due to corruption among tax collectors, who demanded more than the due amount from the hapless population and then kept the excess for themselves. Most rulers were only too happy to receive what they had demanded on time and did not enquire too closely how it was collected.

Mesopotamian records from 2400 B.C. tell of the corruption of tax collectors. When Urukagina became governor of the city of Lagash at that time, he determined that he would stop the terrible oppression of farmers, who were being forced to hand over almost all they produced. Lagash's tax collectors had been cheating by taking much more from the peasants than the law demanded and keeping the surplus.

individual could be worked out. Where these records have survived, they provide historians with a wealth of valuable information about the social structure of the societies concerned.

⇀ EGYPT, ROME, AND CHINA ↽

One of the simplest and most effective systems of taxation was that of Egypt under the pharaohs. The whole of the country in the rich floodplain of the Nile River was seen as the property of the gods and the ruler, who was himself considered a god. Everything produced belonged not to individuals but to Egypt itself. Therefore the entire produce of Egypt was due in tax to the ruler and was regularly collected by an army of tax collectors. The farmers and tradespeople were allowed to keep a certain amount that was seen as a kind of special allowance that enabled the ordinary people to feed and clothe themselves.

The Romans also had tax collectors, who were called publicans, but they administered a very different form of taxation from the Egyptians. There were various kinds of "wealth taxes," which individuals paid according to how many slaves and animals they had, the value of their land and houses, and the furniture and other things that they owned. By modern standards the taxes were very low—only about 0.3 percent of an individual's wealth. Even so, frequent investigations were made to calculate how well off people were and what they had to pay. As the Roman Empire expanded, the cities and peoples that became colonies were forced to pay tithes not as individuals but as communities as a whole.

The amount a colony had to pay was fixed locally, and tax collectors had the responsibility for gathering in the tributes. They paid an advance to the Roman treasury for the right to collect tributes; and even though taxation was often collected in kind—sheep, corn, and so on—the collectors had to convert it into money. The system was often corrupt. It was not hard for publicans to do a deal with the heads of local communities, who would levy more than the official tribute, take a cut for themselves, and give the remainder to the collectors. The burden of these taxes and the corruption were ended by Augustus, the first Roman emperor, who ruled from 27 B.C. to A.D. 14. He got rid of the collectors and imposed a direct tax on the colonies based on one percent of their calculated wealth and a sum per head of population.

From the very earliest times Chinese farmers gave a percentage of their produce to their rulers, the proportion changing dramatically from one dynasty to another. Another important source of government money was the tax levied on salt. It was easy to monitor the amount of salt produced and to put a high rate of tax on something everybody needed. The Chinese also taxed the production of iron in the same way.

⇀ THE INCA EMPIRE ↽

The taxation system of the Incas was only slightly less oppressive than that of Egypt. In the Inca Empire some land and goods were reserved for use by the ordinary people, but most of the land and goods belonged to the emperor and the gods. There was no money, so people had to pay taxes in the form of both tithes and labor.

ABOVE: A third-century A.D. stone relief of a Roman cloth merchant. Roman traders had to pay a proportion of their income to the state as tax.

BELOW: An ancient Mesoamerican manuscript showing the amount of goods that various towns owed as tribute to their Aztec rulers.

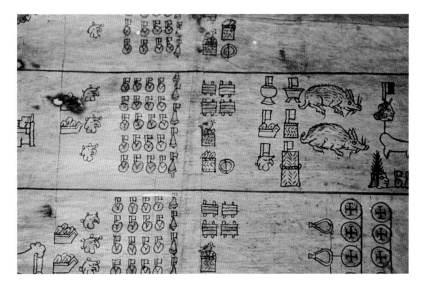

Tools and Technology

The ability of early hominids to fashion and use tools was one of the most important characteristics that distinguished them from other animals. As human beings developed, so did their remarkable ability to devise technical aids to help them in their lives.

LEFT: Iron tools were stronger than those made out of bronze. This collection of Celtic iron farming tools, from the first century B.C., includes a hoe, sickle, and axe heads. They would all have been attached to wooden handles.

Around 2.5 million years ago our ancestors began making sharp-edged stone tools to help them to cut through the tough hides of dead animals they scavenged. The hominids who made stone tools needed planning skills—they needed to be able to think of using a sharp edge for cutting, imagine how to make a tool by striking pieces off the edge of a rock, and then do so, hitting the rock in exactly the correct way to make the pieces come off as wanted.

Stone tools were made by flaking pieces of stone off a small rock. At first, the tool-makers struck the pebble using what is known as a hammerstone. As time went on, however, they discovered that using a softer hammer made of wood or bone gave them greater control over the way they removed the flakes, allowing them to make the shape they wanted more precisely.

Still greater control could be achieved by using a scraping motion on the pebble to remove flakes rather than using the direct force of a blow. These techniques enabled early peoples to create efficient tools using smaller and smaller pieces of stone. Large flakes gave way to smaller blades

from which were made a range of different tools. Stone knives and axes were used to kill animals for food. Some axes were held in the hand; others were attached to wooden handles. Awls were used for piercing leather, scrapers for cleaning hides, and chisels for working wood.

By 8000 B.C. people in many parts of the world were using microliths—tiny sharp pieces of stone used as part of many different tools. For example, a row of microliths fastened into a piece of bone or wood formed a sickle for cutting reeds, grasses, and cereal stalks. Microliths were also used to tip arrows made of wood and were made into drill bits for making holes in stone beads.

◄ WORKING METALS ►

The discovery of how to extract metals from their ores was a major advance in the history of tool-making. The first metal to be smelted, or removed from its ore by heating, was copper. This discovery was made around 6000 B.C. in western Asia and southeastern Europe. However, copper was too soft a material to be used to make effective tools, and it was not until it was mixed

Water Power

While human muscle was the most common source of power in the ancient world, it was not the only one. Water-powered machines are known to have been used by both the ancient Chinese and the Romans by the first century A.D. The Chinese had a highly complex machine in which a waterwheel was used to power a set of bellows. According to the records, the device was invented by a man called Tu Shih in A.D. 31, but it is likely that simpler versions were in use much earlier.

Watermills are known to have been widespread in the Roman world. The most famous example is a flour mill at Barbégal in present-day France. The mill was set on a sloping piece of ground, and water was carried to the top by an aqueduct. It then flowed downhill through two sets of eight waterwheels, turning the wheels, which were connected by a set of gears to machines for grinding corn. It has been estimated that about 27 tons (25 metric tons) of corn were ground daily.

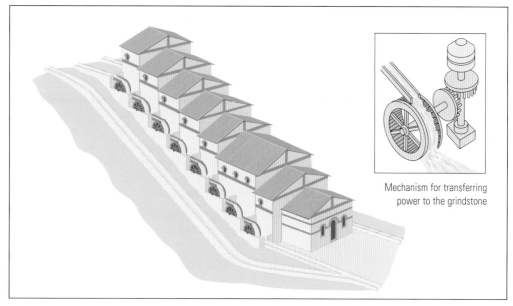

Mechanism for transferring power to the grindstone

A drawing of the Roman watermill at Barbégal, France, which was built around A.D. 300. On each side of the mill a stream of water flowed downhill through a series of eight waterwheels, turning the wheels to power the grindstones that ground the corn.

with tin to make bronze that useful metal tools could be made. Bronze was first produced in the Middle East around 3500 B.C. and was used to make both farming implements and weapons.

Bronze had one major drawback—the tin needed to produce it was not widely available. Another ore, that of iron, was much more widespread. However, it was more difficult to separate the metal from the ore. Once people learned how to do this around 1200 B.C., iron took over from bronze as the metal most commonly used for tools. It was stronger than bronze and could be shaped into a sharp cutting edge more easily.

➤ FARMING TECHNOLOGY ➤

As early civilizations began to evolve, simple pieces of machinery started to appear. Essentially, they served the same basic purpose as hand-held tools, allowing people to farm, hunt, and build houses more efficiently. The primary concern of all ancient peoples was producing enough food to eat, so it is not surprising that many of these technological developments occurred in the realm of agriculture.

One of the most important of these technical advances was the introduction of the ox-drawn plow. This device first appeared in Mesopotamia in around 4000 B.C. and quickly replaced the hand-held wooden hoes that had been used for centuries. The plow consisted of a V-shaped, wooden wedge joined to a wooden beam. Oxen were harnessed to the beam and used to haul the plow over the ground. The invention allowed far greater areas of land to be farmed than had been previously possible, and the design was so efficient that it was used until the 14th century A.D.

Another highly important development was the introduction of irrigation techniques. As early as 5000 B.C. irrigation channels were dug near the Nile River in Egypt and the Tigris and Euphrates rivers in Mesopotamia to use the annual floodwaters. Dams were soon being built to store water during the dry months. To raise water from the canals and reservoirs, a device known as a shadoof was invented. It consisted of a balanced beam with a bucket on one end and a counterweight on the other. It is still used in many parts of the world today.

The need to move water from one place to another became even greater when large cities started to develop. The Romans used an extensive system of aqueducts to serve the needs of the growing urban population in their cities. These aqueducts usually brought water from a high natural source, such as a mountain spring, downhill to the place where it was needed, using the natural force of gravity as propulsion. One famous aqueduct, the Aqua Marcia, was 57 miles (91km) long.

Occasionally water would have to be forced uphill, and for this the Romans used siphons. Siphons were closed pipes that contained no pockets of air. Because of the pressure built up by the flow of water, they could be used to transmit it uphill for small distances. Both aqueducts and siphons were used by the earlier Greeks, but it was the Romans who developed them most fully.

➤ LEVERS AND PULLEYS ➤

In order to put up large structures, ancient builders often had to move huge blocks of stone. They did this either by using slave labor or by using devices and machines that increased the natural strength of human beings. Probably the oldest of these devices was the lever. The simplest form of lever was a plank of wood resting on a point known as a fulcrum. By pressing down on one end of the lever, people were able to lift loads supported on the other end. People soon found

that by moving the fulcrum closer to the load, they were able to lift far greater weights with the same amount of effort. The ancient Egyptians used levers to help them build their pyramids.

Another device that helped people lift heavy objects was the pulley, which consists of a length of rope fitted over the rim of a wheel. A pulley allowed people to lift an object by pulling downward rather than upward. Systems of pulleys, with wheels of different sizes, enabled people to lift large weights with a comparatively small amount of effort. It is recorded that the Greek scientist Archimedes single-handedly pulled a ship into the sea using a system of levers and pulleys.

Roman builders used the pulley as a central part of a machine that has survived to the present day—the crane. In Roman cranes the pulley was attached to the end of a tall pole. The end of the rope was wound around a bar that was turned using a handle—a device known as a windlass. Like the pulley, the windlass reduced the amount of effort needed to move the load. Occasionally, cranes were connected to treadmills—large wheels powered by slaves walking inside them.

ABOVE: An artist's impression of a Roman crane, based on the writings of the engineer Vitruvius, who lived in the first century B.C. The crane is shown lifting building blocks of stone and is powered by a treadmill worked by slaves.

The Compass

The invention of the magnetic compass revolutionized the art of navigation. It works by reflecting the earth's magnetic field, whose north and south poles roughly correspond to the geographic poles. Its invention was based on the discovery of lodestone, a naturally magnetized stone. The first use of lodestone was recorded in China around 400 B.C. When a spoon-shaped piece of lodestone was placed in the middle of a square board, the spoon end always pointed toward magnetic north. The device was not originally used for navigation but for geomancy—the ancient art of aligning buildings with the earth's natural forces. The device was adapted for use on ships around A.D. 900 when an iron needle (rubbed with a lodestone to make it magnetic) was placed in a straw and floated in a waterbowl. The needle always pointed north, so giving the navigator a constant reference point. The marine compass did not reach the West until the 12th century.

Transportation

How to transport people and goods from place to place was one of the major problems confronting ancient peoples. Before the invention of the wheel, water was the best means of transporting heavy loads, and boats were one of the earliest forms of transport used.

For tens of thousands of years walking and running were the only means of transportation open to people on land. However, as the first civilizations began to emerge, people began to develop new means of getting around. Using boats to travel on rivers and seas, riding horses overland, and eventually inventing the wheel meant that people could cover distances more quickly and more easily. These developments also allowed people to transport goods from place to place and thus opened up the possibility of long-distance trade.

The first vehicles of transport to be developed were the log raft on water and the sled on land. Water transport was probably the first advance beyond walking as people took advantage of the currents of rivers and seas. We do not know when the first boats were built, but people probably started floating on logs many thousands of years ago. For example, it is clear that some sort of

watercraft, if only a form of log raft, was necessary for people to cross the water barrier that separated Australia from the Asian continent 40,000 or more years ago. By 8,000 years ago dugout canoes were being used in Europe and North America. One dugout canoe from this period found at Tybrind Vig in Denmark was 30 ft (9.5m) long and could carry six to eight people.

Larger sailing boats have been in use since at least 4000 B.C. The ancient Egyptians used such vessels to transport stone obelisks and other bulky goods up and down the Nile River. As well as sails, these ships also featured rows of oars, so that they could still travel when winds and currents were unfavorable. The Egyptians soon started to sail in the open waters of the Mediterranean and to trade with nearby islands such as Crete. The Phoenicians were another ancient people who quickly mastered the techniques of sailing in the open sea. Between around 1100 and 800 B.C. they

ABOVE: This relief from the palace of the Assyrian king Sargon II shows Assyrian ships carrying imported cargoes of cedarwood. The development of oceangoing ships allowed ancient peoples to build up widespread trading networks.

used their knowledge to develop extensive trading networks, sailing as far as Cornwall in the British Isles.

➤ TRAVELING ON LAND ➤

The first land vehicles were probably the sleds used by migrating hunter-gatherers in snowy areas to carry their belongings. The sleds may have been pulled by people wearing skis—at Vis in Russia archaeologists have found fragments of skis that are about 7,000 years old.

It was not until the invention of the wheel that truly practical vehicles arrived. The wheel was invented around 6,000 years ago in the Middle East and Europe, about the same time that people discovered that animals, especially cattle, could be used to pull heavy things. Plows and wagons are two developments of this period. The earliest wagons were probably used near settlements to haul crops, timber, firewood, and animal carcasses. Between settlements, paths were probably so uneven that it would be quicker to walk.

However, the use of the wheel in ancient times was restricted to a relatively limited part of the world. Wheeled vehicles were unknown in the Americas and in Africa south of the Sahara Desert. Even in Egypt and China such vehicles appeared only after about 2000 B.C.

The domestication of the horse on the steppes of southern Russia by 3000 B.C. led to new possibilities for animal-drawn transport. Around 2000 B.C. horse-drawn wagons came into wider use, and two-wheeled vehicles called chariots were developed for warfare, especially on the open plains of Mesopotamia. Improvements in wheel design, including the use of spokes, led to the adoption of light and fast chariots for personal transportation and for fighting in southeastern Europe, the Middle East, and Egypt.

On the open steppes of southern Russia and Asia horseriding became the standard means of personal transportation among nomadic peoples. Across the deserts of northern Africa, Central Asia, Iran, and the Arabian peninsula camels came into use as pack animals after people started keeping them in about 2500 B.C. Because camels could tolerate dry regions and travel long distances without water they were an ideal means of transportation on trade routes that spanned these deserts. In the Andes Mountains of South America llamas and alpacas were domesticated and were also used for transport.

The harnessing of animal power for transportation did not solve one fundamental problem. How could these animals, the vehicles they pulled, and their riders travel over rough or forested terrain and cross swamps and marshes? Rivers posed yet another problem—they could be crossed only at shallow points or with the help of boats. But even on land the new opportunities provided by animals and vehicles would be very limited unless something was done to provide smooth tracks for vehicles.

The world's first roads were the footpaths worn down by people walking along commonly used trails. These have long since disappeared. The first roads we can identify archaeologically are the wooden walkways built by the people of northern Europe to cross swamps. One such walkway was found in southwestern England. Now known as Sweet Track, it was built to cross a large marsh and was about one mile (1.6km) long. Studies of the rings in the timbers from which it was built have dated the walkway's construction to the winter of 3807–3806 B.C.

One of the earliest major paved roads was the Persian Royal Road. During the Achaemenid dynasty (559–330 B.C.) the road led from the empire's capital of Susa near the Persian Gulf right to Sardis in Lydia (in present-day Turkey), a distance of some 1,550 miles (2,500km).

The greatest road-builders of the ancient world were the Romans. Like all ancient empires, the Roman Empire needed good roads to connect its capital to outlying areas. Roman emperors had to be able to supply and reinforce their armies at short notice, while the empire's administrators needed to be able to move easily back and forth from the capital to the provinces. A vast quantity of goods and products, meanwhile, had to be

BELOW: This Chinese bronze model of a horse and chariot dates back to the second century B.C. Only the very rich could afford to travel in this way, so the figure in the chariot probably represents an powerful court official.

Roads across the Andes

By the time of the arrival of the Spanish in A.D. 1532 the Inca Empire stretched for 2,500 miles (4,000km) along the west coast of South America. A highway system with about 25,000 miles (40,000km) of roads enabled pedestrians and llama caravans to travel anywhere in the empire. Since they were not designed for wheeled traffic, Inca roads could surmount remarkable obstacles. Long flights of steps were used to scale steep slopes. In mountainous areas the roads could be as narrow as 3 ft (1m), although they were more commonly 15 ft (4.5m) wide in flat terrain and sometimes as much as 35 ft (10m) across as they approached cities. Retaining walls and drainage ditches protected the roads from natural disasters such as rockslides and washouts, so ensuring they remained open.

The Inca road leading from the town of Machu Picchu to the empire's capital at Cuzco is still clearly visible after 500 years.

transported back from the outer reaches of the empire to Rome itself.

The Romans began their road network to connect their settlements in Italy. Their first, and most famous, stone-paved road was the Via Appia, or Appian Way, which runs south from Rome and is still in use today. The paving of roads was a significant advance, since it meant that in wet weather vehicles did not get stuck in mud. By A.D. 50 the Roman road system stretched from the Atlantic Ocean in the west to the Euphrates River in the east.

Although the Romans left no map of their roads, enough of them survive today to permit this network to be traced. The Romans also set up milestones along their roads that recorded distance and the dates of construction and repair. Inns and horse-changing posts were established at intervals to serve the travelers.

⬝ CANALS ⬝

The earliest canals were built in Mesopotamia in around 5000 B.C. to irrigate fields. However, water channels were soon being used for transportation as well. One of the most impressive canals constructed in the ancient world was built by the Persian king Darius in around 500 B.C. It connected the Mediterranean and the Red seas and followed much the same route as the present-day Suez Canal.

The ancient Chinese also built many large-scale transport canals. In the seventh century A.D. a 600-mile (960-km) canal was constructed to help transport rice from the delta of the Yangtze River to distant cities. It was constantly rebuilt and lengthened, and forms the basis of a water transport system still used today.

BELOW: One of the most famous of all Roman roads, the Appian Way led south from Rome, stretching 410 miles (660km) to Hydruntum in the southeast of Italy.

Warfare and Weapons

Wars are probably as old as the human race. Even in prehistoric times humans fought over food and land, using hunting tools such as sharpened flints and wooden sticks. Most early battles would have been ambushes or raids that relied on concealment and surprise.

ABOVE: This stone relief from the ninth century B.C. shows the Assyrian king Ashurnasirpal II and his army attacking a city with bows and arrows and siege engines.

The first weapon to be designed specifically for war, around 10,000 B.C., was the club, or mace. A stone was attached to a wooden handle and used to crush the skull of an enemy. In the third millennium B.C. stone gave way to copper and then in about 2900 B.C. to bronze, making the mace much more effective. To counter the mace, men began to develop defensive armor, such as helmets. From then on warfare became a race between ever-more efficient ways of killing and improved methods of defense.

The mace head became more oval in shape so that a blow would be more concentrated and have a greater chance of penetrating a helmet. Gradually the mace evolved into the battleaxe and the poleaxe. The poleaxe was longer than an axe, and the blade was weighted with a metal ball. It took more strength to wield than the battleaxe, but its weight meant that it did a lot more damage to an enemy.

The battleaxe was to be the most important cutting-edge hand weapon until around 1200 B.C., when the discovery of iron smelting meant that swords could be cast in iron. Although the design of the sword changed in different cultures and through the centuries, it was to remain an important weapon until the late 19th century A.D.

When first bronze and then ironworking developed, stabbing spears were one of the first weapons to be made from the new material. A further development of the stabbing spear was the pike—a long, metal-pointed spear with a heavy wooden shaft that could measure as much as 10–20 ft (3–6m).

The mace, axe, poleaxe, stabbing spear, and sword were all shock weapons used in hand-to-hand combat. Equally important were missile weapons that were used to attack the enemy from afar. The simplest of them was the sling, which consisted of two thongs attached to a pouch that held a stone. The sling was whirled above the thrower's head to get maximum power before he let go of one thong and launched the stone. Gradually spears were developed that were specially designed for throwing, and many civilizations, from the Aborigines to the Maya, invented devices for throwing a spear that gave it a greater range.

The most important missile weapon was the bow. Although the appearance of the bow altered very little from 10,000 B.C. onward, two technical developments vastly improved its range and penetration power. Around 3000 B.C. a composite bow made of wood, animal sinew, and horn provided more tension when the string was pulled back and propelled the arrow forward with great force. Around the sixth century B.C. the Chinese invented the crossbow, which had a mechanical winding mechanism and trigger. By the second century B.C. the crossbow was the main weapon of the Chinese army, but the design did not reach the West until the 12th century A.D.

⊷ TYPES OF ARMOR ⊷

The earliest armor known is depicted on the third millennium B.C. box called the Standard of Ur. It shows Sumerian soldiers wearing leather helmets and tunics. In about 2500 B.C. metal helmets were being made by the Sumerians. The earliest body armor known was found in a Mycenaean tomb dating from the late 15th century B.C. It was made of overlapping bronze plates, which would have provided excellent protection but would have been very heavy. Lighter, more flexible armor was invented by the Egyptians and the Chinese around 1400 B.C., when small bronze plates were attached to leather clothing. The Assyrians were the first to use small iron plates instead of bronze.

Flexible mail armor made from small overlapping or linked iron pieces appeared in the third century B.C. in Greece and China, and may also have been used by the nomadic Scythians of southern Russia. Aztec and Mayan soldiers wore thick, quilted cotton clothing, which was effective because of its layered construction.

Alexander's Army

Alexander the Great was one of the greatest generals of ancient times. He began his military adventures with lightning strikes against his enemies in Greece, whom he easily conquered, then he set out to destroy the mighty Persian Empire. The core of his army was the Macedonian phalanx—a unit of foot soldiers each armed with a long pike called a *sarissa*. A heavily armed cavalry unit called the Companions was led by Alexander himself, and a lighter cavalry unit was used for scouting and speedy attacks.

Alexander inspired his men through personal courage and his ability as a leader. He had a gift for improvising under pressure and sensing when to time his attacks. He won his first major victory against the Persian army at Granicus in 334 B.C., for instance, by attacking the Persians immediately he encountered them—despite their strong position on the opposite bank of the Granicus River, the lateness of the day, and the advice of all his generals that he should wait until dawn.

In addition to his fighting men Alexander took with his army a large number of technicians and engineers who contributed to his outstanding successes in siege warfare.

A 19th-century illustration of cavalry being overwhelmed by a Macedonian phalanx.

In about 3500 B.C. steppe nomads started riding horses. Riding horseback gave warriors speed and mobility, but it was difficult to fight effectively on horseback. Without saddles and stirrups warriors did not have much stability. This meant

BELOW: A stone relief from the seventh century B.C. of an Assyrian war chariot. The spoked wheels made it faster.

LEFT: An artist's impression of the largest siege tower of ancient times, which was built in 304 B.C. by the Macedonians to besiege the Greek city-state of Rhodes. It was 130–140 ft (40–43m) high and was wheeled up to within missile range of the walls so that its large stone-thrower could destroy the defenses.

that it was difficult for them to swing heavy weapons and also that they could easily be pulled from their horses.

By 1850 B.C. steppe nomads were using horses to pull light two-wheeled carts. Once this invention reached other ancient peoples such as the Egyptians, the Hittites, and the Macedonians, it made a huge impact on warfare because warriors could now fight from a stable platform. Armies with chariots enjoyed military superiority for about five centuries. However, technical advances

such as better saddles gradually enabled men to fight more effectively on horseback. By the time of the Greek general Alexander the Great (356–323 B.C.) cavalry was gradually replacing the role of the chariot.

⬥ DEFENSE AND ATTACK ⬥

Defensive walls were probably erected around the first houses and settlements ever built. The oldest fortifications yet found were built around the settlement of Jericho near the Dead Sea and date back to around 8000 B.C. Many later ancient civilizations also built strong defensive walls around their towns. The Mycenaean rulers, in particular, sited their towns and palaces on hills where they were easy to defend, and surrounded them with thick walls constructed from huge stones.

Defensive walls prompted people to invent ways of assaulting these fortifications. The Assyrians used a battering ram mounted on a six-wheeled wooden frame. They also used ladders and ramps to get their army over walls. The ancient Greeks used a large number of siege machines, including the *sambuca*, which was a ladder that raised men to the top of the walls within the safety of a covered compartment. They also used large battering rams and fire-raisers, which were long wooden beams that carried cauldrons of lighted coals, sulfur, and pitch for starting fires inside the walls.

Besiegers used mechanical artillery to hurl heavy missiles, such as stones and giant arrows, at the defenders of a town. These devices worked either by pulling on ropes (tension) or by twisting them (torsion).

⬩ ARMIES OF EMPIRE ⬩

Most empires were established and maintained through the use of military power. The three greatest armies of the ancient world were those of the Assyrians, the Macedonians, and the Romans.

The Assyrians were a particularly aggressive people. Led by a series of warrior-kings, the Assyrians fought and defeated many of the neighboring peoples in the Middle East and built a kingdom that stretched from the Mediterranean Sea to the Persian Gulf.

The success of the Macedonian army was largely due to its leader, Alexander the Great, who created an empire that stretched from Greece to India. The Macedonian army would only come up against a superior fighting force in 197 B.C. at the Battle of Cynoscephalae—a victory for the Roman legion, which supplanted the Macedonian phalanx as the ancient world's most flexible military unit.

The Roman army was the best disciplined and most organized of the ancient world. A legion was divided into cohorts and then into centuries (100 men), led by a centurion. The Romans' favored weapon was the short stabbing sword, which made them masters of hand-to-hand combat.

ABOVE: Four swords from the late Bronze Age (about 1250–850 B.C.). Early copper and bronze swords had long, leaf-shaped blades and hilts (handles) that were an extension of the blade in handle form. By Roman times the hilt had become distinct from the short, flat blade. Swords did not become a truly effective weapon until they were forged in iron.

LEFT: This gold ornament on a comb dating from the sixth to fourth century B.C. shows Scythian warriors in combat. The Scythians were a fierce, nomadic people from the steppes whose society was based around warfare.

Weights and Measures

In the ancient past people used their fingers, hands, arms, and feet to represent short units of measurement. However, as societies developed, it became important to develop more reliable systems of weights and measures for trade, paying taxes, building, and measuring land.

As trading contacts increased, it became obvious that standardized, widely accepted systems of weighing merchandise were vital for good trading relationships. At first, small-scale transactions were based on a rough and ready "rule of thumb," but cheating was rife.

Uncovering the measurement systems used in the ancient world can be difficult. Some societies, such as ancient Egypt, left carefully inscribed measurement rods. But more often, measurements have to be figured out from the dimensions of buildings and bricks that were obviously constructed using an accepted system.

➤ EGYPTIAN MEASURES ➤

The measurement system of ancient Egypt was based on the royal cubit (forearm), a length of approximately 20.6 in. (52.3cm). Subdivisions were the palm—about 3 in. (7.5cm)—and the digit—about 0.7 in. (1.7cm). Evidence of this measuring system was found on Philae Island, where the heights of the annual floods of the Nile were recorded on a "Nilometer." Because the Nile floods washed away property boundary markers each year, surveyors had to resurvey the land using ropes, which were knotted to indicate subdivisions of linear measurements.

The official unit of corn, the *hekat*, was about 5.2 quarts (4.9l). Twenty *hekats* were equivalent to one *khar* (sack) of approximately 103.4 quarts (97.8l). The average wage of a fieldworker was

one and a half *khars* per month of emmer wheat, which may have been supplemented by a small allowance of barley.

From about 1550 B.C. metals were weighed in units known as *debens*—each approximately 3.2 oz. (91g). Because there were no coins, *debens* were used as a standard of value.

➤ MESOPOTAMIA ➤

In Mesopotamia linear measurements were also based on the cubit, which was about 19.5 in. (49.5cm). The cubit was subdivided into 30 digits, each of which measured about 0.6 in. (1.6cm). When they were surveying the land in order to build a ziggurat or dig a canal, Mesopotamians used larger units: the reed (6 cubits) and the pole (12 cubits). Evidence of Mesopotamian surveying skills survives on a limestone stela of Ur-Nammu, king of Ur, which shows a land-measuring cord (similar to the one used by the Egyptians) and a pair of compasses.

ABOVE: This wall painting from an Egyptian tomb shows metalworkers using scales to weigh gold rings. Standard weights of precious metals were used as a measure of value in much of the ancient world.

Chinese Measurements

Like many other ancient civilizations, the Chinese used parts of the body as units of measurement, but in no particular order and with many variations in different regions. In addition, a unit with the same name might be a different length depending on whether it was being used by a carpenter, a builder, or a tailor.

This problem was solved when Ch'in Shihuangdi, who became the first emperor of China in 221 B.C., introduced a standard system of weights and measures. The basic weight was called the *shih* or *tan* and weighed about 132 lb. (60kg). The two basic measurements of length were the *chih*, which was 9.8 in. (25cm), and the *chang*—

9.8 ft (3m). The Chinese also had a measurement for the sound made when a measuring vessel was struck. If a vessel was a uniform shape and weight, it would give a standard pitch. Measurements based on the length of a pitch pipe and its subdivisions proved more accurate than measurements based on the human body.

The Babylonians were the first ancient people to attempt to evolve a standardized system of weights and measures. From about 2400 B.C. they introduced a series of standard weights made of stone in the form of a sleeping duck. The Babylonian system of weights reflected their sexagesimal (based on the number 60) counting system. Sixty *shekels*, weighing about 0.3 oz. (8g) each, were equivalent to one *mina*, which weighed 17 oz. (480g); 60 *mina* were equivalent to one *talent*, which weighed 63.5 lb. (28.8kg). The Hittites, Assyrians, and Phoenicians all developed their measurement systems from those of the Egyptians and Babylonians.

The Indus Valley system of weights and measures has been figured out from finds of cube-shaped weights made of a stone called chert. The standard unit of weight was about half an ounce (14g). Historians believe that the smaller weights may have followed a binary system: 1, 2, 4, 8, 16, 32, 64. These smaller weights would be used for weighing foodstuffs, spices, and precious metals, perhaps in a jeweler's workshop. At the other end of the scale weights probably increased as follows: 160, 200, 320, 640, 1,600, 3,200, 6,400, 8,000, 12,800. The larger weights would have been lifted by a rope or metal ring.

Several scales of measurement have been found at Indus Valley excavations; one decimal scale of 1.3 in. (3.3cm) rises to 13.2 in. (33.5cm), which was equivalent to the "foot" that was widespread in western Asia. Another find is a bronze rod marked in lengths of 0.4 in. (1cm), which was probably the equivalent of a half-digit. Sixty half-digits make up a cubit of about 22 in. (56cm). It is possible to see, by measuring excavated Indus buildings, that these units of measurement were actually used in construction. There is a consistency in weights and measures, and even in brick sizes, at sites throughout the Indus region. This indicates that a there was probably a central authority that imposed a system across a wide area of the Indus Valley.

➤ ROMAN MEASUREMENTS ➤

The Romans, like the Greeks before them, based their measurements of length on, in ascending order, the finger's breadth (*digitus*), the palm, and the foot (*pes*), which was equivalent to about 11.5 in. (29cm). Longer units reflect the importance of Rome's marching army: five *pedes* equal one *passus* (pace), while 1,000 *passus* are equivalent to one Roman mile—0.9 miles (1.5km).

Accurate measurements and land surveys were vital tools in Rome's imperial expansion. Land

LEFT: This sculpture from the second century B.C. shows a Roman tradesman using a set of scales to weigh goods. Uniform systems of weights and measures were developed in the ancient world largely to make trading easier.

surveyors used two main instruments, the *groma* (cross-staff) and the *decempeda* (10-foot rod). Using these instruments, newly acquired imperial territory was measured, mapped, and allocated, usually to ex-soldiers or privileged civilians. Military surveyors were responsible for planning fortifications and roads, and they worked with a great degree of accuracy.

The long-distance trade networks of the Roman world are reflected in the measurements they used for capacity. For measurement of liquid the smallest unit was the *cochlearia* ("spoonful"), while the amphora was equivalent to approximately 27.7 quarts (26.2l). Amphoras were the pottery vessels that were used to transport wine and oil all over the empire, mainly by sea. The largest measurement of dry goods was the *modius*—approximately 104.4 quarts (98.7l)—the name given to the cylindrical containers used for transporting corn.

BELOW: A set of weighing scales from the Indus Valley civilization. Cube-shaped stone weights such as those shown in front of the scales would have been used to weigh small amounts of foodstuffs and precious metals.

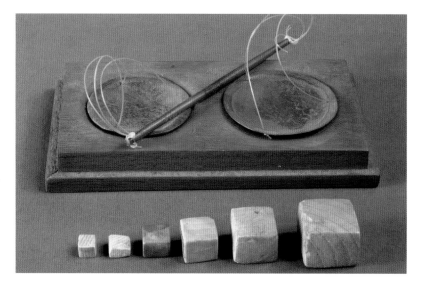

Writing

The invention of writing was one of the most important steps in human progress. It was a powerful tool of government, used for recording laws and rulers' decrees, and was also a means of recording historical events and communicating easily over long distances.

Because writing was a way of communicating easily and reliably over long distances it became a vital element in international trade, diplomacy, and the administration of empires. It was also used to create a historical record, and to record myths and other oral traditions, as well as new literary works.

Without writing it was difficult for a civilization to store its past learning and to pass it on to future generations. At first only a small group of people—scribes, officials, and priests—were able to read and write, but by the time of the ancient Greeks and Romans many ordinary people were able to understand and use the written word.

The world's first writing system was developed by the Sumerians of Mesopotamia. Farmers working the rich soil of the Euphrates and Tigris river valleys began to produce surplus produce, which was stored in temple warehouses. Soon it became essential to keep an accurate record of supplies. Also, as long-distance trading networks extended across the Middle East, it became important to be able to keep records of trading transactions. From about 8000 B.C. clay counting tokens were used to represent goods. By the fourth millennium B.C. the tokens were being sealed into clay envelopes that were marked with signs indicating their contents. These were the first written symbols.

FIRST WRITING SYSTEM

These abstract signs evolved into the world's first writing system around 3300 B.C. Initially, Sumerian script was pictographic—pictures were used to represent words. This system proved both limited and cumbersome, and so symbols gradually came to represent ideas—these were ideograms. For example, a pictogram of a mouth could also be used as a symbol representing the verb "to speak."

The next stage was to develop symbols that indicated the sounds of the spoken language. To begin with, the Sumerians took advantage of the fact that many words sound the same, although they have a quite different meaning. Just as in English the word "belief" could be represented by pictures of a bee and a leaf, so in Sumerian the words for life and arrow sounded the same, and "life" was represented by a pictogram of an arrow. Later, the system came to include symbols that represented different consonants and vowels.

Scribes wrote with a hollow-reed stylus on wet clay tablets. The marks were wedge-shaped; and because the Latin for wedge is *cuneus*, Sumerian writing was called cuneiform. At the end of the second millennium B.C. the Sumerian civilization gave way to that of the Assyrians and the Babylonians, who adopted and elaborated the cuneiform system of writing. Later it spread throughout the Middle East to the eastern Mediterranean coast and as far west as Persia.

⟶ EGYPTIAN WRITING ⟵

The Greeks called Egyptian writing hieroglyphs (meaning "sacred carvings") because it was used for inscriptions on temples, tombs, and monuments. The Egyptian writing system, which appeared from about 3100 B.C. onward, was unique, although it was influenced by Sumerian writing. Like the Sumerian system, it involved a combination of pictograms (where symbols represent words) and hieroglyphs, which represented consonants or groups of consonants. Hieroglyphs were not Egypt's only script; they evolved into two flowing scripts called Egyptian hieratic and demotic, both of which could be written much more quickly than hieroglyphs, using ink and a reed pen. Writing was used to administer and record every aspect of daily life in Egypt, from farming produce to land surveys, court cases, and royal decrees.

Much ancient Egyptian writing is preserved on papyrus, which was made from the flattened inner layers of the stems of papyrus plants that grew along the shores of the Nile River. The earliest surviving papyrus is over 5,000 years old.

To become a scribe in Egypt involved a long training. Students studied the art of writing for 10 to 12 years, practicing on slabs of limestone (because papyrus was too precious to waste). Their reward for this long education was a highly privileged position in Egyptian society and exemption from paying taxes. The ability to write was essential for careers in the higher ranks of the army, the palace, medicine, or the priesthood.

⟶ CHINESE WRITING ⟵

No one knows when writing began in ancient China; the earliest examples to survive date from the Shang dynasty (1766–1100 B.C.). The writing

RIGHT: One of the 20,000 clay tablets inscribed with cuneiform script that were found in the archives of the royal palace of Ebla (in Syria), which was built about 2500 B.C.

Writing Materials

The earliest materials used to write on were clay (in the Middle East), bone and shell (China), palm leaves and birch bark (India), and cotton (Egypt). By approximately 3000 B.C. the Egyptians had begun writing on sheets or rolls of papyrus, which became the most widely used writing material of ancient times. When the pharaohs banned the sale of papyrus to other countries in the second century B.C., the shortage of writing materials led to the invention of parchment in the city of Pergamum (in present-day Turkey).

Parchment was made from the prepared skins of animals, and it gradually became more popular than papyrus. The Chinese had been using silk, bamboo strips, and wooden tablets to write on, but in about A.D. 200 they invented paper. The Maya also invented paper, made from fig bark, in the fifth century, but the art of paper-making did not spread to Europe until about the eighth century A.D.

Plant juices and mineral pigments have been used as paints or inks since prehistoric times by many societies. Writing inks date from about 2500 B.C. in both Egypt and China. A mixture of lampblack (soot collected from burning lamps) and liquid gum or glue was molded into sticks and allowed to dry. Before use, the sticks were moistened with water on an ink stone. The Sumerians and Egyptians used sharpened reeds as pens, while the Chinese were writing with brushes by the first millennium B.C. The Maya also used brushes or feather pens. Feather pens were the forerunners of the quill pens that would revolutionize writing in the sixth century A.D.

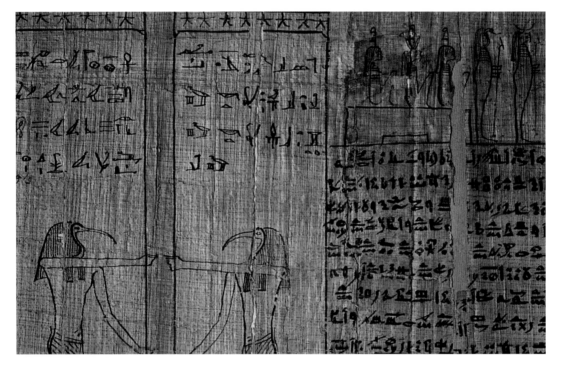

LEFT: A section from an Egyptian *Book of the Dead* written on papyrus. The text on the left above the illustration is in hieroglyphs, while the text on the right is written in hieratic script.

BELOW: Chinese script was the basis of all Eastern writing systems, and until the 18th century more than half of all the world's books were written in Chinese. This 17th-century Chinese text is written in ink on paper.

was found on oracle bones, which were used for divination. Questions were first written on fragments of animal bones, which were then heated to produce cracks. The cracks were examined and interpreted by a diviner in much the same way that people read tea leaves today. The predictions were then inscribed onto the oracle bones.

The Chinese writing system was a complex combination of pictograms, ideograms, and signs that indicated sounds. There are more than 50,000 Chinese signs, or characters. They have changed very little over the last 4,000 years, making ancient Chinese texts quite easy to interpret, in contrast to many other ancient writing systems. The Chinese writing system spread over much of East Asia.

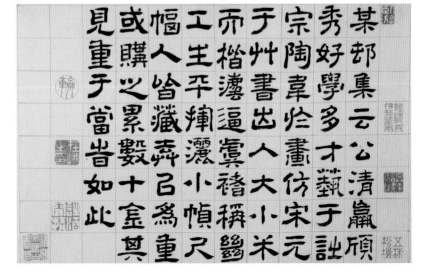

The alphabetic system is the most common form of writing in the world today. Alphabets use a limited number of letters to represent consonants and vowels, which can then be combined together to form words. This compact system involves learning only 26 letters to write all the words in the English language—a much easier system than the 800 cuneiform signs or several thousand Chinese characters.

It is probable that the earliest forms of alphabetic systems were evolving on the coast of the eastern Mediterranean around 1400 B.C. The Phoenicians, a maritime trading people whose base was the coast of present-day Syria and Lebanon, had evolved an alphabetic system by 1100 B.C. that used only 22 characters, each representing a consonant. But it was the Greeks who, in the eighth century B.C., developed the world's first truly alphabetic system, with letters representing both vowels and consonants. Phoenicians and Greeks had close trading contacts, especially in the eastern Mediterranean, where the Greeks encountered the Phoenician writing system. They adopted the Phoenician alphabet, but as it had too many consonant symbols for their own language, they used the extra symbols to represent the vowel sounds.

The Etruscans, who lived in western central Italy in the seventh century B.C., adapted the Greek alphabetic script and introduced their alphabet to the region of Latium and its Latin-speaking inhabitants. Several changes had to be made to accommodate the Latin language, including, in the first century B.C., the introduction of the letters Y and Z. As the Romans colonized the Italian peninsula and then built their empire, the influence of the Latin alphabet extended well beyond the borders of Italy.

⤚ ALTERNATIVE ALPHABETS ⤚

By the second century A.D. the Celts in Britain and Ireland had developed an alphabetic script called Ogham that consisted of 20 linear characters. Meanwhile the Germanic peoples were using a runic system consisting of 24 symbols arranged in an alphabetic order called a futhark, after the first six characters (f, u, th, a, r, k). But as the Romans advanced farther into northern Europe, these scripts gradually gave way to Latin. The arrival and spread of Christianity reinforced the importance of Latin, and it became the written language of the monasteries.

The Maya, who flourished in Central America around A.D. 250–900, developed their own system of writing, which has yet to be fully deciphered.

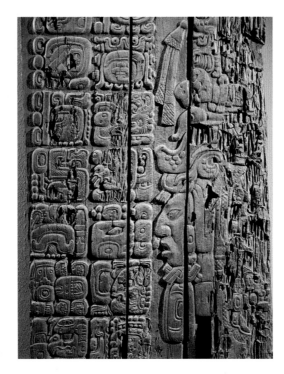

LEFT: This section of a carved wood doorway comes from a Mayan temple at Tikal (in present-day Guatemala). It shows a Mayan lord with a panel of glyphs (the Mayan form of writing) on the left. Mayan writing is read in double columns from left to right and from top to bottom.

Mayan symbols, or glyphs, combined pictograms with syllabic symbols. Inscriptions carved in stone recorded key facts about royalty and wars. Four books called codices, written on tree bark paper, have also survived. Other Mesoamerican peoples, such as the Aztecs and Mixtecs, also developed their own scripts.

LEFT: A ninth-century A.D. Viking stone engraved with lines of runes, a form of writing used by the early Germanic peoples.

Timeline

6500 B.C. | 6000 | 5500 | 5000 | 4500 | 4000 | 3500

EUROPE

Neolithic Europe: Megalithic Monuments 6500–1500 B.C.

Steppes: Sredny Stog 4400–3500 B.C.

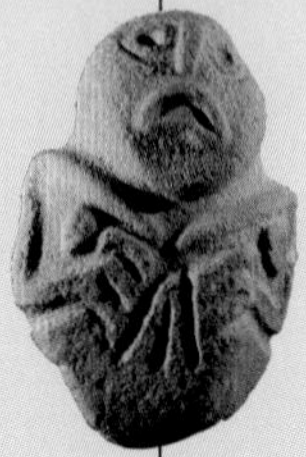

OCEANIA

Aborigine culture 40,000 B.C.–present day

INDIA AND THE FAR EAST

AMERICAS

MIDDLE EAST AND AFRICA

Jericho 10,000–6000 B.C.

Çatal Höyük 6250–5400 B.C.

Mesopotamia 5000–3000 B.C.

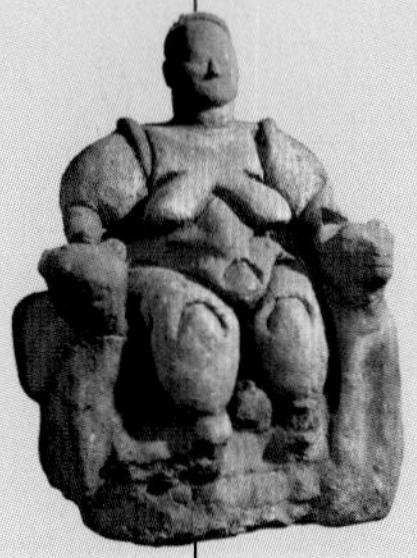

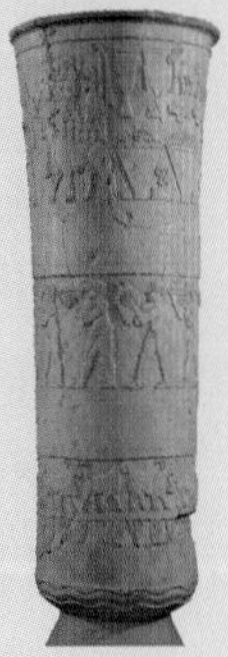

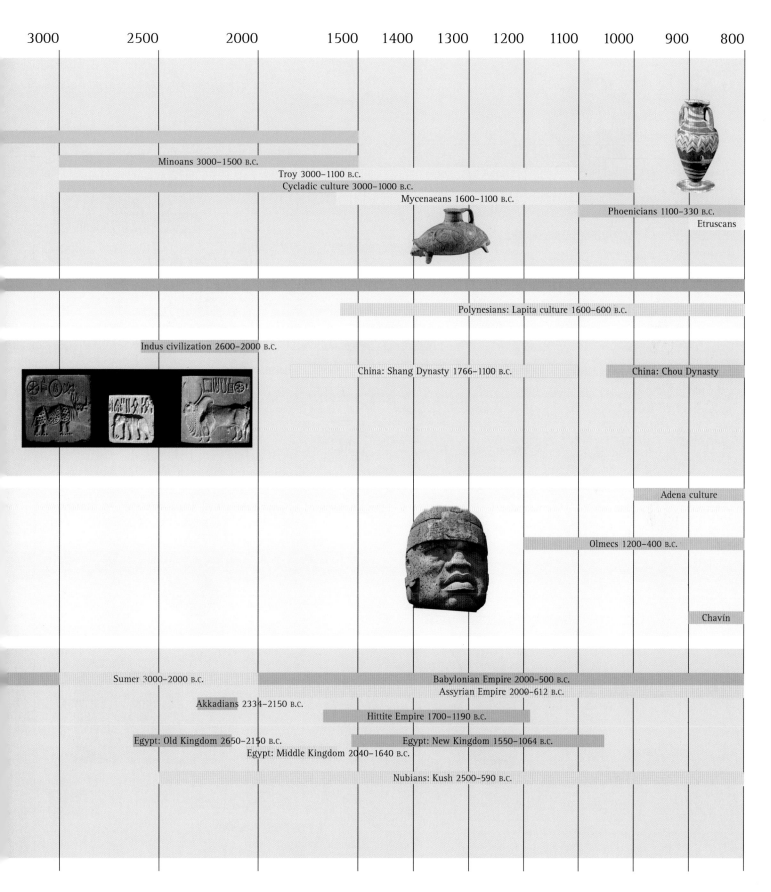

| 3000 | 2500 | 2000 | 1500 | 1400 | 1300 | 1200 | 1100 | 1000 | 900 | 800 |

Minoans 3000–1500 B.C.

Troy 3000–1100 B.C.

Cycladic culture 3000–1000 B.C.

Mycenaeans 1600–1100 B.C.

Phoenicians 1100–330 B.C.

Etruscans

Polynesians: Lapita culture 1600–600 B.C.

Indus civilization 2600–2000 B.C.

China: Shang Dynasty 1766–1100 B.C.

China: Chou Dynasty

Adena culture

Olmecs 1200–400 B.C.

Chavín

Sumer 3000–2000 B.C.

Babylonian Empire 2000–500 B.C.

Assyrian Empire 2000–612 B.C.

Akkadians 2334–2150 B.C.

Hittite Empire 1700–1190 B.C.

Egypt: Old Kingdom 2650–2150 B.C.

Egypt: New Kingdom 1550–1064 B.C.

Egypt: Middle Kingdom 2040–1640 B.C.

Nubians: Kush 2500–590 B.C.

800 B.C.	700	600	500	400	300	200	100	A.D. 1	100	200	300	400

Celts 500 B.C.–A.D. 50

Phoenicians 1100–330 B.C.
Etruscans 900–250 B.C.
Greece 800–338 B.C.
Roman Republic 509–27 B.C.

Roman Empire 27 B.C.–A.D. 476

Aborigines 40,000 B.C.–present day

Polynesians: Lapita culture
Polynesian colonization of Pacific 300 B.C.–A.D. 1000

India: Mauryan Empire 320–185 B.C.
India: Gupta

China: Chou Dynasty 1050–256 B.C.
China: Han Dynasty 202 B.C.–A.D. 220

Southeast Asia: Dong Son culture 500 B.C.–A.D. 43

Korea:

Adena culture 1000 B.C.–A.D. 100

Southwestern peoples 250 B.C.–A.D. 1450
Hopewell 100 B.C.–A.D. 500

Olmecs 1200–400 B.C.

Teotihuacán 200 B.C.–A.D. 650

Chavin culture 900–200 B.C.

Moche 50 B.C.–A.D. 750

Persian Empire 550–331 B.C.
Babylonian Empire 2000–500 B.C.
Assyrian Empire 2000–612 B.C.

Nubians: Kush 2500–590 B.C.
Nubians: Meroe 590 B.C.–A.D. 350
Nubians:

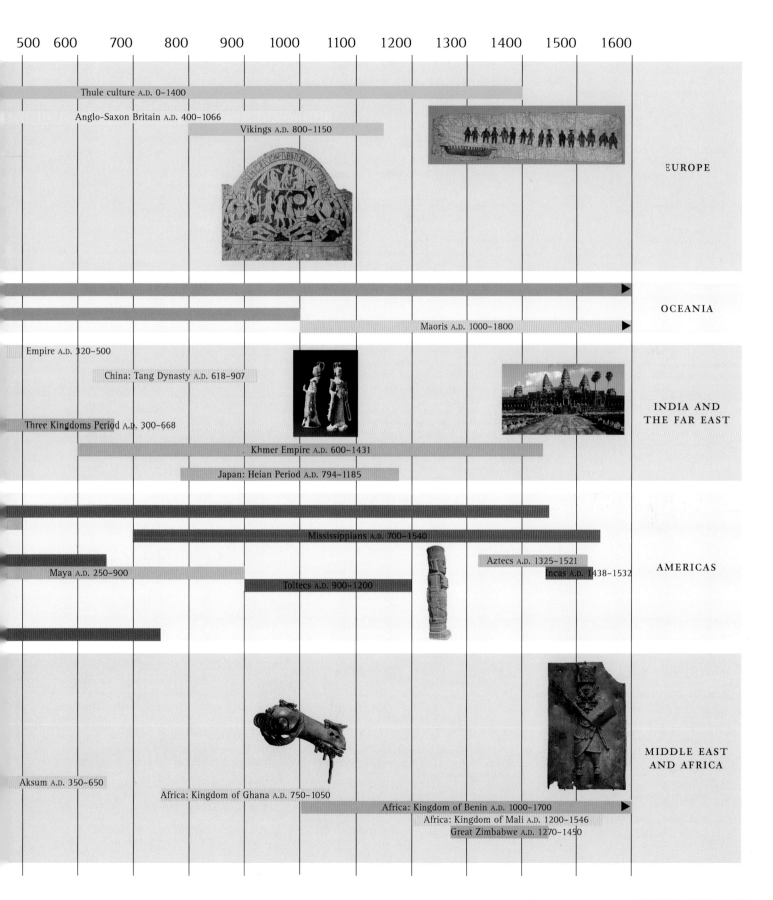

500 600 700 800 900 1000 1100 1200 1300 1400 1500 1600

Thule culture A.D. 0–1400

Anglo-Saxon Britain A.D. 400–1066

Vikings A.D. 800–1150

EUROPE

OCEANIA

Maoris A.D. 1000–1800

Empire A.D. 320–500

China: Tang Dynasty A.D. 618–907

INDIA AND
THE FAR EAST

Three Kingdoms Period A.D. 300–668

Khmer Empire A.D. 600–1431

Japan: Heian Period A.D. 794–1185

Mississippians A.D. 700–1540

Aztecs A.D. 1325–1521

AMERICAS

Incas A.D. 1438–1532

Maya A.D. 250–900

Toltecs A.D. 900–1200

MIDDLE EAST
AND AFRICA

Aksum A.D. 350–650

Africa: Kingdom of Ghana A.D. 750–1050

Africa: Kingdom of Benin A.D. 1000–1700

Africa: Kingdom of Mali A.D. 1200–1546

Great Zimbabwe A.D. 1270–1450

Further Reading

Aldred, Cyril. *The Egyptians*. London: Thames & Hudson, 1998.

Allchin, F.R. *The Archaeology of Early Historic South Asia: The Emergence of Cities and States*. Cambridge: Cambridge University Press, 1995.

Bahn, Paul G. (editor). *The Cambridge Illustrated History of Archaeology*. Cambridge: Cambridge University Press, 1996.

Bahn, Paul G. (editor). *The Story of Archaeology*. London: Weidenfeld & Nicolson, 1996.

Barker, Graeme, and Tom Rasmussen. *The Etruscans*. Oxford: Blackwell Publishers, 1998.

Barker, Graeme (editor). *The Routledge Companion Encyclopedia of Archaeology*. London: Routledge, 1999.

Barnes, Gina L. *The Rise of Civilization in East Asia*. London: Thames & Hudson, 1999.

Barnett, Jo Ellen. *Time's Pendulum: The Quest to Capture Time—From Sundials to Atomic Clocks*. New York: Plenum Press, 1998.

Barnett, William, and John Hoopes (editors). *The Emergence of Pottery: Technology and Innovation in Prehistoric Societies*. Washington, DC: Smithsonian Institution Press, 1995.

Bawden, Garth. *The Moche*. Oxford: Blackwell Publishers, 1996.

Bogucki, Peter. *The Origins of Human Society*. Oxford: Blackwell Publishers, 1999.

Burger, Richard L. *Chavín and the Origins of Andean Civilization*. London: Thames & Hudson, 1992.

Castleden, Rodney. *Minoans: Life in Bronze Age Crete*. London: Routledge, 1993.

Chang, Kwang-Chih. *The Archaeology of Ancient China*. New Haven: Yale University Press, 1986.

Chippindale, Christopher. *Stonehenge Complete*. London: Thames & Hudson, 1994.

Coe, Michael. *Mexico: From the Olmecs to the Aztecs*. London: Thames & Hudson, 1994.

Connah, Graham. *African Civilizations*. Cambridge: Cambridge University Press, 1987.

Cunliffe, Barry. *The Ancient Celts*. Oxford: Oxford University Press, 1997.

Cunliffe, Barry (editor). *The Oxford Illustrated Prehistory of Europe*. Oxford: Oxford University Press, 1994.

Cunliffe, Barry, and Colin Renfrew (editors). *Science and Stonehenge*. New York: Oxford University Press, 1997.

Dickinson, Oliver. *The Aegean Bronze Age*. Cambridge: Cambridge University Press, 1994.

Dodson, Aidan. *After The Pyramids: The Valley of the Kings and Beyond*. London: Rubicon Press, 2000.

Fagan, Brian. *Ancient North America: The Archaeology of a Continent*. London: Thames & Hudson, 1995.

Fagan, Brian (editor). *The Oxford Companion to Archaeology*. Oxford: Oxford University Press, 1996.

Fash, William L. *Scribes, Warriors, and Kings: The City of Copan and the Ancient Maya*. London: Thames & Hudson, 1991.

Fiedel, Stuart J. *Prehistory of the Americas*. Cambridge: Cambridge University Press, 1987.

Harrison, Peter. *The Lords of Tikal: Rulers of an Ancient Maya City*. London: Thames & Hudson, 1999.

Higham, Charles. *The Archaeology of Mainland Southeast Asia from 10,000 B.C. to the Fall of Angkor*. Cambridge: Cambridge University Press, 1989.

Ifrah, Georges. *The Universal History of Numbers: From Prehistory to the Invention of the Computer*. New York: John Wiley & Sons, 1999.

Imamura, Keiji. *Prehistoric Japan: New Perspectives on Insular East Asia*. Honolulu: University of Hawaii Press, 1996.

Irwin, Geoffrey. *The Prehistoric Exploration and Colonisation of the Pacific*. Cambridge: Cambridge University Press, 1992.

Keatinge, Richard W. (editor). *Peruvian Prehistory: An Overview of Pre-Inca and Inca Society*. Cambridge: Cambridge University Press, 1988.

Keeley, Lawrence H. *War Before Civilization*. Oxford: Oxford University Press, 1996.

Kemp, Barry J. *Ancient Egypt: Anatomy of a Civilization*. London: Routledge, 1989.

Kenoyer, Jonathan Mark. *Ancient Cities of the Indus Valley Civilization*. Oxford: Oxford University Press, 1998.

Kirch, Patrick Vinton. *The Lapita Peoples: Ancestors of the Oceanic World*. Oxford: Blackwell Publishers, 1997.

Kolata, Alan L. *The Tiwanaku: Portrait of an Andean Civilization*. Oxford: Blackwell Publishers, 1993.

Macqueen, J.G. *The Hittites*. London: Thames & Hudson, 1986.

Milner, George. *The Cahokia Chiefdom: The Archaeology of a Mississippian Society*. Washington, DC: Smithsonian Institution Press, 1998.

Noble, David. *The Hohokam: Ancient People of the Desert*. Santa Fe: School of American Research Press, 1991.

Oates, Joan. *Babylon*. London: Thames & Hudson, 1986.

Phillipson, David W. *African Archaeology*. Cambridge: Cambridge University Press, 1993.

Plog, Stephen. *Ancient Peoples of the American Southwest*. London: Thames & Hudson, 1998.

Pollock, Susan. *Ancient Mesopotamia*. Cambridge: Cambridge University Press, 1999.

Potts, D.T. *Mesopotamian Civilization: The Material Foundations*. London: The Athlone Press, 1997.

Powell, T.G.E. *The Celts*. London: Thames & Hudson, 1980.

Price, T. Douglas (editor). *Europe's First Farmers*. Cambridge: Cambridge University Press, 2000.

Renfrew, Colin, and Paul G. Bahn. *Archaeology: Theories, Methods and Practice*. London: Thames & Hudson, 1996.

Robinson, Andrew. *The Story of Writing*. London: Thames & Hudson, 1995.

Rudgley, Richard. *Lost Civilisations of the Stone Age*. London: Century, 1998.

Sabloff, Jeremy. *The New Archaeology and the Ancient Maya*. New York: W.H. Freeman, 1994.

Sawyer, Peter (editor). *The Oxford Illustrated History of the Vikings*. Oxford: Oxford University Press, 1998.

Scarre, Chris. *The Seventy Wonders of the Ancient World*. London: Thames & Hudson, 1999.

Schick, Kathy D., and Nicholas Toth. *Making Silent Stones Speak*. New York: Simon & Schuster, 1993.

Schmandt-Besserat, Denise. *Before Writing: From Counting to Cuneiform*. Austin: University of Texas Press, 1992.

Sharer, Robert J. *Daily Life in Maya Civilization*. Westport, Connecticut: Greenwood Press, 1996.

Smith, Bruce D. *The Emergence of Agriculture*. San Francisco: W.H. Freeman & Company, 1995.

Taylour, Lord William. *The Mycenaeans*. London: Thames & Hudson, 1983.

Thorpe, I.J. *The Origins of Agriculture in Europe*. London: Routledge, 1999.

Van De Mieroop, Marc. *The Ancient Mesopotamian City*. Oxford: Oxford University Press, 1997.

Wells, Peter S. *Farms, Villages, and Cities: Commerce and Urban Origins in Late Prehistoric Europe*. Ithaca: Cornell University Press, 1984.

Wells, Peter S. *The Barbarians Speak: How the Conquered Peoples Shaped Roman Europe*. Princeton: Princeton University Press, 1999.

Wenke, Robert. *Patterns in Prehistory: Humankind's First Three Million Years*. Oxford: Oxford University Press, 1999.

Whittle, Alasdair. *Europe in the Neolithic*. Cambridge: Cambridge University Press, 1996.

Index

Page numbers in **bold** refer to main articles; those in *italics* refer to pictures or their captions.

A

abacuses 222–23
Aborigines of Australia 4, **198–99**
Achaemenid Empire 42–43, 236
acupuncture 133
Adad (god) 30, 33–34, 37
Adena culture 165, 167, 168
adobe 169
Aeneid (Virgil) 217
Aeschylus 92
Africa **46–50**
Agamemnon, *king of Mycenae* 74, 77
agriculture 4, **207–8**
    Anglo-Saxon 119–20
    in Babylonia 32
    at Çatal Höyük 7
    in China 128, 207, *208*
    in Egypt 17, 208
    Hittite 39–40
    implements 219, *232*
    Indus civilization 126, 208
    Iron Age 103
    Mayan 172
    Mycenaean 76
    in Neolithic Europe 52, 54
    Polynesian 202
    in Sumeria 14
    See also irrigation; and under names of crops
Ah Cacao, *Mayan king* 178
Akhenaten (Amenhotep IV), *king of Egypt* 22, 24
Akhetaten 22, 24
Akkadian Empire **28–29**
Akrotiri *62*
Aksum 27
Alexander the Great 34, 42, *45*, 82, 95, 142, 213, 241
    army 239, 240
Alexandria 112, 229
Alfred the Great 118
alphabets 82, 247
Alps, "Iceman" found in 54
Amanishakhete, *queen of Meroe* 27
Amenhotep IV, *king of Egypt* 22, 24
Americas *See* Mesoamerica; North America; South America
amphitheaters, Roman 110
amphoras 226, 243
Amun (god) 21, 22, 24
Analects, The (Confucius) 131
Anasazi people *162*, 163–64, 227
Anatolia *See* Çatal Höyük; Hittites
Anaxagoras 91
Anaximander 91
Andes Mountains
    roads 237
    See also Chavín culture; Incas; Moche/Mochica civilization
Angkor 151, 152
Angkor Thom 150
Angkor Wat 153
Anglo-Saxons **115–16**
animals 207
    for transportation 55, 104, *206*, 207, 236
Anittas 38
Ankhesenpaaten, *queen of Egypt* 25
Antonius, Marcus (Mark Anthony) 108
Anuradhapura **139–40**
Anyang 128
Apache 181
Appian Way 237
aqueducts
    Moche 169
    Roman *107*, 111, 234

Archaeology
    and pottery 227
Archimedes 229
architecture, Greek 93
Arctic, Thule people **104–5**
Ariadne 64
Aristarchus 229
Aristophanes 92
Aristotle 91, 229
armies/soldiers
    Akkadian 29
    Assyrian 36–37
    Greek *90*, 91
    Hittite 39
    Inca 194
    Roman 109, 241
    Sumerian *14*
    See also warfare and weapons
armor 228, 239
art
    Aboriginal 199
    Celtic 101
    Chavín 161
    Egyptian 23
    Etruscan *83*, 85
Arvad 80
Aryans 126, 141
Ashoka, *Mayan king 141*, 143, 146
Ashur (city) 36
Ashurbanipal II, *king of Assyria* 35
Ashurnasirpal II, *king of Assyria 36*, 37, *238*
Ashur-uballit I, *king of Assyria* 35
Asia, Southeast **137–38**
    See also Khmer Empire; Korea; Polynesians
Askia Mohammed, *Songhai ruler* 48
Assyrians **35–37**, 228, *235*, 243
    warfare 36, *238*, *239*, 241
astronomy 228
    in Babylonia 30
    Mayan 177
    and the Nazca Indians 171
    and the Olmecs 159
    and Stonehenge 57
    See also calendars
Atahualpa 194
Aten (god) 22
Athene (goddess) 75, 90
Athens 73, 86, 91–92, 93, 94–96
    laws 215
    Parthenon *51*, *86*, 90
    pottery 225–26
    and science 229
Attic ware 225–26
Attila, *Hunnish king* 61
Aubrey holes 57
Augustus, *Roman emperor* 108–9, 231
Australia, Aborigines 4, **198–99**
Avebury 55, *58*, 59
Aztecs 159, **184–89**, *231*
    calendars 186–87, *209*

B

Babel, Tower of 34
Babylon 11, **33–34**
Babylonia **30–32**, 228
    calendars 32, 209
    capital *See* Babylon
    clocks 210
    numbers and counting 221, 222
    and the Persians 43
    weights and measures 243
ball games, Central American 175, 182
barbarians, and the Roman Empire 112
bards 100, 216
barley 207
barrows, Neolithic 59
Basketmaker people 163–64
baths, Roman 111

batteries 228
Battle-Axe culture 226
Beaker Folk 226
Behistun, inscriptions at 43
Belshazzar 31–32
Benin 49
Berytus 80
Beserkers 121
Bindusara, *Mauryan emperor* 143
Bingham, Hiram 195, 196
Blanchard Bone 209
bloodletting 159, 175–76
blood money 116
Book of the Dead 216, *217*, *246*
Bo tree 140
Boudicca, *queen of the Iceni* 99–100
bows 239
brahmans 143, 145, 146
Brattahlid *120*
bridges 193, 228
Britain
    Anglo-Saxons **115–16**
    hill forts *101*, **102–3**
    Neolithic *See* Avebury; Stonehenge
    and the Phoenicians 80
    See also Celts
bronze 219
    in Africa 47, *48*
    Celtic *100*, 213
    in China *128*, 219
    Etruscan *85*
    in Mesopotamia 11
    and the people of the Aegean and Crete 62, 65
    in Southeast Asia 137
    tools 233
    weapons 238, *241*
Bronze Age 62, 65, 78, 79, 219
Buddha (Siddhartha Gautama) 140, 142, *145*, 146, 151
Buddhism
    in India 141 15, 146
    in Japan 154, 155
    in the Khmer Empire 152
    in Korea *147*, 148
    on Sri Lanka 139, 140
bulls, and the Minoans 66, 72
burial rites *See* tombs and burial rites
Byblos 79, 80
Bylany 53

C

Caesar, Julius 97, 107–8, 210
Cahokia 179–80, 181
calendars **209–10**
    Aztec 186–87, *209*
    in Babylonia 32, 209
    Celtic 100
    Mayan 177
Caligula, *Roman emperor* 109
calligraphy 156
Cambyses, *king of Persia* 43
camels *206*, 236
Canaanites 79
canals 237
cannibalism 159
canoes *197*, 203, 235
Carnac, standing stones 59
Carnarvon, Lord 25
carnelian 125
Carter, Howard 25
Carthage 80, *82*, 107
carts 240
castes 141, 143
Çatal Höyük *5*, **7–8**, 224
Catullus 217
Celts **97–101**, *212*, 213, *232*
    alphabet 247
centurions 109, 241
ceremonial sites, Neolithic 55
    See also Avebury; Stonehenge

Ceres (goddess) 110
Chaco Canyon 164
Champa 151
Champollion, Jean F. 245
Chams 151
Chandragupta I, *king of India* 145
Chandragupta II, *king of India* 145
Chandragupta Maurya, *Mauryan king* 142–43
Changan 133, 134
chariots 39, 236, *239*
Charon 96
chaski 193
Chavín culture **160–61**
Cheddar 116
Cheng *See* Ch'in Shihuangdi
Cherokees 181
Chiapa de Corzo 159
Chichén Itzá 175, 177, 183
China **128–34**
    agriculture 128, 207, *208*
    calendars 209–10
    Ch'in dynasty 131–32, *133*, 215
    Ch'in Shihuangdi's tomb 132, **135–36**, 228
    Chou dynasty 129–30, 131
    Han dynasty *131*, 132–34, 136, 138
    influence on Japan 154–55
    jewelry 212, *213*
    and legalism 215
    literature 216
    and lodestone 234
    metals *128*, 219, 220
    pottery *134*, 224, 225, 226–27
    science 228, 229
    Shang dynasty 128, *130*, *133*, 219, 225, 245–46
    and Southeast Asia 138
    Sui dynasty 134
    Tang dynasty 134, 227
    taxes 230–31
    transportation *236*, 237
    warfare and weapons 228
    water power 233
    weights and measures 242
    writing 128, 245–46
Ch'in Shihuangdi (Cheng of Ch'in; Shihuangdi) 131–32, 135, 242
    tomb 132, **135–36**, 228
chocolate 177, 187
Choctaws 181
Choson 148
Christianity, and Rome 112
Ch'u Tzu (poems) 216
cities, first 4, 10–11
Claudius, *Roman emperor* 109
Cleisthenes 87
Cliff Palace *162*, *163*, 164
clocks 210
clothing
    Aztec 187
    Celtic 98
    Chinese *134*
    at Great Zimbabwe 50
    Greek 94
    Hittite 40–41
    Hopewell 168
    Mayan 173
    Minoan *65*, 66
    Mycenaean 75–76
    Roman 108
    Thule 104–5
coins 141
Colosseum 110
Comanche 181
compass, magnetic 234
Confucius/Confucianism 130–31, 133, 148
Constantine, *Roman emperor* 112
Constantinople 112
Copán 174, *175*
copper 55, 167, 218–19

extraction 11, 232–33
Corinth 88, 94
corn 172–73, 179, *180*
Cortés, Hernán 188
cotton 208
crafts
  Assyrian 37
  Celtic *97, 100*, 101
  Hittite 40
  Iron Age 103
  Mississippian *179, 180*, 181
  Mycenaean *74, 76, 224, 225*
  Phoenician 81
  See also art; glass; jewelry;
    lacquering; pottery
cranes 229, 234
Creeks 181
Crete
  and the Mycenaeans 73–74
  pottery 224
  See also Minoans
Croesus, *king of Lydia* 43
Crow 181
Ctesibius 210, 229
cubits 242
Culhuacán 184
Cunliffe, Barry 102
Cuzco 191, *192*, 237
Cyclades **62–63**
Cyclopean stonework 75
cylinder seals 10
Cyrus the Great, *king of Persia*
  42–43

D
dagobas 140
daimyo 156
dams 234
dances, Japanese 156
Danebury hill fort **102–3**
Darius I, *king of Persia 42*, 43–44,
  237
Darius III, *king of Persia* 44, *45*, 95
David, *king of Israel* 80
Deir el-Medina 23
Delian League 92–93
Delphi *89, 90*, 93
democracy
  Greek 86–88
  Roman 107
Desborough *101*
Devanampiyatissa, *king of Sri Lanka*
  139, 140
dogs, used for transportation 104
Dong Son culture 137
Dorians 63
Dörpfeld, Wilhelm 77
drainage systems 125, 127
Dreamtime 199
Druids 59, 101
Dutugemunu, *king of Sri Lanka* 139,
  140
dye, purple 79, 80

E
earthenware 225
Easter Island 202, 208
Ebla, clay tablets of 29
education
  Greek 93
  Sumerian 14
Edward the Confessor 117
Egypt **17–23**
  agriculture 17, 208, 234
  boats 235
  calendars 209, 210
  jewelry 211–12
  legal codes 214–15
  literature 216, *217, 246*
  metalwork 212, *220*
  numbers and counting *221*, 222
  taxes *214*, 230–31
  Tutankhamun's tomb 22, **24–25**
  weights and measures 242

writing 21, *221, 244, 245*, 246
Elam/Elamites 13, 16, 42
Elara, *Indian ruler* 139
electricity 228
electrum 219
El Mansur 48
Epic of Gilgamesh 216, 217
Epidaurus 92
Eridu 12
Erik the Red 120
Eriksson, Leif 120
Es-Saheli 48
Ethelfled 116
Etowah 181
Etruria 83, *84*
Etruscans **83–85**, 106–7, 247
Euripedes 92
Europe 51–121
  Neolithic **52–55**, 224
Evans, Arthur 64, 65, 67, 69–72
Ezana, *king of Aksum* 27

F
faience *65*, 123, 212
farming *See* agriculture
Fertile Crescent *208*
filigree 211
Fiorelli, Giuseppe 114
flint 123, *198*
flower arranging, Japanese 155
footwear, Greek 50
frescoes
  of the Cycladic culture *62, 63*
  Minoan *66, 68, 70, 72*
Fujiwara clan 156
Funan 138, 150
futhark 247

G
Gades 80
Gaozong, *emperor of China* 148
Gaul 97
Ghana, kingdom of 47–48, *49*
Gla 73
gladiators, Roman 110
glass, Phoenician 81
gods and goddesses
  Assyrian 37
  Aztec 185, *209*
  Babylonian 30, *31*
  Celtic 101
  Egyptian 21, 22, 24, *217*
  Etruscan 84
  Greek 90
  Hindu 146
  Hittite *39*
  Inca 191
  Mayan *173*, 174–75
  Mesopotamian *9, 10*, 11
  Minoan 65–66
  Mycenaean 75
  Nubian 27
  Persian 45
  Phoenician 81
  Roman 109–10
  Viking 121
gold 218
  Egyptian 212, *220*
  at Great Zimbabwe 50
  Inca *194*
  Minoan 65
  Moche *169*, 170
  Scythian *60*
  Sumerian *218*
Goths 112
Gournia 68
government
  Greek 86–88
  Roman 107–9
Grand Canal (China) 134
granulation 211
Great Death Pit 16
Great Serpent Mound 168
Great Sun 180, 181

Great Wall of China 132, *133*, 136
Great Zimbabwe 49–50
Greece **86–96**
  alphabet 82, 247
  architecture 93
  clocks 210
  clothes 94
  colonies and trade 89–90
  daily life 93–94
  government 86–88
  jewelry 213
  justice 215
  literature 94, 216, 217
  numbers and counting 222
  and the Persians 44, *45*,
    90–91
  pottery 50–52, *90*, 94–96, *224,
    225*–26
  sanctuaries and gods 90
  science 228
  scientists and philosophers 91,
    228–29
  sculpture 96
  taxes 230–31
  theaters 92
  tombs 96
  warfare and weapons *228*
  See also Athens; Cyclades;
    Mycenaeans
Greenland 120
greenstone 204, *205*
Gupta Empire 145–46
Gutians 13

H
Hades (god) 90
Halloween 100
Hallstatt culture 97–98
Hambledon Hill 55
hammerstones 232
Hammurabi, *king of Babylon* 30, 31,
  33, 35, 214
Hanging Gardens of Babylon 31,
  34
Hannibal 107
Harappa *124*, 125
Harappan civilization *See* Indus
  civilization
Harsha, *king of Kanauj* 146
Hastings, Battle of 117
Hathor (goddess) 81
Hatshepsut, *queen of Egypt* 21
Hattusas 38, *39*, 41
Hatusilis, *Hittite king* 38
Hawaii 202
Heian 155–56
Heijo 155
Hera (goddess) *73*, 90
Herculaneum 114
Hermes (god) 75
Herodotus 33, 45, 80, 217
Heron 229
hieroglyphics *See* writing
hill forts *101*, **102–3**
Hinduism 145, 146, 152, 153
Hippocrates 217
Hiram, *king of Tyre* 80
Hissarlik 77
Hittites 30, **38–41**, 100, 220, 243
Hohokam culture 162–63
Homer 74, 77, 217
Hopewell **165–68**
hoplites *90*, 91
horses 60, 181, 236, 239–40
huacas 191
Huangdi 129
Huari 171
Huascar 194
Huemac, *Toltec king* 183
Huitzilopochtli (god) 185
Huns 61, 146
hunter-gatherers, Neolithic 52, 53,
  54
hunting 105, 198
Hurrians 38, 39

Hwanung (god) 147

I
Ice Age 198
Iceland, Vikings 121
"Iceman," the 54
Iceni 98–99
Ife 48–49
Igbo-Ukwu 47
Iliad (poem) 74, 77, 94, 217
Ilium 78
Inanna (goddess) *9*, 10
Incas **190–94**, 213, 223, 231
  roads 237
  See also Machu Picchu
India 138, **141–46**
  and Alexander the Great 95, 142
  literature 144, 217
  See also Indus civilization; Sri
    Lanka
Indus civilization **123–27**, 208, 212,
  243
initiation rites 49
Ionians 63
iron 46, 100, 220
  tools *232*, 233
  weapons 238, *241*
Iron Age 98
  Danebury hill fort **102–3**
Iron Gates settlement 52, *53*
irrigation 207, *208*, 233–34
  and the Hohokam 163
  in Mesopotamia 9, 12, 14, 234
Ishtar (goddess) 30, 33, 37
Ishtar Gate 33–34
Isis (goddess) 27, 109
Issus, Battle of *45*
Italy *See* Etruscans; Pompeii;
  Rome/Romans

J
jade *133, 159*, 212, *213*
Jains 142
Janus (god) 109
Japan **154–56**, 224
Jayavarman II, *Khmer king* 150–51,
  152
Jayavarman VII, *Khmer king* 152
Jenné-Jeno 46–47
Jericho *6*, 8, 240–41
Jerusalem 31
jewelry **211–13**, 219
  Celtic *98, 212, 213*
  Chinese *133*
  Hopewell *165, 167, 168*
  Indus civilzation 125
Jimmu, *emperor of Japan* 154
Juno (goddess) 109
Jupiter (god) 109
Justinian, *Roman emperor* 215

K
Kachina religion 164
Kadesh, Battle of 39
Kamares ware 66, 225
Kanesh 38
Karnak, temple of 21, *22*
Kassites 30
Kastri 62
Kausambi 141
kayaks *105*
kendo 156
Kenyon, Kathleen 6
Kerma 26
Khmer Empire **150–53**
Khufu, *king of Egypt 18*, 19
Kija 147
kilns 218
Kings, Valley of the 20, 22
  Tutankhamun's tomb **24–25**
kivas 162, 163
Knossos, palace of Minos 65, *66, 68*,
  69–72, 224–25
Koguryo 148, 149

Koldewey, Robert 33
Korea **147–49**
Koryo 149
Kumbi Saleh 48
Kush 26
Kushans 144–45
Kyongju *147*
Kythnos 62

L
Labarnas, *Hittite king* 38
lacquering *131*
Lagash 12, *13*, 28
language
    Etruscan 84
    See also writing
Lanzón monolith 161
Laozi 130
Lapita culture 200–201
La Tène culture 97, 101
Latins 106
La Venta 158, 159
laws *See* legal codes
legal codes **214–15**
    Babylonian 31
Lepenski Vir 52
levers 229, 234
Linear A script 67
Linear B script 67, 74
Linear pottery settlements 53–54
literature 156, **216–17**, 217
    Egyptian 216, *217*, *246*
    Greek 94, 216, 217
    Indian 144, 217
Liu Bang, *emperor of China* 133
llamas 160, 192, 236
lodestone 228, 234
longboats, Anglo-Saxon 115
longhouses, Viking *119*, 121
longships, Viking 118–19
lost-wax process 14, 47, *48*, *128*, 220
Lugalzagesi, *king of Uruk* 28
Lullubi 29
Luoyang 134
Lyceum 91, 229
Lydenburg heads 49
Lydia 43

M
Macedonia 93, *240*, 241
Machu Picchu **195–96**, 237
Magadha, kingdom of 142
magnetism 228
Mahabharata (poem) 144, 217
Mahavira 142
Mali 46–47, 48, *49*
mandalas 137–38
Manishtusu, *king of Akkad* 28–29
Maoris **203–5**
Mapungubwe 49
Marathon, Battle of 91
Marduk (god) 11, 30, 34
Mars (god) 109
Marshall, John 127
martial arts 148, 156
Marzabotto 83
mastaba tombs 19–20
mathematics 228
Mauryan Empire 141, 142–44
Maya 159, **172–78**
    numbers and counting 174, 221, 223
    pottery *176*, 227
    writing 176, 246, 247
Medes 42
Media 42
medicine, Chinese 133
megalithic tombs 55
Mellaart, James 7
Melos 65
Memphis 18, 24
Menerva (goddess) 84
Menes, *king of Egypt* 18

Mercury (god) 110
Meroe 26–27
Mesa Verde *162*, *163*, 164
Mesoamerica
    calendars 210
    See also Aztecs; Maya; Olmecs; Toltecs
Mesopotamia **9–11**
    calendars 209
    cylinder seals 10
    legal codes 214
    literature 216
    numbers and counting 222
    taxes 230
    weights and measures 242–43
    writing 11, *13*, 29, 37
    ziggurats 11
    See also Akkadian Empire; Assyrians; Babylonia; Sumerians
metals 137, **218–20**
    tools 232–33
    See also bronze; copper; gold; iron
metics 88
Mexica 184
Mexico *See* Aztecs; Maya; Toltecs
mica *165*, 167
microliths 232
millet 207
Milos 62, 63
Minamoto family 156
mining 218–19
Minoans 62, **64–68**, 73
    pottery *65*, 66–68, 224–25
Minos, palace of *See* Knossos
Minotaur 64, 66, 69, *71*, 72
Mississippians **179–81**, 227
Mitannians 35
moa 205
Moche/Mochica civilization 161, **169–71**, 213
    metalwork *169*, 170, 219–20
Mogollon people 163, 227
Mohenjodaro 125, 126, 127, 208
Monk's Mound 180
Montezuma I, *Aztec emperor* 185
Montezuma II, *Aztec emperor* 188
Mouhot, Henri 153
Mound Builders 165
mounds, Mississippian 179, 180
Moundville 181
Mursilis I, *Hittite king* 38
Mursilis II, *Hittite king* 39
Musa, *emperor (mansa) of Mali* 48
Muwatallis, *Hittite king* 39
Muyol, *king of Silla* 148
Mycenae 73, 74, 75
Mycenaeans 63, 72, **73–76**, 80, 241
    pottery *74*, 76, 224, 225

N
Nabonidus, *king of Babylon* 31–32
Nabopolassar 30, 33
Napata 26, 27
Naram-Sin, *king of Akkad* 29
Narmer, *king of Egypt* 17–18
Natchez tribe 180
Nazca 161, 171
Nazca lines 171
Nebhepetre Mentuhotep 20
Nebuchadnezzar II, *king of Babylonia* 30–31, 80
    and Babylon 33–34
Nefertiti, *queen of Egypt* 24
Neolithic Europe **52–55**, 224
Nero, *Roman emperor* 109
New Zealand 201–2, 208
    See also Maoris
Ngo Quyen 138
Nigeria 47
Nile River 17, 22, 208
Nimrud *36*, 37
Nineveh *35*, 36, 37, 42
Nippur 12

Nok culture 46, *49*
Norsemen *See* Vikings
North America
    Adena culture 165, 167, 168
    agriculture 208
    Hopewell **165–68**
    metals 218
    Mississippians **179–81**, 227
    pottery 227
    Southwestern peoples **162–64**, 227
Nubians **26–27**
numbers and counting 174, **221–23**

O
Oba 49
obsidian 8, 62, 65, 186
Oceania 197–205
Oc Eo 138
Odin (god) 121
Odoacer 112
Odysseus 77
Odyssey (poem) 94, 217
Olmecs **158–59**
Olympia 90, 96
Olympic games 90
oracle bones 128, *130*, 246
origami 155
Orkney Islands, Skara Brae *52*, 55
ostracism, Greek system of 88
"Otzi" (the "Iceman") 54
Ovid 217

P
Pacal, *Mayan king* 176
Pachacutec 190
Pachuca 182
Pacific islands, colonization 201–2
Paekche 148, 149
paintings *See* art
Palenque 174, *176*
paper 134, 246
papyrus *244*, 245, 246
parchment 246
Parthenon *51*, *86*, 90
Parthians 228
Pasargadae 45
Pataliputra 143
Pawnee 181
Pazyryk 60, *61*
Peloponnesian War 93
Pericles 92
Persepolis 43, *44*, 45
Persian Empire **42–45**, 142, 236
Persian Wars 90–91
Philip II, *king of Macedonia* 61, 93
Philon 229
philosophers 91, 228–29
Phnom Penh 152
Phoenicians 63, **79–82**, 243
    alphabet 247
    ships *80*, 235–36
Phylakope 63
Piankhi, *Nubian king* 26
pictograms 11, 244–46
Picts 115
pillars
    of Ashoka *141*, 143–44
    stelae of Aksum 27
pipes (smoking) *166*, 167, 168, 180, *181*
Pizarro, Francisco 194
Plataia, Battle of 91
Plato 91
Pliny the Elder 114
Pliny the Younger 114
plows 11, 207, 233, 236
polis 86
Polynesians *197*, **200–202**, 208
Pompeii **113–14**
Pompey 107–8
porcelain 134, 227

Poseidon (god) 75, 90
pottery **224–27**
    Anasazi *163*
    and archaeology 227
    Chinese *134*, 224, 225, 226–27
    Greek 50–52, *90*, 94–96, 224, 225–26
    Indus civilization *125*
    Linear 53, 224
    Mayan *176*, 227
    Mimbres 164
    Minoan *65*, 66–68, 224–25
    Mississippian *179*
    Moche 170–71
    Mogollon 163, 164
    Mycenaean *74*, 76, 224, 225
    Polynesian 200, 202
    Roman 226
    Trojan *78*
Priam, *legendary king of Troy* 77, 217
    treasure 77, *78*
Ptolemy II, *king of Egypt* 229
Pueblo Bonito 164
Pueblo culture 164
pulleys 229, 234
Punjab 123
Pylos 73
pyramids
    Aztec 186, *187*, 189
    Egyptian 18–19, *20*
    Korean 149
    Moche 169
    Olmec 159
    stepped *See* ziggurats
    Toltec 182
Pythagoras 229

Q
Quetzalcoatl (god) 183, *185*, 188, 189
quipu 194, 223

R
Raedwald, *king of East Anglia* 117
Rajaraja I, *Indian ruler* 140
Ramayana (poem) 144, 217
Rawlinson, Henry 43
Red River Valley 137, 138
Reisner, George 26
religion
    Etruscan 84
    Inca 191
    in India 146
    Olmec 159
    See also gods and goddesses; ritual and sacrifice; temples; and under names of various religions
rice 122, 128, 137, 207, *208*
Rimush, *king of Akkad* 28
ritual and sacrifice
    Aztec 186, 188
    at Danebury hill fort 103
    Incas 191
    Mayan 175–76
    Olmec 159
    Phoenician *82*
    See also tombs and burial rites
roads
    Inca 193, 237
    Roman 109, 236–37
Roman Empire 27, 97, 111–12
    and the Celts 97
Rome/Romans *4*, **106–12**
    alphabet 82
    aqueducts *107*, 111, 234
    armies 109, 241
    calendars 210
    clothes 108
    jewelry 213
    legal codes 215
    measurements 243
    numbers and counting 222

pottery 226
roads 109, 236–37
taxes 230–31
technology 233, 234
trade 100, 145, 226, *231*, 243
water power 228, 233
See also Pompeii; Roman Empire
Rosetta Stone 245
runes 247

S
sacrifice *See* ritual and sacrifice
Sahara Desert, trade across 46
salt 47–48, 231
Samian ware 226
Samoa 201
samurai 156
San Lorenzo 158, 159
Sanni Ali, *Songhai ruler* 48
Sanskrit 138, 141
Santorini 63, 68, 72
Sargon, *king of Akkad* 12–13, 28, 29
Sargon II, *king of Assyria* 235
Sasanians 44
sati 143
scales 243
Schliemann, Heinrich 74, 77, 78
Schroda 49
Schwanfeld 53
science 32, 91, 145, **228–29**
Scythians *60*, 61
Sea Peoples 39, 79–80
seismoscopes *229*
Seleucus 34
Sennacherib, *king of Assyria* 37
Senusret, *king of Egypt* 26
sewers 125
Shamshi-Adad 35
Shar-kali-Sharri, *king of Akkad* 29
Shih Ching (poems) 216
Shihuangdi *See* Ch'in Shihuangdi
Shinto 154
ships and boats 68, *80*, 115, 117, 118–19, 235–36
Shiva (god) 146, 152
Shona people 50
Shotoku 154–55
Shulgi, *king of Ur* 214
Sidon 80
siege machines *238*, *240*, 241
Silbury Hill 59
silk 129
Silk Road *133*, *206*
Silla kingdom *147*, 148–49, 225
silphium *96*
Sind 123, 127
siphons 234
Skara Brae *52*, 55
skis 236
skulls, plastered *6*
slaves
   Anglo-Saxon 116
   in Babylonia 32
   Greek 88, 93
   Roman *108*, 111
   Viking 120
sleds 236
smelting 40
Smenkhkare 24
Snaketown 163
Snefru, *king of Egypt* 19
Socrates 91, 217
soldiers *See* armies/soldiers
Solomon, *king of Israel* 80
Solon 86–87
Songak 149
Songhai 48, *49*
Soninke people 47
Sophocles 92
South America
   Chavín culture **160–61**
   jewelry 213
   metalwork 219–20
   See also Incas; Moche/Mochica civilization

Southern Cult 181
Sparta 88–89, 93
Spina 85
Spiro *180*, 181
sports *87*, 90
   bull-leaping 66
Sredny Stog 60
Sri Lanka
   Anuradhapura **139–40**
   writing 141–42
stamps, stone 124
Standard of Ur *14*, *15*, 16, 239
standing stones
   Chavín 161
   See also stone circles
stelae 27, 176, 178, 242
steppe nomads **60–61**, 239–40
Stone Age(s) 52, 147
stone circles, Neolithic 55, 56–59
Stonehenge 55, **56–59**, 228
stoneware 225
Strato 229
stupas 143, *144*, 145
Suiko, *empress of Japan* 154
Sumerians **12–14**
   armor 239
   cities *See* Ur; Uruk
   jewelry 211
   kings 11, 12
   literature 216
   metals 211, *218*
   temples 13
   writing 244–45
Suppiluliumas, *Hittite king* 38–39
Suryavarman II, *Khmer king* 151, 153
Susa *42*, 43, 44, 45
Sutton Hoo 117
Swahili people 49
Sweet Track 236
Syros 62

T
taekwondo 148
Tahiti 202, 203
Taira family 156
Tale of Genji (novel) 156, 217
Tangun 147
Taoists 130
Tao Te Ching (book) 130
Tarquinia *83*, 85
Tarquin the Proud (Lucius Tarquinius) 106–7
tattooing, Maori 204
taxes *See* tithes and taxes
technology and tools 198, **232–34**
Telemon, Battle of 97
Tell al Muqayyar 15
temples
   Aztec 186
   Buddhist *147*, 155
   at Chavín de Huantar *160*, 161
   Etruscan 83–84
   Greek *51*, *86*, *88*, 90
   Hindu 145
   Hittite *40*
   Inca 191
   Khmer *150*, 151, 153
   Mesopotamian *See* ziggurats
   Moche 169–70
Tenochtitlán 185, 186, 187, 188
Teopantecuanitlan 159
Teotihuacán *157*, 183, 189
terracotta army *See* Ch'in Shihuangdi, tomb
Thailand, Ban Lum Khao cemetery 227
theaters
   Greek 92
   See also amphitheaters
Thebes 20, 21–22, 73
   Tutankhamun's tomb **24–25**
Theodosius, *Roman emperor* 215
Theseus 64
Thirty Tyrants 93

tholos tombs 75
Thor (god) 121
Three Kingdoms, Korean 148
Thule people **104–5**
Tiberius, *Roman emperor* 109
Tiglath-pileser III, *king of Assyria* 35
Tikal 174, 178, *247*
Timbuktu 48
Tiryns 73
tithes and taxes 194, **230–31**
Tlatilco 159
Tollan 182
Toltecs 159, **182–83**
Tomb of the Reliefs 85
tombs and burial rites
   Anglo-Saxon 117
   at Çatal Höyük 8
   Ch'in Shihuangdi's tomb 132, **135–36**
   and the Cycladic culture 62
   in Egypt 19–20, 22, 24–25
   Etruscan *83*, 85
   Greek 96
   at Jericho *6*
   Korean 149
   Mayan 176
   and Mimbres pottery 164
   Mississippian *180*, 181
   Moche 170
   Mycenaean *73*, 74, 75, 239
   Neolithic 55, 59
   in Nigeria 47
   North American burial mounds 165–67
   Nubian 26
   steppe nomad 60, 61
   in Thailand 227
   at Ur 16
Tonga 201, 202
tools and technology 198, **232–34**
Topiltzin, *Toltec king* 183
trade
   across the Sahara 46
   Anglo-Saxon 117
   Celtic 100
   in Egypt 20–21
   Etruscan 84–85
   Greek 89–90
   Indian 145
   Mayan 177
   in Mesopotamia 9–10
   Mycenaean 76
   Olmec 158–59
   Phoenician 79, 80, 81
   Roman 100, 145, 226, *231*, 243
transportation **235–37**
   animals for 55, 104, *206*, 207, 236
Tres Zapotes 158
Trojan War 77
Troy 76, **77–78**
Trung Trac 138
Tula 182, 183, 188
Tutankhamun's tomb 22, **24–25**
Tyre 80

U
Ugarit 79
umiaks *105*
Umma 28
Ur 12, **15–16**, 28, 211
Ur-Nammu, *king of Ur* 11, 13, 15, 16, 242
Ur-Nanshe, *king of Lagash* 12
Uruk 10–11, 12, *13*, 14

V
Vandals 112
Vedas (texts) 141, *144*, 217
Vedic period 142, 143
Vedic tribes (Aryans) 126, 141
Ventris, Michael 67
Venus (goddess) 109
Vespasian, *Roman emperor* 110
Vesta (goddess) 110

Vietnam 138
Vikings 104, 117, **118–21**, *247*
Vinland 120
Virgil 217
Vishnu (god) 143, 146
Visigoths 112
Vitruvius *234*
Vlasac 52

W
wagons 236
walls 240–41
   Great Wall of China 132, *133*, 136
Wang Kon 149
warfare and weapons 228, **238–41**
   See also armies/soldiers
"Warrior," the 61
water power 228, 233
weapons *198*, 199, 238–39, 241
weights and measures 126, **242–43**
West Stow *115*
whaling 105
wheat 207
wheel 11, 13, 236
   potter's 11, 224, *225*
William the Conqueror 117, 121
Wiman 148
windlasses 234
women
   Anglo-Saxon 116–17
   Celtic 99–100
   Egyptian 19
   Greek 93–94
   in India 143
   Minoan 66
   Roman 108
   Spartan 89
   Viking 121
Woolley, Sir Leonard 15, 16, 211
wrestling, Greek *87*
writing 11, 14, **244–47**
   Aztec 187
   in Babylonia 32
   Chinese 128, 245–46
   cuneiform 11, *13*, 14, 29, 32, 37, 41, 43, 82, 245
   Egyptian 21, *221*, *244*, 245, 246
   Etruscan 84
   hieratic 21, *246*
   hieroglyphics 21, 41, 67, 176, *221*, 245, *246*
   Hittite 41
   Indian 141–42
   Indus civilization 126
   Mayan 176, 246
   in Mesopotamia 11, *13*, 29, 37
   Minoan 67
   Mycenaean 74
   Phoenician 82
   pictographic 11, 187, 244–45
   Sumerian 244–45
   See also literature
Wu Ti, *emperor of China* 133

X
Xerxes 44
Xilingshi 129

Y
Yamato clan 154
Yasovarman, *Khmer king* 151, 153
Yeavering 116
Yoritomo 156
Yoruba people *48*, 49
Yu (Chou ruler) 129–30

Z
Zeus (god) 75, 90
ziggurats 11, 12, 13, 16, 37
Zimbabwe Tradition 49
Zoroaster 45